Topics in Regulatory Economics and Policy

More information about this series at http://www.springer.com/series/6646

Pier Luigi Parcu • Timothy J. Brennan
Victor Glass
Editors

The Changing Postal Environment

Market and Policy Innovation

Springer

Editors
Pier Luigi Parcu
Badia Fiesolana
European University Institute
Fiesole, Italy

Timothy J. Brennan
Baltimore County (UMBC)
University of Maryland
Baltimore, MD, USA

Victor Glass
Rutgers Business School
Newark, NJ, USA

Topics in Regulatory Economics and Policy
ISBN 978-3-030-34531-0 ISBN 978-3-030-34532-7 (eBook)
https://doi.org/10.1007/978-3-030-34532-7

This Springer imprint is published by the registered company Springer Nature Switzerland AG
The registered company address is: Gewerbestrasse 11, 6330 Cham, Switzerland

Preface and Acknowledgments

This book is a set of papers presented at the 27th Conference on Postal and Delivery Economics, which was held on May 22–25, 2019, in Dublin, Ireland. The Conference was a joint effort of the Florence School of Regulation – Communications and Media (FSR C&M) at the European University Institute and the Center for Research in Regulated Industries (CRRI) at the Rutgers Business School.

The Conference continues to provide a valuable opportunity for the researchers and stakeholders to share knowledge and best practices, as well as testify to the evolution in the postal and delivery sector. Reflecting this evolution, the Universal Postal Union, e-commerce, competition, pricing, the challenges and opportunities of digitalization and new technologies, the changing role of postal operators, and the Universal Service Obligation in a blended (physical-digital) environment were all subjects for study and debate.

The Conference was made possible by the contribution of generous supporters. We would like to thank them not only for their financial support but also for their helpful advice in their role on the organizing committee as well as, along with others, intellectual contributions, advice, and encouragement: Virginie Alloo, Mattias Almqvist, Antonin Arlandis, Kamak Arzhangi, Bruno Basalisco, Olga Rocio, Bohorquez Suarez, Stephen Brogan, David Brown, Mindaugas Cerpickis, Julien Crutzen, Sophie De Schrevel, Barbara Delaney, Peter Denley, Peter Dunn, Blandine Eggrickz, Colm Farrelly, Nathan Francis, Jimmy Gårdebrink, Marina Gibbs, Stefano Gori, Philip Groves, Adam Houck, John Hearn, Marine Lefort, Gerdis Marquardt, Leonardo Mautino, Sandro Mendonça, Jade Neveu, Henrik Ballebye Okholm, Alain Roset, Luigi Stammati, Sophie Van Besien, Tim Walsh, Paul Walsh, and Özhan Zurel.

This year's conference benefited greatly from the efforts of the Conferences Unit of the Robert Schuman Centre for Advanced Studies and, in particular, Elisabetta Spagnoli and the team of the FSR C&M, who were incredibly helpful during the Conference, enabling it to operate very smoothly. They and colleagues provided both advice and assistance on numerous occasions and contributed greatly to the success of the event. We are very grateful to Chiara Carrozza, FSR C&M Coordinator, for her superb management of the editing process for this book.

We would like to thank our distinguished keynote speakers: Raphaël Goulet, Head of Unit, DG Growth, European Commission; João António Cadete de Matos, President of ANACOM and Chair of the European Regulators Group for Postal Services; and Garrett Blaney, Chairperson at ComReg. We would like to also thank An Post for hosting the farewell cocktail at the GPO/Witness History Centre. In particular, we thank Damian Quinn for his warm welcome and Stephen Ferguson for telling with such passion the story of the building and its historical significance in the creation of the Irish Republic.

In addition, we thank all the authors and participants of the Conference. Without their contributions, the Conference and this book would not have been possible. The usual disclaimers are applicable. In particular, the views expressed reflect the views of the authors and are not necessarily those of the editors or supporters.

Fiesole, Italy — Pier Luigi Parcu
Baltimore, MD, USA — Timothy J. Brennan
Newark, NJ, USA — Victor Glass

The Conference was Kindly Supported by

United Parcel Service
Pitney Bowes
Ofcom
Poste Italiane
Swiss Post
Le Groupe La Poste
Copenhagen Economics
Bpost
IBM
An Post
ComReg
Oxera
Cullen International
Postal Hub Podcast

Contents

Postal and Electronic Communications Services: Together Again?

Paula Gori and Pier Luigi Parcu

1 Introduction

The future of the postal sector remains a major topic. The Internet continues to alter the mix of mail and parcels in postal and delivery markets. Digital disruptions continue to reshape the habits of users and consequently all the underlying markets.

From a policy perspective, postal and telecommunications regulation have remained separate even though their services are substitutes (e.g., e-mail replacing mail) or complements (e.g., hybrid mail). Both industries have a common mission: to deliver "communication services" from one given user to another. Markets and technology provided these personal contacts through two different kinds of, often monopolistic, companies: one focusing on voice contact and the other on written communication. In addition, in the European Union, the same kind of National Regulatory Authorities (NRAs) was and usually still is often responsible for both sectors.[1]

In the last two decades, the Internet revolution reached all communications markets, by completely changing the habits and standards of the final users and necessarily also the business strategies of both postal and telecommunications operators. Digital disruption is having a decisive impact in both sectors, with instant messaging replacing SMS, digitalization changing the characteristic of many postal services, and e-mail substituting for letter delivery. The reaction to these profound changes leads to some kind of inter-sectoral convergence: such as e-billing or hybrid mail solutions. In many cases, the same service, to survive, was moved from the

[1] The same NRAs often are also responsible for media regulation, i.e., communication to the public.

P. Gori (✉) · P. L. Parcu
European University Institute, Fiesole, Italy
e-mail: paula.gori@eui.eu

P. L. Parcu et al. (eds.), *The Changing Postal Environment*, Topics in Regulatory Economics and Policy, https://doi.org/10.1007/978-3-030-34532-7_1

physical to the digital word, i.e., from the postal infrastructure to the telecommunications one.[2]

This convergence between the postal and the telecommunications services needs to be recognized and reflected at a regulatory level. This paper moves from a comparative analysis between the newly approved EU Electronic Communications Code (with its revised Universal Service Obligation) and the present EU postal legislation, to discussing the basic rationale, or better the lack of it, for maintaining distinct requirements for the Universal Service Obligation (USO) in different communications markets. The more immediate aim is to understand the logical overlaps between USO in postal services and in telecommunications and to explore which type of regulation could best take advantage of the continuing market convergence of these sectors. We sketch, in light with new market developments and users' needs, the essential elements of a modernized intermodal universal service, in order to identify a possible framework for a future full convergence of USO regulation in the postal and telecommunications fields.

In Section 2, we summarize the main changes in consumers' habits and, consequently, in the postal and telecommunications service offers. In Section 3, we focus on regulation, with particular attention to present USO principles, in both the electronic communications and postal sectors. This analysis will set the scene for Section 4, where we attempt to conceptualize a new intermodal definition of USO and Section 5 where we design a simple proposal. Section 6 briefly concludes.

2 Common Trends Affecting Postal and Electronic Communications Markets

In the European Union, the recent 10–15 years saw a sharp decline in letter volumes that went almost in parallel with a rapid growth of broadband penetration. Avoiding buying a stamp and physically going to a mailbox, as well as the advantage of instantaneous delivery, are clearly the main reasons why e-mails are almost completely replacing traditional letters. Instant messaging and social networks broke the habit of sending postcards when travelling. Tailor-made advertising campaigns, and the decline of paper journals, have also heavily impacted other kinds of bulk mails

[2] In 2016, the ERGP issued a *Report on Universal Services in light of changing postal end users´ needs*. Its aim was precisely to understand users' want and needs, in other words to look at the USO from the demand side. To do so, it gathered a number of study issues in various Member States to compare them and identify common sets. However, the methodologies used in the different reports were so different that a clear comparison turned out to be hard, which made the ERGP propose a suggestion to design users' surveys. In 2017, an ERGP *Report on the quality of service, consumer protection, and complaint handling – an analysis of trends* followed. An interesting discussion, on the concept of "postal user's needs," well related to our paper, is in Gottschalk (2019), in this volume.

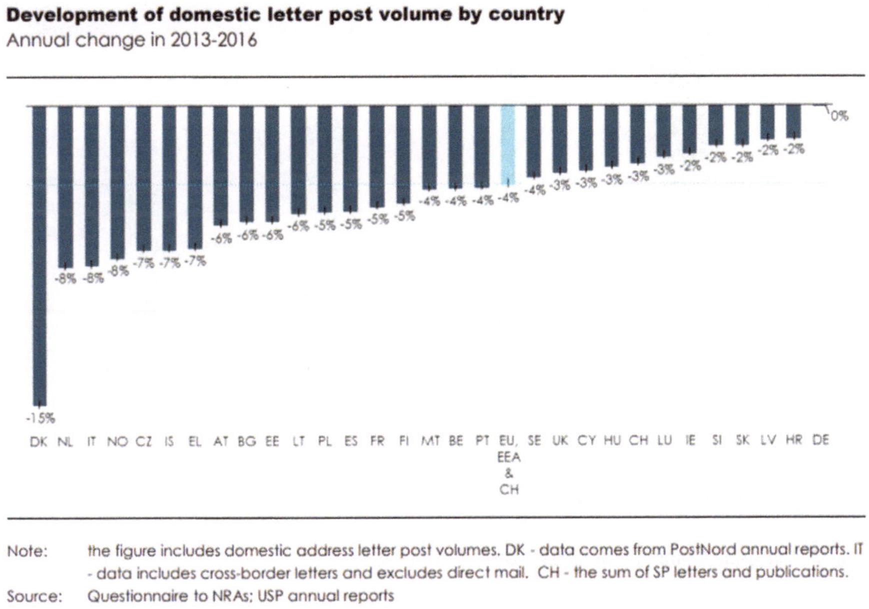

Fig. 1 Domestic letter volumes in the European Union. Copenhagen Economics (2018): Main Developments in the Postal Sector (2013–2016) Study for the European Commission, Directorate-General for Internal Market, Industry, Entrepreneurship, and SMEs

and publication distribution. Figure 1 displays the substantial mail decline in the last few years across all EU countries.

Digital substitution has been undoubtedly disruptive for previous mail business, such as letters and bulk mail. However, a careful distinction for particular cases, such as rural areas, needs to be recognized. This is particularly relevant considering that the focus of this paper is on the need to update the Universal Service Obligation in the postal sector and the possibility of a single USO valid for all communications services. To ensure an effective right of access to postal services, the USO provider has to guarantee that a minimum range of services of a given quality are provided at affordable prices, irrespective of the geographical location of the user.[3]

A bridge toward the electronic communications sector is already contained in postal regulation. Recital 19 of the Postal Services Directive[4] affirms that:

> Rural postal networks, in, inter alia, mountain and island regions, play an important role in integrating businesses into the national/global economy and in maintaining cohesion in social and employment terms. Furthermore, rural postal points in remote regions can provide an important infrastructure network for access to new electronic communications services.

[3] Postal Services Directive (97/67/EC, amended by Directives 2002/39/EC and 2008/6/EC).

[4] *Id.*

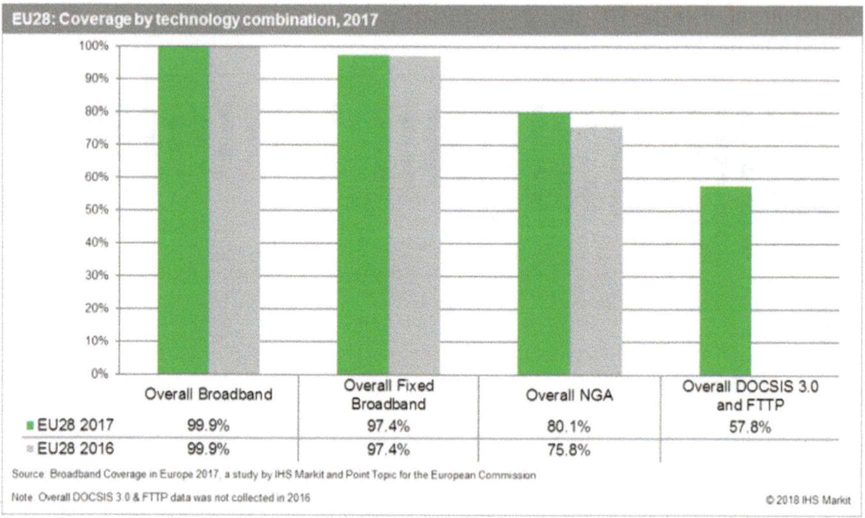

Fig. 2 European Commission (2017): Broadband Coverage

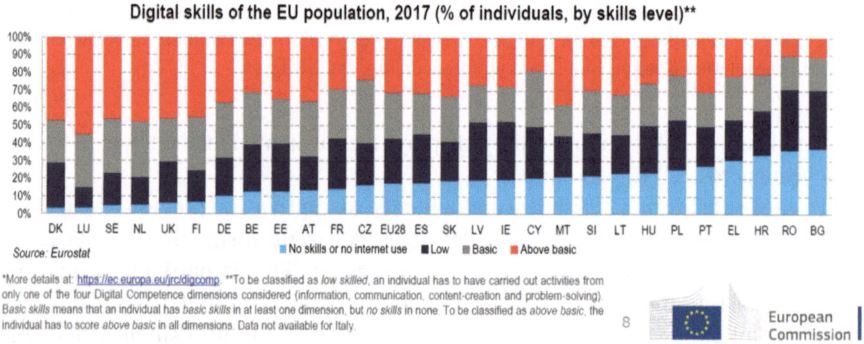

Fig. 3 Digital skills of the EU population (2017). European Commission (2018): Digital Economy and Society Index Report Human Capital

Nonetheless, as shown in Fig. 2, recent EU Commission data indicate that Internet access is widely available within EU countries.[5]

What is still seriously lagging in part of the EU Member States, shown by Fig. 3, is widespread digital literacy. According to the European Commission, around 40% of the EU population has an insufficient level of digital skills and 22% have none at all. These are usually older citizens, less educated young people, lower-income families, and migrants.[6]

[5]European Commission (2017), COMMISSION STAFF WORKING DOCUMENT, Europe's Digital Progress Report.

[6]https://ec.europa.eu/social/main.jsp?catId=1315&langId=en (last access 31/07/2019).

One interesting instance is Denmark. Since 2014, it has been mandatory for all citizens to have an e-box to receive communications from the Danish authorities as well as from other institutions. Even there, however, an exception is made for elderly and disabled people, who can still use traditional postal services for the same purpose (Falch and Henten 2018).

This specific issue is connected to our previous research on diversification and business models of postal operators (Gori and Parcu 2018). Because of the historic trust users attribute to postal operators (POs), and because of their local presence and proximity to the citizens, POs could play a role in providing digital literacy skills and acting as an e-government access point, as well as in being active in any inclusive e-government strategy.

3 The Market Reaction of Operators and the Expected Evolution of the USO

While volume of letters is decreasing, e-commerce is growing and the parcel delivery sector along with it. Differences across countries within the EU in this growth are related to issues such as trust in online purchasing and customer traditions. ERG (2015) emphasized that increased consumers' willingness to buy goods online means not only that parcel delivery will grow but also that their habits will continue to change. Consumers are demanding higher quality of service including faster speed, track and trace, and more delivery flexibility. They are also becoming more familiar with complementarity of use between physical and digital communications.[7] However, in respect to all these activities, it is important to remember that in the letter market there is still evidence of considerable concentration—usually with the legacy Universal Service Provider—while things are different in the parcel services, where competition is strong and the USO providers are rarely the main actors in the markets.

These developments constitute an opportunity for the Universal Service Providers to speed up innovation and enhance their customer care. e-Commerce is a sector in which electronic communications and postal markets naturally converge. In this case the service originates on the electronic communications network to then move to the postal one. Most importantly, this is a case in which both markets need to be involved in order to finalize the service.

Referring again to the comparison with the telecommunications sector, Falch and Henten (2018) draw an interesting parallel between the growth of parcel delivery to private consumers and its positive impact on postal operators' revenue, with broadband penetration favoring OTT services that replace video services from traditional telecom

[7] "The role of postal services is significantly changing. Their significance as a means of communication or exchange of information is diminishing due to e-substitution. In contrast, the relevance of postal services as a means to deliver goods is continuingly increasing due to the growth of e-commerce," ERGP (2019a at *t*).

players but at the same time provide new revenues from broadband access. The new businesses, e-commerce or broadband access, connect markets and provide revenues, expertise, and finally time for traditional operators to change.

The decline in letter volumes that goes almost in parallel with the growth of e-commerce and parcel delivery is only one, albeit certainly the most important element of a more general convergence. Acknowledging that letter delivery remains a market in which concentration is still quite high, while parcel delivery is quite competitive, it may be worth looking at the phenomenon from a broader perspective.

The online revolution has a double effect: on one side the telecommunications market is replacing the postal one (e-substitution), and on the other it is complementing it (e-commerce and hybrid solutions). We are witnessing an increasing demand for communications services in its most general dimension, which, in the way it is approached by users, is rather technologically neutral and not sector specific. The disruption of the Internet and the consequent change in users' habits are having an impact on business strategies of the different postal operators. One particular example is the so-called hybrid and reverse hybrid mail. In the first case, the sender prepares a message online, which is then printed and physically delivered to the recipient. In the second case, the postal operator receives the physical letter from the sender and if the recipient agrees, opens, scans, and sends the message to the recipient via electronic means.

This kind of services is strictly related to the spread of PO boxes. Home delivery becomes less frequent. Users are informed, via SMS or e-mail, about the arrival of a mail and can ask for it to be scanned and sent via e-mail (and then delivered when planned by the PO) or can pick it up at the post office.

The Universal Postal Union (2015) classified new e-services offered by postal operators into four groups: (i) e-post and e-government, (ii) e-commerce, (iii) e-finance and payments, and (iv) support services. e-Post and e-government includes services such as e-mailboxes, e-invoicing, hybrid and revers hybrid mail, digital signatures, digital identities, etc. e-Commerce covers shopping portals, analytics and performance reports, virtual international addresses, etc. Online account management, e-bill paying, escrow services for e-commerce, etc. are all services that fall in the e-commerce group. Support services include track and trace, online change of address, digital personalized postage, electronic notifications, online chats, and customer service.

What emerges from this long list of mixed services is that postal operators, by leveraging their traditional assets and capabilities, are trying to react to the convergence between telecommunications and postal markets in order to profit from it rather than being destroyed. They are developing and exploiting complementarity, with different degrees of success, to avoid outright substitution for their services.

As mentioned by Maegli et al. (2010), the presence of externalities, both in the telecommunications and in the postal market, triggers the regulatory need for Universal Service Obligation. On the one side, (positive) externalities are linked to the network: the more users on a network, the more it is valuable and useful for other users. In this case, USO aims at connecting all the users to the most effective network for their specific needs. On the other side, there are externalities linked to specific services (postal or telecom operators offer a number of different products), in which case USO may be needed to guarantee a minimum quality and accessible prices to certain essential services, irrespective of technology or geographical location.

Currently, following the Postal Services Directive, Member States have to ensure that the general public is provided with a postal service of a specified quality (regardless to where a person lives) at an affordable price. This requires that contact and access points are able to cope with the foreseeable needs of users as interpreted by regulation. Presently, the principle is ensured by specifically requiring that the universal service is guaranteed at least five working days a week (including one collection and one delivery per day). While the Directive leaves some flexibility to Member States on what to include or not include in the USO, Article 3 lists a minimum set of services that are still mandatory: (i) insured and registered mails; (ii) clearance, sorting transport, and distribution of postal items up to 2 kg; and (iii) clearance, sorting transport, and distribution of postal packages up to 10 kg.

In the telecommunications sector, the EU has recently adopted the European Electronic Communications Code (European Parliament and Council 2018b). This comes after the European Commission assessed that the current regulatory framework (the updated telecoms package) was becoming obsolete in the face of market developments, particularly the spread of the Internet, with new players offering services similar to those offered by traditional suppliers.[8] The Code revised the Universal Service Obligation by attempting to update regulation in response to technology and market evolution. Old obligations such as public payphones and user directories were removed, replaced by obligations for Member States to guarantee that consumers have access, at an affordable price, to an adequate broadband service and that no discrimination should be made on the basis of the technology used. According to Article 84.2 of the Code, "Member States may also ensure the affordability of the services referred to in paragraph 1 that are not provided at a fixed location where they consider this to be necessary to ensure consumers' full social and economic participation in society." This evolution sounds similar to the requirement of the Postal Services Directive, where Article 5 states that Universal Service Obligation "[…] shall evolve in response to the technical, economic and social environment and to the needs of users."

In summary, there appears to be a guiding pattern from how operators respond to the technological challenge and the best evolution of the regulatory requirements related to the USO. The origin of this common thread lies in the evolution of consumers' habits and needs. Regulation of the USO should follow this same evolution. It is up to the USO regulation to ensure that behind the digital disruption are not hidden new exclusions and digital divides that can be as dangerous as those in the past. USO regulation should be maintained but only in the presence of proven market failures or explicit distributive public choices. Where the evolving communications market and competition not able to guarantee economic and social inclusion of the public in the new digital environment, then an adapted USO regulation should continue to fill the gap.

[8] http://europa.eu/rapid/press-release_IP-18-4070_en.htm (last access 31/07/2019).

4 Toward an Intermodal USO Definition?

Rapidly changing users' communication habits and new complementarities are being created between telecommunications and postal networks and services. It is worth considering whether a separated Universal Service Obligation for the two markets is still socially needed and economically justified. Parcu and Silvestri (2017) argued that USO standards should be regularly updated, considering both the substitutability and the complementarity between the postal delivery and the online instruments. In the Internet era, the mission of assuring to citizens an effective *right to communication* calls for a single, technologically neutral, universal obligation for communications services (De Streel and Peitz 2015). This today, to be truly effective and economically viable, could only assume an intermodal characteristic. For example, if one considers a service that encompasses both communication networks, combining immediate electronic delivery with reliable postal physical delivery, a request to postal operators to deliver letter mails 5 days per week becomes obsolete.

As mentioned by Maegli et al. (2010), proximity and complementarity between the telecommunications and postal network could lead to a win-win situation for both the operators and the users. On the one hand, the electronic communications network would speed up the delivery process of most communication by mainly acting as an immediate last-mile delivery tool. On the other hand, postal operators have the means, among which users' trust, to ensure citizens that any hybrid solution combining electronic/physical elements is secure and will not violate their privacy. On the same theme, De Streel and Peitz (2015)[9] proposed to revise the USO, precisely because of intermodal competition of postal services with other communications services. In doing so, they suggested to consider a broader concept, to which they referred to as a "right to communicate." Finally, as it was also underlined in the above-quoted report by the Universal Postal Union (2015), postal operators, as providers of a trusted communication infrastructure, could be of great help for governments to fill the data protection and security issues behind any successful e-government strategy.

Within the framework of the services of general economic interest (SGEI), the basis for this common Universal Service Obligation could be found in what, in the EECC, is referred to as the requirement of "full social and economic participation in society." To this end, the new USO in communications services would carry the mission to guarantee that no citizen is excluded from the possibility to getting and sending communication/information. In this context, technological neutrality should be applied in its broader sense: the right is to be assured without any exogenous preference for using traditional postal networks, electronic communications networks, or any combined solution. The result should be that every citizen, irrespective of age, education, health status, and geographic location, should have the right to send and receive communication, according to some minimum standards of quality and affordability embodied in an intermodal USO.

---

[9] De Streel and Peitz (De streel and Peitz 2015, p. 3).

It is interesting to note how policy approaches reflected contemporaneous market situations. The review in the telecoms sector started moving the USO toward the social embeddedness principle, while the Green Paper for postal services slightly mentions the social aspects but is still pretty much oriented to the market dimension, with a focus on access, quality of service, and tariffs. This was then the approach in the first Postal Services Directive. In its last revision (2008), Article 4 was then modified to state that Member States shall make sure that the Universal Service Obligation is, among other things, "taking into account the important role it plays in social and territorial cohesion." The evolution also continued in the telecommunications sector. While the 2002 framework was referring to a risk of social exclusion and to public interest, the Electronic Communications Code (Article 84.2) now mentions "full social and economic participation in society."

A smart converging regulation, aligned with market evolution, with this special focus on USO widely interpreted needs, would also be in line, and clearly helped, by the trend in the EU countries to have the same National Regulatory Authorities responsible for both the postal and the telecommunications sectors. Regulatory thinking is also rapidly evolving under the pressure of market reality, recently the European Regulators Group for Postal Services (ERGP) (2019b, p. 20) affirmed: "The fact that in certain areas the provision of postal services is not economically viable may provide a rationale for maintaining a universal service. But e-connectivity may also be an important instrument to ensure genuine inclusion of citizens in a future society."[10]

A unified intermodal USO could also foresee tailored solutions that depend on the particular status of a given groups of citizens. For example, a 5-day home delivery rule could be preserved, as a special service, which is hard or impossible for the specific user to receive communication via electronic means (e.g., elderly, disabled people, household without Internet connection) or where an official written communication is still required. Nonetheless, with inter-modality one could significantly reduce delivery frequency while increasing innovation and quality. It will be important to understand whether this could apply to both residential and business users or whether different policies should address these two groups.

This unified strategy consequently will impact USO volumes, reducing some activities and increasing others, as well as the economic sustainability of USO items for the Universal Service Provider (and for Member States). Following a reform of the USO in New Zealand, delivery in the country is now 3 days per week in urban areas and at least 5 days per week to PO boxes and in rural areas (ERGP 2014). It is this kind of smart adaptation of regulation that could be strengthened and refined by the simultaneous exploitation of the telecoms and postal networks, exploiting both their substitutability and their complementarity.

---

[10] ERGP (2019b, p. 20) continues, "In this respect also, Member States show significant differences. It is therefore important that a regulatory framework affords Member States sufficient flexibility to find solutions suitable to their respective national circumstances. This may for example include that specific measures are taken to provide for the interests of specific users' groups, instead of imposing a general universal service obligation on one or more postal operators."

In summary, a new concept of USO, founded on a right to communication, could better incorporate modern public service needs. Some, if not all, of the resources for financing the new USO could come from already existing general funds. As already mentioned, this new USO could comprise additional features but could save on others.

5 A Simple Proposal

In order to design a single comprehensive definition of the Universal Service Obligation, finalized to a new right to communications services, one should start from a few main principles. Three simple and well-known concepts, access, quality, and price, could constitute the fundamental social and economic elements that the new universal service should ensure:

A. Citizens shall be granted an effective right to communications services, i.e., they should always be able to communicate from one to another.
B. This right to continuous communication should be guaranteed using different networks, regardless of the technology used.
C. Communications services should be affordable, to guarantee that every citizen can fully participate in the society.

While broadband penetration is high, digital skill may not be, as shown in Fig. 3. The cultural digital divide, still higher than the technological and infrastructural one, should be adequately protected in the new USO during this era of transition. As an indispensable complement to this new general USO, a fourth element should be:

D. An appropriate special regime should be set up to protect people with special needs, not only the elderly, disabled people, and citizens living in particular rural areas but also those people who do not have sufficient digital skills to be able to rely on an intermodal universal service.

With regard to procedure, a smart proposal would require regular frequent review of the scope of the unified USO. In the EU, the current regulatory framework for the postal market is essentially based on a 1997 directive, slightly revised in 2002 and in 2008. Consequently, the USO is regulated by a legislative text that was elaborated when the market and users' habits were extremely different compared to nowadays. The speed of digitalization and technological development shows how fast markets can evolve. Therefore, we should have a further principle:

E. A revision, at least every 3 years, of the content and extension of the intermodal Universal Service Obligation should be mandatory, as is currently the practice in electronic communications.

Finally, on the institutional side, an effective principle would simply require that:

F. A single independent regulatory authority should supervise the application of the intermodal USO for the right to communication.

Since all NRAs in the EU, with the only exception being in Denmark, are already responsible for both electronic communications and postal markets, this part of the reform should not have a big impact. One might also consider if, at the EU regulatory level, it may be worth unifying the postal sector and the electronic communications sector under the umbrella of a revised DG Connect. The European Regulators Group for Postal Services (ERGP) and the Body of European Regulatory for Electronic Communications (BEREC) are already collaborating. The latter has a more solid status, with the BEREC office, an EU agency, providing administrative and professional support. One could think of both institutions evolving toward a single body, responsible for coordinating regulation and USO in the postal and the electronic communications sector.

6 Conclusions

The aim of this analysis is to consider converging toward a single Universal Service Obligation utilizing both the electronic communications and the postal sector and the principles for such a change. The elements triggering this process are to be found in the spread of broadband penetration and in the consequent change in users' habits. e-Mails and instant messaging are replacing letters (substitution); on the other hand, online purchase of goods is enhancing the physical parcel delivery markets (complementarity). Overall, citizens are using more and more communications services and are becoming more demanding in terms of digital solutions, flexibility, and high-quality standards. Moreover, present Universal Service Obligation, in both sectors, represents a significant cost, both private and public, for Member States economies.

The conceptual proposal contained in this work is to reconsider the approach to the USO from an overall communications markets and rights perspective, while keeping in mind its very essence, which is the need for social and economic inclusion of all citizens. We propose to redesign and unify the USO of both sectors by creating and ensuring, with an intermodal solution, a new right to communication. This evolution would require a technologically neutral solution, which also takes into full consideration the transitional phase we are currently living. This means taking into consideration also the gaps in broadband penetration, especially in digital skills—a factor that will change slowly. In any case, our proposal purports the need of a regular refit exercise of the changing USO.

References

Batura, O. (2016). *Liberalisation of telecommunications services: Social embedding of the liberalised market as a regulatory challenge, universal service in WTO and EU law*. Legal Issues of Services of General Interest.

Copenhagen Economics. (2018). *Main developments in the postal sector (2013–2016)*. Study for the European Commission, Directorate-General for Internal Market, Industry, Entrepreneurship and SMEs.

De Streel, A., & Peitz, M. (2015). *The right to communicate: Redefining universal service obligations in postal and electronic communications markets*. CERRE Discussion Paper.

European Commission. (1987). *Communication from the commission to the council and the European Parliament*. Towards a dynamic European Economy—Green Paper on the development of a common market for telecommunications services and equipment, COM(87) 290 final.

European Commission. (1992). *Communication from the commission*. Review of the situation in the telecommunications services sector.

European Commission. (1993). *Green Paper on the development of the single market for postal services*.

European Commission. (2015). Report from the commission to the European parliament and the council on the application of the postal services directive (Directive 97/67/EC as amended by Directive 2002/39/EC and 2008/6/EC).

European Commission. (2017). *Commission staff working document*. Europe's Digital Progress Report.

European Commission. (2018). *Digital economy and society index report human capital*.

European Parliament and Council. (2018a). Directive 2008/6/EC of the European Parliament and of the council of 20 February 2008 amending Directive 97/67/EC with regard to the full accomplishment of the internal market of Community postal services.

European Parliament and Council. (2018b). Directive (EU) 2018/1972 establishing the European Electronic Communications Code.

European Regulators Group for Postal Services. (2014). *Discussion paper on the implementation of Universal Service in the postal sector and the effects of recent changes in some countries on the scope of the USO*.

European Regulators Group for Postal Services. (2015). *ERGP report on the outcome of the ERGP public consultation on the evolution of the universal service obligation*.

European Regulators Group for Postal Services. (2016a). *ERGP report universal services in light of changing postal end users' needs*.

European Regulators Group for Postal Services. (2016b). *ERGP medium term strategy 2017–2019 discussion paper for public consultation*.

European Regulators Group for Postal Services. (2017). *Report on the quality of service, consumer protection and complaint handling – an analysis of trends*.

European Regulators Group for Postal Services. (2019a). *Medium term strategy 2020–2022 (for public consultation)*.

European Regulators Group for Postal Services. (2019b). *Developments in the postal sector and implications for regulation*.

Falch, M., & Henten, A. (2018). *Universal service obligation in a digital world: The demise of postal services*. https://www.riverpublishers.com/journal.php?j=NBJICT/2018/1/11

Finger, M., Brand-weiner, I., & Swars, E. (2012). Revisiting the European universal service obligation, *1st European Postal Regulation Forum, Florence School of Regulation*.

Gori, P., & Parcu, P. L. (2018). *Postal operators as "ground based" online platforms?* New Business and Regulatory Challenges in the Postal Sector.

Gottschalk, G. (2019). *A note on "postal users' needs" and their role in postal regulation*. in this volume.

Maegli, M., Jaag, C., Koller, M., & Trinkner, U. (2010). *Postal markets and electronic substitution: What is the impacts of convergence on regulatory practices and institutions?* Competition and Regulation in Network Industries.

Parcu, P. L., & Silvestri, V. (2017). *Lessons learnt from the postal sector to telecommunications and vice versa*. The Changing Postal and Delivery Sector.

Universal Postal Union. (2015). *Measuring postal e-services development: A global perspective*.

Universal Postal Union. (2016). *Research on postal markets, trends and drivers for international letter mail, parcels, and express mail services, final report*.

Potential Insights for US USO from Recent Federal Communication Commission's Broadband Auctions

Victor Glass

1 Introduction

The United States Postal Service (USPS) is losing billions and missing service targets. Both the Postal Regulatory Commission (United States Postal Regulatory Commission 2017, 2017a) and a special task force ("Presidential Commission") initiated by President Trump (White House 2018) have developed proposals to make USPS financially healthy "while meeting the needs of urban and rural communities, large mailers, and small businesses" (White House 2018, p. 68).

This paper is a follow-up to the author's previous chapter (Glass 2019) on last-mile delivery options that the USPS might consider. That article used as a case study the Federal Communications Commission's (FCC) proposed use of auctions to extend broadband services in unserved areas. Since that time, the FCC conducted its auction, which proved highly successful. Many new carriers have promised to provide service in these areas at service levels rejected by incumbents as too costly. The actual design of the broadband auction may convey important lessons for subcontracting last-mile postal service delivery through the use of auctions.

Section 2 summarizes the current debate on how to improve USPS's financial condition while meeting customer needs for postal services. Section 3 reviews Crew and Kleindorfer's views on postal privatization and contrasts them with reactions by interested parties that oppose privatization. This discussion foreshadows the conflicts that will likely surface if the USPS actually decided to use auctions to subcontract or possibly spin off last-mile delivery. Section 4 describes the FCC's broadband auction and analyzes its outcome. Section 5 considers how these results could be translated into a proposal to subcontract last-mile postal services. Section 6 has concluding remarks.

V. Glass (✉)
Rutgers Business School, Newark, NJ, USA
e-mail: vglass@business.rutgers.edu

P. L. Parcu et al. (eds.), *The Changing Postal Environment*, Topics in Regulatory Economics and Policy, https://doi.org/10.1007/978-3-030-34532-7_2

2 Current Political Debate over Restoring USPS to Financial Health and Privatizing It

Competition is already fierce for portions of last-mile parcel delivery service. Besides major parcel competitors such as FedEx and UPS, USPS is facing the prospect that large e-commerce companies will deliver more of their own parcels. Amazon, for example, has its own direct delivery business, including "Shipping with Amazon" and Amazon lockers located in apartment buildings, gas stations, and grocery stores.

Unlike other parcel delivery and e-commerce companies, USPS is mired by a web of regulations associated with mail delivery, burdened with its universal service obligation, and pre-funding its employee retirement funding program. On top of this, its cash cow, first-class mail, is a rapidly declining business. As a result, USPS is hemorrhaging funds. Something has to give: USPS knows it, and the government knows it; the question is what to do.

The USO, in particular, illustrates the problem with defining alternatives for returning the Postal Service to financial health. The Presidential Commission cites having to delivering mail to 150 million locations 6 days per week as not supportable, as mail volume declines (White House 2018, p. 68). Crew and Kleindorfer (2003, pp. 187 and 191) had already cited delivery in noneconomic areas as a challenge to USPS's solvency. Geddes (2004, p. 64) cited sources claiming that rural and urban delivery costs are comparable but later pointed out that roadside delivery in rural areas is inferior (Geddes 2005, p. 224).

Solvency itself is also debatable. The Presidential Commission noted that the USPS has $100 billion in unfunded liabilities, a capital investment backlog, and has no clear road to profitability (White House 2018, p. 68). Buc (2018), however, pointed out that USPS has $326.7 billion in retirement assets invested in Treasury securities. If these funds were invested like other public pension funds, the assets would generate $13.7 billion of additional funds per year. By contrast, USPS reported a $3.9 billion loss in 2018.

As might be expected in the current US political environment, there are partisan differences in solutions to USPS's persistent reported losses and declining mail volumes. Democrats see USPS as a national treasure. It must never be privatized. It must maintain a 6-day, door-to-door delivery. The solution is to end pre-funding of retirement benefits and allow USPS to offer new services such as paycheck cashing (Democratic Party Platform 2016, p. 6).

Republicans want to privatize USPS (White House 2018, p. 68). It would allow USPS to adapt to changing customer needs without political interference. It could also cut costs by delivery fewer days per week to more central locations. It should have the ability to adjust prices as necessary. It could negotiate pay and benefits with its workforce more effectively. The key challenge is to make the Postal Service profitable. Then it could be spun off as an investor-owned utility (White House 2018, p. 69).

In a follow-up report, the executive branch described near-term reforms, which included expanded private sector contracting in areas such as processing and sortation (Report of Task Force 2018, p. 5). Last-mile subcontracting would fit this vision. Subcontracting is already a big business. In 2016, USPS spent $14 billion on outside purchase. About half was spent on transportation services, for example, with Federal Express paying $1.68 billion to USPS. Other companies provide telecommunications and energy billing services (Hendel 2017). Pitney Bowes presorts approximately 15 billion pieces of mail per year and delivers them to designated locations to gain discounted postage costs, effectively allowing USPS to subcontract presorting.[1]

USPS currently subcontracts last-mile postal delivery in rural areas. Its Contract Delivery Service allows independent contractors in rural areas to sort and deliver mail and parcels and collect mail, sell stamps, and offer other services (DeSimone 2018).[2] The issue to be considered here is whether subcontracting the last-mile can be expanded to all service areas, whether they are profitable or not.

3 Crew and Kleindorfer and Interested Party Perspectives

Many economists have favored privatization for more than a decade but made little headway in persuading the Congress to consider converting USPS into an investor-owned utility. Crew and Kleindorfer wrote a string of articles citing the need for privatization even before the turndown in mail volume. They pointed to USPS's inefficient organizational and governing structure that "precludes alignment of market and efficiency incentives with investment and operations" (Crew and Kleindorfer 2003, p. 187). The record shows that major decision-making is politicized, such as closing post offices and downsizing its labor force. The basic problem is that these political decisions were unfunded. As a result, the Universal Service Obligation (USO) continues at high service levels despite draining resources.

According to Crew and Kleindorfer (2000), internal inefficiency is likely because of the lack of residual claimants. Residual claimants – stockholders and upper management in a private organization – are subject to pressures to keep labor costs down and keep borrowing costs low (Crew and Kleindorfer 2000, p. 6). Other networked industries – telecom and electric utility companies – are privately owned (Crew and Kleindorfer 2000, p. 4). Other countries have privatized their postal services (Crew and Kleindorfer 2003, p. 187).

Crew and Kleindorfer (2000, p. 1) said that the continued monopoly on local mail delivery and mailbox control and current delivery service levels should be revisited because of alternative delivery systems such as e-mail and e-commerce. In

---

[1] See Pitney Bowes website, available at https://www.pitneybowes.com/us/shipping-and-mailing/mail-and-parcel-sorters/presort-services.html

[2] Instructions for becoming a Contact Delivery Service are available online (WikiHow, *How to become a Contact Delivery Service*).

their view, the postal sector arguably fits the competitive model with minimum externalities (Crew and Kleindorfer 2013, p. 3). Intermodal competition is growing rapidly, and USPS must be nimble enough to respond to market changes. They observed that USPS has focused mainly on cost cutting. They do not believe cost cutting is the way to greatness (Crew and Kleindorfer 2013, p. 11). The Freedom Foundation, a conservative think tank, supports Crew and Kleindorfer's view. They point out that Deutsche Post was able to implement policies that saved a vast amount of money and still delivers letters to all areas of the country, meeting a policy requirement that no one be excluded (Hunter 2018).

Others see the results of privatization through different lenses, as an attack on its universal service obligation. The Center for Economic and Policy Research warned that privatization means staff reductions, wage reductions, shortened postal retail hours, decreases in delivery access, and higher postal rates (Barber 2018). USPS employees believe USPS management is slashing costs, but at the expense of service quality and worker security. Between 2004 and 2018, postal employment has dropped from approximately 700,000 to 500,000.[3] In 2009, USPS had 4800 offices, but was reviewing 3200 to determine whether to keep them open. There were 304 closures in 2017 and 378 offices under suspension. In their view, no discontinuances occurred between 2013 and 2015 because USPS did not want to raise public concerns. USPS wants to close permanently the suspended post offices during fiscal years 2018 and 2019. Notably, three out of four office closings were in rural areas (Save the Post Office 2018).

Bittle (2018) made the case that USPS is already collapsing in rural areas. More than 100,000 postal employees are responsible for delivering mail in rural areas. About half are part-time employees. Rural Carrier Associates (RCAs) are part-time substitutes for full-time employees, and Assistant Rural Carriers (ARCs), a position created in 2015, work only on weekends and holidays. Pay for part-time employees was $21/hour before 2010. It now stands at $17/hour, based on the estimated time it takes to complete a route. Once package volume started to ramp up after 2010, rural delivery became difficult. The pay did not consider extra delivery time for parcels. Built into the pay system is a 30-second estimate to deliver a parcel in a rural area. Many stations are understaffed; 12-hour days are frequent. In North Dakota, rural carrier overtime has increased 241 percent between 2011 and 2014 (Bittle 2018).

4 FCC's Approach to Last-Mile Unserved Areas

The FCC has also been grappling with assuring universal service in rural, high-cost areas. The Telecom Act of 1996 requires that services and rates in rural areas must be of comparable quality to those in urban areas. The problem is that rural areas are

[3] Source Number of Postal Employees. Available at https://about.usps.com/who-we-are/postal-history/employees-since-1926.pdf

much more expensive to serve and, in a competitive environment, carriers cannot cross-subsidize rural areas by raising rates in competitive urban areas. In response, the FCC has had a universal service fund to subsidize service in high-cost areas. The actual funding of unserved areas was based on a forward-looking cost model, which was designed to estimate the cost that a putatively efficient carrier would incur to build a fiber to the premises of the broadband network in unserved areas. The subsidies were offered to incumbent carriers. They chose not to accept the offer to serve almost 500,000 census blocks (Glass and Tardiff 2019).[4]

As a result, the FCC introduced an auction using the cost estimates from its forward-looking cost model to set a reserve price (maximum price) for building and maintaining a network in an unserved territory. The FCC hoped to attract new satellite, wireless, and landline carriers that would be willing to provide broadband services in unserved areas. The problem facing the FCC was that each technology has difference capabilities, with satellite having the most limitation on speed and latency (delay) and landline fiber having the highest capabilities. As a result, the FCC developed a set of penalties attached to a bid (see note to Table 1), which effectively lowered support for service offerings with inferior performance compared to a high-speed fiber optic connection.

Performance tier	Speed	Monthly usage allowance	Weight (penalty)
Minimum	≥10/1 Mbps	≥150 gigabytes (GB)	65
Baseline	≥25/3 Mbps	≥150 GB or US Median, whichever is higher	45
Above baseline	≥100/20 Mbps	≥2 terabytes (TB)	15
Gigabit	≥1 Gbps/500 mbps	≥2 TB	0

Mbps ≡ megabits per second
Gbps ≡ gigabits per second
GB ≡ Gigabyte (8 bits to a byte)

Latency	Requirement	Weight (penalty)
Low latency	≤100 ms	0
High latency	≤750 ms and median opinion score ≥ 4	25

Source: Federal Communications Commission 2018, par. 12
ms ≡ miliseconds

The FCC used the following formula to evaluate bids.

$$\text{Support}_i = \text{Reserve Price}\left(\text{percentage bid} - w_i\right)$$

where w_i is the penalty weight.

[4] Census blocks, the smallest geographic area for which the Bureau of the Census collects and tabulates decennial census data. In a city, it typically refers to a block surrounded by streets. For more information, see https://www.census.gov/newsroom/blogs/random-samplings/2011/07/what-are-census-blocks.html

The actual bidding process began with the first offer of support per line based on a cost simulation model that the FCC had adopted to estimate the cost of construction. The "percentage bid" is less than 100%. In other words, the bidder is offering to discount the reserve price to win the bid. The penalty weight reduces support further if the carrier is offering to build a network with low-speed/high-latency connections.

The FCC intended to give lower-capability technologies the chance to win bids in remote areas that are very costly to serve with landline technology.[5] However, if the going percentage bid declined to 65% of the reserve price, satellite companies would no longer be able to receive support. In other words, the winning bid would go to the technology capable of producing higher speeds and lower latency.

The results of the auction were very encouraging. Glass and Tardiff (2019) report that close to half of the bidders offered baseline speed levels, about 35 percent offered speeds above the baseline, and approximately 20 percent offered gigabit speeds. Only 0.3 percent of the locations included in the winning bids were won by firms offering the minimal speed level that subsidized incumbents had been obligated to provide. Their analysis also supported the hypothesis that the initial reserve price was a good starting point for the bidding process because winning bids were somewhat below the reserve price after holding other factors constant. In other words, FCC's simulation model estimated build-out costs well, and its penalty weights worked effectively. Wireless companies and electric utility companies offering fiber won a large majority of the bids (see Glass and Tardiff 2019, Tables 6 and 7).

5 A Roadmap for Subcontracting Last-Mile Delivery

Any carryover from the FCC's auction to postal rural area delivery would require a major change in government policy. First of all, it would require the establishment of an explicit fund to subsidize high-cost routes. The PRC would need to develop a simulation model to estimate the costs of delivering mail using likely alternative technologies. Then it would have to set tiered service levels. Moreover, it would need buy-in from unions.

While USPS has detailed cost information for last-mile service routes, policy makers would benefit from a simulation model that would estimate the cost of alternative service delivery methods for mail and parcels. The model may include larger mailboxes, lockers located in highly trafficked business locations, mobile post offices, crowd sourcing, and collaborative efforts with other industries. For example, Glass (2012) proposed that rural telco offices and rural post offices could work

[5] The actual term used was a technologically neutral auction. See Connect America Fund Phase II Auctions highlights at https://www.fcc.gov/auction/903

together to lower joint costs while introducing new services such as viewing mail online and receiving credits for viewing follow-up advertisements online after a physical advertisement was delivered. The simulation model would serve as the basis for developing penalty weights for alternative last-mile delivery methods.

Setting labor rates would be crucial for setting the reserve price. For an auction to have any prospect of success, current USPS employees should not be disadvantaged by the auction. One nonstarter would be if competing carriers could set wages for full-time employees below current union rates. Another problem area is the use of part-time employees. USPS is already using CRAs and ARCs to cut costs. Again, to forestall postal employees claiming union busting, ground rules for these types of employee categories need to be addressed.

Weighting of the Postal Regulatory Commission's (PRC's) general service objectives and factors would have to be balanced to develop service tiers. The PRC would have to weight 9 performance objectives and 14 factors to evaluate specific target objectives that would define baseline service (PAEA 2017 or 2017a). For example, what penalty should be assigned to delivery of mail 1 day slower than the current benchmark?

An explicit Universal Service Obligation fund would be necessary. It would require either ear-marked government tax funds or an assessment on users of the postal system. The funds would be used to fund winning bids for subsidy funding. Total funding would be, at the most, the estimated reserve cost of a service route. If the auction fails in certain service territories, the cost model would need to be revisited and funding resized if a new auction is desired.

6 Concluding Remarks

Auctions could be a way of satisfying both Democrats and Republicans. Subcontracting would keep USPS as a public corporation. Fulfilling an explicit USO through an auction could reduce USPS losses in high-cost areas. However, as opponents would rightly say, subcontracting is a form of piecemeal privatization. Crew and Kleindorfer recognized that privatization has a range of meaning: from complete sale of assets to subcontracting (Crew and Kleindorfer 2003, p. 188).

Nonetheless, the auction would be an opportunity for postal workers and others to improve their employment prospects. The auction would open new delivery opportunities foreclosed by current service restrictions such as offering smart city sensing services while delivering mail. A winning bidder could conceivably add a variety of new services not efficiently exploited by the USPS such as same-day parcel delivery, offer pickup parcel returns, and offer new mailbox types and new combinations of online and physical delivery services. The list is as long as a realistic imagination.

References

Barber, A. (2018). The future of our postal service. Center for Economic and Policy Research, July 26, 2018. Available at http://cepr.net/publications/briefings/testimony/the-future-of-our-public-postal-service

Bittle, J. (2018). In Rural America, the postal service is already collapsing, *The Nation*, May 3, 2018. https://www.thenation.com/article/in-rural-america-the-postal-service-is-already-collapsing/

Buc, L. (2018). *USPS retirement fund investment restrictions*, SLS Consulting, Available from author.

Crew, M., & Kleindorfer, P. (2000). Privatizing the Postal Service. In E. Hudgins (Ed.) *Mail @ Millennium: Will the Postal Service Go Private*. Cato Institute. Available at https://www.google.com/search?rlz=1C1GCEA_enUS802US802&ei=hneSXKXgNbC7ggfi9a-QDQ&q=crew+and+kleindorfer+privatizing+the+postal+service+2000&oq=crew+and+kleindorfer+privatizing+the+postal+service+2000&gs_l=psy-ab.3...3403.17049..17516...9.0..0.175.3128.24j10......0....1..gws-wiz.9pDN_BLPXgc

Crew, M., & Kleindorfer, P. (2003). Postal privatization: In general and for the United States postal service. In D. Parket & D. Saal (Eds.), *Handbook of privatization*. Cheltenham, UK/Northampton, MA: Edward Elgar.

Crew, M., & Kleindorfer, P. (2013). Privatization of postal operators: Old arguments in new realities. In M. Crew & P. Kleindorfer (Eds.), *Reforming the postal sector in the face of electronic competition*. Cheltenham, UK/Northampton, MA: Edward Elgar.

Democratic Party Platform. (2016). Available at https://democrats.org/wp-content/uploads/2018/10/2016_DNC_Platform.pdf

DeSimone, N. (2018). *Last mile delivery: Tough road for USPS, opportunity for private sector*, Reason Foundation, March 7, 2018. Available at https://reason.org/commentary/last-mile-delivery-tough-road-for-usps-opportunity-for-private-sector/

Federal Communications Commission (2018). *Connect America Fund Phase II Auction Scheduled for July 24, 2018 Notice and Filing Requirements and Other Procedures for Auction 903*, AU Docket No. 17–182 and WC Docket No. 10–90, Public Notice, February 1, available at https://docs.fcc.gov/public/attachments/FCC-18-6A1_Rcd.pdf

Geddes, R. (2004). Postal reform. *Economic Journal Watch, 1*(1), April 2004. Available at file:///C:/Users/vglass.BUSINESS/Downloads/2004-04-geddes-reach_concl%20(3).pdf

Geddes, R. (2005). Policy watch: Reform of the U.S. Postal Service. *Journal of Economic Perspectives, 19*(3), Summer 2005. Available at https://www.aeaweb.org/articles?id=10.1257/089533005774357879

Glass, V. (2012). *Delivering the goods to your door: RLEC/Postal connections*, CRRI Postal Workshop 2012. See, *A Possible Pilot Collaboration between Rural Telecom Providers and the Postal Service,* issued by United States Postal Service, Office of Inspector General, February 8, 2013. Available at https://www.uspsoig.gov/sites/default/files/document-library/2013/rarc-ib-13-001.pdf

Glass, V. (2019). Creating last-mile incentives from inside-out. A template drawn from rural telecom. In P. L. Parcu, T. J. Brennan, & V. Glass (Eds.), *New business and regulatory strategies in the postal sector*. Switzerland: Springer.

Glass, V., & Tardiff, T. (2019) *The federal communications commission's rural infrastructure auction: What is hidden in the weeds?* Available from the authors.

Hendel, D. P. (2017). *Transportation subcontractors lead list of top U.S. Postal Service suppliers,* March 17, 2017. Posted by Postal Service Contracting. Available at https://www.contractorsperspective.com/postal-service-contracting/transportation-contractors-lead-list-of-top-u-s-postal-service-suppliers/

Hunter, B. (2018). It's time to privatize the postal service. *Foundation for Economic Education*, June 28, 2018. Available at https://fee.org/articles/its-time-to-privatize-the-united-states-postal-service/

Report from the Task Force on the United States Postal System. (2018). *United States Postal Service: Sustainable Path Forward*, December 2018. Available at https://home.treasury.gov/system/files/136/USPS_A_Sustainable_Path_Forward_report_12-04-2018.pdf

Save the Post Office. (2018). *Post Office discontinuances and suspensions: A decade in review*, February 26, 2018. Available at https://savethepostoffice.com/post-office-discontinuances-and-suspensions-a-decade-in-review/

Save the Post Office. (2018a). *How to privatize the Post Office: Piece by piece, step by step?* June 24, 2018. Available at https://savethepostoffice.com/how-to-privatize-the-post-office-piece-by-piece-step-by-step/

United States Postal Regulatory Commission. (2017). Statutory review of the system for regulating rates and classes for market dominant products, Docket No. RM2017–3, Notice of Proposed Rulemaking for the System for Regulating Rates and Classes for Market Dominant Products, Order No. 4257, Issued December 1, 2017. Order No. 4257, (PAEA, 2017) Retrieved from https://www.prc.gov/docs/102/102709/Order%20No.%204257.pdf. "PRC Order 4257".

United States Postal Regulatory Commission. (2017a), Statutory review of the system for regulating rates and classes for market dominant products, Docket No. RM2017–3, Notice of Proposed Rulemaking for the System for Regulating Rates and Classes for Market Dominant Products, Order No. 4258, (PAEA, 2017a) Issued December 1, 2017. Retrieved from https://www.prc.gov/docs/102/102715/Order4258.pdf. "PRC Order 4258".

White House (OMB) Office of Management and Budget (2018), *Delivering government solutions in the 21st century*, June, 2018. Available at https://www.performance.gov/GovReform/

Postal Services: Quo Vadis?

John Hearn

1 Introduction

This paper examines the dramatic changes that postal services and postal service providers worldwide have undergone over the last 50 years and assesses what changes the future may hold. By way of background Section 2 notes that the changes proposed in Rowland Hill (1837) – the introduction of a Universal Penny Post and the prepayment of postage by means of stamps – were copied worldwide very rapidly. Those services remained unchanged for more than a century.

1969 marked an important turning point. In Britain provision of postal services was delegated to a newly established statutory corporation.[1] Globally the Tokyo Congress of the UPU[2] introduced a system of "terminal dues" to remunerate the delivery of international letters. 1969 also marked the emergence of electronic communications as a competitor for postal services.[3] Since then the status of postal service providers worldwide has changed radically. The most significant change is corporatization, the establishment of statutory corporations or state-owned limited liability companies to provide postal service. In more recent times, private capital has acquired some or all of the share capital of a few of these companies

[1] "The Post Office" was established by the Post Office Act 1969 UKPGA 1969 c48 as an autonomous public authority. Section 6(5) of the Act declared that "… the Post Office is not to be regarded as the servant or agent of the Crown, or as enjoying any status, immunity or privilege of the Crown, or (subject to the express provisions of this Act relating to stamp duty) as exempt from any tax, duty, rate, levy or other charge whatsoever, whether general or local, and that its property is not to be regarded as property of, or property held on behalf of, the Crown."

[2] Universal Postal Union.

[3] In 1970 35 per cent of households in the UK owned a telephone; by 1985 penetration had reached 81%. Source: https://www.statista.com/statistics/289158/telephone-presence-in-households-in-the-uk/

J. Hearn (✉)
Formerly ComReg and vice-chair CERP, Dublin, Ireland

P. L. Parcu et al. (eds.), *The Changing Postal Environment*, Topics in Regulatory Economics and Policy, https://doi.org/10.1007/978-3-030-34532-7_3

(privatization). Of course it has always been the case that privately owned companies have been contracted to provide specific services to the postal service provider. Different responses to the changes demanded by the users of postal services and policy makers and the emergence of competing services, particularly those driven by electronic communication, are noteworthy. No longer is the scope of postal service providers' activities homogeneous. These and the other changes are discussed in Section 3.

Quo Vadis? Is there a role for government in the provision of postal services in the future? And what will those services look like? Will there be vertical or horizontal diversification or both? Section 4 examines the options.

2 Background

Postal services have been in existence since ancient times. The Roman Empire had a well- organized service – *cursus publicus*. By the fifteenth century, organized services between Britain, the Low Countries, the Hanseatic League, and the towns of the Rhine and northern Italy existed, in addition to private and governmental posts within individual countries.[4] The middle of the seventeenth century saw the amalgamation of private and governmental posts and the establishment of postal monopolies. The Swedish Royal Postal Agency was established in 1636, and in 1657 Britain's "General Post Office" was established by Act of Parliament.

There were two objectives in establishing a state monopoly. The first was to enable surveillance of potential conspirators by state security and the second to secure a source of revenue for the government of the day. The latter offers an early example of franchising with individuals paying a fixed sum to the government for the contractual right to gather postal revenues as their own.[5] For the next two centuries, postal services evolved to better meet the needs of users, but as Feldman and Kane (1975) observed, "It is one of the remarkable facts of Post Office history that all the really important innovations and reforms were the work of outsiders, who usually did not achieve success until the strenuous opposition of Post Office Officials was overcome." One such innovation was William Dockwra's "New and Useful Invention." No service for local letters within London existed until Dockwra launched a Penny Post in March 1680.[6] It featured prepayment of charges and insurance cover and was unrivalled in terms of frequency and geographical scope. The service was eventually suppressed in November 1682 but reopened within a matter of days as a subdivision of the government's General Post Office.

The changes brought about by the Industrial Revolution had significant implications for national economies and citizens. The introduction of machine-based man-

[4] See Duncan Campbell-Smith (2011) p. 5.

[5] See Duncan Campbell-Smith (2011) p. 37.

[6] See Duncan Campbell-Smith (2011) p. 59–60.

ufacturing gave rise to increased commercial activity and improved standards of living, although it might well be argued that it took over a hundred years for the full benefits to be achieved. An important consequence, so far as the Posts were concerned, was the consequential migration from rural to urban areas and also, for example, migration from Europe to North America and from Britain and Ireland to Australia and New Zealand. All this gave rise to the need for cheap, reliable, and efficient postal services.

In Britain, the campaign for Postal Reform gathered pace during the 1830s. In his pamphlet on Postal Reform, Rowland Hill (1837) presented a detailed business case for the introduction of a Universal Penny Post within the UK, based on simplified tariffs, faster services, and the prepayment of postage. The Penny Post started in January 1840, but postage stamps for the prepayment of postage, which became synonymous with the reforms, were not introduced until 6 May 1840.

The concept of postal service as we have known it until very recently has its origins in this pioneering work. As well as meeting the needs of commerce and trade, postal services played a vital part in cementing the social fabric of the nation, whether in Europe, which witnessed significant urbanization, or in new countries such as the USA, Canada, and Australia, which needed not only to ensure cohesion between vastly dispersed settlements but also to provide links with families still living in Europe. Postal services also played an important part in promoting culture and education, for example, the distribution of newspapers and books (Britain introduced a *Book Post* in 1855), and it fostered fiscal probity (Britain opened its Post Office Savings Bank in 1863). Postal services also played a key role in the development of railways, shipping, and, during the twentieth century, airlines by offering contracts for the conveyance of mails.[7]The Posts were also willing to compete with the private sector, for example, in providing parcel services and in nationalizing services such as telegrams and telephones (see below).

The reforms introduced by Rowland Hill, and especially the use of postage stamps for the prepayment of postage, were copied worldwide very rapidly. By 1855 21 countries across the globe had adopted Rowland Hill's principles – see Table 1.

A postal conference organized in Paris in 1864 to introduce similar reforms in the international service led to the Treaty of Bern 1874 and the establishment of the UPU (Universal Postal Union). In its early years, the UPU was a significant driver of reforms. For example, the 1878 Congress recommended the establishment of an international parcel post at a time when the carriage of parcels in many countries was the prerogative of the private sector. A postal parcel service within the UK was introduced very soon following this recommendation, in 1882, but the USA did not introduce such a service until 1913.[8] While the services were organized by govern-

[7] See AIRMAIL CREATES AN INDUSTRY: Postal Act Facts Smithsonian National Postal Museum USA https://postalmuseum.si.edu/airmail/airmail/public/airmail_public_postal_long.html

[8] See Hearn (2014) for further details.

Table 1 Introduction of prepayment by means of postage stamps

Year	Country
1840	UK (Britain and Ireland)
1843	Brazil
1847	USA
1849	France
1849	Belgium
1849	Bavaria
1850	Austria
1850	Lombardy (Italy)
1850	Spain
1850	Switzerland
1850	New South Wales and Victoria (Australia)
1851	Canada
1851	Denmark
1851	Sardinia (Italy)
1852	Luxembourg
1852	The Netherlands
1853	Chile
1853	Portugal
1855	New Zealand
1855	Norway
1855	Sweden

ments, important elements such as conveyance between post offices were outsourced to the private sector.

The emergence of new communications media such as the telegraph and the telephone was initially championed by the private sector. However, in many countries these services were eventually provided by the state's postal services. In such countries private companies lacked the resources to provide a reliable nationwide service. The labels P&T (Posts and Telegraphs) or PTT (Posts Telegraphs Telephones) became synonymous with the provision of postal and telephone services.

The homogeneous principles for the provision of postal services established during the second half of the nineteenth century went unchallenged for more than a century. There are eight key principles. The services were provided directly by governments. The services were provided on a non-contractual basis under public law. "Postage" was a nonnegotiable fixed charge. There were uniform charges within the state. Prepayment of "postage" was the norm. The "Post" acted as an intermediary between sender and addressee, rather than as the agent of either sender or addressee. "Postage" was a government tax payable by users of the service. The cost of providing the service was a charge on the Exchequer; which meant there was no matching of income and expenses. Hearn (2018) discusses the legal status of postal services in more detail.

3 The Last 50 Years

The last 50 years have witnessed different responses to the changes demanded by the users of postal services and policy makers and the emergence of competing services, particularly those driven by electronic communication. No longer is the scope of postal service providers' activities homogeneous.

3.1 Corporatization and Privatization

The status of postal service providers has changed radically. The most significant change is corporatization – the establishment of statutory corporations or state-owned limited liability companies to provide postal service. In more recent times, private capital has acquired some or all of the share capital of a few of these companies (privatization). Of course it has always been the case that privately owned companies have been contracted to provide specific services to the postal service provider. Table 2 summarizes the situation in the industrialized countries as defined by the UPU[9]:

Within the EU in only one country, namely, Cyprus, are postal services still provided by a government department.

3.2 Business Volumes

Hearn (2018) noted that there has been a significant reduction in the number of letters being sent since the EU's Postal Directive came into force. Copenhagen Economics (2018) reported that during the period 2013–2016, addressed letter post products declined by on average 4.2 per cent annually in the 31 countries surveyed. The UPU (2019) reports that the compound rate of decline worldwide in the last decade has been 3.1 per cent annually. About 87% of the total worldwide volume is attributed by the UPU to the group of industrialized countries.[10] In these countries the annual rate of decline over the same period was 2.4%, but in 2017 there was a positive growth rate of 1.8 per cent.

[9] 23 countries as listed in the table, but notably only including 14 of the 28 EU member states.

[10] See footnote 9 supra.

Table 2 Status of postal service providers in UPU industrialized countries

Country	Autonomous state enterprise	Limited liability company	Extent of state ownership
Australia	Yes		100%
Austria		1999	52.8%
Belgium		Yes	50% + 1
Canada	1981		100%
Denmark		PostNord	40% Denmark; 60% Sweden
Finland		Yes	100%
France		Yes	100%
Germany		1995	20.5%
Greece		1996	90%, remainder Postal Savings Bank
Iceland		1998	100%
Ireland		1984	100%
Israel		2006	100%
Italy		Yes	64.3%
Japan		Yes	Fully privatized
Luxembourg	Joint P&T corporation		
Netherlands		Yes	Fully privatized
New Zealand		Yes	100%
Norway		Yes	100%
Portugal		1992	100%
Spain		2000	100%
Sweden		1994, then PostNord	60% Sweden; 40% Denmark
Switzerland	1997		100%
UK	1969	2001	Fully privatized

Sources: UPU website, Status and structures of postal entities (See http://www.upu.int/en/the-upu/status-of-postal-entities/about-status-of-postal-entities.html) and annual reports of postal service providers

3.3 *Service Provision*

As already noted postal services have traditionally been provided under public law with the postal service provider acting as an intermediary between sender and addressee, the features of the services being nonnegotiable, and postage being prepaid.

Prepayment by postage stamps is no longer the norm, having been challenged by the use of online postage, franking meters, credit accounts, and other innovative payment methods. Stamps are now normally used only by private individuals and SMEs.[11]

[11] According to the OECD, SMEs (small- and medium-sized enterprises) are non-subsidiary, independent firms which employ fewer than a given number of employees, normally 250 employees, as in the European Union, but as high as 500 employees as in the USA.

Analysis of An Post's 2017 Regulatory Accounts[12] shows that only 18.5% by volume and 20.2% by value of national postal services are prepaid by stamps.[13] According to Copenhagen Economics (2018), the proportion of mail posted by private individuals has declined very significantly and, based on data from 13 countries, is now about 11 per cent of the total by volume.

Larger businesses, public authorities, and nongovernmental organizations[14] (NGOs) generate most mail items. An Post's 2017 Regulatory Accounts show that 16.5% by volume and 16.1% by value of postal items are prepaid using franking machines. By inference at least 65% of national items are now paid for using non-traditional methods, including credit and other accounts.

Credit facilities are now a very important part of the offer by postal service providers. Royal Mail, the UK's postal service provider, offers a credit account, advertised as "The fast and easy way to pay for your mail." The key selling point is to "Take control of your budget and your cash flow with a credit account. You'll benefit from convenient payment terms - up to 30 days and volume-related discounts."[15] This necessitates an increase in working capital. In the case of Royal Mail, trade receivables as of 25 March 2018 stood at GB£999 m or 9.8% of annual revenues. Six years earlier trade receivables as of 25 March 2012 stood at GB£759 m or 8.7% of annual revenues.[16]

It is not just the method and terms of payment that have changed. Business users often prefer provision of postal services under contract law, meaning that the postal service provider has a legal responsibility to the customer (normally the sender but sometimes the receiver). The EU Consumer Rights Directive (2011) requires the seller to be fully responsible for all aspects of the supply of goods, including delivery. Hearn (2014) observed that this is inconsistent with the use of the traditional postal services for delivery. Competing delivery services are invariably provided under private contract law.

Larger businesses often require postal service providers and competing delivery services to provide services which are specifically tailored to meet their requirements in terms of speed, pickup and delivery times, packaging, insurance, etc. The traditional "one size fits all" approach is inconsistent with these requirements. The challenge for postal service is to develop the capability to negotiate with such businesses rather than to sell the inflexible, in terms of price and features, traditional services.

[12] An Post has been used as an example solely because of the availability of information.

[13] It should be borne in mind that 12.4% of An Post's delivered traffic originates abroad, and because of this, the proportion of stamped mail may be overstated.

[14] Including charities and other "not for profit" organizations.

[15] See, for example, https://www.royalmail.com/corporate/services/account.

[16] Figures taken from Royal Mail plc Annual Report and Financial Statements 2017–2018 and Royal Mail plc.

Prospectus 27 September 2013.

3.4 Mail (Letter) Services

As quantified in Section 3.2, volumes have fallen significantly, but letters are still a very significant business. 271bn letters were posted in the industrialized countries during 2018.[17] Although mail is more expensive than electronic communication media, mail remains one of the most effective channels for connecting with customers and generating new leads. According to Royal Mail, "In-depth studies into the effect of direct mail show that it makes customers feel more valued than other channels. Not only that, but mail is read, kept in the home, referred back to and shared with others."[18] There are emerging signs that it may be possible to halt the decline in letter volumes, including a small increase in business volume in the industrialized countries reported by UPU (2019).

The British Post Office introduced a two-tier letter service offering a choice between a D + 1 (next day) service and a slower D + 3 service as long ago as 1967, and many of the larger operators followed this trend. With the decline in business volumes, some operators have decided to reduce the quality of service provided by reducing the number of days on which letters are delivered or offering a very slow service, e.g., D + 5. Some operators, e.g., Poste italiane, Correos (Spain), and Post Danmark, have introduced a premium service similar to registered post and offering a D + 1 service.

3.5 Parcel and packet services

The decline in the letter business has been offset to some extent by a growth in packet and parcel volumes. According to the UPU (2019), parcel post volumes have increased by 7.1% per annum over the decade 2007–2017. There are however a number of caveats. In the past, packets and in some instances postal parcels were delivered along with the letter post. As parcel volumes increase, this model of delivery may no longer be sustainable. Furthermore, parcel delivery is a very competitive business, so while it is attractive to postal operators to exploit, there is no guarantee of profits sufficient to make up for losses from declining letter volumes.

A key issue that has to be addressed is the difficulty in delivering parcels at the first attempt as many addressees may not be at home when the postman calls. Alternatives implemented by some operators include the use of lockers,[19] delivery to a parcel shop open 7–11 or 24/7,[20] and evening or weekend delivery.[21] Postal

[17] See footnote 9 *supra*.

[18] See https://www.royalmail.com/corporate/marketing-data/marketing/benefits-marketing-mail

[19] For example, Deutsche Post/DHL, Post Danmark, La Poste (France), bPost (Belgium), and Poczta Polska (Polish Post).

[20] For example, Posten Se.

[21] For example, Royal Mail (UK), An Post (Ireland).

operators are often disadvantaged by obligations to deliver to the specified address and the limited opening hours of post offices and delivery offices.

3.6 International Services

The 1969 Tokyo Congress of the UPU introduced a system of "terminal dues" based on a flat rate charge per kg on the excess weight received.[22] The following 50 years saw postal service providers compete with one another, developing services such as Remail[23] and acquiring regional and international networks for packets and parcels.

The distortions caused by the terminal dues system both in the postal markets and in related markets such as printing and distance selling have been well documented in Campbell (2016), but there has been a reluctance by governments to resolve the issues. However, the recent growth in ecommerce imports from Asia has prompted both the EU and the USA to take action.

The EU is focused on eliminating the low value tax exemptions on postal imports and ensuring that value added tax and customs duties are paid by commercial senders before the goods are dispatched.[24] The UK already has similar arrangements with certain territories, including Jersey.[25] Both these initiatives are bad news for postal operators. The elimination of the low value tax exemptions leads to a significant increase in the number of items to be presented to customs and therefore adds to costs. The new arrangements for the prepayment of VAT and Customs Duty will be more attractive to commercial operators and the Posts risk being left with expensive to handle C2C parcels.

The USA is taking a different tack. In October 2018, the US President decided that the USA should withdraw from the UPU because of concerns that the highly subsidized rate set by the UPU for delivery of lightweight packages from countries, such as China, puts American businesses engaged in e-commerce – from small retailers to large manufacturers – at a disadvantage.[26] Proposals to address the distortions caused by the UPU terminal dues system have not yet been approved by the UPU. On 7 June 2019, the UPU announced that 128 valid postal ballots had been received from UPU member countries in support of convening an Extraordinary

[22] Payment was not paid for all mail delivered but only for the imbalance. For example, if Country B receives 100 tons of mail from Country A but sends 50 tons to Country A, it would be paid for 50 tons, and Country A would receive nothing.

[23] Arranging for mailings to be posted in a foreign company to avail of international rates cheaper than domestic rates in the destination country.

[24] See Council Directive (EU) 2017/2455 of 5 December 2017 amending Directive 2006/112/EC and Directive 2009/132/EC as regards certain value added tax obligations for supplies of services and distance sales of goods.

[25] See House of Commons Library Briefing Paper 4155 (2017).

[26] See "State Dept. Backs Plan for U.S. to Set Own Global Package Rates" https://about.bgov.com/news/state-dept-backs-plan-for-u-s-to-set-own-global-package-rates/

Congress to discuss the UPU terminal dues system in September 2019.[27] There are parallels with IATA[28] which, like the UPU, was an intergovernmental organization representing state enterprises. As the industry was liberalized, the price fixing and related regulations came under attack.[29] Within 5 years all those elements of the IATA regulations which might be considered to be anti-competitive were repealed. Will the UPU follow the same path?

3.7 *Divesting*

As discussed in Section 2, in the nineteenth and early twentieth centuries, new services such as telegrams, telephones, etc. were often provided by the postal service provider. During the last 50 years, this business model has been challenged. The main drivers were the necessity for dedicated management teams, the capital-intensive nature of the services, and the introduction of economic regulation within the EU (European Union). Most postal service providers have by now been divested of telecommunications services.

It might be observed, with hindsight, that divesting electronic communications has created the biggest threat to the long-term survival of postal services by facilitating the emergence of competing services. Hearn (2018) has noted that the traditional postal services are losing the competitive battle with electronic communication services such as text messaging (SMS), email, and mobile voice communication.

In some cases, postal service providers have also been divested of the network of post offices and some financial services. The main driver appears to be the need to allow postal service managers to focus on the development of the postal services but also to facilitate the retention of socially necessary services that might not be provided on a commercial basis. In the UK, the Post Office Ltd. was separated from Royal Mail Group in 2012 on foot of a recommendation in the Hooper Report[30]; the former remained a state-owned company, and the latter was subsequently privatized. In Sweden, Postgirot Bank AB was divested in 2001. In 2018 An Post, the Irish postal operator, announced a structural separation between post offices and mail services.[31] In Germany, the financial services of Deutsche Post were divested in 1990 with the formation of Deutsche Postbank AG.

[27] See http://news.upu.int/no_cache/nd/upu-member-countries-vote-to-hold-geneva-extraordinary-congress-on-terminal-dues-system/

[28] The International Air Transport Association.

[29] See Order 2007-3-23 issued by the USA Department of Transportation on the 30th day of March 2007.

[30] See House of Commons Briefing Paper Number 7550, 12 April 2019 "The Post Office."

[31] See An Post Annual Report 2017, p. 6.

3.8 *Diversification*

As the core mail services have declined in importance, many postal service providers have diversified into other activities. Unlike the reforms of the nineteenth century, however, a variety of approaches are discernible. These include diversification into logistics, marketing, printing, IT, and even financial services. Also some postal companies have diversified geographically, with one operator developing a global network[32] and two operators developing substantial regional networks.[33] Many of the world's leading postal companies have positioned themselves to be successful in the coming decades. Table 3 provides examples of these diversification strategies.

These nine examples demonstrate that there is no consensus about the form of diversification that should be followed. What the examples show is that those service providers that have diversified into financial services have relatively small exposure to international markets and that access to capital and a significant domestic base is important for developing global or regional networks.

4 Quo Vadis

The changes of the last 50 years have been merely a transitioning toward a new order. The key assets of postal service providers are their conveyance and delivery networks, with their nationwide coverage and a committed, trusted, and well-trained workforce. There are two types of networks. The first is the letter (and small packet[34]) delivery network, which normally aims to serve every delivery point on a fixed route. The other type of network, used for the delivery of parcels,[35] is more variable in routing. In practice there is some overlap between these two networks. In rural areas where letter delivery routes use vehicles, these routes will also deliver parcels. In urban areas when the percentage of packets is large, some items may be delivered by the parcel network, particularly those that require a signature to be obtained on delivery or if the item cannot be delivered through the delivery box at the house.

From the regulatory viewpoint, although the letter delivery network can be replicated, both legally and practically, there is no example where this has been done on a nationwide basis. Regulators must therefore ensure that postal service providers do not use the de facto monopoly over the letter delivery network to foreclose on upstream competition. The position concerning the parcel delivery network is somewhat different in that there are often competing networks and the postal service

[32] Deutsche Post (DHL).

[33] Royal Mail (GLS) and La Poste (France) (DPD).

[34] Volume not greater than 0.027 m^3 and weight not exceeding 2 kg.

[35] That is, items larger than the limits for packets and normally with an upper limit of. 0.1875 m^3 and 30 kg.

Table 3 Diversification strategies

Operator/country	See note	State ownership	Total external revenue 2018	Product diversification[a]	Geographical diversification[b]
Deutsche Post (Germany)	1	20.5%	€61.5bn	€18.3bn (29.8%)	€18.8bn (30.6%)
Poste italiane (Italy)	2	64.3%	€10.9bn	€3.6bn (33.0%)	No material diversification
Swiss Post (Switzerland)	3	100%	CHF 7.7bn	CHF 2.7 BN (35.1)	84.5%
bPost (Belgium)	4	50% + 1	€3.9bn	€1.7bn (43.6%)	€2.5% (64.1%)
La Poste (France)	5	100%	€24.7bn	€11.3bn (45.7%)	€12.5bn (50.6%) Mail €5.5bn (22.2%) Banking
An Post (Ireland)	6	100%	€0.9bn	€0.6bn (66.7%)	€0.8bn (88.9%)
PostNord (Sweden and Denmark)	7	100%	SEK 37.7bn	SEK 35.8bn (87.7%)	SEK 22.1bn (58.6%) Sweden SEK 8.1bn (21.5%) Denmark
Royal Mail (UK)	8	NIL	GB£10.2bn	No material diversification	GB£7.6bn (74.5%)
PostNL (The Netherlands)	9	NIL	€2.758bn	€1.672bn (50.8%) Mail €1.547bn (47%) Parcels	€2.483bn (90.0%)

Note 1
International brand DHL
PRODUCT DIVERSIFICATION Post eCommerce Parcel Division
Other divisions: Express, Global Forwarding Freight, Supply Chain
Note 2
PRODUCT DIVERSIFICATION Mail, Parcels and Distribution segment
Other segments: Payments, Mobile and Digital, Financial services, Insurance services
Note 3
PRODUCT DIVERSIFICATION PostMail
Other segments: Swiss Post Solutions, PostalNetwork, PostLogistics, PostFinance, PostBus
Note 4
PRODUCT DIVERSIFICATION Mail and Parcels segment
Other segments: Logistic Solutions, Banking and financial products, Distribution, Retail and Other
Note 5
International brand DPD
PRODUCT DIVERSIFICATION Services-Mail-Parcels segment
Other segments: GeoPost (DPD), La Banque Postale, Digital Services, La Poste Network
Note 6
PRODUCT DIVERSIFICATION Letters and parcels, etc.
Other segments: Retail and Financial services, printing and database services
Note 7
PRODUCT DIVERSIFICATION Mail, logistics and eCommerce
Other products: Information logistics
Note 8
International brand GLS
Note 9
The Parcels segment includes the international activities of Spring. The product segments include an element of overlapping revenue streams that are eliminated on consolidation.
[a]% of revenue *from* postal services as defined by operator in annual report
[b]% of revenue from home country

providers' market share is not great.[36] For example, in Ireland, DPD, UPS /Nightline, GLS, Fastway, and DHL all have competing networks. The key concern for regulators must be to ensure that the terminal dues payable to postal service providers do not distort the market for the delivery of packets, i.e., items less than 2 kg in weight.

Although there has been a significant reduction in the volume of letter post items, there is still a sufficient volume of letters to support the retention of the letter delivery networks of most postal service providers. The reduction in the frequency of delivery in some countries may be imprudent. The volume of packets appears to be increasing as a result of the growth in ecommerce. Daily deliveries are essential to meet the needs of this market.

However, the traditional postal service model providing for the collection, sorting, transport, and delivery of postal items under public law at a nonnegotiable tariff may not be sustainable for the vast majority of business customers. Rather the need must be to redefine the relationship between postal service provider and business customer as a partnership offering bespoke services under private contract law. To fully meet the needs of their customers and to maximize the potential of their delivery networks – including achieving the necessary economies of scale and scope – they will need to consider vertical diversification into upstream markets such as printing, database management, ecommerce platforms, etc.[37] The latter is quite important in that already some ecommerce platforms are in the process of acquiring delivery networks. As already identified this will need strong regulatory surveillance to ensure there is no abuse of a dominant position. Moreover, the need to address the issue of climate change will lead to significant changes in operational processes including the use of electric vehicles and the use of real-time software systems to ensure flexible routing and other efficiency measures.

The current international arrangements are not sustainable. Several postal service providers own and operate global or regional networks for parcel delivery.[38] And there are other global networks operated by private sector companies.[39] The UPU arrangements cannot compete with these networks in terms of price/cost and quality of service. Many smaller countries might find themselves unable to offer international services if these trends continue. As a minimum they would need to negotiate a business relationship with one or other of the global networks.

---

[36] See TPR (2015) and The European Economic and Social Committee (2016) which suggest market shares varying between 10% and 25%.

[37] Asendia, the joint venture between La Poste (France) and Swiss Post, is a 40% shareholder in eShopWorld, an eCommerce company that provides a technology platform to brands and retailers that wish to sell online into global markets.

Also the An Post website provides links to facilities to help new e-retailers, including a link to the platform "www.Iloveshopping.ie." See https://www.anpost.ie/AnPost/GeneralTemplates/AboutUsStandard.aspx?NRMODE=Published&NRNODEGUID=%7b2C5300D3-CF17-4CB7-AACB-BEA4D9DDF8CD%7d&NRORIGINALURL=%2fAnPost%2fMainContent%2fBusiness%2bCustomers%2fecommerce%2feCommerce%2bExperts%2ehtm&NRCACHEHINT=Guest#Getting

[38] Deutsche Post, La Poste, Royal Mail.

[39] UPS, FedEx.

The global and regional parcel operators do not generally offer services for letters, other than premium products for important documents. There is no obvious alternative to the UPU arrangements in letter post markets, but these are threatened by the American decision to withdraw from the UPU. Furthermore international letter markets are declining faster than domestic letter markets – down by 5.5% per annum compared with 2.4% nationally over the 10 years to 2017. The threat to the UPU is its role in price setting. It is clearly undesirable for governments to be involved in price setting when it causes distortions in competitive markets, but governments have a role to play in ensuring international connectivity for written communications and cultural material – books, educational material, etc. The extraordinary Congress of the UPU to be held in September 2019 should put in place a process to reform the UPU, focusing on ensuring international cooperation and avoiding any involvement in price setting. If this is agreed, then the USA might withdraw its notice of resignation.

The observations above relate specifically to mail and parcel services. The services provided at "post offices" present a completely different set of issues. Post offices have an obsolescent business model – very limited opening hours during the week and limited or no activity at the weekend. Postal service providers can, and do, offer their services over the Internet or by arrangement with other retailers operating 24/7 or 7 till late[40]. In those countries that have been able to leverage the network of post offices to provide a viable range of financial and government services, it may be preferable, as in the UK, to divest these to separate government-owned companies. This would allow appropriately focused management teams address the future of two very different activities.

A key issue that will need to be addressed is "Is there a role for government in the provision of postal services in the future?" Although there is a demonstrable need to reduce, but not eliminate, government involvement in international postal services, the proper role of governments in providing national services is more abstruse. In the developed world, there are now very few examples where governments are directly involved in the provision of postal services. That is not to say that governments have ceased to have any involvement, but as in so many other areas of government activity, they have delegated their involvement to state agencies, including independent regulators.

A follow on is to ask what type of state agency and to what extent should these have access to private capital. The data presented in Table 2 suggests that the limited liability company is the preferred model in 19 of the 23 countries analyzed. There is less consensus as to the involvement of private capital; only 3 of the 23 postal service providers have been fully privatized. In Germany there is a relatively small (20%) state shareholding; in Belgium a 50/50 arrangement with the state holding a controlling share but elsewhere private capital is in a minority. The analysis in Table 2 suggests that private investors are willing to participate on the basis of a minority interest.

[40] The term 7 till late is used as the normal opening times for such shops as the closing time varies considerably from country to country but typically would be 10 pm, 11 pm, or midnight.

Private capital may be needed in the future to ensure that operators adapt to the new order. All too frequently governments do not have sufficient funds for such investment, and, even when they do, the requirements of state aid rules, and similar antitrust legislation, present significant obstacles. Moreover, market changes may involve a greater degree of risk than governments are comfortable with. Finally, private capital perhaps can bring expertise in terms of risk management, income generation, and cost control without the need for day-to-day involvement in management.

To conclude, both mail and parcel services retain a significant future. Postal service providers will have a de facto monopoly over letter delivery, but in reality they will be competing, as they do now, with electronic communications services. To be successful postal service providers will need a more commercial focus on forming partnerships with business customers rather than offering nonnegotiable tariffs on a take it or leave it basis. The challenge for regulators will be to ensure that postal service providers do not use their de facto monopoly over letter delivery to compete unfairly on parcel markets. Given the international nature of ecommerce, it is difficult to identify a role for postal service providers in smaller countries other than as an agent for one of the global/regional networks. But this could lead to the introduction of capital to facilitate investment to develop the networks.[41] Also there is a need to look at opportunities for vertical diversification similar to the investment by Asendia in eShopworld.

References

Campbell. (2016). A quantifying the distortive effects of UPU terminal dues. In M. Crew & T. J. Brennan (Eds.), *The future of the postal sector in a digital world* (p. 2016). New York: Springer.

Consumer Rights Directive. (2011). Directive 2011/83/EU of the European Parliament and of the Council of 25 October 2011 on consumer rights, amending Council Directive 93/13/EEC and Directive 1999/44/EC of the European Parliament and of the Council and repealing Council Directive 85/577/EEC and Directive 97/7/EC of the European Parliament and of the Council.

Copenhagen Economics. (2018). *Main Developments in the Postal Sector (2013–2016) Study for the European Commission*. Directorate-General for Internal Market, Industry, Entrepreneurship and SMEs.

Duncan Campbell-Smith. (2011). *Masters of the post: The authorized history of the royal mail penguin Allen lane.*

European Economic and Social Committee. (2016). Opinion, Proposal for a Regulation of the European Parliament and of the Council on cross-border parcel delivery services [COM(2016) 285 final – 2016/0149 (COD)], INT/799 Parcel delivery, 19 October 2016.

Feldman, D., & Kane, W. (1975). *Handbook of Irish postal history to 1840*. Dublin: David Feldman (I) Ltd.

---

[41] See, for example, the acquisition of UK Mail by Deutsche Post and the subsequent investment over GB£21 m to support recent and future growth. See https://www.theguardian.com/business/2016/sep/28/deutsche-post-agrees-to-buy-uk-mail and https://ukmail.com/news/2017/08/21/uk-mail-invests-over-21m-(-23m)-in-regional-network-to-support-growth

Hearn. (2014). Delivering the goods to households – Would further regulation help or hinder? In *The role of the postal and delivery sector in a digital age*. Cheltenham: Edward Elgar Publishing Cheltenham.
Hearn. (2018). Regulation. Quo vadis? In P. L. Parcu et al. (Eds.), *The contribution of the postal and delivery sector, topics in regulatory economics and policy* (p. 2018). Cham: Springer.
House of Commons Library Briefing Paper 4155. (2017). *VAT on postal packages By Antony Seely*.
Rowland Hill. (1837). *Post office reform: Its importance and practicability*. London: Charles Knight and Co.
TPR. (2015). *Cross-border parcel delivery operations and its cost drivers, department of transport and regional economics*. University of Antwerp, for the European Commission.
UPU. (2019). *Postal economic outlook 2019 latest trends in an evolving sector*. Cham: UPU Berne.

How the Fragmentation of the Postal Supply Chain Leads to New Business Models

Ozhan Zurel and Luigi Scorca

1 Introduction

The postal sector is changing at a fast pace induced by many innovations and disruptive technologies. We aim to explain how the postal supply chain is increasingly fragmenting into modules, where some of these modules are virtualized and no longer needed to be carried out physically in order to offer end-to-end delivery services.

Section 2 describes the traditional postal supply chain. Section 3 illustrates how the traditional postal supply chain is under pressure, while Section 4 describes the new postal reality. Section 5 then illustrates innovations on different postal stages: clearance, sorting, transport and delivery. This section looks at the introduction of different types of platforms in the delivery market. Section 6 concludes, outlining some implications for postal operators and policy makers regarding the postal supply chain fragmentation.

The views expressed in this paper are personal and do not necessarily represent the position of the institution to which the authors belong.

O. Zurel (✉)
BIPT, Brussels, Belgium
e-mail: Oezhan.Zurel@bipt.be

L. Scorca
Bocconi University, Milan, Italy

P. L. Parcu et al. (eds.), *The Changing Postal Environment*, Topics in Regulatory Economics and Policy, https://doi.org/10.1007/978-3-030-34532-7_4

2 The Traditional Postal Supply Chain

Postal items have a few general characteristics: they are addressed in their final form[1] and can weigh up to 31.5 kg. The address might be linked to the item in different forms (e.g., a QR code), but it must indicate who is entitled to receive the item and where it should be delivered.

The traditional postal supply chain consists of an end-to-end system, based on a hub-and-spoke model, where a single postal operator, usually state-owned, covers all postal stages. Within the framework of the European Postal Services Directive 97/67/EC (hereafter: PSD), the postal supply chain is organized by these four postal stages: clearance, sorting, intercity transport, and delivery.[2] By clearance, postal items are collected through different modalities and then carried out to the distribution center of the area. By sorting, postal items are sorted by homogeneous groups of items (according to product, format, and destination) and then conveyed (the transport step) to the distribution center of the area of destination. In the hub located near to the destination, items are sorted again, finally by destination, routed, and finally distributed/delivered to the customers by different modalities; see Fig. 1.

3 The Pressure on Traditional Post

3.1 *Technological Innovation*

The Internet has had, and is still having, a twofold effect on traditional postal markets. Firstly, the Internet has enabled the growth of e-commerce retailers (e-tailers), through webshops and e-commerce platforms. This translated into the volume and revenue of parcels witnessing double-digit growth rates throughout the past decade.

Secondly, social communication, which was before done mainly by social mail, has been significantly e-substituted by web and smartphone applications such as Skype, Whatsapp, Snapchat, Messenger, etc. The current letter mail market is mainly characterized by direct mail advertisements and administrative mail, including invoices, registered items, and legal notifications. These mail segments, however, are increasingly falling subject to e-substitution as well through initiatives such as e-government and electronic registered items on the one hand and online direct mail on the other (Corredera and Leta 2019).

[1] It does not necessarily mean they should be labelled with an address, as unaddressed mail are postal services too, nor that it is compulsory that postal items need to be delivered in an envelope or in a box.

[2] Transport also takes place between the clearance and sorting stage, and – as mentioned in the ECJ jurisprudence (DHL International NV, formerly Express Line NV vs. Belgisch Instituut voor Postdiensten en Telecommunicatie), as well as in the EU Regulation n. 2018/644 – can be considered a postal activity only if undertaken with one of the other activities already mentioned.

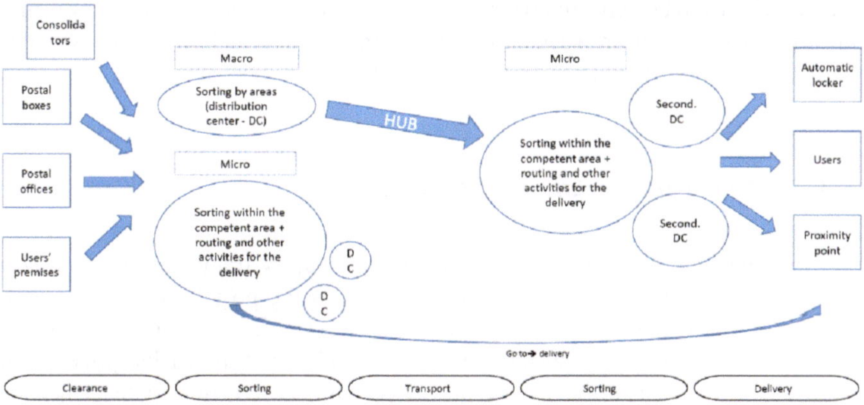

Source: (Scorca, 2019)

Fig. 1 Postal service supply chain. (Source: Scorca (2019))

Postal market supply chains are also witnessing pressure from disruptive technological innovations such as enhanced connectivity (geolocation and real-time tracking information), blockchain (verified digital labelling),[3] and artificial intelligence (highly accurate demand forecasting and intelligent interfaces).[4] These innovations offer efficiency improvements as well as increased operational model reliability for the provision of postal services.

3.2 *Demographic Evolutions*

In 1950 approximately one-third of the world population (or less than 1 billion citizens) lived in urban areas, but by 2050 this proportion is expected to rise to two-thirds (or over 6 billion citizens) (United Nations 2014). This increasing population density creates a significant challenge for last mile delivery. The preference of most consumers for home delivery, from an inner-city logistics point of view, is a major concern. The growth in e-commerce, combined with a preference for home delivery, has led to a fragmentation of shipments in the "last mile" (Morganti et al. 2014).

At the same time, consumers are becoming more time-sensitive regarding delivery, especially for parcels containing commercial goods. Whereas traditional postal operators used to indicate only the day of delivery, a growing number of postal operators communicate more narrow delivery time slots. This creates pressure on supply chain management and requires complex forecasting models. Consumers also wish

[3] See www.mpost.co.ke for a nice example of blockchain use in postal services.

[4] https://www.singpost.com/about-us/news-releases/singpost-integrates-loginext%E2%80%99s-artificial-intelligence-next-gen-logistics-platform-lamp

their purchases to be delivered when they are actually at home, meaning they want it mostly in evenings or on weekends (Zurel 2016). Evening delivery, moreover, falls during rush hours, creating an extra challenge for on-time delivery.

3.3 A New Interpretation of Inclusivity

In 1997, the first PSD established a common regulatory framework for European postal services. The main purpose of EU policy in the postal sector has been to gradually complete the single market for postal services and to ensure that reliable, efficient, and high-quality postal services are available at affordable prices to all European citizens. This inclusivity aspect is, with the creation of the Universal Service Obligation (hereafter: USO), one of the main *raisons d'être* of the PSD. The main rationale behind this is to ensure that every citizen should be able to communicate both at a domestic and at an intra-EU level.

Communication in 1997 was mainly performed through social mail (with mostly letter mail items). However, the function of letter mail as a means of social communication has eroded over the past decade. For digitized EU Member States, in the near future, a discussion may arise as to whether the USO is still required and/or at what level this USO might be required.

EU Regulation 2018/644 on cross-border parcel delivery services (hereafter: Regulation), which complements the PSD, contains some noteworthy additional references to the notion of inclusivity: Recital 9 says, "In order to improve cross-border parcel delivery services, especially for individuals and micro and small businesses, *including those in remote or sparsely populated areas*, and for *individuals with disabilities or with reduced mobility*, it is necessary to improve the access to and transparency of public lists of tariffs for a limited set of cross-border parcel delivery services." Art 6, 2, D says, "The likely impact of the applicable cross-border tariffs on individual and small and medium-sized enterprise users *including those situated in remote or sparsely populated areas*, and on *individual users with disabilities or with reduced mobility*, where possible without imposing a disproportionate burden" (emphases added).

Contrary to the PSD, which was initially published in 1997 and focused on social mail streams, the Regulation focuses mainly on commercial mail streams. This has paved the way to approach inclusivity from a different angle, as social mail and commercial mail have completely different mail characteristics. Social mail, consisting mainly of letter mail items, is easier to standardize and distribute. Commercial mail, especially when containing goods, is subject to a large range of dimensions and weight. Traditional postal operators have to adapt their operational model in order to meet changing postal behavior and consumer needs.

Assuming that the inclusivity rationale for social mail will eventually fade out due to digitization, the *raison d'être* for the USO might shift from social communication to e-commerce. This discussion is taking place at the moment and will play an important element within the new (or revised) PSD (ERGP and European Commission 2018).

4 Post 2.0

4.1 The Era of the Postal Consumer

4.1.1 An Emotional Shift

Traditionally, letter mail has always had a high emotional value since it contained mainly social mail as a way of communication between (far-away) citizens with an emotional bond. With the outflux of social mail from the letter mail segment, the remaining segments (direct and administrative mail) evoke less (positive) emotions. Parcel mail, consisting mostly of e-commerce items, has become the segment that consumers are eager to receive (BIPT 2017a).

Consumer needs have changed together with this shift of emotional value from letter mail to parcel mail. In Belgium, postal end users approach a diminution of the delivery frequency for letter mail rather positively. Delivery speed of these letter mail items can decrease as long as a faster premium option remains available for urgent mail (BIPT 2017b).

4.1.2 Fast and Free Delivery

Because of the high emotional value of e-commerce items, consumers tend to prefer the fastest possible delivery method. Whereas traditionally a parcel used to be delivered within a week, a next-day delivery equipped with a track and trace barcode is becoming the new standard. Within city centers and in densely populated areas, pilots have started to provide 2 or even 1 hour delivery services.[5,6] In order to participate to this race to the front door, parcel delivery service providers are required to optimally decentralize their network with regional parcel sorting centers, local warehouses, and inner-city delivery hubs.[7]

4.2 Sustainable Delivery Models

Postal operators also face ecological limits in city centers. Firstly, restricted traffic areas have been put into place in many cities. In the Belgian city of Ghent, for example, this has been named "The Circulation Plan" and is aimed at opening up

[5] https://www.channelengine.com/company/marketplace-blog/dutch-marketplace-bolcom-starts-2-hour-delivery-in-the-netherlands/

[6] https://primenow.amazon.co.uk/onboard?sourceUrl=%2Fhome

[7] In addition, e-consumers often get low-cost or free delivery. Although the sustainability of this model of free delivery (and returns) is contested, e-tailers seem to be prepared to reduce their profit margin in order to gain market share.

space for pedestrians, cyclists, and public transport while it hampers motorized vehicles to travel freely within the city center.[8] This implies that bicycle delivery has an advantage as compared to car or truck delivery within these city centers.

A second possible barrier is the installation of low emission zones (in major cities such as London, Paris, and Antwerp). To reduce CO_2 emission within city centers, low emission zones encourage the most polluting vehicles to become cleaner. This type of regulation seems to be the first step, as cities plan to move toward ultralow emission zones.[9] The city of Amsterdam even plans to phase in a ban on petrol and diesel cars and motorbikes by 2030.[10] Parcel delivery service providers are directly affected by city access regulation, as they will have to shift toward emission-free delivery, likely combined with inner-city distribution hubs, in order to offer a sustainable yet fast delivery service.

5 The Impact of Technology on the Postal Stages

New operational postal models are mainly based on the decentralization of the postal stages that previously needed to be bundled: in these innovative models, the activities of the postal supply chain are organized in separate modules interacting in different ways, and postal services might be provided differently according to users' needs. Technology is, in fact, leading to the fragmentation of the postal supply chain into parts that can be then re-bundled in different ways, according to the needs of operators and users (Scorca 2019). An example is the case of e-commerce platforms (e.g., eBay and Amazon), which integrate both retail services and only some of the postal activities (as the sorting both between and within warehouses, as well as the successive routing and delivery of the items): in some areas, in fact, e-commerce platforms are developing their own network in order to deliver goods ordered at their electronic marketplace. These infrastructures might one day also be used to deliver postal items from different sources, not necessarily e-commerce orders.

A consequent manifestation of the fragmentation of the postal supply chain is that operations can be organized by a model of point-to-point services operated by local delivery units, which are managed by a third party as a sort of a virtual platform. The operator in charge of the efficiency of the whole supply chain manages warehouses and the relationship with logistic companies, carrying out bulk items from different locations within the primary sections of the infrastructure, and, at last, organizes the last-mile (point-to-point) segment. This paper will look a bit deeper on the technological impact on each postal stage.

[8] https://stad.gent/ghent-international/mobility-ghent/circulation-plan

[9] https://tfl.gov.uk/modes/driving/ultra-low-emission-zone

[10] https://www.theguardian.com/world/2019/may/03/amsterdam-ban-petrol-diesel-cars-bikes-2030

5.1 Clearance

The clearance process has mainly become more granular. It used to be rather centralized, with local collection points, owned by the postal operator, such as postal offices and sorting centers. The introduction of platforms, parcel lockers, and Pick Up Drop Off (PUDO)[11] points has, however, increased the granularity of clearance points. This implies that while a higher burden is put on traffic (and mobility), generally the customer can decrease its transport needs.

5.2 Sorting

Sorting activities involve separation of postal items into specific groups (according to product, format, weight, and destination). Then, these groups of postal items are assigned to a routing-based courier. The assignment itself is a sort of (virtual) sorting as it determines the destination address. Technology plays an essential role in the (virtual) sorting as point-to-point delivery services generally make use of an algorithm that optimizes the last mile delivery process.

5.3 Transport

Although the general increase of postal item volume (from letter to parcel post) has brought post closer to transport, the transport phase does not necessarily have to be part of the postal supply chain. Case law has cleared out that transport can only be interpreted as postal services if it is performed in conjunction with clearance, sorting, or delivery activities.[12]

5.4 Delivery

5.4.1 In-Car and In-Home Delivery

The delivery phase of the postal supply chain has been subject to many innovations. Many alternatives to traditional home or postal office delivery have been put into place in order to optimally meet consumer demand and control delivery costs.

[11] Pick Up Drop Off locations are manned postal points (mostly local enterprises) where the consumer can collect its postal item.

[12] Confederazione Generale Italiana dei Trasporti e della Logistica (Confetra) and Others v Autorità per le Garanzie nelle Comunicazioni and Ministero dello Sviluppo Economico.

Consumers can opt for in-car or in-home delivery, where the postal operator acquires access to the vehicle or premises through applications with or without cameras.[13,14] The postal end user, who does not need to be present, can then follow the delivery through the application.[15]

5.4.2 PUDO Point Delivery

A second option is a delivery in a PUDO point.[16] These are locations, usually small convenience stores or warehouses, where postal end users can receive and/or return their e-commerce items. PUDO points generally offer between 2- and 4-weeks' time for the postal end user to collect their item.

5.4.3 Parcel Locker Delivery

In contrast to PUDO points, which are accessible only during the hours in which the convenience store or warehouse is open, parcel lockers offer a service with a 24/7 availability. There exist many facets of parcel lockers may have, including static vs. autonomous parcel lockers and public vs. private parcel lockers (Zurel et al. 2019). Parcel lockers can be provided by postal operators (as do Deutsche Post, Correios, and Omniva), by e-tailers (as does Amazon), and by private enterprises (as do Bringme and Swipbox). Usually, a combination of PUDO points and parcel lockers is the optimal solution (Zurel and Rozycki 2019).

5.4.4 Crowdsourced Delivery

A fourth delivery option is crowdsourced delivery. Deliveries are allocated to couriers within a crowdsourced network in order to optimize the efficiency of this (virtual) infrastructure. Delivery agents participating in such networks indicate their time availability (time slots) and usually paid per performed delivery. The amount of work is the result of a match between the needs of the platform and of the local courier. The platform examines the work of the local couriers by different metrics and navigates the couriers through incentives (monetary, as a bonus on the work performed, or nonmonetary, as the privilege to obtain more time slots or more work assignments/deliveries).

The local courier receives accurate and detailed instructions on how to perform the deliveries, using a smartphone application that indicates (through geolocation)

[13] https://incardelivery.volvocars.com/#/

[14] https://www.amazon.com/gp/help/customer/display.html?nodeId=202104360

[15] https://parcify.com/smartlocks

[16] https://www.pudopoint.com/about.aspx

the most efficient routing to be followed. Even though routing is made by a virtual platform and the modalities by which the delivery service might be slightly different from the traditional ones (e.g., the use of crowdsourced networks or of an applicative indicating the rides and the routes to take), essentially it has the same features of the activities undertaken by traditional postal operators.

Crowdsourced delivery is generally preferred and possibly viable in urban areas (UberEATS, Grubhub, Instacart) or along high-traffic routes (PiggyBee). The main benefit of crowdsourcing is that it can drastically speed up deliveries, a characteristic that aligns well with the rising expectations of postal end users. Also, crowdsourced delivery is tech-heavy and asset-light, giving companies an additional access to faster delivery options, next to delivery through e-commerce giants such as Amazon.

5.4.5 Autonomous Vehicle Delivery

Automation and the introduction of autonomous vehicles are a fifth possible delivery option (Joerss et al. 2016). After locating the customer, these autonomous vehicles drive to the customer's desired location. When the vehicle stops at a certain point, the customer can access the secure package compartments by using a smartphone or entering a PIN code. Different enterprises are developing such self-driving cars. Google, for example, has been granted a US patent for the development of a self-driving parcel delivery truck, which it named "autonomous delivery platform."[17] Ford's CEO stated that by 2021, parcel delivery can, next to ride hailing, be one of the key commercial applications for the first fleet of fully autonomous vehicles.[18]

5.4.6 Drone Delivery

A final delivery option this paper discusses is drone delivery. Although there are many regulatory barriers to this type of delivery in urban areas, some pilot programs have been launched in rural areas. Wing Aviation LLC, a subsidiary of Google's parent company Alphabet, was the first company to receive Federal Aviation Administration approval in the USA. The company has plans to begin routine deliveries of small consumer items in two rural communities in Virginia within months.[19] Drone delivery can be one among many delivery options, especially in rural areas and disaster relief.

---

[17] Patent named "autonomous delivery platform" with patent number 9.256.852 B1 granted on 09/02/2016.

[18] https://postandparcel.info/74935/news/ford-ceo-sees-parcel-delivery-as-important-application-for-fully-autonomous-vehicles/

[19] https://www.bloomberg.com/news/articles/2019-04-23/alphabet-s-drone-delivery-business-cleared-for-takeoff-by-faa

6 The Introduction of Platforms

Virtual platforms may be able to organize networks that provide point-to-point delivery services by local, self-employed delivery units as opposed to traditional postal operators which use employees to perform delivery services. However, both the traditional postal operator and the platform exert a level of control over their delivery agents. First, we look at e-commerce delivery platforms, where the platform is able to offer a holistic end-to-end solution through complete vertical integration. Then, we look a bit deeper into crowdsourced delivery platforms.

6.1 E-commerce Delivery Platforms

The activities undertaken by the platform involve the placement of the stock of goods received, the allocation of deliveries between its own service and external providers (services are allocated outside if their cost is minor), and, in case the delivery is undertaken by its own operative arm, how the operations are performed eventually by a crowdsourcing network of local couriers. Vertical infrastructures empowering different postal activities are increasingly replaced by flexible networks that can adjust their operations and processes quickly with negligible cost. Modularity of those networks allows both the segmentation of the postal chain into separate activities and the integration of those services with e-commerce platforms (Scorca 2019).

E-commerce platforms as Amazon and eBay are developing their own network of hubs to provide ancillary services to the sellers (Amazon Logistics and Shutl). Products on the marketplace are proactively sent to the warehouses managed by the platform. Once in deposit, goods are classified and stored. Using predictive algorithms based on potential demand, the platform deposits part of the stock near where buyers might require it.

In some cases, e-commerce platforms might decide to integrate their virtual infrastructure with a system of physical urban stores. In urban areas, deliveries are concentrated in smaller spaces and bring higher returns in the provision of the delivery service. E-commerce platforms perform delivery, often using the service of traditional postal operators to cover the remaining regions, in particular those with higher operating costs.

When deliveries are performed directly by the e-commerce platform, the platform manages completely the operations performed by the courier. As in the case of crowdsourced operations, the duties of the courier are strictly defined. The courier must follow the instructions of the applicative, which is in charge of the communication with the client, and it defines the routing to be followed in order to perform the task as well as the precise time of delivery.

6.2 Crowdsourced Delivery Platforms

Crowdsourced point-to-point services might take different forms.[20] Operations are usually organized through an algorithm, which automatically assigns the ordered product to the agent closest to the locations where the item needs to be picked up and delivered (citywide distances). The platform might also organize multiple deliveries, where a local courier collects different postal items and the platform manages the routing activity which the agent follows for final delivery. In this case, the local courier would be carrying out its activity on behalf of the platform, which is responsible for the whole service.

The modalities by which crowdsourced operations are instituted and managed are one of the main innovations of recent years. The decentralization of the traditional postal supply chain and the centralization in innovative solutions are concurrent tendencies that redefine how postal services are provided. Innovative operators, which focus on the provision of premium services using crowdsourced operations and iterative optimization, are competing on the most profitable areas with traditional postal operators.

Crowdsourced delivery platforms distinguish themselves from e-commerce delivery platforms as they focus on the final part of the postal supply chain, notably routing and delivery of postal items. These operators do not manage facilities for the storage of goods that need to be brought to destination. After the route is determined by the platform, items are collected and then delivered to the user by the agents operating on behalf on the virtual platform. In some cases, crowdsourced platforms have an agreement with mass retailers in order to deliver last-mile goods bought in their shops.[21]

From a physical point of view, only the collection and delivery phases take place. As is the case with e-commerce platforms, sorting is undertaken virtually through an algorithmic calculation that optimizes the use of the local couriers in order to offer the most efficient delivery service as possible.

There is a growing use of crowdsourced delivery platforms to deliver food items. These food items range from basic grocery products to meal kits, catering services, and prepared meals. From an operational point of view, however, it does not matter to the local courier what is inside the delivery box. Local couriers will focus mainly on the required delivery speed and the weight of the delivery box.

---

[20] https://www.ipc.be/en/News-Portal/operations-logistics/2018/05/08/07/38/crowd-sourced-delivery

[21] https://mobile.reuters.com/article/amp/idUSKCN1UC0KS?

7 Conclusions on the Implications of the Postal Supply Chain Fragmentation

7.1 *Implications for Postal Operators*

The rise of logistic networks managed by virtual platforms, as well as new services within the delivery phase of the postal supply chain, are changing postal services and how they are provided. Crowdsourced operations might be both a threat and an opportunity for traditional postal operators covering the entire vertical supply chain. Networks of traditional postal service providers might need to be reshaped to enable adaptability and flexibility, allowing real-time routing optimization. There should also be space for alternative forms of delivery, in order to offer a wider range of delivery options to optimally meet diverging users' needs. Traditional postal operators might therefore need to increase the variability of their cost structure to survive in a competitive environment where margins will probably decrease.

Competition between traditional postal operators and e-commerce platforms might reduce the profitability of the postal sector as took place in telecommunication. Some platforms have started to offer their clients a subscription to an unlimited delivery service, Amazon Prime being an example. Furthermore, e-commerce platforms have more market flexibility than traditional postal operators as they bundle different services (e-commerce and delivery). Platforms possess data on users (as their preferences on products purchased and on the type of delivery service required) that are not available to both off-line retail shops and postal operators. Vertical integration of e-commerce and delivery services might allow the platform to leverage information gained to price discriminate between consumers or to exclude competitors from the market.

Given the volumes handled, e-commerce platforms can influence the entire postal market lowering the profitability of the sector. Traditional postal operators might be keen to develop business ties with e-commerce platforms in order to deliver items ordered by the platform, as such volumes might help to fill up their network capacity. Such agreements might have risky implications, however. If volumes become too important, postal operators might find themselves in a position where platforms acquire some sort of monopsony power and thus can negotiate low delivery prices. The consequence might be that e-commerce platforms will capture most of the value coming from delivery, with only a relatively small profit is left to traditional postal operators. Furthermore, automatization of activities will affect the need for manual labor, as standardized micro-tasks will open the way for automation. In the future, some postal activities might be performed on an increasing scale by drones or self-driving vehicles.

7.2 *Implications for Policy Makers*

As postal and transport services, driven by e-commerce, are converging, postal legislation needs to redefine more precisely the boundaries of postal services, especially if there remains a reason to insulate the postal market within the transport market. Current definitions in the PSD treat the postal stages as a traditional postal supply chain. Technology, however, has made it possible to carry out sorting through different modalities. This may require establishing a new definition of "postal item," taking into consideration the fact that letter mail is declining and, at the same time, the commercial delivery of goods is becoming predominant. Regulatory measures might be revised in light of the fragmentation of postal activities. The integration of delivery and e-commerce services might lead to new market failures and a distortion of the competition between e-commerce platforms and traditional postal operators due to the issues expressed in the previous paragraph.

New services and operational models might require a new way to approach postal regulation. Regulators should take technological disruption into consideration. Postal markets might need regulatory guidance to ensure a minimum level playing field between operators and to address potential competitive constraints emerging from the vertical integration of delivery services within the activities performed by e-commerce platforms. The discrepancy of working contracts between postal employees working for traditional operators and those employed by innovative platforms should also be addressed to ensure minimum appropriate conditions throughout the sector and competition based on merits amongst postal operators.

Recent ECJ jurisprudence[22] indicates that activities of virtual platforms are not merely an intermediation. They exercise a decisive influence over the conditions under which the service is provided, determining fares, processing payments, and controlling the quality of service. E-commerce platforms and, more in general, virtual platforms managing deliveries by crowdsourcing networks might be then considered postal operators.

References

BIPT. (2017a). *Communication by the BIPT Council of 7 February 2017 on the qualitative survey of consumer perceptions within the Belgian postal market*. Brussels: BIPT. Retrieved from https://www.bipt.be/en/operators/postal/universal-and-non-universal-postal-services/communication-by-the-bipt-council-of-7-february-2017-on-the-qualitative-survey-of-consumer-perceptions-within-the-belgian-postal-market.

BIPT. (2017b). *Communication by the BIPT Council of 13 February 2017 on an overall analysis about postal needs in Belgium*. Brussels: BIPT. Retrieved from https://www.bipt.be/en/operators/postal/universal-and-non-universal-postal-services/communication-by-the-bipt-council-of-13-february-2017-on-an-overall-analysis-about-postal-needs-in-belgium.

Corredera, D. N., & Leta, T. B. (2019). *The digital economy and digital postal activities – A global panorama*. Berne: Universal Postal Union.

ERGP, & European Commission. (2018). *Stakeholder Forum: When digital meets postal – Evolution or revolution?* Brussels. https://ec.europa.eu/growth/content/ergp-stakeholder-forum-when-digital-meets-postal-evolution-or-revolution_en.

Joerss, M., Schröder, J., Neuhaus, F., Klink, C., & Mann, F. (2016). *Parcel delivery, the future of last mile*. McKinsey & Company. New York.

[22] ECJ C-434/15 Asociación Profesional Élite Taxi v Uber Systems Spain SL. http://curia.europa.eu/juris/liste.jsf?num=C-434/15

Morganti, E., Seidel, S., Blanquaert, C., Dablanc, L., & Lenz, B. (2014). The impact of e-commerce on final deliveries: Alternative parcel delivery services in France and Germany. *Transportation Research Procedia, 4*, 178–190.

Scorca, L. (2019). The transformation of postal services in light of technological developments and users' needs. In P. L. Parcu, T. J. Brennan, & V. Glass (Eds.), *New business and regulatory strategies in the postal sector* (pp. 3113–3325). Cham: Springer. https://doi.org/10.1007/978-3-030-02937-1_23.

United Nations. (2014). *World Urbanization Prospects: the 2014 Revision*. New York: United Nations.

Zurel, O. (2016). *A systematic review of postal consumers' needs within the USO framework*. Florence: 24th Conference on Postal and Delivery Economics.

Zurel, O., & Rozycki, M. (2019, May 5). Why lockers and PUDOs are the future of the last mile. *Parcel & Postal Technology International*. Retrieved from https://www.parcelandpostaltechnologyinternational.com/analysis/why-lockers-and-pudos-are-the-future-of-the-last-mile.html

Zurel, O., Van Hoyweghen, L., Braes, S., & Seghers, A. (2019). Parcel lockers, an answer to the pressure on the last mile delivery? In P. L. Parcu, T. J. Brennan, & V. Glass (Eds.), *New business and regulatory strategies in the postal sector* (pp. 299–312). Cham: Springer. https://doi.org/10.1007/978-3-030-02937-1_22.

The Fading of the Traditional Postal Market Boundaries and a New Role for Postal Operators: A European Perspective

S. Romito, I. Vacca, A. Rovero, and S. Gori

1 Introduction

Exogenous structural phenomena have affected the postal industry in recent years. Mail volumes have dramatically decreased due to digitalization, while parcel volumes have increased mainly due to e-commerce growth. These trends will continue to shape the industry in Europe. In this context, universal service providers (USPs) have diversified their sources of revenues and profits, aiming to grab all the opportunities coming from new businesses such as the growth of parcels and to exploit the economies of scope from the post office network.

Another primary element affecting the industry is competitive pressure the traditional postal market is experiencing on both the "communication side" and the "parcel side." Moreover, on the "parcel side," many European postal operators (POs) sell e-commerce deliveries that are generally low-priced and interchangeable, with universal parcels included in the universal service (US) as described in the European postal directive. Hence the competitive field is unbalanced, as the USPs

The views presented are those of the authors and not of the affiliated institutions. We would like to thank our session chairman Prof. Pier Luigi Parcu and discussant Soterios Soteri for the constructive comments and suggestions. Furthermore, we would like to thank Prof. Tim Brennan for providing us, during the discussion in Dublin, a critical assessment of the paper and comments about SSNIP (small but significant and non-transitory increase in price) test. He believes that it is still a topic of debate how much the SSNIP test is a test on market dominance versus a test to identify the availability of substitute services or even more if the objective is to identify specific elasticity. We have taken into account his comments in our paper.

S. Romito (✉) · I. Vacca · A. Rovero
Poste Italiane, Rome, Italy
e-mail: SIMONA.ROMITO@POSTEITALIANE.IT

S. Gori
Poste Italiane, CeSPI, Rome, Italy

P. L. Parcu et al. (eds.), *The Changing Postal Environment*, Topics in Regulatory Economics and Policy, https://doi.org/10.1007/978-3-030-34532-7_5

face competitive pressure in this growing market but have to bear universal service obligations (USO), while their competitors have no constraints. As a result, USPs have to exploit their operational infrastructure in other markets where this infrastructure may not be the best one.

Recently, in Europe, with regard to the communication side, the Netherland Court of Appeal (College van Beroep voor het bedrijfsleven or CBb 2018) reversed a decision of the National Authority (Autoriteit Consument & Markt or ACM), which certified the existence of significant market power (SMP) by PostNL in a 24-h bulk mail letter consignments market (§7.1.0, §8, §9, §10). According to the Court, the inclusion of electronic communication within the relevant market would have radically altered the conclusions of the Authority regarding PostNL's alleged dominance. The ACM should have considered the analysis conducted using the SSNIP[1,2] test (small but significant and non-transitory increase in price) showing the potential substitution between physical and digital communications (§7.5, §7.6.1; §7.6.2; §7.8; §7.9.2). One can ask whether the SSNIP test applies to market dominance of a single firm, as opposed to understanding when a merger would increase market power, the purpose for which it was originally designed.[3] With regard to parcels, recently in the aftermath of important decisions and evolution of the European regulatory framework including the European Court of Justice Judgment (2018), Cases Confetra and others (§ 76), the European Regulation on transborder parcels,[4] the Decision SA.38869 (2014/N), and Resolution (Delibera AGCOM 2018a) N.399/18/CONS,[5] there has been a debate on the parcel delivery market especially on the effects of e-commerce.

Section 2 of this paper analyzes the main dynamics of the postal industry, such as e-substitution, parcels' growth, and diversification of revenues. Section 3 raises questions about CBb's judgment and relevant market definition (from §7.6.2 to §7.9.4), based on "Commission notice on the definition of relevant market for the purposes of Community competition law (European Commission 1997)." The same section provides empirical evidence on the substitution between physical and digital communications. This may generate a peculiar outcome, on one side the new technology can vastly reduce demand for an old technology and the same time, on the other side this

---

[1] The US Antitrust Division (1982), Horizontal Merger Guidelines, Department of Justice, indicates the hypothetical monopolist test has an instrument to define the relevant market. The SSNIP test is used in this kind of analysis as it measures the customer reaction to a hypothetical permanent small price increase (from 5% to 10%).

[2] This analysis is applied in a conceptual framework defined as a test of the hypothetical monopolist. In short, the analysis investigates, with empirical data and related evidences, whether product A finds sufficiently strong/close substitutes, for example, the product B.

[3] The US Antitrust Division (1982), Horizontal Merger Guidelines, Department of Justice, https://www.justice.gov/archives/atr/1982-merger-guidelines

[4] Regulation (eu) 2018/644 of the European Parliament and of the Council on cross-border parcel delivery services, 18/04/2018.

[5] It is worth including the "Compensation of Poczta Polska for the net of USO 2013–2015" (Decision of European Commission 2015) (§2.2) (analyzed in the paper by Romito et al. (2019) (§3, §4)).

may lead to a dominant position in a rapidly fading-out market. Section 4, observes the growth of e-commerce and some features of e-commerce parcels that make them substitutable with the universal parcel as outlined in the paper by Romito et al. (2019) and in line with the Polish case on the compensation fund cited above. Section 5 tries to imagine, based on the evidence, a new role for the PO in the changing postal industry. In Section 6, we discuss the fading of boundaries of the traditional postal sector and the development of a modern postal sector.

2 Main Dynamics of the Postal Industry

Like many economic sectors, the postal industry has been heavily affected by digitalization in recent years. More specifically, communication processes have been digitalized with a noticeable reduction in postal volumes. Unfortunately for the POs, this trend will not be reversed. Copenhagen Economics (2018a, p. 34–35) observed that interacting with the public administration electronically is "quickly becoming commonplace in many countries" in the EU. Public administration authorities will make it easier for citizens and companies to communicate with them electronically, e.g., change of residency, hospital appointments, and judiciary notifications. Access to the public sector via an electronic identification system is widespread, and in many EU countries, the same electronic identification can be used to interact with both public and private sector (e.g., Austria, Denmark, Iceland, Norway). Copenhagen Economics (2018a, p. 36) points out that the main reasons for the digitalization of communications are the "cost-saving potential for senders" and "the convenience to access, save, and store communication."[6] These reasons affect both the public and private sector. Table 1 shows the impact of e-substitution at EU level that affected the postal industry.

The data clearly show the significance and persistence of the negative trend that has affected mail volumes over the last 10 years.

The recent positive phenomenon for the sector is the increase in the parcel volumes, which can become an opportunity for USPs. This trend will continue as it is mainly determined by e-commerce rapid growth which will not end in the next

Table 1 The decline of mail volumes

	Average change rate per year: Letter post volumes		Letter post items per capita	
	2007–2011	2013–2016	2011	2016
EU countries	−4.10%	−4.20%	163	112

Source: Copenhagen Economics (2018a), WIK Consult (2013)

[6] Relative to the public administration reasons for not digitalizing communications are privacy concerns, technical difficulties with e-government platforms, and cultural preferences for traditional postal services.

years. Most European USPs benefit from this new volume flow, but they need to adapt their operational infrastructure. This change of the volume mixed with a growing weight of parcels and a lower weight of mail will determine new business opportunities but at the same time new operational challenges for USPs. According to a study carried out by Copenhagen Economics on European operators, many USPs have indicated in a questionnaire that the most efficient solution is to integrate single steps of production chains (Copenhagen Economics 2018a, p. 59–60) creating a combined network, for example, using postmen to deliver both small parcels and mail.

USPs will also face fierce competition from the existing players, which are also experiencing rising e-commerce-driven volumes. Copenhagen Economics (2018a, p. 81) observes that of about 17 national regulatory authorities, none of them notice a decrease of market shares of USPs' competitors.[7] USPs have also to cope with bigger e-commerce players developing their own delivery network subtracting precious volumes. Specifically, Copenhagen Economics (2018a) reports that in EU countries, parcel volumes increased 13% per year from 2013 to 2016.

Many European USPs have faced the decrease in profits coming from mail volumes, and they have used their assets to offer services in areas completely different from mail. An example is the offering of higher-margin services (than mail) such as financial services and insurance services (e.g., France, Italy, Switzerland) through the post office network. The USPs have thus exploited the scope economies related to the sale of financial services through a large number of post offices, ensuring themselves a generous source of profits. Copenhagen Economics (2018a) shows that among EU countries, an average of only 53% of USP revenues come from postal services, with a maximum of 90% in Poland and as little as 16% in Germany.[8]

3 The Competitive Pressure of Electronic Communication on the Mail Market

The Commission notice on relevant market definition for the purposes of Community Competition Law (97/C 372/03) states that "market definition is a tool to identify and define the boundaries of competition between firms. ....The main purpose of market definition is to identify in a systematic way the competitive constraints that

[7] "Nine out of 17 NRAs replied to our survey that the incumbent's three main competitors' market shares in the national parcel segment are growing at an at least moderate pace and 3 classified the growth pace as strong. Eight of the responding NRAs considered the market stable. Not a single market was considered to exhibit declining market shares of the incumbent's competitors" (Copenhagen Economics (2018a, p. 81)).

[8] Regarding these data the report specifies: "Countries that include other postal services not just letter post, FR, IE, and IT, – includes letter and parcel service; DE represents postal business revenues in total group's revenues; NO represents the mail segments; HR, IS, LT, LU, and MT include other not specified postal services; PL includes all USO services; SE and CH revenues for communication services. The EU, EEA, and CH average is an unweight average."

the undertakings involved face." The Commission notice identifies three main sources of competitive constraints: demand substitutability, supply substitutability, and potential competition. The definition of a relevant market implies the definition of the "alternative source of supply for the customers…in terms of products/services and geographic location of suppliers."

On the demand side, potential substitution may arise from a small and permanent change in prices.[9] Competitive pressure from e-substitution on mail is relevant for the definition of the relevant market in the recent CBb's judgment that annulled ACM's decision. ACM found an abuse of a dominant position by PostNL in the multiple mail market with the delivery in J + 24 h. As a result, to PostNL's network mandatory conditions for access by other POs were imposed. In defining the relevant market, ACM considered only simple qualitative comparison. ACM excluded a study that aimed to quantitatively define the boundaries of the relevant market using the SSNIP test and that showed potential substitution between PostNL services and the electronic communications. CBb ruled in favor of PostNL in its appeal of the ACM's decision, rejecting ACM's definition of the relevant market because of what it deemed insufficient evidence to support the exclusion of electronic communications (§ 7.8, § 7.10). Inclusion of electronic communications in the relevant market would change the outcome of the investigation, as it could revise the assessment of PostNL's dominance.

In light of this, the Court considered it important that the evidence presented to support a specific definition of the relevant market be robust and convincing. The Court stated that the definition of the relevant market cannot be based only on the listing of the different characteristics of electronic communications with respect to postal services (§ 7.5; § 7.10). The ACM's definition was challenged by the presentation of empirical evidence that produced different results based on the SSNIP (§7.6.4; §7.7; §7.8). Moreover, the Court did not accept ACM's finding the alleged independence of digitalization from the competitive dynamics in the postal sector. In the past, when the ACM defined the relevant market in other sectors, it often used the SSNIP test. The Court found that a lack of data on long-term margins was not sufficient to justify ACM's failure to carry out the SSNIP test (CBb, § 7.9.). Finally, ACM did not carry out all checks in order to decide whether the prices of multiple items were competitive, including an international comparison.

CBb's judgment indicated that evidence showing the substitution between physical mail and electronic communications and that the analysis to determine the boundaries of the markets is increasingly complex. Market boundaries between digital and physical services are increasingly blurred. Electronic communications exert a competitive pressure that is ever more relevant to the point that the boundaries may disappear.

---

[9]Commission notice (1997, §17),"The question to be answered is whether the parties' customers would switch to readily available substitutes or to suppliers located elsewhere in response to a hypothetical small (in the range 5–10%) but permanent relative price increase in the products and areas being considered. If substitution were enough to make the price increase unprofitable because of the resulting loss of sales, additional substitutes and areas are included in the relevant market."

Table 2 Why digitalize communications

Elements that make business senders to shift to electronic communications	% of respondents that indicated the element
Cost-efficiency	70%
Service quality	40%
Consumer's preferences	35%
Operational needs	29%
Information security and privacy	15%

Source: Copenhagen Economics (2018b)

Other evidence for substitution come from a study developed by Copenhagen Economics (2018b) for Poste Italiane (Il ruolo delle Comunicazioni Digitali in Italia), aimed at better understanding the evolution and the role of digital communications in the Italian postal market. The study also developed a survey focusing on the main kind of communications between companies and users.[10] It is worth noting that in private use (consumers to consumers), postal communication has long been associated with telephone communications (i.e., calls, SMS, chat) and in general via Internet. The survey showed that the overwhelming majority of companies, 98%, communicate with their customers using both mail and digital communications, and only 2% use exclusively paper to communicate.[11] Moreover, the survey showed that even small businesses[12] found no barriers in terms of IT-fixed costs in digitalizing, indicating no barriers to shifting between media. Table 2 shows the main reasons of the survey.

Another important element found in another survey in Copenhagen Economics (2018b)[13] is the power of a bulk sender to encourage its customers to adopt digital communications. The survey also examined the consumers' point of view (the communications recipients). This is important because electronic communications can become a valid alternative to the paper communications only when consumers already use digital channels. The survey pointed out that 48% of the communications received by consumers who have current bank and utilities accounts are digitalized, with 52% paper-based. Three to 4 years ago, 34% of communications were digital, and 66% were paper-based.

[10] The survey tested more than 400 Poste Italiane's customers and considered the main uses for communications (such as invoices, periodic reports, bank statements, quotations).

[11] It is worth noting that the data above exclude firms that have already completely digitalized their communications and are no more Poste Italiane's customers.

[12] Small businesses are defined as small office home office (SOHO) from 1 to 9 employers (Copenhagen Economics 2018b, p. 50).

[13] The survey measures the experience of a representative sample of all Italian consumers and in particular those who have a relationship with a company providing B2C services (utilities, telecommunications companies, banking institutions).

Copenhagen Economics (2018b) also followed the SSNIP test to define the relevant market.[14] The SSNIP test has been applied to bulk mailer, and it has been tested by examining the volume decrease linked to a 10% increase in price. To measure correctly the volume decrease, it is important to notice also the inertial volume reduction of the market as the volume decrease is made of two phenomena: the decrease strictly linked to the price increase and the autonomous market trend. The test divided and measured both these phenomena, and the results show a relevant switch of bulk mailers to digital communications linked to a price increase of 10%. However, this could be an incorrect inference of a lack of market power, as analyzed extensively in the US antitrust literature, or it is better known as "Cellophane fallacy."[15]

Both the Dutch case and Copenhagen Economics (2018b) support a finding of substitution between postal service and digital communications. Another piece of evidence is the observation in the Court of Justice Judgment (2015), in Case Bpost SA C-340-13, where bpost and the French Government noted that "postal services [...] are currently faced with a growing choice of competing methods of sending, particularly that of electronic mail." Moreover, ERPG (2018, §5) found that there is a "fundamental shift of interpersonal communication to digital modes of communication, new businesses and business strategies (e-commerce, innovative delivery services, e-substitution)." The Fondazione Ugo Bordoni's (FUB) study (2019) ("E-substitution nel mercato postale della corrispondenza") found that the boundaries of the postal industry market are blurring due to electronic communications. Hence, certain specific electronic communications should be correctly included in the postal industry market. The study observed that electronic communications partly "hybridize" traditional mail services, such as the registered mail replaced by certified electronic mail, and the bulk (B2C and B2B) mail.[16]

The evidence above indicates advanced and strong substitution between paper and electronic communications. Traditional relevant postal markets should be redefined by enlarging the boundaries. Economic studies could be used to redefine these boundaries.

4 The Role of E-Commerce on the Parcel Side

On the other side of the mail market, there is growth in parcel volumes due to the significant increase in e-commerce shipments. Eurostat (2017)[17] showed that the percentage of turnover on e-sales in 2017 was 17% of the total turnover of enterprises

[14] This analysis is applied in a conceptual framework defined as a test of the hypothetical monopolist. In short, the analysis investigates, with empirical data and related evidences, whether product A finds sufficiently strong/close substitutes, for example, the product B.

[15] "Undertaking a market definition analysis at monopolistic prices can lead one to define too broad a market and fail to identify market power when it is present, which is known as the 'Cellophane Fallacy'," United States Department of Justice, Monopoly Power, Market Definition and the "Cellophane" Fallacy, https://www.justice.gov/atr/monopoly-power-market-definition-and-cellophane-fallacy

[16] "E-substitution nel mercato postale della corrispondenza" (p. 22–23).

[17] Data are related to 2017.

with ten or more employers. In the EU-28, the percentage of enterprises making e-sales is about 20%, with Ireland (35%), Sweden and Denmark (32%), Belgium (30%), and the Netherlands (27%) having higher percentages.

Important new elements in the legal landscape are emerging. "The parcel delivery services are changing fast," as observed by the recital 30 of the Regulation (eu) 2018/644. This recital recognized the importance of the change in these services set rules in order to improve them "especially for individuals and micro and small businesses."[18] Another important recent development was the Court of Justice Judgment, Cases Confetra, and others (§ 76), which also allowed requiring the contribution from firms to a USO compensation fund if they provide services interchangeable "to a sufficient degree with the universal service." Moreover, the same judgment has stated (§ 76) that national legislation can define "haulage, freight-forwarding and express mail undertakings providing services involving the clearance, sorting, transport and distribution of postal items constitute, except where their business is limited to the transport of postal items, postal service providers." The European Commission in UPS/Tnt Express (2013, at §207) noted that both express and standard parcel deliveries have been increasing, with standard shipments having grown more.

This growth may be linked to the rise of e-commerce, the growth of B2C deliveries, as these deliveries "are predominantly shipped by deferred shipments," that is, standard deliveries. In Italy, the NRA has started an analysis of the delivery market also aimed at examining the effects of the e-commerce growth on the market. This trend of increasing e-commerce volumes is destined to continue, and therefore, it becomes fundamental to understand the characteristics of these items. The proper understanding of these characteristics allows to correctly classify such mailings and to correctly define the boundaries of the mail market on the "parcel side." Recently Romito et al. (2019) attempted to classify these items by analyzing the characteristics of these shipments. Several EC Decisions have identified price and delivery time as the main features to classify these items. Most of the e-commerce shipments appear to have the same characteristics of the universal parcel (low price and no committed delivery).[19] Services interchangeable with universal services have to contribute to the compensation fund.

FUB's study (2019) found that the majority of e-commerce shipments are similar to universal services, so that they should be included in the postal industry market.[20] Furthermore, the Dutch State Secretary for Economic Affairs and Climate's letter "An affordable postal letter in a digital society" (2018) observed that e-commerce shipments are growing and they should be included in a "broader" market that could

[18] Recital 9, Regulation (Eu) 2018/644.

[19] UPS/Tnt Express, 2013, at § 156, "In line with its decisional practice, the Commission identifies the relevant product markets on the basis of the speed of delivery (that is to say, express delivery services - commonly understood as services with a next day delivery commitment, and standard/deferred delivery services)". In the most recent Decision, Fedex/Tnt Express (2016 at § 90), the Commission defined "deferred delivery services" as those "with a longer delivery time" comparing to express deliveries which are "also considerably more expensive.

[20] FUB (2019), E-substitution nel mercato postale della corrispondenza, p. 22–24.

include even logistic services.[21] Finally, WIK Consult (2019) noticed that in the delivery market, "the boundaries between standard parcel and express services are blurred – and will become more so."[22]

It is worth noting that recital 15 of the EU Regulation 2018/644 observes about e-commerce parcels that "they are often processed in the letter post mail stream." In Resolution (Delibera AGCOM 2018b) 452/18/CONS (§ 4.2.6. – V.15; V.17), the Italian national regulatory authority (here after AGCOM) pointed out that about 80% of e-commerce parcels weigh less than 2 kilos. They undergo the same operational processes of registered mail if there is the signature and regular mail otherwise. Both e-commerce parcels and mail can be delivered to receivers if there is the signature or in the postbox (when there is no signature) by the postmen together with other universal services. Both the Regulation and the Italian NRA AGCOM's Decision (§ 4.2.6. – V.15; V.17) show that the overwhelming majority of e-commerce parcels use the same operational processes of universal services, which is another element that shows the substitutability of majority e-commerce parcels with universal parcels.

5 The PO's New Role in the New Age of the Postal Industry

The postal industry continues to change. Both universal and other services are seeing the competition from other services such as electronic communications, which can substitute for different kinds of physical communications. In this new era, the PO is seeing the blurring of the boundaries of its traditional postal markets and should consider what steps to take. Figure 1 tries to describe the new postal operator's role considering communication and the delivery markets in which they operate.

The Incumbent Postal Operator could become the "link" between the communication and delivery markets that are being heavily impacted by digitalization, and physical communication has been more and more displaced by digital communication, while the delivery market has experienced an enhanced role due to digitalization. A primary role can be played by the post office network as a strategic asset that can become a tool to promote social inclusion (in some cases contributing to reduce the digital divide by bringing digital services inside the premises of the post office), as Gori (2018) showed,[23] due to its network that ensures a physical presence in both

[21] "On the other hand, adjoining markets driven by e-commerce are growing, especially in the parcels market and the broader delivery services market......... possibly becoming a market for the delivery of products or services, such as letters, parcels, and weekly meal boxes or an even wider logistics services market" Ministry of Economic Affairs and Climate Nederland (2018), An affordable postal letter in a digital society, p. 1.

[22] Slide 24.

[23] Gori (2018), (§ 6), "The specific characteristic of widespread physical presence and consumers' trust of the Postal Operators, i.e. once again building on their legacy assets, can lead to a new strategy that fully integrates them in the digital world" (p. 13).

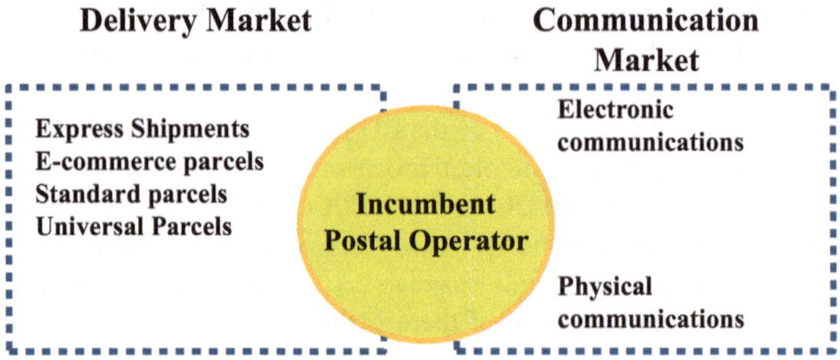

Fig. 1 The new PO's role in the delivery and communication markets

rural and urban locations. UPU (2018) emphasized that the delivery network used for the universal services can deliver e-commerce parcels. Along this line, the Italian NRA AGCOM in Resolution 452/18/CONS (§ 4.2.6. – V.16) underlines that players in the postal market are delivering e-commerce parcels and are reorganizing the delivery network to better exploit the synergies from the joint delivery of mail (especially registered mail) and e-commerce parcels (AGCOM 2018b).

The FUB Foundation goes a step forward and envisions even a "digitalized post office" where other services besides mail and parcels delivery are available such as services delivered on behalf of the local and regional postal administration (e.g., Spain and Italy). The PO can perform its new role in different ways, following the different business models developed in response to digitalization. Gori (2018) observed different reactions of USPs to the Internet revolution, and they have clustered them into two groups, those who "embrace primarily digitalization and technological development with the aim to improve their traditional business model, and the second group choosing a radical diversification of the business models adjacent of other market area" (Gori 2018, p. 6).

6 Conclusions

The progressive digitalization and the e-commerce development are reshaping the postal industry. The shift is so deep that it must be reflected in a change in the regulatory and legal context in all its different aspects. Recently the ERPG (2018, §4.1) underlined in a report that an important issue that the European legislator has to bear in mind:

> is whether there is still a specific postal market and, if so, how this market may be determined. The elements to consider in doing this exercise are the "convergence… between postal services and electronic communications on the other hand, the diversification of services provided by postal operators, the most recent technological innovations, the new business models and strategies deployed by postal operators and other market players (e.g. vertical integration etc.) and changing consumer behavior and demand.

Moreover UPU (2018) stated that:

> it is important to consider the recent trend in some countries to give a wider definition of the postal market in their national regulations which also incorporates digital communications. This interpretation implies a resizing of traditional postal services' share in this new wider market, thus opening a reflection on the re-definition of the role of postal operators.

A new role of the PO seems to emerge at the same time a change of the regulatory context becomes a need. The PO is becoming the link between the delivery and communication markets exploiting its primary assets the delivery network, the post office/acceptance point network, and proximity services. An updated regulatory outlook is necessary to support the PO's new role. Obsolete regulations run the risk of damaging the PO's evolution. A first step in Europe might be a new definition of relevant markets in antitrust analysis/cases taking into account the digitalization of the communications. Another step in Europe might be analysis of parcel markets and e-commerce shipments by NRAs in order to properly regulate these new streams of deliveries. These new regulatory frameworks will have to take into account the specificities of two groups described above by Gori 2018, ((1) those embracing digitalization but without changing the business model and (2) those taking a more radical business approach) to avoid a "one fit for all" model.

References

AGCOM. (2018a). Delibera N.399/18/CONS Avvio dell'analisi del mercato dei servizi di consegna dei pacchi.

AGCOM. (2018b). Delibera n. 452/18/ CONS Definizione del test di replicabilità delle offerte di servizi di recapito di invii multipli di Poste Italiane e dei criteri per la sua conduzione.

College van Beroep voor het bedrijfsleven. (2018). Case numbers: 17/1385, 17/1387, 17/1389, 17/1390 https://uitspraken.rechtspraak.nl/inziendocument?id=ECLI:NL:CBB:2018:440

Copenhagen Economics. (2018a). *Main developments in the postal sector (2013–2016), Study for the European Commission*. Directorate-General for Internal Market, Industry, Entrepreneurship and SMEs.

Copenhagen Economics. (2018b). *Il ruolo delle comunicazioni digitali nel mercato postale*. Study for Poste Italiane.

Court of Justice Judgment. (2015). Bpost Sa, C 340/16.

Court of Justice Judgment. (2018). Confetra and Others, *C 259/16.*

Decision of European Commission. (2013). Case No COMP/M 6570 UPS/TNT Express.

Decision of European Commission. (2015). SA.38869 (2014/N) – Compensation of Poczta Polska for the net of USO 2013–2015.

Decision of European Commission. (2016). Case No COMP/M7630 Fedex/TNT Express.

Directive 97/67/EC of the European Parliament and of the Council with amendments, (15 December 1997).

ERPG. (2018). *Developments in postal sector and implications for regulation.*

European Commission. (1997). *Commission notice on the definition of relevant market for the purposes of Community competition law* (97/C 372/03).

Eurostat. (2017). *Eurostat statistics*. https://ec.europa.eu/eurostat/statistics-explained/index.php?title=E-commerce_statistics#The_share_of_turnover_from_EDI-type_sales_is_greater_than_that_from_web_sales

Fondazione Ugo Bordoni. (2019). *E-substitution nel mercato postale della corrispondenza*, February, 2019. http://www.fub.it/it/News/Eventi/La_trasformazione_digitale

Gori, P. (2018). Postal operators as "Ground Based" online platforms. In *New business and regulatory strategies in the postal sector*. Cham: Springer.

Ministry of Economic Affairs and Climate Nederland. (2018). *An affordable postal letter in a digital society*, 15 June 2018.

Regulation (eu). (2018). *2018/644 of the European Parliament and of the council on cross-border parcel delivery services*, 18/04/2018.

Romito, S., Gori, S., & Rovero, A. (2019). Compensation fund in postal service: A step forward after the Polish case. In *New business and regulatory strategies in the postal sector*. Cham: Springer.

United States Department of Justice. *Monopoly power, market definition and the "cellophane" fallacy*. https://www.justice.gov/atr/monopoly-power-market-definition-and-cellophane-fallacy

UPU. 2018. *Digital policy and regulatory considerations for postal operators – White paper – Document from the Electronic Services Development Group*.

US Antitrust Division (1982). Horizontal Merger Guidelines. Department of Justice. https://www.justice.gov/archives/atr/1982-merger-guidelines.

WIK Consult. (2013). *Main developments in the postal sector (2010–2013)*. Study for the European Commission.

WIK Consult. (2019). *Development of cross –border e-commerce through parcel delivery. A study for DG GROW*.

European Postal Operators' Diversification Strategies and Implications for Cost Allocation

Antonin Arlandis

1 Introduction

As with other sectors of the economy, the postal sector is impacted by the digital revolution. During recent years, the postal sector has been characterized by two major opposing trends: the decline in letter post volume and the growth in e-commerce parcels volume. Many types of communication that were traditionally based on letter post have been digitalized. As a result, domestic letter volumes dropped in all European countries.

Even if letter post still plays an important role in the postal and express market, according to a study by Copenhagen Economics (2018), the growth in parcel and express segment does not outweigh letter revenue decline for most of postal operators in Europe. Therefore, postal operators are actively pursuing growth opportunities in new business areas in which economies of scope could be reached, mainly in logistics and freight, financial services, digital services and telecommunications, which are the largest sources of global postal revenues after traditional letter post and parcels and express delivery services. Postal operators also invest other markets such as local services or silver economy.

These diversification strategies may raise a competitive issue because postal operators (PO) will likely maintain significant market power in the declining letter post segment in contrast to their limited market shares in the parcel delivery market and in the new business segments they are investing. In this context, POs must be able to show that they are not distorting competition in a market by unduly abusing of their market power on the letter one despite the fact that this market is quickly

This paper represents the personal views of the author and should not be taken to represent the position of La Poste.

A. Arlandis (✉)
Le Groupe La Poste, Paris, France
e-mail: antonin.arlandis@laposte.fr

P. L. Parcu et al. (eds.), *The Changing Postal Environment*, Topics in Regulatory Economics and Policy, https://doi.org/10.1007/978-3-030-34532-7_6

disappearing and that the power postal operators could extract from it is theoretical, not to say fictional.

To prove they do not abuse of their market power by, for instance, cross-subsidizing new activities or activities in highly competitive markets by their historical, less competitive, activity of mail delivery, it is crucial to identify the costs for each activity. While some costs can be easily traced to individual product or line of business, there are important common costs, between historical and new activities, that need to be properly allocated between the different products sold by postal operators.

Accurate cost allocation principles serve multiple purposes: they divide joint costs to set tariffs to comply with competition law, but knowledge of costs is also a key to success and efficiency in new markets. The need to create value implies knowing the costs in order to optimize them and invest and innovate profitably.

Several cost methodologies are examined in this paper: notably methods based on game theory and methods based on the value of the activity. To our knowledge very few studies have analysed and compared all those different methods from an operational point of view. After this introduction, Section 2 performs a benchmark analysis of European postal operators' diversification strategies. Section 3 presents the different cost allocation methods that postal operators can use in order to allocate costs to their diversified product mix. Section 4 presents the advantages and disadvantages of the different cost allocation methods. Section 5 concludes.

2 Postal Operators' Diversification Strategies

2.1 Overview

Aggregate turnover of the 11 postal operators presented in Table 1 grew slowly between 2014 and 2018 (1.5% on average per year). By contrast, revenue of the giant e-commerce firm Amazon, which disrupted the parcel delivery market, grew on average by 27% over the same period (Amazon turnover has increased from 78 billion euros in 2014 to 204 billion euros in 2018[1]). Many European postal operators (Austrian Post, Post NL, Posten Norge, Posti, PostNord and Swiss Post) have seen their incomes decline during the 2014–2018 period.

In order to respond to the rapid evolution of consumer needs, European postal operators have embraced innovation and pursued growth opportunities in several business areas. They have chosen different models (Table 2).

Levels of diversification differ across operators. Copenhagen Economics (2018) conducted a survey on 32 European universal service providers showing that the share of total revenues collected outside the letter segment (including advertising mail) varies from 84% (Deutsche Post DHL) to 10% (Poczta Polska).

[1] Source: Amazon Financial Statements

Table 1 Evolution of revenue of postal operators between 2014 and 2018

M€	2014	2015	2016	2017	2018	CAGR
Austrian Post	2364	2402	2031	1939	1959	−4.6%
Bpost	2465	2408	2425	3024	3850	11.8%
CTT	719	727	697	714	717	0.0%
Deutsche Post DHL	56,630	59,230	57,334	60,444	61,550	2.1%
Gruppo Poste Italiane	10,553	11,056	10,643	10,629	10,864	0.7%
Le Groupe La Poste	22,163	23,045	23,294	24,110	24,699	2.7%
Posti	1859	1649	1608	1647	1610	−3.5%
PostNord	3886	3828	3743	3600	3664	−1.5%
Posten Norge	2450	2517	2487	2478	2399	−0.5%
PostNL	4251	3461	3413	3495	2772	−10.1%
Royal Mail	10,364	10,279	10,862	11,302	11,757	3.2%
Swiss Post	7441	7310	7278	7168	6836	−2.1%
Total	125,144	127,912	125,815	130,550	132,678	1.5%

Source: Author's calculations based on operators' financial reports

Table 2 Diversification of revenue among postal operators (2018)

	Mail and associated services	Media and advertising	Digital, local services and other products	Financial services	Parcel, packets and eCommerce	Express	Logistics
Austrian Post	41%	26%	5%		28%		
Bpost	35%	6%	13%	4%	13%		28%
CTT	71%			9%	20%		
Deutsche Post DHL	15%				14%	26%	45%
Gruppo Poste Italiane	23%	1%	5%	64%	7%		
Le Groupe La Poste	31%	6%	3%	22%	8%	30%	
Posten Norge	30%				33%		37%
Posti	48%			4%	18%		4%
PostNL	51%		2%		47%		
PostNord	45%				55%		
Royal Mail	28%	10%			35%	27%	
Swiss Post	34%		24%	25%	17%		

Source: Author's calculations based on operators' financial reports

2.2 Telecommunications Services

Several postal operators use their post office networks also to commercialize telecommunications services. In 2007 Gruppo Poste Italiane launched a mobile virtual network operator, PosteMobile, in order to provide mobile phone services. Providing telecommunications services in their post office network allows operators to benefit from scope economies. In 2011, Le Groupe La Poste joined forces with the French telecommunications operator SFR in order to create La Poste Mobile, a joint venture between the two companies. La Poste Mobile offers telecommunication and Internet services thanks to the network of SFR. In the same way, Austrian Post has a service branch that provides telecommunications contracts and products for its business partner A1 Telekom Austria AG.

2.3 Digital Services (E-Government Services, Dematerialized Solutions, Hybrid Mail and Virtual Mail)

In 2018, hybrid mail was offered by 23 of the 30 postal operators responding to the survey of Copenhagen Economics.[2] Poste Italiane provides mail digital services such as hybrid mail and digital collection of registered letters (when letters cannot be delivered due to the absence of the addressee, the latter can collect the registered letter through digital identification).

La Poste offers several digital services, including secure and dematerialized solutions, through its subsidiary DOCAPOST. La Poste provides a service called Digiposte which offers a certified digital identity tool and an electronic safe to store pay slips, tax forms and other important documents. This service can be accessed through an online application certified as secure, encrypted and with the users' personal data hosted in France. La Poste has also launched a dedicated business online services platform, offering electronic administrative services such as e-signature, e-invoices and archiving. La Poste's mobile app also includes the possibility to have a webmail address and to send and receive e-registered letters (Alloo 2018). In 2018, digital services turnover represents 2.2% of the total turnover of Le Groupe La Poste.

PostNord is restructuring its business to focus more on digital communication, combining physical and digital products and services. PostNord offers a secure electronic mailbox service, E-Boks, used by citizens to communicate with public authorities. Bpost subsidiary Speos manages outgoing financial and administrative document flows, such as invoices, bank statements and pay slips. The services offered include document generation, printing and enclosing, electronic distribution

[2] Hybrid mail refers to items that are dispatched in electronic form by the sender and are subsequently printed, packed, sorted and delivered by the postal operator to the recipient. Virtual mail refers to the digitalization (scanning) by the postal operator of a paper-based item dispatched by the sender and its electronic delivery of the item to the recipient (source: Copenhagen Economics (2018)).

and archiving. In addition, bpost's Certipost service provides document security, digital certification and Belgian e-ID activities (Alloo 2018).

E-government services in 2018 was provided by 15 of the 30 postal operators responding to the survey of Copenhagen Economics. Poste Italiane strives to become the key service provider for the public sector in Italy thanks to the digitalization of access to the public sector and digital identification. In Spain, Correos provides a range of digital services and has a network of post offices which can securely verify individuals' identity when required for certain digital transactions or to provide e-Government services.

2.4 *Financial Services*

Financial services in 2018 were offered by 25 of the 30 postal operators responding to the survey of Copenhagen Economics, e.g. bpost, CTT, Poste Italiane, Le Groupe La Poste, Poczta Polska, Posten Norge and Swiss Post. However, revenue shares of postal financial services vary widely among these postal operators. In 2018, financial services represent respectively 25% and 64% of Swiss Post and Poste Italiane total revenue. The share of financial services in total turnover is lower than 25% for bpost, CTT, Le Groupe La Poste and Posti.

Gruppo Poste Italiane uses the convergence of banking and telecom to provide several innovative financial and insurance digital services such as a payments portal for bills and dues owing to enterprises and the public sector. Poste Italiane is also developing new service models for home insurance and third-party liability car insurance thanks to the Internet of Things. Poste Italiane has elaborated several mobile apps that offer numerous features, including the ability to manage bank accounts, pay utility bills and transfer money. According to its own estimates, Poste Italiane holds 25% of the Italian market share in e-commerce payments. In Finland, Posti's subsidiary OpusCapita offers software solutions for sourcing, payment and cash management either by selling licenses or software as a service.

2.5 *Parcel and Express Delivery Services*

The continued move from offline to online shopping is leading to the rapid growth in e-commerce and creates new opportunities for postal operators to respond to and to minimise the negative impact of letter volume decline. Almost all European postal operators provide parcel express services. This is one of the main diversification strategies implemented by postal operators across Europe. According to Copenhagen Economics, the growth in parcel and express segment clearly does not outweigh letter revenue decline for most of postal operators in Europe. However, for few operators (Deutsche Post DHL, Le Groupe La Poste or Royal Mail), parcel and express delivery services revenues already exceed letter revenues (see Annex).

Many operators see a strong increase in the global cross-border e-commerce market.[3] National European postal operators like Deutsche Post DHL, Royal Mail, PostNL or Le Groupe La Poste (thanks to its subsidiary GeoPost) have expanded their business in the European parcels and express market through acquisition of established players of the market. Many other new operators also entered the parcels and express market in several European countries. All this has increased competition between incumbents and new entrants. As a result, the parcels market is becoming more and more competitive and fragmented in many countries such as Cyprus, Greece, Italy and Croatia, even if it remains concentrated in few other countries.[4]

2.6 *Logistics and Freight*

A good 80% of postal operators responding to the survey of Copenhagen Economics reported providing logistics and freight services. Main examples include Deutsche Post DHL, PostNord, Posten Norge and Posti. In 2018, Deutsche Post DHL logistics revenue represents 45% of the total group revenue. Deutsche Post DHL logistics revenue remained relatively stable for the past few years. Deutsche Post DHL states that it focuses upon market segments that offer higher margins and growth rates especially in the service logistics business. In 2018, Deutsche Post DHL logistics revenue fell slightly because Deutsche Post sold its subsidiary Williams Lea Tag to Advent International in 2017.[5]

Between 2017 and 2018, logistics services sales of the PostNord Group increased by 14 percent. In 2018, bpost acquired several logistics companies.[6] Bpost also manages the order, the stock, the packaging and the delivery of the licence plates in Belgium.

2.7 *Local Services, Silver Economy and Circular Economy*

Within its services mail and parcel division, Le Groupe La Poste sells several local services. La Poste implemented a recycling of office waste thanks to a joint venture with the company Suez. La Poste uses its network of postal service outlets to

[3] According to DHL analysis, cross border items are growing at about 20–25% each year.

[4] According to OFCOM, Royal Mail retains a very high share of single piece parcels weighing 2 kg or below. OFCOM estimates this was between 80% and 90% of both volumes and revenues in 2017/2018. The market share of DHL in the German parcel market is equal to 45.5% according to the company estimates. The German parcel market is nevertheless characterized by fierce price competition.

[5] Source: reuters.com

[6] In 2018, bpost acquired the companies Leen Menken Foodservice Logistics BV, IMEX Global Solutions, LLC, M.A.I.L., Inc., and Anthill BV.

conduct the highway code. Postmen can install at home electronic equipment and deliver shopping and meals.

La Poste offers the service "Veiller sur mes parents" for elderly persons which includes a 24 hours a day teleassistance and regular visits of postmen at home. In 2017, Le Groupe La Poste acquired Asten Santé a company that provides home care services. Between 2017 and 2018, sales of local services offered by La Poste have increased by 200%.

In the Netherlands, PostNL has expanded its range of services and now supplies pharmaceuticals, flowers, fresh food and bulky products (furniture, appliances) that it installs at home. In 2018 PostNL coinvested with Henkel, a chemical and consumer goods company, in Dobbi, an online laundry and dry cleaning service. Dobbi was recognised as the most innovative new business in its market and currently has a coverage of around 70% of the Netherlands. PostNL also coinvested in 2018 in Roamler Care, a home care platform that connects self-employed home care providers with sick or elderly people connected to care institutions. This is a business-to-business service that aims to improve matching, planning and administration between care institutions and home care providers.

Poste Italiane has elaborated a digital platform enabling users to assess their future pension position and build the return on their supplementary pension fund. Poste Italiane is also developing new service models for e-health.

3 How to Properly Allocate Costs of New Activities?

Properly estimating the incremental costs of new activities and allocating the common costs between new and historical activities are essential to allow postal operators to make efficient decisions in terms of pricing and to comply with competition law as well.

3.1 Some Costs and Regulation Concepts

A "cost object" is a managerial term for a product, process, department or customer from which some costs originate from it or are associated with it. In other words, they are costs that can be identified with and traced back to an originator.[7] Total cost refers to the total expense incurred in reaching a particular level of output; if total cost is divided by the quantity produced, average or unit cost is obtained. A portion of the total cost known as fixed cost—e.g. the costs of a building lease or of heavy

[7] Source: www.myaccountingcourse.com

machinery—does not vary with the quantity produced in the short run. Variable costs, like the costs of labour or raw materials, change with the level of output.[8]

Direct costs are expenses that a company can easily connect to a specific cost object, which may be a product, department or project. Indirect costs go beyond the expenses associated with creating a particular product to include the price of maintaining the entire company. These overhead costs are the ones left over after all direct costs have been computed.[9] Common costs are costs which are incurred for more than one product, job, territory or any other specific costing object.[10]

An aspect of cost particularly important in economic analysis is marginal cost, or the addition to the total cost resulting from the production of an additional unit of output.[11] Incremental cost refers to a discrete change instead of a marginal change. It could be in the volume of a particular product or a new product. It is similar to marginal cost, except that marginal cost refers to the cost of the next unit. Incremental cost might be the additional cost from the next 200 units.[12]

Fully distributed costs consist in allocating categories of costs, which can be directly or indirectly attributed to products. These categories of costs are direct volume-sensitive costs, or direct variable costs, direct fixed costs and a share of the joint and common costs. Stand-alone cost is a cost standard that measures the cost of providing a product or service by the operator in isolation from the other productive activities of the company (ERGP 2015).

The greater the difference between the incremental and the stand-alone costs, the greater the possibility of conflicts and disagreements on how to best allocate indirect costs (Oxera 2005).

On December 2008, the European Commission issued a Guidance paper on its enforcement priorities in applying Article 102 TFEU (then Article 82 EC) to abusive exclusionary conduct by dominant undertakings. In this Guidance paper, the Commission identifies two cost benchmarks that it is likely to use in determining whether a dominant firm's pricing should be regarded as exclusionary: average avoidable cost (AAC) and long-run average incremental cost (LRAIC).[13]

Average avoidable cost is the average of the costs that could have been avoided if the company had not produced a discrete amount of (extra) output. Long-run average incremental cost is the average of all the (labour and capital) costs that a company incurs to produce a particular product (OECD 2004).

According to the European Commission (2009), failure to cover AAC (black zone) indicates that the dominant undertaking is sacrificing profits in the short term and that an equally efficient competitor cannot serve the targeted customers without incurring a loss. If a dominant undertaking charges a price below AAC for all or part

[8] Source: universalium.academic.ru

[9] Source: businessnewsdaily.com

[10] Source: yourarticlelibrary.com

[11] Source: universalium.academic.ru

[12] Source: www.myaccountingcourse.com

[13] Temple Lang and Renda (2009)

of its output, it is not recovering the costs that could have been avoided by not producing that output: it is incurring a loss that could have been avoided. Pricing below AAC by a dominant company is in most cases viewed by the Commission as a predatory price.

LRAIC is usually above AAC because, in contrast to AAC (which only includes fixed costs if incurred during the period under examination), LRAIC includes product specific fixed costs made before the period in which the allegedly abusive conduct took place.[14] Failure to cover LRAIC indicates that the dominant undertaking is not recovering all the (attributable) fixed costs of producing the good or service in question and that an equally efficient competitor could be foreclosed from the market. Therefore, if the price covers AAC but does not cover LRAIC (grey zone), there is a risk that it would be considered as a predatory price by the competition authorities. If the effective price is between AAC and LRAIC, the Commission can carry out additional investigations to determine whether entry or expansion even by equally efficient competitors is likely to be affected or not.

3.2 *Proportionality and Accounting Methods*

Various proportionality methods are used to allocate overhead costs to units of production. Some methods consist of allocating all or part of the common costs according to a proportionality rule. The Equi-Proportionate Mark-Up (EPMU) is an approach sometimes used by regulated firms. With this quite simple approach, the mark-up for indirect costs is applied across all products based on the direct costs of each product. For example, if 50M€ of indirect costs has to be allocated across two products, with 40M€ and 60M€ of direct costs respectively, 20M€ would be allocated to the first product (i.e. 50M€*40M€/(40M€ + 60M€)), and 30M€ to the other product (i.e. 50M€*60M€/(40M€ + 60M€)). That is, an equal mark-up of 50% would apply to each product (Oxera 2005).

Other accounting methods use either input-based cost drivers (labour hours consumed in making the product, floor space used, etc.) or output indicators such as production volumes as allocation keys in order to allocate indirect costs.

Another widely used method, the Activity-Based Costing, or ABC system, is based on the analysis of specific costs related to every activity performed by a firm in the manufacturing of its products. Based on these activities, resources are allocated to various products, markets, etc.[15]

[14] Average avoidable cost is the average of the variable and fixed costs that could have been avoided if the company had not produced a discrete amount of (extra) output. For a single-product company AAC and the average variable cost (AVC) will be the same, as it is only variable costs that can be avoided. For a multi-product company, AAC includes fixed costs incurred during the period of examination. Long-run average incremental cost is the average of all the (variable and fixed) costs that a company incurs to produce a particular product (European Commission (2009)).

[15] Source: www.myabcm.com

Under the ABC system, an activity can also be considered as any transaction or event that is a cost driver. A cost driver, also known as an activity driver, is used to refer to an allocation base. Examples of cost drivers include machine setups, maintenance requests, consumed power, purchase orders, quality inspections or production orders. There are two categories of activity measures: transaction drivers, which involves counting how many times an activity occurs, and duration drivers, which measure how long an activity takes to complete.[16]

Unlike traditional cost measurement systems that depend on volume count, such as machine hours and/or direct labour hours, to allocate indirect or overhead costs to products, the ABC system classifies five broad levels of activity that are, to a certain extent, unrelated to how many units are produced. These levels include batch-level activity, unit-level activity, customer-level activity, organization-sustaining activity and product-level activity.[17]

Activity-based costing expands the number of cost pools that can be used to assemble overhead costs. Instead of accumulating all costs in one company-wide pool, it pools costs by activity. ABC creates new bases for assigning overhead costs to items such that costs are allocated based on the activities that generate costs instead of on volume measures, such as machine hours or direct labour costs. ABC alters the nature of several indirect costs, making costs previously considered indirect—such as depreciation, inspection or power—traceable to certain activities.[18]

3.3 *Methods Inspired by Cooperative Game Theory*

The problem of the allocation of common costs can be seen as a cooperative game (a cost game). The entities of the set N are the players. By cooperating (forming coalitions, subsets S of N), they can reduce their total production costs. An important concept in the use of allocation methods inspired by cooperative game theory is that of the "core". The core is the set of feasible allocations that cannot be improved upon by a coalition of the economy's agents.

Among the proposed allocation rules by cooperative game theory, the most frequently used is the Shapley value (Shapley 1953). Shapley's idea is to look at the marginal value of all the coalitions of players that can be formed from the n players and to determine the value of a player from each of the coalitions. Shubik (1962) considered the Shapley value as a method of joint cost allocation. This method allows each player to assess a priori the benefits (in terms of cost reduction) he would reap if he decides to join the coalition. To show its application to the problem of assigning joint cost, let us suppose that the full cost of some common costs (e.g. finance, regulation or network costs) is shared among n products designed by

[16] Source: www.investopedia.com

[17] Source: www.investopedia.com

[18] Source: www.investopedia.com

$N = \{1, 2, \ldots, n\}$. The function $C(S)$ describes the net total cost of the coalition S when those products "cooperate". The Shapley value for product i is given by:

$$x_i = \sum_{S \cup N} \frac{(s-1)!(n-s)!}{n!}\left[C(S) - C(S \setminus \{i\})\right]$$

where s is the number of products in the coalition S and n is the total number of products. The Shapley value can be computed by calculating the average marginal cost which product i brings to a coalition under the assumption that coalitions are formed randomly. Thus there are $(s-1)!\,(n-s)!$ orderings of the products, such as product i comes after all the other products in a given coalition S (which contains i), but before any product which is not in the coalition S. The incremental cost of product i is $C(S) - C(S\setminus\{i\})$.

There are also variants or extensions of the Shapley method. The nucleolus measures the attitude of a coalition towards a proposed allocation by the difference between the cost it can secure and the proposed cost (Lemaire 1984). This allocation rule is not additive, unlike the Shapley value, but always selects a core application when it is not empty. The nucleolus, part of the core, is immune to threats of withdrawal.

Owen (1977) defined the Shapley value of a game with a priori unions and created an allocation rule known as the Owen value. Owen takes into account the possibility that some players because of their political or economic affinities may act together more often than others. In this case, the unions play a game among themselves, called the quotient game, and after that the players in each union play an internal game. In the Owen value, the payoffs for the unions in the quotient game and the payoffs for the players inside the union are given by the Shapley value (Lorenzo-Freire 2017).

The equal allocation of non-separable costs rule is based on the marginal contribution of the agents to the grand coalition, also called the separable costs. The non-separable costs are what remains of the cost incurred by the grand coalition after deleting the sum of these marginal contributions. The equal allocation of non-separable costs first assigns to each agent his/her separable cost and then equally splits the non-separable costs[19] (Béal et al. 2014).

3.4 *Methods Based on the Value of the Activity*

The idea of this approach is to bear a larger share of the common costs to activities for which demand is less elastic. In other words, more (less) costs are allocated to activities that are less (more) price sensitive. Ramsey pricing was applied by varying

[19] The equal allocation of non-separable costs rule neglects the contributions of players to the coalitions. However, this rule satisfies three axioms of the Shapley value (efficiency, symmetry and linearity).

the amount of common and fixed costs allocated to user type based on the likely impact of such a cost change on user behaviour. Ramsey pricing techniques have been used to assign fixed and common costs in large networks, such as electrical utilities, telecommunications, etc. (Fiertz and Monico 1998).

4 Advantages and Disadvantages of the Different Methods

Frisk et al. (2010) examine cost allocation between eight forest companies in Sweden using data taken from a case study done by the Forestry Research Institute of Sweden. When forest companies collaborate, they benefit from cost savings. These authors compare the cost allocation results of different methods (the Shapley value, nucleolus, non-separable costs and volume weights). The simplest solution for the forest companies would be to split the common cost equally among the participants based on volumes. However, this cost allocation is not to be considered as fair; some participants pay more with this allocation than with the Shapley value, the nucleolus or the allocation of non-separable costs. The concepts based on Shapley, nucleolus and non-separable costs provide stable cost allocations and are interesting as a basis for splitting costs.

Owen (1982) analyses the fees policy of the Birmingham airport between 1968 and 1969. He shows that the allocation of the common costs of landing fees used by the Birmingham airport resulted in large aircraft being subsidized by small aircraft over what would have been prescribed by the nucleolus and the Shapley value.

Cost allocation rules can be used for different goals (pricing, competition law analysis, net cost calculation, etc.). Proportional cost allocation methods have the advantage of simplicity and are easy to implement. The simplest proportional cost allocation method is EPMU. The ABC method produces a more accurate picture of the distribution of the costs than the EPMU method. However, the ABC method tends to transfer overhead costs from high-volume products to low-volume products, raising the unit cost of low-volume products.[20] In the postal sector, parcels tend to have higher cost than letters due to their handling characteristics (size, weight, etc.). The EPMU method tends to allocate more overhead costs to parcels instead of letters as parcels increase as a share of total traffic in postal networks.

Unlike approaches using value-based drivers, such as Ramsey pricing, proportional cost allocation methods neglect consumers' willingness to pay and in general demand-side factors. Firms wishing to use Ramsey pricing need to obtain reliable estimates of the elasticities of demand (Oxera 2005).

Proportional cost allocation methods and methods based on the value of the activity do not carry out the calculation of the whole combinatory between the various coalitions of entities (divisions or products of an enterprise, the partners of a project, etc.). With these methods, the share of common costs attributed to an

[20] Source: www.investopedia.com

activity does not take into account the common costs actually induced by that activity (in limit cases, stand-alone costs could be lower that fully distributed costs obtained with these methods).

Methods inspired by cooperative game theory present the advantage of generating a better distribution of economies of scope than proportional cost allocation methods and approaches using value-based drivers. The use of cooperative game theory rules such as the Shapley Value allows a more accurate regulatory compliance and even a stronger competitiveness in terms of pricing.

Methods inspired by cooperative game theory, however, are more complex to implement from an operational perspective. These methods require estimates of counterfactual scenarios for stand-alone costs and common costs shared by the different coalitions of products. A postal operator selling, for example, letters, parcels and a new product has to estimate the stand-alone costs of the three products and the common costs of letters and parcels, letters and the new product, parcels and the new product and the common cost of the three products. Therefore, firms wishing to use those methods need to invest in information technology and engineering.

To our knowledge, methods inspired by cooperative game theory have been very rarely used by firms.[21] However, in the future these methods might be more used thanks to technological progress.

5 Conclusion

For many European postal operators, the growth in parcel and express segment does not outweigh letter revenue decline. Postal operators are obliged to find new growth drivers. They are actively pursuing growth opportunities in new business areas, mainly in logistics and freight, financial services, digital services and telecommunications, which are the largest sources of global postal revenues after traditional letter post and parcels and express delivery services. Postal operators also invest in other markets such as local services or the silver economy.

Letters are declining because of the competition of electronic communications. The European parcels market is becoming more and more competitive. As a result, postal operators have now less market power than a few years ago. Even if postal operators have now less market power, diversification strategies raise competition issues. When diversifying or entering new markets, postal operators should firstly cover incremental costs. Determining incremental costs implies to establish adequate methods to allocate fixed and common costs in the case of multi-product firms. Allocating indirect costs such as overheads and network costs is not an easy task.

[21] Long-distance telephone call pricing proposed by Billera et al. (1978) was adopted by Cornell University. A community of 18 Swedish agglomerations used the Shapley value to spread the increase in water supply costs. Aadland and Kolpin (1998) show that Shapley value is sometimes used to share the costs of cleaning irrigation channels for ranch groups in the United States.

Choosing an adequate cost allocation method will enable firms to make efficient decisions in terms of pricing, product mixes, outsourcing or internal development, research and development investments, automation, marketing, campaigns, etc..[22] The different methods presented in this paper have each specific advantages and drawbacks. Proportional cost allocation methods have the advantage of being simple to use. Methods based on the value of the activity allocate more costs to activities that are less price sensitive. Methods based on game theory are more difficult to apply in practice, but they give more accurate results.

On the basis of my analyses, I recommend to use methods inspired by cooperative game theory, such as the Shapley value, anytime operators are able to reasonably estimate counterfactual scenarios for stand-alone costs and common costs shared by the different coalitions of all the products they sell.

If it is too complicated to estimate counterfactual scenarios for stand-alone costs and common costs, it seems advisable to use the ABC method rather than EPMU. A further option is to use methods based on the value of the activity in order to take into account demand-side factors. But this solution can be adopted only if reliable estimates of the elasticities of demand are available.

Annex

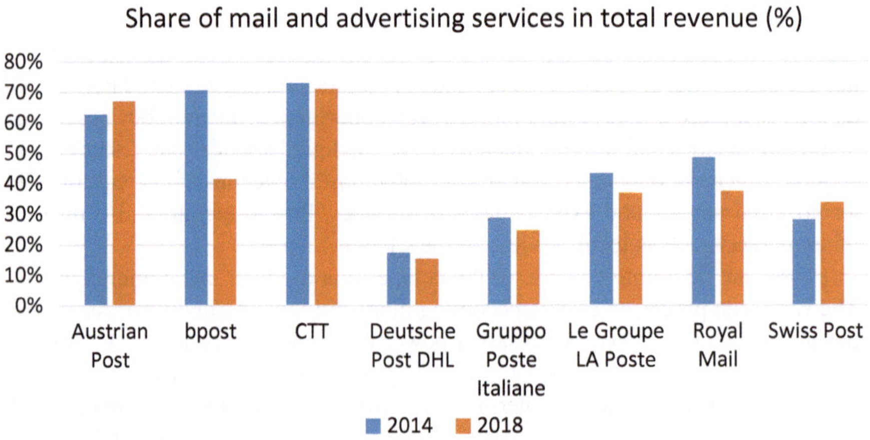

Source: author's calculations based on operators' financial reports

[22] Source: www.myabcm.com

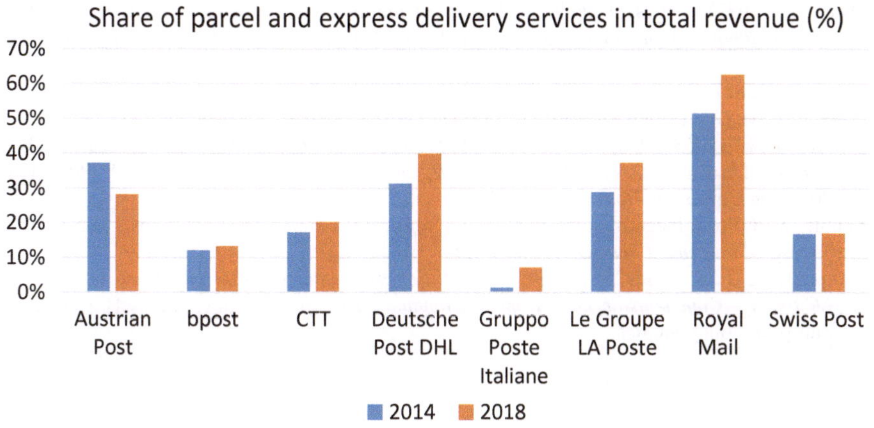

Source: author's calculations based on operators' financial reports

References

Aadland, D., & Kolpin, V. (1998). Shared irrigation costs: An empirical and axiomatic analysis. *Mathematical Social Sciences, 35*(2), 203–218.

Alloo, V. (2018). Postal industry diversification: Exploring new worlds and facing new regulations. In P. L. Parcu, T. Brenan, & V. Glass (Eds.), *New business and regulatory strategies in the postal sector*. Cham: Springer.

Béal, S., Deschamps, M., & Solal, P. (2014). *Balanced collective contributions, the equal allocation of non-separable costs and application to data sharing games*. Working Papers 2014-02, CRESE.

Billera, L. J., Heath, D. C., & Raanan, J. (1978). Internal telephone billing rates — A novel application of non-atomic game theory. *Operations Research, 26*, 956–965.

Communication from the European Commission. Guidance on its enforcement priorities in applying Article 82 of the EC Treaty to abusive exclusionary conduct by dominant undertakings. OJ C 45, 24.2.2009, p. 7–20.

Copenhagen Economics. (2018). *Main Developments in the Postal Sector (2013–2016)*. Study for the European Commission, Directorate-General for Internal Market, Industry, Entrepreneurship and SMEs.

ERGP. (2015). (12) 28 Rev. 1. Common position on cost allocation rules, Ref. Ares 5491994. 01/12/2015.

Fiertz, R., & Monico, C. (1998). *Cost Allocation Paper*. United States Department of Transportation, National Transportation Library's Repository and Open Science Access Portal.

Frisk, M., Göthe-Lundgren, M., Jörnsten, K., & Rönnqvist, M. (2010). Cost allocation in collaborative forest transportation. *European Journal of Operational Research, 205*(2), 448–458.

Lemaire, J. (1984). An application of game theory: Cost allocation. *ASTIN Bulletin: The Journal of the International Actuarial Association, 14*(01), 61–81.

Lorenzo-Freire, S. (2017). New characterizations of the Owen and Banzhaf–Owen values using the intracoalitional balanced contributions property. *TOP, 25*(3), 579–600.

OECD. (2004). *Predatory Pricing – Issue for a balanced and practical enforcement policy – Roundtable discussion on predatory foreclosure*. Note by the European Commission.

Owen, G. (1977). Values of games with a priori unions. In O. Moeschlin & R. Hein (Eds.), *Mathematical economics and game theory: Essays in honor of Oskar Morgenstern*. New York: Springer.

Owen, G. (1982). *Game theory*. San Diego, CA: Academic Press.

Oxera. (2005). *One size fits all? Cost allocation in postal services*. August 2005.

Shapley, L. S. (1953). A value for n-person games. In H. W. Kuhn & A. W. Tucker (Eds.), *Contribution to the theory of games vol. II, annals of mathematics studies 28*. Princeton: Princeton University Press.

Shubik, M. (1962). Incentives, decentralized control, the assignment of joint costs and internal pricing. *Management Science, 8*, 325–343.

Temple Lang, J., & Renda, A. (2009). *Treatment of exclusionary abuses under article 82 of the EC treaty – Comments on the European Commission's guidance paper*. Brussels: Centre for European Policy Studies.

Pricing "Competitive" Postal Products

Timothy J. Brennan

1 Introduction

The US Postal Service (USPS) provides "market-dominant" services on an exclusive basis, e.g., first class mail, and "competitive" services in markets with other rivals, e.g., parcel delivery. Rivals in the competitive market have long complained that USPS cross-subsidizes its competitive offerings.[1] In the USA, the Supreme Court on May 20, 2019, declined to hear a challenge by the United Parcel Service (UPS), a leading rival to USPS in parcel delivery, to the authority of the US Postal Regulatory Commission (PRC) to determine USPS's attributable cost of providing parcel delivery.[2] Bradley et al. (1999) and others have argued that as long as USPS's competitive offerings cover their incremental cost, there is no cross subsidization.

[1]Postal Regulatory Commission, Revised Notice of Proposed Rulemaking, Institutional Cost Contribution Requirement for Competitive Products, Docket No. RM2017-1, Order No. 4742 (Aug. 7, 2018).

[2]United Parcel Service, Inc. v. Postal Regulatory Commission, Petition for a Writ of Certiorari, Supreme Court of the United States (Dec. 26, 2018), available at https://www.supremecourt.gov/DocketPDF/18/18-853/77552/20181226122249306_UPS%20Petition%20for%20Cert.pdf. The Supreme Court's denial of a writ of certiorari is at https://www.supremecourt.gov/orders/courtorders/052019zor_1bn2.pdf. The opposing brief filed by the Solicitor General of the US Department of Justice on behalf of the Postal Regulatory Commission is at https://www.supremecourt.gov/DocketPDF/18/18-853/95477/20190405110310785_18-853%20UPS%20-%20Opp.pdf. The central legal issue is whether the PRC has the discretion under PAEA to define attributable costs as it did, a question of administrative law more than economics as such.

I thank, for comments, Peter Bernstein, Larry Buc, Victor Glass, Krish Iyer, Pier Luigi Parcu, and participants at the 27th FSR Postal Conference and the 38th Rutgers Eastern Conference. All errors remain my responsibility.

T. J. Brennan (✉)
School of Public Policy, University of Maryland Baltimore County, Baltimore, MD, USA
e-mail: brennan@umbc.edu

P. L. Parcu et al. (eds.), *The Changing Postal Environment*, Topics in Regulatory Economics and Policy, https://doi.org/10.1007/978-3-030-34532-7_7

On the other hand, a 2018 report by a Presidential Task Force on the United States Postal System concluded, "While there is no direct financial subsidy of competitive products, mail products and the mailbox monopoly allow for an indirect delivery subsidy. The USPS needs to provide full transparency and fully distribute costs."[3]

I examine this debate by asking what prices of the market-dominant and competitive services maximize net economic welfare across the market-dominant and competitive service markets.[4] Section 2 provides the basic Ramsey pricing model (Baumol and Bradford 1970), which points out that a service's welfare-maximizing price need not cover its fixed costs. Section 3 discusses Ramsey pricing with perfect competition in one market and monopoly in the other, finding that the monopoly PO should charge the market price for its competitive products and use the profits to fund reductions in market-dominant service prices. Section 4 shows that when the PO firm sets price facing a competitive fringe of rivals with an upward-sloping supply curve for an identical product, the optimal prices fit the Ramsey formula based on the elasticity facing the PO in the competitive market, as calculated by Landes and Posner (1981).

Section 5 shows how this result should be modified if the rival in the competitive market offers a differentiated product. Prieger (1996) addressed the question of optimal pricing by a regulated firm in an unregulated market. He examined this optimization problem when the regulated firm is the price leader and the rivals are the followers in the competitive product market. With differentiated products, the regulated firm's price in the competitive market should be adjusted upward from that Ramsey level because the rival is producing too little output. Increasing the regulated firm's price in the competitive market increases demand for the rival's product, which produces a first-order welfare gain from marginally increasing the regulated firm's price.

Section 6 discusses modeling when both the regulated firm's and rival's prices are endogenous in the competitive market. Since the rival's price is that which maximizes profits given the regulated firm's price in that unregulated market, this Bertrand equilibrium price is unlikely to be the price that maximizes welfare overall. Since given demands and the Bertrand interaction, prices are determined by marginal cost, the only instrument available to the regulator would be to change the dominant firm's marginal cost in the competitive market, either through a subsidy or tax. The regulator should implicitly tax (subsidize) output in the competitive market only if the Bertrand price in that market is below (above) the PO's welfare-maximizing price as determined above, since the rival's price always equals the price that maximizes its profits given the regulated firm's price in that market. Section 7 offers concluding observations.

---

[3] Task Force on the United States Postal System, United States Postal Service, A Sustainable Path Forward (Dec. 4, 2018) at 54, available at https://home.treasury.gov/system/files/136/USPS_A_Sustainable_Path_Forward_report_12-04-2018.pdf

[4] In general, net economic welfare includes both producer and consumer surplus. In the models below, I assume that the regulator is maximizing welfare subject to a requirement that the PO is just covering cost, that is, it is getting no producer surplus. However, when we add in rivals, I include any surplus they may get in the overall welfare calculation.

2 Basic Ramsey Pricing

Ramsey prices are markups over marginal cost that maximize net economic welfare subject to a constraint that the revenues raised by those markets reaches a specified amount. Originally found by Ramsey (1927) in the context of per unit taxes to provide a given amount of revenue, Baumol and Bradford (1970) applied the idea to finding optimal markups to cover the revenues of a multiproduct firm with sufficient economies of scale that prices equal to marginal cost do not generate enough revenue to cover the firm's total cost. We assume that the goods or services provided by the firm are neither substitutes nor complements, so that the price of one good does not affect demand for the other.[5] With this simplification, if the firm sells N products, the optimal prices P_i, $i = 1, \ldots, N$, are given by the familiar "inverse elasticity" rule, that is, that price-cost margins are proportional to the absolute value of the elasticity of demand. That is,

$$\frac{P_i - MC_i}{P_i} = \frac{K}{|e_i|},$$

where MC_i is the constant marginal cost of producing good i and e_i is the elasticity of demand for good i.[6] K, constant across all products, is set just large enough for the firm to cover its total cost.

This basic relationship illustrates some of the controversies regarding cost recovery. Suppose there are two products, X and Y, and the cost of producing X and Y is given by

$$C(X,Y) = F + F_X + F_Y + MC_X X + MC_Y Y,$$

where F is the common fixed cost, F_X is the fixed cost associated with producing X, F_Y is the fixed cost associated with producing Y, and MC_X and MC_Y are respectively the marginal costs of producing X and Y. The optimal markups $P_X - MC_X$ and $P_Y - MC_Y$ generate revenue together to cover the sum of $F + F_X + F_Y$. Those optimal markups are the same regardless of how that sum is divided among F, F_X, and F_Y. Hence, there is no guarantee that optimal markups for both X and Y generate revenues sufficient to cover their respective incremental costs $F_X + MC_X$ and $F_Y + MC_Y$, that is, optimal Ramsey pricing need not be subsidy-free.

This effect highlights what has become a central issue in the dispute between UPS and the PRC—the appropriate time frame for defining marginal cost. The above result could be an artifact of the use of short-run marginal cost, and that the appropriate marginal cost to use is longer run, perhaps even the average incremental

[5] This rules out applications where the market-dominant service is an input to the competitive service, in particular, where the USPS's "mail" service is used to deliver "parcels" or is provided under other worksharing arrangements.

[6] If goods are substitutes or complements, the elasticity expressions here become matrices of own price and cross price elasticities (Scott 1986).

cost, including fixed costs, of adding a particular service to the mix. I do not resolve the question of the right time frame here. However, if one believes that MC_Y, for example, should be larger because regulators should be using a longer run marginal cost, then the same argument should be used in principle to increase MC_X. When all "marginal" costs are similarly adjusted to reflect a common time frame, be it instantaneous, eternity, or sometime in between, it may well be that P_Y should fall. Calculating which prices go up and which go down depends on the demand curves for the products as well as how changing the time frame over which marginal costs are measured and differences in how changing the time scale affects marginal cost across products.

3 Perfect Competition for Competitive Products

To garner insights more in line with postal disputes, treat one of the two products as that for which the PO is market-dominant, and simplify by treating this as a monopoly, e.g., letter delivery. Indicate this by the subscript "*M*." The other product will be "competitive," with subscript "*C*"—parcel delivery as the stereotypical example—although the competition need not be perfect. The market is competitive in the sense that there are rivals to the PO that independently set prices to maximize their profits—perhaps waiting to see the price the PO charges and perhaps choosing prices strategically anticipating the price the PO would charge in that market.

Here, though, suppose that the market is perfectly competitive, in the sense that the PO takes the price in that market P_C, as given. Rivals in this competitive market may have constant and equal minimum average cost equal to P_C, making that the equilibrium price. For this case to differ from the above, assume that the PO's marginal cost of supplying the competitive product is increasing and reaches P_C at a level of output below market demand at the price. Figure 1 displays the PO's operations in the competitive market.

Figure 1 illustrates the optimal course of action for the regulator. Since demand is perfectly elastic at P_C, the PO should charge P_C for its competitive product, supplying Q_{PO}. Operating profits, indicated by the shaded area, would then be used to contribute to covering aggregate fixed cost across both the market-dominant and competitive product, as in the previous section. The regulator would set the price for the market-dominant product, P_M, just high enough to cover the remaining fixed cost. In effect, the regulator has only one instrument, P_M, as the price in the other market, P_C, is dictated by competition. The regulator, along with the regulated firm, takes P_C as given.[7]

[7] Even with this ambiguity, if a PO cannot cover its incremental—fixed and variable—costs of supplying the competitive service at the optimal price, it should not enter if the market is already competitive. The optimal entry question is more complex in settings below where, because of product differentiation, the "competitive" market is less than fully competitive. If so, PO entry can cause price to fall, generating consumer benefits that it does not capture.

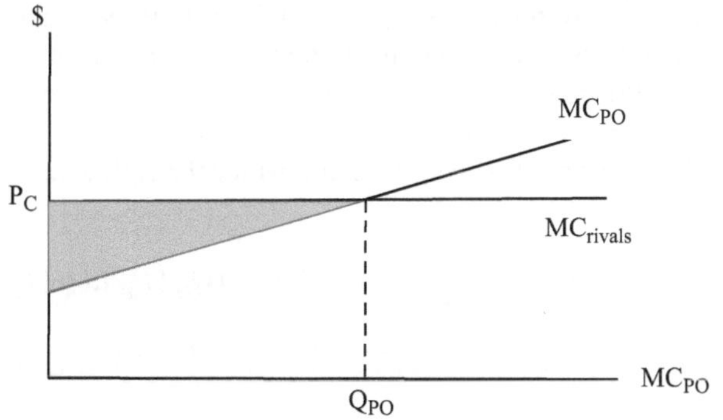

Fig. 1 PO supply in a perfectly competitive market

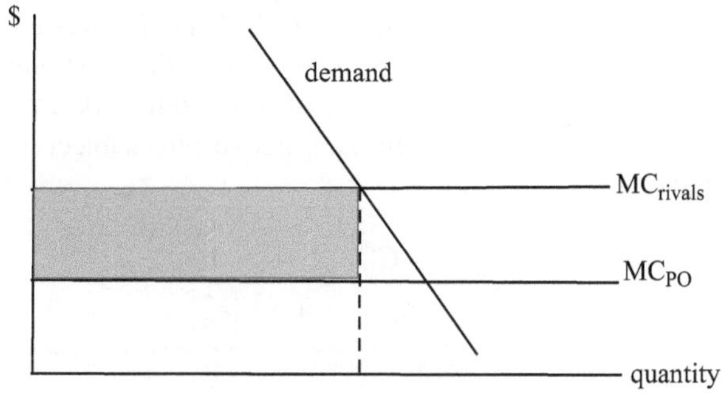

Fig. 2 Revenue capture when matching competitive product price

The result that operating profits be used to reduce price of the market-dominant service also holds if the PO could meet all competitive market demand at a price above its marginal cost but that demand in the competitive market is not so elastic as to have the Ramsey markup at a price below P_C, at which point demand becomes perfectly elastic. This implies that the Ramsey price would be P_C. Figure 2 illustrates this possibility.

The shaded area indicates the profits that would be used to hold down the price of the market-dominant service when the PO sets price just below that would induce entry by the rivals.

4 The PO as Dominant Firm Facing a Competitive Fringe

The next step is to treat the PO's rivals in the competitive market as taking the PO's price as the market price and supplying to the point where their marginal cost just equals the PO's price. To model this, let $Q_C(P_C)$ be demand in the competitive product market, and let $S_F(P_C)$ be fringe supply, dictated by the quantity where the marginal cost for the fringe's supply equals P_C. The PO's sales of the competitive product are thus $Q_C - S_F$. The PO's costs in both markets thus depend on Q_M, the sales of its market-dominant product, and $Q_C - S_F$, the sales of its competitive product. Prices P_C and P_M in the market-dominant or monopoly market that maximize net economic welfare subject to the PO's revenues covering its total cost are those that solve the first-order conditions for the following:

$$\int_0^{Q_M(P_M)} P_M(z)\,dz + \int_0^{Q_C(P_C)} P_C(z)\,dz - C^{PO}\left(Q_M(P_M), Q_C(P_C) - S_F(P_C)\right) - C^F\left(S_F(P_C)\right)$$
$$-\lambda\left[P_M Q_M(P_M) + P_C\left[Q_C(P_C) - S_F(P_C)\right] - C^{PO}\left(Q_M(P_M), Q_C(P_C) - S_F(P_C)\right)\right].$$

The top line is total surplus less costs for the market-dominant and competitive product, where Q_M is demand for the monopoly product, C^{PO} is the PO's cost as a function of its production of both products, and C^F is the fringe's cost of producing the competitive product. The bottom line represents the constraint that the PO's revenues from both markets cover its total cost from both markets.

The first-order conditions for maximizing net surplus subject to this constraint for P_M and P_C give:

$$P_M : \frac{P_M - C_M^{PO}}{P_M} = \frac{-\lambda}{1-\lambda}\frac{1}{\left|e_M^d\right|}.$$

$$P_C : \frac{P_C - C_C^{PO}}{P_C} = \frac{-\lambda}{1-\lambda}\frac{Q_C - S_F}{\left|Q'_C - S'_F\right|}\frac{1}{P_C}.$$

The first of these is of the familiar format, with the price-cost margin equal to a constant across markets times the inverse of the elasticity of demand in the monopoly market. The second of these is the same, under closer inspection, as the last two terms together equal the inverse of the elasticity of demand facing the PO for the competitive product. $Q_C - S_F$ represents its sales in that market, and $Q'_C - S'_F$ is the change in the PO's sales of the competitive product as it changes its price.

Following Landes and Posner (1981), the elasticity of demand facing the PO can be decomposed into its component parts as follows:

$$\left[\frac{-Q_C' + S_F'}{Q_C - S_F}\right]P_C = \frac{-Q_C' P_C}{Q_C - S_F} + \frac{S_F' P_C}{Q_C - S_F}$$

$$= \frac{-Q_C' P_C}{Q_C}\frac{Q_C}{Q_C - S_F} + \frac{S_F' P_C}{S_F}\frac{S_F}{Q_C - S_F}$$

$$= \left|e_C^d\right|\frac{1}{SHARE_{PO}} + e_F^s\frac{1 - SHARE_{PO}}{SHARE_{PO}},$$

where $e^d{}_C$ is the elasticity of demand for the competitive product at P_C, $e^s{}_F$ is the elasticity of supply of the competitive fringe at P_C, and $SHARE_{PO}$ is the market share of the PO in the competitive market, given by $[Q_C - S_F]/Q_C$. $1 - SHARE_{PO}$ is the market share of the competitive fringe. With $SHARE_{PO}$ less than one, that is, when the fringe makes some sales in equilibrium, this demand facing the PO in the competitive product market will be more elastic than demand for that competitive product as a whole.

One needs to be careful making inferences from an equilibrium condition in which all of the terms are endogenous. That said, the larger is the elasticity of demand facing the PO in competitive market, the smaller will be its price-cost margin. In turn, that elasticity facing the PO will be larger, all else equal, the more elastic is the fringe supply and the larger share of the market the fringe holds, that is, the smaller is $SHARE_{PO}$. This suggests that the stronger is the competition facing the PO for the competitive product, the lower the PO's price for it and the higher should the PO's price be in the market in which it holds a monopoly. This welfare-maximizing behavior is qualitatively the same as if the PO were cross-subsidizing its competitive product with revenues from its monopoly market-dominant product. A regulator that wants to set prices to maximize welfare will likely be vulnerable to arguments that it permits cross-subsidization.[8]

5 PO Price Leadership with Differentiated Products

We drop the assumption that there is a single price in the market for the competitive product. Rather, there are different prices, the one that the PO charges for its product, and those the rivals choose in response. To simplify the analysis, we assume that there is just one rival, which sets its price to maximize profits given the price the PO charges for its (differentiated) product.

Even with just one rival, having two different products on the competitive side requires modifying the above model. Instead of an integral to measure gross surplus, designate W^C as welfare in the competitive market. This welfare will be a function of the output of the postal service in that market, Q^{PO}, and the output of the rival, Q^R. These, in turn, are both functions of the price the PO charges, P_{PO}, and the rival's profit-maximizing price in response, $P_R(P_{PO})$. Putting this all together gives welfare in the competitive product market as

$$W^C\left(Q^{PO}\left(P_{PO}, P_R\left(P_{PO}\right)\right),\ Q^R\left(P_{PO}, P_R\left(P_{PO}\right)\right)\right).$$

The partial derivatives of this gross welfare measure are the respective prices, that is, ${W^C}_{PO} = P_{PO}$ and ${W^C}_R = P_R$.

[8]There should be a test to see if PO entry increases welfare, which if the entered market is competitive will be equivalent to asking if the price in the competitive market is sufficient to cover the PO's fixed and variable costs of entry. See *supra* n. 7.

The PO's cost of providing quantity Q^M market-dominant monopoly service and quantity Q^{PO} of its competitive product becomes

$$C^{PO}\left(Q^M\left(P_M\right), Q^{PO}\left(P_{PO}, P_R\left(P_{PO}\right)\right)\right).$$

The rival's cost is

$$C^R\left(Q^R\left(P_{PO}, P_R\left(P_{PO}\right)\right)\right).$$

With these notational adjustments, the equation describing choosing P_M and now P_{PO} to maximize welfare across the market-dominant and competitive market, subject to revenues from both markets covering the PO's cost, becomes:

$$\int_0^{Q_M(P_M)} P_M(z)dz + W^C\left(Q^{PO}\left(P_{PO}, P_R\left(P_{PO}\right)\right), Q^R\left(P_{PO}, P_R\left(P_{PO}\right)\right)\right)$$
$$-C^{PO}\left(Q^M\left(P_M\right), Q^{PO}\left(P_{PO}, P_R\left(P_{PO}\right)\right)\right) - C^R\left(Q^R\left(P_{PO}, P_R\left(P_{PO}\right)\right)\right)$$
$$-\lambda\left[P_M Q_M\left(P_M\right) + P_{PO}\left[Q^{PO}\left(P_{PO}, P_R\left(P_{PO}\right)\right)\right] - C^{PO}\left(Q^M\left(P_M\right), Q^{PO}\left(P_{PO}, P_R\left(P_{PO}\right)\right)\right)\right].$$

The first-order condition for P_M in for this constrained welfare maximization is the familiar

$$P_M : \frac{P_M - C_M^{PO}}{P_M} = \frac{-\lambda}{1-\lambda}\frac{1}{\left|e_M^d\right|}.$$

To derive and interpret the first-order condition for P_{PO}, define

$$\frac{dQ^{PO}}{dP_{PO}} = Q_{PO}^{PO} + Q_R^{PO}P'_R$$

as the total derivative of the PO's output in the competitive market as a function of the price it charges, taking into account the effect of its change on the rival's price P_R and the effect of the change in that price on demand for its competitive product. Similarly, define

$$\frac{dQ^R}{dP_{PO}} = Q_{PO}^R + Q_R^R P'_R$$

as the total derivative of the rival's output when the PO's price changes, taking into account both the direct effect of the PO's price on demand for the rival's output and the effect on the rival's output when it changes its price in response to the change in the PO's price.

With this notation, and recalling that the marginal effect on gross welfare in the competitive market from increasing output of either product is that product's price in that market, the first-order condition for P_{PO} is

$$P_{PO}:\frac{P_{PO}-C_{PO}^{PO}}{P_{PO}}=\frac{-\lambda}{1-\lambda}\left[\frac{-Q^{PO}}{\frac{dQ^{PO}}{dP_{PO}}}\frac{1}{P_{PO}}\right]+\frac{1}{1-\lambda}\frac{P_R-C'_R}{P_R}\frac{P_R}{P_{PO}}\left[-\frac{\frac{dQ^R}{dP_{PO}}}{\frac{dQ^{PO}}{dP_{PO}}}\right].$$

The fraction in the brackets is just the inverse of the absolute value of the elasticity of demand facing the PO in the market for the competitive products, taking into account the effect of its price on rival's price. This is the same as the term in the first-order condition for the PO's price for the competitive product in the case where a competitive fringe supplies an identical product.

Were this all, one would have the Ramsey inverse elasticity rule, adapted for the higher elasticity of demand facing the PO in the market for the competitive product because of rivals' supply response. The second term on the right, however, changes the results.[9] Because λ is negative,[10] $1 - \lambda$, the first denominator, is positive. The second term is the rival's price-cost margin, which we can presume is positive if it offers a differentiated product. The next term is the ratio of the price of the rival's competitive product to the price of the PO's competitive product.

The fraction in the brackets is the ratio of the change in output of the rival to (the absolute value of) the decrease in output of the PO when the PO increases the price of its product. In merger analysis, this is known as the "diversion ratio" (U.S. Department of Justice and Federal Trade Commission 2010). Increasing the PO's price will generally increase demand for the rival's product, but it could be negative, if an increase in the PO's price reduced the elasticity of demand for the rival's product, leading it to increase its price so much that sales fall.[11] However, one would expect that when one competitor increases price, rivals, as suppliers of substitutes, would increase output, leading to a positive diversion ratio.

If the diversion ratio is positive, then the first-order condition for PPO says that the price-cost margin for the PO's competitive product should be *greater* than that

---

[9] Prieger (1996) finds a somewhat similar term.

[10] See *supra* n. 8.

[11] These remaining three terms constitute what Salop and Moresi (2009) call, in the context of merger analysis the "Generalized Upward Pricing Pressure Index" or "GUPPI." There is an important difference, however. The GUPPI is calculated taking the rival's price as fixed, because it is applied to simultaneous pricing models where one price does not influence another. When the rival sets price based upon the dominant firm's price, in a sequential model as here, the diversion ratio needs recognized that the rival will raise price. Hence, in this setting the diversion ratio can be negative, whereas it is always positive in the simultaneous pricing models used in merger assessment.

dictated by the Ramsey inverse elasticity rule alone.[12] The first-order condition supplies the intuition, which is essentially a "second best" argument.[13] Suppose the PO's price in the competitive market was set to satisfy the Ramsey rule. With a positive diversion ratio, incrementally increasing that price would increase output of the rival's product. Because price exceeds marginal cost for that product—the first part of this term in the first-order condition—the rival is supplying too little of that product, hence increasing supply increases welfare. At the price that satisfies the Ramsey rule, the direct effect on welfare ignoring the effect from the rival's product is zero at the margin, so increasing P_{PO} increases overall welfare. The magnitude of that welfare loss is rival's price-cost margin; all else equal, the larger is that margin, the greater is that welfare loss.

Measuring the size of that marginal effect requires measurement of the diversion ratio and the difference between price and cost for the rival, or rivals as the case may be. Merger simulation techniques (Werden and Froeb 1994; Berry 1994; Nevo 2000) may be of use in estimating this in practice. However, this is only a marginal effect and in and of itself tells us little about how much above the Ramsey price the PO should set for its competitive product. However, assumptions about the specific form of the demand functions (linear, constant elasticity) may allow calculations of those prices (Salop and Moresi 2009, p. 47).

6 Differentiated Bertrand Equilibrium for Competitive Products

The last complication is to go from a sequential equilibrium, in which the rival in the competitive product market sets price after observing the PO's price, to a simultaneous (Bertrand) equilibrium, in which both the PO and the rival set prices at a Nash equilibrium, where each supplier's price maximizes its profits given the price the other charges. In such an equilibrium, the PO's price is endogenous, which implies that it is not directly under the regulator's control.

Consequently, if the postal regulator wishes to manipulate pricing in the competitive product market to maximize welfare, it must do so indirectly. As the controversy on the PO's competitive product pricing centers is in part over its contribution to institutional cost—that is, costs that cannot be attributed to a specific product—one might approach this not as requiring a minimum contribution from sales of the competitive product but limiting the contribution to institutional cost from sales of the market-dominant product. However, this is highly unlikely to be optimal. In one

[12] Conversely, to the extent that the PO's competitive product is a complement to differentiated services in other markets, its price should be lower than that prescribed by the Ramsey inverse elasticity rule, also to increase output in market where differentiation implies too little. Prieger (1996) makes this point as well.

[13] One could say, because Ramsey pricing is itself second-best, that this is a "third best" pricing argument.

direction, the PO's variable profits from the competitive product Bertrand equilibrium could be too low for the PO to cover its cost. In the other direction, the PO's variable profits from sales in the Bertrand equilibrium could be more than enough to cover its total cost, implying that welfare could be increased by reducing the PO's prices for both the market-dominant and competitive products.

Two more direct possibilities present themselves. One is for the regulator to add a per-unit contribution to the PO's marginal cost for its competitive product, thereby changing the equilibrium price in that market. A policy and modeling question is whether that per-unit contribution or the PO's entire profit from the competitive product market should count toward that contribution toward institutional cost. A second possibility would be for the postal regulator to impose a fixed cost requirement on the PO's provision of the regulated product. This could lead the PO to withdraw from the competitive product market, which would reduce welfare in the competitive market. To the extent competitive market profits contribute to common costs, withdrawal would reduce welfare in the monopoly market as well.[14] If the PO continues to supply the competitive product, this requirement would be either nonbinding or, in effect, set a floor on the PO's competitive market price, forcing a sequential rather than Bertrand equilibrium.

In either case, the relevant comparison is with the result in the previous section. In any differentiated Bertrand equilibrium, the rival's price will be their best response to the price it expects the PO to charge for its product. Therefore, the optimal differentiated Bertrand equilibrium will be where the PO charges the prices that satisfy the first-order conditions in the sequential model where the PO sets its competitive product price first and the rival follows.[15] To the extent that either adding an amount to (or subtracting an amount from) the PO's marginal cost, it will lead to lower total welfare if it leads to a different outcome. Similarly, a minimum contribution requirement will reduce welfare if it leads to a different set of prices chosen by the PO and rival in the market for competitive products.

This does not mean that the differentiated Bertrand equilibrium is itself optimal; however, one must proceed with caution. As Fig. 3 shows, because prices are strategic complements (Bulow et al. 1985), a policy, such as requiring greater per unit contributions to covering institutional costs, which increases the PO's optimal price given the rival's price, will lead to both charging higher prices.

The response functions $P_{PO}(P_R)$ and $P_R(P_{RO})$ are both increasing, with prices as strategic complements. If a policy intervention increases the price the PO would charge in response to the rival's expected price from $P_{PO}(P_R)$ to $P{*}_{PO}(P_R)$, the

[14] In practice, these potential benefits accruing from economies of scope—the existence of common costs—have to be weighed against potential harms from discrimination and cross-subsidization that can follow regulated firm participation in unregulated markets (Brennan 1987).

[15] In a repeated game, perhaps the PO and its rival would institute the collusive price. I am not considering that here, in part because models of firm interaction used in merger analyses, as noted above, use one-shot games. If one thinks tacit collusion between a PO and its rivals in, say, parcel delivery, is likely, one might expect that a welfare-maximizing regulator might effectively prevent it by forcing the PO to charge the one-shot equilibrium price. But this could be a subject for future investigation.

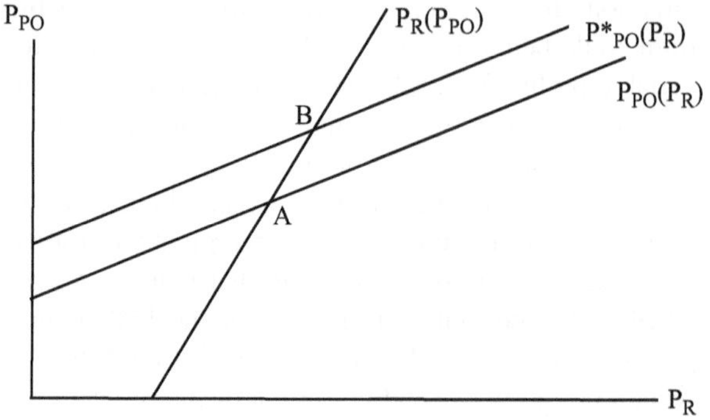

Fig. 3 Effect of increasing per unit contributions on competitive product prices

Bertrand equilibrium would move from point *A* to point *B*, with both charging higher prices.

This reduces welfare in the market for competitive products. That could be offset if the per unit contributions to institutional costs or, more generally, the PO's profits in that market would be offset by a lower price for the market-dominant product. However, the simultaneous Bertrand prices for the differentiated competitive products could be too high relative to the sequential prices found above, for example, if demand for the market-dominant product is very inelastic at the price that, with the PO's price for its competitive product, generates just enough revenues to cover the PO's total cost. In that case, it would increase overall welfare to reduce the contribution to institutional costs from the competitive product, to reduce prices of both the PO and rival's competitive products below those that would prevail in the differentiated Bertrand equilibrium. Simpler models above indicated that the stronger is competition from a rival's competitive product, the higher is the elasticity of demand facing the PO in that market, and thus the lower is its price in that market that maximizes total economic benefit net of the PO's costs.

7 Concluding Observations

The above traces out considerations in setting optimal prices for a regulated firm, here a postal operator, that operates in a market for competitive products. It is not surprising that increased competition for competitive products justifies lower prices by the regulated firm in that market. It may be surprising that those optimal prices should be tweaked upward when the rival offers a differentiated product, when increasing the PO's price in that market increases the rival's supply. When the rival offers a differentiated product, its price will be above marginal cost, indicating too little supply.

All of these results are in a framework where the regulator can use profits from competitive product sales to defray overall costs so as to reduce price for the market-dominant products. This implies that prices of those products are tied to net costs.

This is not the case with price caps, which are designed to be separated from costs to give the regulated firm the incentive to control costs and to remove incentives to cross-subsidize based on misallocating competitive product costs to the regulated product (Brennan 1989, 1990). However, the PRC's proposal "to revisit a [price cap] plan's performance quickly enough to prevent either persistent windfalls to the firm that harm consumers or persistent revenue shortfalls that damage the producer" suggests that to some extent prices will be tied to costs.[16] This renders the Ramsey pricing framework relevant, at least as a periodic target.

An additional concern is that the analysis, particularly of the Bertrand equilibrium, presupposes that the PO maximizes profits or at least minimizes costs. Pragmatically, profit maximization is necessary to apply the market simulation models noted above that might be used to estimate the appropriate prices if parcel carriers offer differentiated services. Michael Crew extensively advocated for privatizing USPS because it was not a profit-maximizing enterprise (Crew and Kleindorfer 2008; Crew and Brennan 2015). Sappington and Gregory Sidak (2003a, b) more generally argued that state-owned enterprises may be well-positioned to cross-subsidize operations in competitive markets, as they may be able to draw on public resources to cover losses from pricing below costs. That, and the lack of incentive to be efficient when costs are covered by the treasury—or by ratepayers, when prices are tied to costs—inevitably complicate the persistent legal and policy debates on pricing by dominant firms in competitive markets. Whether one can model optimal regulation in the face of these complexities remains a task for future research.

References

Baumol, W. J., & Bradford, D. (1970). Optimal departures from marginal cost pricing. *The American Economic Review, 60*(3), 265–283.

Berry, S. (1994). Estimating discrete-choice models of product differentiation. *RAND Journal of Economics, 25*(2), 242–262.

Bradley, M., Colvin, J., & Panzar, J. (1999). On setting prices and testing cross-subsidy with accounting data. *Journal of Regulatory Economics, 16*(1), 83–100.

Brennan, T. (1987). Why regulated firms should be kept out of unregulated markets: Understanding the divestiture in *U.S. v. AT&T*. *Antitrust Bulletin, 32*(3), 741–793.

Brennan, T. (1989). Regulating by 'capping' prices. *Journal of Regulatory Economics, 1*(2), 133–147.

Brennan, T. (1990). Cross-subsidization and cost misallocation by regulated monopolists. *Journal of Regulatory Economics, 2*(1), 37–51.

Bulow, J., Geanakoplos, J., & Klemperer, P. (1985). Multimarket oligopoly: Strategic substitutes and strategic complements. *Journal of Political Economy, 93*(3), 488–511.

[16] Postal Regulatory Commission, Notice of Proposed Rulemaking for the System for Regulating Rates and Classes for Market-dominant Products, Statutory Review of the System for Regulating Rates and Classes for Market-dominant Products, Docket No. RM2017-3, Order No. 4258 (December 1, 2017), at 37.

Crew, M., & Brennan, T. (2015). Business models: Some implications for USPS. In M. Crew & T. Brennan (Eds.), *Postal and delivery innovation in the digital economy* (pp. 1–15). New York: Springer.

Crew, M., & Kleindorfer, P. (2008). Regulation and the USO under entry. In M. Crew & P. Kleindorfer (Eds.), *Competition and regulation in the postal and delivery sector* (pp. 3–22). Cheltenham: Edward Elgar Publishing.

Landes, W., & Posner, R. (1981). Market power in antitrust cases. *Harvard Law Review, 94*(5), 937–996.

Nevo, A. (2000). A practitioner's guide to estimation of random-coefficients logit models of demand. *Journal of Economics and Management Strategy, 9*(4), 513–548.

Prieger, J. (1996). Ramsey pricing and competition: The consequences of myopic regulation. *Journal of Regulatory Economics, 10*(3), 307–321.

Ramsey, F. (1927). A contribution to the theory of taxation. *The Economic Journal, 37*(145), 47–61.

Salop, S. C., & Moresi, S. (2009). *Updating the merger guidelines: Comments*. Georgetown Law Faculty Publications and Other Works, 1662. Available at https://scholarship.law.georgetown.edu/facpub/1662

Sappington, D., & Gregory Sidak, J. (2003a). Incentives for anticompetitive behavior by public enterprises. *Review of Industrial Organization, 22*(3), 183–206.

Sappington, D., & Gregory Sidak, J. (2003b). Competition law for state-owned enterprises. *Antitrust Law Journal, 71*(2), 479–523.

Scott, F. (1986). Assessing USA postal ratemaking: An application of Ramsey prices. *Journal of Industrial Economics, 34*(3), 279–290.

U.S. Department of Justice and the Federal Trade Commission. (2010). *Horizontal merger guidelines*. August 19, 2010.

Werden, G., & Froeb, L. (1994). The effects of mergers in differentiated products industries: Logit demand and merger policy. *Journal of Law, Economics, and Organization, 10*(2), 407–426.

Assessing the Recommendations of the President's Task Force on the Postal Service

Michael D. Bradley, Jeff Colvin, and Mary K. Perkins

1 Introduction

Over the years the US Postal Service (USPS) has undergone several major legislative overhauls, including the Postal Reorganization Act (PRA) in 1970 and the Postal Accountability and Enhancement Act (PAEA) in 2006. Each change in regulatory regime has had substantial impacts on USPS operations, pricing, strategy, and regulation. Recently, the President's Task Force (TF) on the US Postal System released its report summarizing the recent history of the institution along with a set of recommendations that, put together, may constitute the outline for another round of regime changes, via legislation or by USPS policy actions or both.

The TF report identifies the cause of USPS's financial difficulties to be its reliance on its statutory letter monopoly to fund its Universal Service Obligation (USO) and argues for a Sustainable Business Model (SBM). The TF's proposed SBM would target a set of USO "safety net" (Task Force 2018, p. 34) services for continued government protection, as these Essential services have a strong social rationale for such protection (Task Force 2018, p. 40). Such products include personal correspondence, bills, and pharmaceutical packages and would be protected by a legal monopoly and their prices constrained by a cap.

The views presented in this paper are those of the authors and do not necessarily represent those of the Office of the Inspector General, the US Postal Service, or any other organization.

M. D. Bradley
Department of Economics, George Washington University, Washington, DC, USA

J. Colvin (✉)
USPS Office of Inspector General, Arlington, VA, USA
e-mail: jcolvin@uspsoig.gov

M. K. Perkins
Graduate Faculty, Department of Economics, Howard University, Washington, DC, USA

P. L. Parcu et al. (eds.), *The Changing Postal Environment*, Topics in Regulatory Economics and Policy, https://doi.org/10.1007/978-3-030-34532-7_8

The TF recommended that Commercial services, mainly package delivery and direct mail, would have no statutory price limits and quality requirements but rather be priced so as to provide funding for the targeted USO products, needed capital expenditures, and balance sheet liabilities (Task Force 2018, p. 38). Toward this end, the Task Force would allow USPS to determine delivery frequency, implement new business lines, eliminate nonessential products that lose money, and expand third-party logistic relationships to reduce costs. In addition, the SBM would eliminate collective bargaining, make postal wages commensurate with those of other federal employees, redefine mail classes by type of sender, introduce a fully allocated cost system (Task Force 2018, p. 65), establish a separate balance sheet for packages, and possibly license the use of the mailbox to third parties.

The TF argues that the statutory monopoly system for financing the USO is defunct due to the rise of digital services and strong competition in the parcel delivery market.[1] It further argues that the failure of this regulatory structure has created financial instability for the USPS. To correct this problem, it puts forth a regulatory structure that would replace the current so-called "urban-rural" subsidy, in which profitable activities finance loss-making ones, with a different subsidy in which the customers of Commercial services (CS), primarily admail, both in FCM and in marketing mail, and commercial parcels would subsidize the loss-making activities of Essential services (ES).[2]

The ES would be a type of new "universal service" obligation for the Postal Service. The TF defines ES, in "market failure" language, as those socially necessary services that it claims the market cannot provide. Such products would be covered under a statutory monopoly, and the customers of such products would be protected by a price cap and mandated service standards. Under the TF's proposal, losses from provision of ES products would be funded by customers of Commercial products.

To accomplish this, USPS would redefine mail classes by creating products defined by the type of sender (admail, gov't mail, correspondence, etc.) and the "declared purpose of the mail item." Unlike ES products, the prices of CS products, along with the delivery frequency, the service standards, and the mode of delivery, would be set by the Postal Service to maximize net revenue. USPS would have to exit any business line that cannot be priced to cover its "direct" costs.

Costs would be contained in the SBM model by:

- Expanding third-party relationships, such as midstream processing and logistics.

---

[1] A firm with declining demand nevertheless can retain considerable market power if intermodal substitution is not sensitive to price (Brennan and Crew 2014).

[2] While the Postal Service has profit-making and loss-making activities, it is not at all clear that they can be divided into "urban" and "rural" groupings. For example, there are low-volume loss-making routes in urban areas. The Task Force report adopts this "urban-rural" view without producing any evidence to support it.

- Lowering wages, by ending collective bargaining and/or conforming wage agreements to the President's Management Agenda.[3] In addition, USPS would measure costs based on FDC principles and construct separate balance sheets for letters/flats and packages to prevent cross-subsidization.

While some commenters have welcomed aspects of the approach taken by the TF, especially its warnings about the Postal Service's financial instability and emphasis on redefining the USO (see Steidler 2018; Taub 2019), others have raised considerable criticism of the SBM along lines of practicality. Plunkett (2019) notes that the TF report would categorize account statements as Essential and advertising mail as Commercial, with admail paying a higher rate. This would be true even where the sender and the recipient are the same in both cases. Plunkett further points out that account statements contain promotional material and advertising mail contains personalized information. He predicts that the proposed price differential would cause admail to migrate from marketing mail, its current home, to first-class mail (now dubbed Essential and offered at a lower rate) where it would masquerade as account statements, causing the Postal Service to hemorrhage revenue. Plunkett also argues that similar identification and enforcement issues may arise with the TF's recommendation to subsidize prescription parcel mailing.

It is probably safe to say that a reclassification of this magnitude would confront significant practical difficulties in identifying mail by sender intention and enforcing the rate differential.

Bradley et al. (2008) built a model of the Postal Service embodying the regulatory and pricing structure dictated by the 2006 law. The paper examined its key elements and their likely impact on the US postal industry, in particular projecting financial instability in the absence of successful cost control. In this paper, we put aside the practical difficulties discussed above and perform an exercise similar to Bradley et al. (2008), constructing a new model of the Postal Service that reflects the assertions put forth in the Task Force recommendations. We use that model to identify and quantify the key elements of the SBM and draw out the implications for future USPS behavior and results. We calibrate the model with USPS data to approximate current USPS costs, volumes, and demand sensitivities.

In this paper, we assume that, somehow, Essential and Commercial services are identified and charged rates according to the TF vision. We ask then, under such Panglossian circumstances, whether the TF goal of sustainability is attainable. Section 2 describes our model of the TF's approach to postal reform. Section 3 presents the calibration of our model, designed to approximate USPS results under the TF recommendations. Section 4 presents three scenarios illustrating the pricing behavior of the USPS implied by the TF's recommendations and its results. Concluding remarks are found in Section 5.

[3] This refers to plans to make the Federal workforce more like the private sector: performance goals, no across-the-board raises, reduced retirement benefits, and other policy changes. See United States Office of Management and Budget (2018).

2 The Model

The Task Force includes the following economic recommendations, which go a long way to defining the regulatory/economic environment in which USPS would operate. We model the three of them together to assess the implications for USPS performance in the hypothesized regime.

First, USPS products would be regrouped into those services which are "Essential" (ES) and those which are "Commercial" (CS). According to TF, ES are those products which would not be provided by private sector competitors in sufficient quantity and/or are sufficiently important socially that the Postal Service would retain its monopoly over them. CS are products for which USPS faces competition. Second, the USPS would maximize profit on Commercial services and use that profit to subsidize its Essential services. Third, the Postal Service would use fully distributed costing (FDC) in which all costs are allocated to products to prevent cross-subsidy of CS by ES.

To model these characteristics, we assume that there are two Postal Service products, Essential (V_E) and Commercial (V_C). They are produced with constant marginal cost but with economies of scope. The Postal Service has product-specific fixed costs for each group (N_E and N_C) and common network costs (N).

Costs for the Postal Service are thus captured by the following equation:

$$C = \alpha_1 V_C + \alpha_2 V_E - \alpha_3 V_C V_E + N + N_C + N_E \tag{1}$$

There are separate, independent demands for the two products:

$$V_C = \beta_0 - \beta_1 P_C ; V_E = \gamma_0 - \gamma_1 P_E \tag{2}$$

In the Task Force vision, the Postal Service maximizes profit on its Commercial product. That profit is defined as:

$$\pi_C = P_C \left(\beta_0 - \beta_1 P_C\right) - \alpha_1 V_C + \alpha_3 V_C V_E - N_C \tag{3}$$

Once the price that maximizes Commercial product profits is set, USPS will set the price of the Essential product just large enough to cover the Essential product costs, less the subsidy from the profits made on Commercial products. If the profit from selling the Commercial product exceeds network costs, the price for the Essential product will be below its average incremental costs:

$$P_E V_E = \alpha_2 V_E - \alpha_3 V_C V_E + N_E - \left(\pi_C - N\right) \tag{4}$$

Putting these two conditions together demonstrates that in this setup as long as $\pi_C > N$, the Postal Service is breaking even:

$$\pi = P_C \left(\beta_0 - \beta_1 P_C\right) - \alpha_1 V_C + \alpha_3 V_C V_E - N_C + P_E V_E - \alpha_2 V_E + \alpha_3 V_C V_E - N_E - N = 0 \tag{5}$$

Before investigating the implications of FDC in this structure, we first find the profit-maximizing Commercial product price (and thus its quantity and profit):

$$P_C^* = \frac{\beta_0 - \alpha_1\beta_1 - \alpha_3\beta_1 V_E}{2\beta_1} \tag{6}$$

We can then solve for the subsidized Essential product price:

$$P_E^* = \alpha_2 + \frac{N_E - \alpha_3 V_C^*}{V_E} - \frac{\pi_C^*}{V_E} \tag{7}$$

This shows that the Essential product price is equal to its average incremental cost less the Commercial profit per piece of Essential mail. Using our demand specification, the expression for the Essential good's price can be expressed as a function of the optimal Commercial good price and quantities:

$$P_E^*\left(\gamma_0 - \gamma_1 \mathrm{P}_E^*\right) + \alpha_2\gamma_1 P_E^* = \alpha_2\gamma_0 + N_E - \alpha_3 V_C^* - \pi_C^* \tag{8}$$

where

$$\pi_C^* = \frac{\left(\beta_0 + \alpha_1\beta_1 - \alpha_3\beta_1 V_E^*\right)^2}{4} - \frac{\left(\alpha_1 - \alpha_3 V_E^*\right)\left(\beta_0 + \alpha_1\beta_1 - \alpha_3\beta_1 V_E^*\right)}{2} \tag{9}$$

and

$$V_C^* = \frac{\beta_0 + \alpha_1\beta_1 - \alpha_3\beta_1 V_E^*}{2} \tag{10}$$

Equations 6 and 8 form a two-equation system that permits simultaneous solution for the profit-maximizing Commercial good's price and the associated Essential good's price.[4]

We now turn our attention to implementing the third recommended characteristic of the Task Force, fully distributed costing. Under FDC, all costs are allocated to products on some arbitrary basis. There is no causal basis for the allocation. To calculate the FDCs for the two products, we first need to find the "institutional" cost (IC), the cost which is not causally attributed to each of the two products. The general form is given by:

$$IC = C - C_E - C_C \tag{11}$$

Substitution yields the expression which shows that the institutional cost is the sum of overall network costs and the cost savings from economics of scope:

[4]The existence of scope economies causes the need for simultaneous solution. Otherwise the profit-maximizing price for the Commercial good could be set and the price for the Essential good set subsequently.

$$IC = N + \alpha_3 V_E V_C \tag{12}$$

In the break-even scenario envisioned by the Task Force, each product's price is set equal to that product's fully distributed cost. Then all costs are allocated to products, and total revenue equals total cost. If the FDC allocation is made on the basis of relative volumes, then the two product prices (and FDC unit costs) are given by:

$$P_C^{F_1} = \text{FDC}_C^1 = \alpha_1 V_C - \alpha_3 V_E V_C + N_C + \frac{V_C}{V_C + V_E}\left(N + \alpha_3 V_E V_C\right) \tag{13}$$

and

$$P_E^{F_1} = \text{FDC}_E^1 = \alpha_2 V_E - \alpha_3 V_E V_C + N_E + \frac{V_E}{V_C + V_E}\left(N + \alpha_3 V_E V_C\right) \tag{14}$$

These two equations can be solved simultaneously for the prices for the Commercial and Essential goods. Those solutions can then be used to calculate the volumes under a volume-based FDC system.

Alternatively, the FDC system could allocate institutional cost on the base of relative product costs. In this application of FDC, the two product prices would be set by the following equations:

$$P_C^{F_2} = \text{FDC}_C^2 = \alpha_1 V_C - \alpha_3 V_E V_C + N_C + \theta\left(N + \alpha_3 V_E V_C\right) \tag{15}$$

and

$$P_E^{F_2} = \text{FDC}_E^2 = \alpha_2 V_E - \alpha_3 V_E V_C + N_E + (1-\theta)\left(N + \alpha_3 V_E V_C\right) \tag{16}$$

where

$$\theta = \frac{\alpha_1 V_C - \alpha_3 V_E V_C + N_C}{\alpha_1 V_C + \alpha_2 V_E - 2\alpha_3 V_E V_C + N_C + N_E}$$

Given the complexity of the solutions under profit maximization and the two FDC scenarios, it is difficult to infer quantitative implications for the TF model of "sustainability." We thus calibrate the model to values associated with USPS and solve numerically. This approach also allows us to examine the sensitivity of the results to different assumptions about relative costs and our demand parameters.

3 Calibration

The model in Section 2 is designed to capture the key aspects of the Task Force's economic recommendations. The TF report is vague in places, with only general suggestions about how the recommendations should be implemented, so we have isolated the three TF recommendations that are clear. To accurately assess their implications, we calibrate our model with recent Postal Service data.

The first step is to implement TF's division of products into Essential and Commercial groups. The TF report lists the following classifications of mail as being Essential:

- Personal correspondence
- Transaction mail (bills, financial statements)
- Government mail (election and tax)
- Parcels containing pharmaceuticals
- Person-to-person parcels

The Task Force does not implement this listing by identifying which current mail products would migrate, so our calibration exercise must undertake that effort, and we make a first cut at determining which current products move to the two proposed groupings. The TF appears to place all advertising mails, magazines, and competitive packages in the Commercial group, so we start by putting all of USPS marketing mails, periodicals, package services, and competitive products and services in the Commercial group. It then remains to split first-class mail between the two groups. To do so, we use the Postal Service's survey data (2018a) which records the type of first-class letter and flats sent and received by households. It also provides an estimate of the total amount of household first-class mail, allowing us to infer the amount of business first class. That study thus provides the following proportions for first-class letters and flats (Table 1):

To be consistent with the Task Force recommendations, we place correspondence and transactions mail in the Essential group, along with other. We also place first-class parcels in the Essential category, in order to capture parcels containing pharmaceuticals, which are sent via first class.[5] That means that we put advertising and business first-class letter and flats in the Commercial group.

Table 2, from USPS (2018b), shows the mapping of existing Postal Service products into the two groups proposed by the Task Force.

We can now use these data, along with the Postal Service's total cost, to calibrate the model. We start on the cost side and find values for α_1 and α_2, the marginal costs for the Commercial and Essential products.[6] From the table we use the weighted

Table 1 Proportions of first-class letters and flats

Correspondence	25.9%
Transactions	39.1%
Advertising	6.2%
Other	4.7%
Business	24.1%

[5] Not all first-class packages are for medicine, but we still include the total amount and let the balance be our measure of person-to-person parcels.

[6] There are no measures available for the degree of economies of scope between the two products, so we drop that term from the numerical analysis.

Table 2 Putting USPS products into Task Force groups

Product	Revenue	Attributable cost	Volume variable cost	Volume	Revenue/ piece	VVC/ piece
Essential						
FC parcels	546.6	478.7	477.8	190.9	$2.863	$2.502
Correspondence	6765.3	3163.2	3087.8	15,334.9	$0.441	$0.201
Transactions	10,235.2	4785.5	4671.5	23,200.0	$0.441	$0.201
Other	1234.8	577.3	563.6	2798.9	$0.441	$0.201
MD services	1818.4	1323.4	1301.6	5459.0	$0.333	$0.238
Total essential	**20,600.3**	**10,328.1**	**10,102.2**	**46,983.6**	**$0.438**	**$0.215**
Commercial						
FC advertising	1623.2	759.0	740.9	3679.4	$0.441	$0.201
FC business	6302.8	2946.9	2876.7	14,286.5	$0.441	$0.201
Total periodicals	1374.7	1982.8	1977.0	5300.7	$0.259	$0.373
Total USPS marketing mail	16,671.8	10,917.7	10,748.5	78,369.8	$0.213	$0.137
Total package services	801.1	773.0	771.1	619.9	$1.292	$1.244
Total competitive mail and services	20,689.5	13,538.1	13,318.7	5103.4	$4.054	$2.610
Total commercial	**47,463.3**	**30,917.4**	**30,432.8**	**107,359.8**	**$0.442**	**$0.283**

average volume-variable costs for the two groups as our values for marginal costs, as volume-variable cost per piece is USPS's measure of marginal cost. We note that the Commercial marginal cost is about seven cents higher than the Essential marginal cost. This reflects the presence of competitive package services in the Commercial group. We next find the two product-specific fixed costs and the overall network or "institutional" cost. For each product, the Postal Service computes both the volume-variable cost and the attributable fixed cost.

For our calibration, we will take the difference between the two to be a measure of each product's product-specific cost. This effort yields a product-specific fixed cost of $225.9 million for the Essential product group and $484.6 million for the Commercial group. Finally, total institutional or network cost is found by subtracting the total attributable costs for the two product groups from Postal Service total costs, yielding a value of 30.8 billion.

We next calibrate the demand side of the model. We find values for the parameters in the demand functions that produce results consistent with Postal Service's actual volumes in 2017. We start the calibration exercise with the actual price (average revenue per piece) and volume for each of the product groupings. For the Commercial group, we have a price of 0.442 and a volume of 107.4 billion pieces:

$$107.4 = \beta_0 - \beta_1 0.442.$$

To solve for both coefficients, we use the current estimated elasticity of demand (USPS 2018c). Although the Postal Service does not explicitly calculate a demand elasticity for the Commercial group, review of the demand elasticities for the products in the group suggests an overall elasticity of 1.1. This allows us to write the second required equation:

$$\varepsilon_c = \frac{\partial V}{\partial P}\frac{P}{V}, \quad or \ \ 1.1 = \beta_1 \frac{0.442}{107.4}.$$

With these two equations, we find that $\beta_0 = 225.54$ and $\beta_1 = 267.23$. With these coefficients, inserting the price of 0.442 yields the existing CS volume of 107.4 billion. A similar exercise is done for the Essential product group using its assumed elasticity of 0.70. The next table provides the calibrated values for the model (Table 3).

To assess the accuracy of the calibration, we compare the model's computed values to the actual values for the Postal Service in FY 2017. That comparison shows the model is within rounding error of the actual values (Table 4).

4 Numerical Solutions

We now use the model to assess the implications of the Task Force recommendations, and we do that in several steps. We first look at just the proposed product reclassification scheme and the suggestion to use Commercial product profits to subsidize Essential products. We then add the proposed, but undefined, cost savings.

Table 3 Parameter values

Parameter	Calibrated value
α_1	\$0.215
α_2	\$0.283
β_0	225.5
β_1	267.2
γ_0	79.9
γ_1	75.0
N_C	\$0.48
N^E	\$0.23
N	\$30.80

Table 4 Baseline values (billions)

Measure	Commercial	Essential	Total	USPS values
Volume	107.40	46.98	154.38	154.34
Revenue	\$47.46	\$20.60	\$68.08	\$68.07
Attributable cost	\$30.92	\$10.33	\$41.26	\$41.25
Contribution	\$16.55	\$10.27	\$26.82	\$26.81
Profit			–\$3.97	–\$3.90

Finally, we look at the implications of imposing fully distributed costing in the Task Force's regulatory structure.

4.1 *Scenario 1: Profit Maximization and Cross Subsidy*

In this scenario, we investigate part of the Task Force suggestions, setting the profit-maximizing price for the Commercial products and using the profit to subsidize Essential products. While the Task Force is silent on the mechanism, the logical approach is that profit made on the Commercial product is first used to defray institutional costs and then any remaining balance is used to subsidize the Essential products. After all, the primary focus of the Task Force is "sustainability," meaning the Postal Service is self-sustaining and not earning losses. We investigate this scenario first to understand the opportunities for this approach to provide sustainability and then, secondly, to understand the implications of fully distributed costing for achieving sustainability (Table 5).

With an initial elasticity of (negative) 1.1, allowing USPS to maximize profits on the Commercial products leads to a higher price and reduced volume. The reduction in revenue is smaller than the reduction in attributable cost because marginal cost is constant and the price is higher. This means that the Commercial product group produces an extra $4 billion in contribution. This is used first to cover the institutional costs, and the remaining balance then subsidizes Essential products. Because the Postal Service had a deficit of $4 billion in FY 2017, there is no subsidy available to support the Essential products. In fact, for the Postal Service to break even, Essential products must contribute $10.3 billion to defraying institutional costs (Table 6).

Table 5 Changes from baseline

Measure	Commercial	Essential
Price	$0.122	$0.001
Volume	−32.5	−0.1
Revenue	−$5.3	$0.01
Attributable cost	−$9.2	−$0.01
Contribution	$4.0	$0.02

Table 6 Aggregate measures

Measure	Commercial	Essential	Total	USPS Values
Volume	74.9	46.9	121.8	154.9
Revenue	$42.2	$20.6	$62.8	$68.5
Attributable cost	$21.7	$10.3	$32.0	$41.6
Contribution	$20.5	$10.3	$30.8	$26.9
Profit			$0.0	−$3.9

That amount is almost identical to the contribution made by Essential products in FY 2017, so the price of Essential products is virtually unchanged (it increases by one-tenth of one cent). Without the requirement of FDC, maximizing profits on the Commercial goods closes the Postal Service's deficit but leaves the price of Essential product unchanged. Note that this is dependent upon the assumed Commercial elasticity of 1.1 (which rises to 2.01 after the price increase).

If the elasticity were higher, then Commercial products would not be able to raise sufficient contribution to close the deficit. In reality, things are more complicated because the different products within the Commercial group have different elasticities, so there would not be a common across-the-broad increase.

4.2 *Scenario 2: Effects of Cost Savings*

To get a better sense of how the Task Force's proposed product realignment might work, we look at a scenario in which the Postal Service is able to save $3.5 billion a year in institutional costs. To provide some perspective, the requirement for the Postal Service to prefund its retiree health benefit was $4.3 billion in FY 2017. With the $3.5 billion savings, the contribution from the Commercial products is sufficiently large to allow a material cross subsidy to the Essential products. Thus, the Essential product price falls by nine cents, and its volume increases by seven billion pieces. The volume increase is not big enough to offset the price decline so Essential product revenue falls by about $2 billion. The higher volume also causes a higher

Table 7 Changes from baseline

Measure	Commercial	Essential
Price	$0.122	–$0.093
Volume	–32.5	7.0
Revenue	–$5.3	–$1.97
Attributable cost	–$9.2	$1.51
Contribution	$4.0	–$3.48

Table 8 Aggregate measures

Measure	Commercial	Essential	Total	USPS values
Volume	74.90	53.99	128.89	154.90
Revenue	$42.22	$18.63	$60.85	$68.50
Attributable cost	$21.71	$11.83	$33.55	$41.60
Contribution	$20.51	$6.79	$27.30	$26.90
Profit			$0.0	–$3.9

attributable cost, and total contribution from the Essential product falls by $3.5 billion (Table 7).

As in Scenario 1, the Postal Service breaks even, showing that this scenario is consistent with sustainability. The difference is that the cross subsidization is effective in lowering the price for Essential products and thus increasing their volume. If these products are socially preferred or underproduced due to market failure, this shift could increase welfare (Table 8).

4.3 *Scenario 3. Introducing Fully Distributed Costing*

Ignoring substantial economic research on the topic, the TF recommends the use of the FDC approach to product costing. Rather than tracing costs to the products that cause them, the Task Force approach relies upon an arbitrary costing scheme to assign institutional costs to products.[7] This mechanism thus attributes common fixed costs to products and acts as if they are volume-related.

In a break-even enterprise, the use of FDC eliminates pricing flexibility. For a product to cover its cost, its price must equal its unit fully distributed cost. But because all costs have been distributed, an FDC approach means total revenue will just equal total cost. This is not true in a loss-making enterprise in which prices will be below unit FDC costs or a profit-making enterprise in which the opposite will be true.

Since there is no "correct" way to implement FDC, we will look at a number of different alternatives.

In the first approach we look at, network cost is distributed on relative volume. In this version of FDC, Commercial products are assigned 69.6% of network cost because they comprise 69.6% of volume. Essential products are assigned the remaining 30.4%. Under this flavor of FDC, the unit cost for the Commercial product is 48.7 cents, well above its marginal cost of 28.3 cents. Similarly, the FDC cost for the Essential product is 41.9 cents. Multiplying these unit costs by the base volumes equals the $72.06 billion of total Postal Service costs. Setting prices equal to these costs should, in FDC thinking, allow the Postal Service to break even. But

Table 9 Aggregate measures under a volume-based FDC

Measure	Commercial	Essential	Total	Profit max values
Volume	95.27	48.42	143.69	121.82
Revenue	$46.44	$20.30	$66.75	$62.83
FDC cost	$48.92	$20.01	$68.93	$32.03
Contribution	−$2.47	$0.29	−$2.18	$30.80
Profit			−$2.18	$0.0

[7] The literature on this topic is vast. For a recent summary of the research in this area, however, see Mayo and Willig (2018).

that does not occur, because the FDC approach does not account for the demand response to higher prices, unlike the profit maximization approach in Scenario 1.

Running the model with the volume-based FDC prices demonstrates the point that adding the FDC requirement to the Task Force recommendations precludes those recommendations from producing "sustainability" in the sense of a break-even Postal Service. Under volume-based FDC, the Postal Service earns losses on its Commercial product, when FDC costs are included, despite a decline in volume. FDC costing precludes the Postal Service from charging the profit-maximizing price. Those results are shown in Table 9. Note that the final FDC costs per piece will differ from the original ones because charging FDC-based prices will change the relative volumes. Commercial products fall from 69.6% of volume to 66.3%. Yet FDC cost per piece rises because the fall in volume is 11.2% and the fall in FDC cost is 6.5%.

As mentioned above, there is no unique FDC set of costs. As a check on the results found above, we examine two other FDC approaches. In the first, the network costs are allocated to products on the basis of their relative attributable costs; then we examine allocation-based network purpose. This approach is sometimes put forward by FDC advocates through the specious argument that the products responsible for producing attributable costs are also necessarily the products responsible for producing network costs.[8]

The third approach we examine attempts to allocate network costs based upon the assumed purpose of the network. To the extent the Postal Service's network was established and is maintained for the acceptance, transportation, and delivery of first-class mail, then the responsibility for network costs arises from first-class products. Under this approach the network costs are allocated to Commercial and Essential products based upon their relative first-class mail volumes.[9] This approach would thus assign more network costs to the Essential product than the Commercial product. Of course, some may object that this approach is "unfair," so this example also serves to illustrate the arbitrariness of FDC.

The results show the cost-based FDC is even worse for the Task Force goal of sustainability. The losses under this FDC method are nearly $3 billion dollars, providing little gain over the current situation. Because Commercial products have, on average, higher unit costs than Essential products, this FDC method shifts more

[8]Network costs, by definition, are common costs and are not caused by individual products. This is true whether they are fixed or variable costs. Consider a letter carrier walking from the sidewalk to a customer's mailbox while carrying two first-class letters, a piece of priority mail, and three marketing flats. The cost of that walk is identical if the first-class mail was removed, or if the priority mail was removed, or if the marketing flats are removed. None of those products are responsible for creating the cost.

[9]A similar approach to FDC might argue that all, or most of, the network exists for the acceptance, transportation, and delivery of Essential mail, so all, or nearly all, network costs should be allocated to that product. This approach to FDC completely reverses the avowed goals of the TF of sustainability and support for Essential products. While some might consider this approach to be extreme, it does highlight the fact that FDC costing can produce an extremely wide range of results.

Table 10 Aggregate measures under a cost based FDC

Measure	Commercial	Essential	Total	Profit max values
Volume	91.13	51.07	142.21	121.82
Revenue	$45.84	$19.61	$65.45	$62.83
FDC cost	$49.41	$18.92	$68.33	$32.03
Contribution	−$3.57	$0.69	−$2.88	$30.80
Profit			−$2.88	$0.0

Table 11 Aggregate measures under a network purpose-based FDC

Measure	Commercial	Essential	Total	Profit max values
Volume	126.26	28.53	154.79	121.82
Revenue	$46.91	$19.53	$66.44	$62.83
FDC cost	$45.25	$28.19	$73.44	$32.03
Contribution	$1.66	−$8.66	−$7.00	$30.80
Profit			−$7.00	$0.0

costs to Commercial products. This shift decreases Commercial product revenue more than it increases Essential product revenue so total revenue falls compared to the volume-based FDC method (Table 10).

The results under the network purpose approach are even more drastic, actually making things worse than they are currently. Under this FDC method, the Postal Service loses $7 billion per year. The much higher price for the Essential product ($0.68) drives that product into its elastic range and substantially lowers its volume. At the same time, the lower cost for the Commercial product means a lower price and a large increase in its volume. This drives the demand for the Commercial product into its inelastic range, so the price decline does not materially increase revenue. But it does increase cost, so contribution falls (Table 11).

Finally, even a $3.5 billion cost saving is not enough to rescue the Postal Service from FDC, as under all three FDC methods, the Postal Service continues to earn losses. The distortion caused by FDC is sufficiently large so that the Postal Service is not "sustainable" under the Task Force's proposed product structure. Under a volume-based FDC, the best the Postal Service can do is to lose $500 million a year. Under the cost-based approach, it loses $1.1 billion a year, and under the network purpose approach, it loses $4.4 billion annually.

5 Conclusions

This paper examines three central recommendations of the President's Task Force report on the *United States Postal Service: A Sustainable Path Forward*: (1) regrouping of USPS products into Essential and Commercial products, (2) pricing so that customers of Essential products are subsidized by Commercial products' customers, and (3) FDC pricing. These recommendations are meant by TF to ensure that USPS will be financially sustainable. We develop and calibrate a model of economic behavior under these assumptions to illustrate the conditions when, and when not, such an outcome is likely. The calibration is based on USPS data reconfigured to fit the TF approach.

Under USPS-based calibration, the model shows that an increase in the price of competitive products to a profit-maximizing level will not be sufficient to subsidize the customers of Essential products, and in fact USPS would require substantial contribution from Essential products to attain the TF sustainability goal of breaking even, and the price of Essential products is the same as the actual FY 2017 price.

To reach breakeven and provide a subsidy for customers of Essential products, USPS would have to make dramatic cost savings. Such savings would, along with a price increase in the competitive products' price, allow USPS to lower the price of Essential services and increase ES volume, which is the TF goal. Of course, if the Postal Service could achieve such savings, it could break even without having to reclassify its product groupings.

Finally, we use the model to show that FDC pricing is incompatible with TF's sustainability. It is of course true that setting prices to fully distribute all the costs will produce breakeven in some static sense, but only if prices have no effect whatsoever on demand, a very dubious notion. As shown by the scenarios we investigate above, even a truly large cost saving cannot render USPS sustainable under FDC pricing.

References

Bradley, M. D., Colvin, J., & Perkins, M. (2008). An economic model of the regulatory structure created by the Postal Accountability and Enhancement Act of 2006. In *Handbook of worldwide postal reform*. Northampton: Edward Elgar.

Brennan, T., & Crew, M. (2014). Gross substitutes vs. marginal substitutes: Implications for market definition in the postal sector. In M. Crew & T. Brennan (Eds.), *The role of the postal and delivery sector in a digital age* (pp. 1–15). Cheltenham: Edward Elgar.

Mayo, J. W., & Willig, R. (2018). *Economic foundations for 21st century freight rail rate regulation*. Washington, DC: Georgetown University.

Plunkett, M. (2019). An essential dilemma. *Consumer Postal Council.*

Steidler, P. (2018). *Postal service task force report: Seven things to know*. Lexington Institute, Arlington, VA, USA.

Task Force on the United States Postal Service. (2018). *United states postal service: A sustainable path forward. Advanced workshop on regulation and competition*. Rutgers Business School, Washington, DC in April of 2019.

Taub, R. (2019). *The President's report on USPS reform. Advanced workshop on regulation and competition*. Washington, DC: Venable LLP, 2001. April. (Presentation).

United States Office of Management and Budget. (2018). *The President's management agenda: Modernizing government for the twenty-first century*. Washington, DC: OMB.

United States Postal Service (2018a). Household Diary Study: Mail Use and Attitudes in FY 2017, Washington, DC June.

United States Postal Service (2018b). Cost and Revenue Analysis Report, FY 2017, Washington, DC April. 2018.

United States Postal Regulatory Commission (2018c), Econometric demand equation tables, in Documenting the United States Postal Service Demand Equation Estimation and Volume Forecasting Methodologies. Washington, DC. January.

On Correcting the Cross-Subsidies Caused by the US Postal Tariff

Edward S. Pearsall, Margaret M. Cigno, and Lyudmila Y. Bzhilyanskaya

1 Introduction

Cross-subsidies are evidence of defects in the prices charged by a multi-product public enterprise (Pearsall 2009). A cross-subsidy occurs whenever the revenue derived from a proper subset of products, or a single product, fails to cover incremental cost (IC).[1] IC is the cost that would be avoided if the products in the subset were not produced. The difference between IC and the revenue from the subset at the stipulated prices is the amount of the cross-subsidy.

An enterprise's tariff does not cause cross-subsidies when IC does not exceed added revenue for any subset of services. This is the complete IC test as described by Faulhaber (1975). It is usually impractical to apply the test directly to a complex tariff. Even a fairly small number of broadly defined individual product categories can be combined into a great many subsets—far too many to be tested individually.

[1]This is the conventional definition of a cross-subsidy found in Faulhaber (1975) and Pearsall (2009). It entails no specific designation of the parties bearing the cost of a cross-subsidy. As a whole the cost of a cross-subsidy must be borne by some combination of the enterprise's other customers and its residual claimants.

Edward S. Pearsall is an independent consultant. Margaret M. Cigno is the director of the Office of Accountability and Compliance of the US Postal Regulatory Commission (PRC). Lyudmila Y. Bzhilyanskaya is a senior staff member of the PRC. The views expressed in this paper are those of the authors and do not necessarily represent the opinions of the PRC.

E. S. Pearsall (✉)
Independent Consultant, Alexandria, VA, USA

M. M. Cigno · L. Y. Bzhilyanskaya
U.S. Postal Regulatory Commission (PRC), Washington, DC, USA

P. L. Parcu et al. (eds.), *The Changing Postal Environment*, Topics in Regulatory Economics and Policy, https://doi.org/10.1007/978-3-030-34532-7_9

In addition, the procedure usually does not unambiguously identify those products whose prices are responsible for the cross-subsidies.[2]

In this paper we show how these difficulties may be overcome for a postal service with a sub-modular cost function.[3] The US Postal Service (USPS) employs a cost accounting system that supports a single-driver model of USPS costs that is sub-modular (Pearsall 2019). Postal costs are characteristically sub-modular because they exhibit economies of scope and scale and because some fixed costs are specific to particular subsets of services.[4] With such a cost function, we can find the smallest proper subset of services receiving the maximum cross-subsidy using a simple "myopic" algorithm described in Pearsall (2009). The algorithm has previously proven to be effective on the USPS tariff (Fenster et al. 2008).

We apply the myopic algorithm to identify the maximizing subset and then extend the complete IC test to describe the calculation of upper and lower bounds for the price increases needed to correct cross-subsidies. ICs for single-service categories, which denote the lowest level of aggregation, are used to calculate the lower bounds. These are the smallest increases needed to correct any of the cross-subsidies for the services in the maximizing subset. Complementary upper bounds are calculated as the price increases needed to individually remove each of the included services from the maximizing subset. These are the largest increases that would ever be needed to eliminate a single-service's price as a cause of cross-subsidies given the levels of output of all services. We also show how these upper and lower bounds can be adjusted to account for the demand effects of raising rates. The adjusted bounds are then employed to calculate Ramsey-Boiteux price increases that maximize welfare subject to the bounds and the constraint that the cross-subsidy for the maximizing subset is eliminated.

This paper describes the mechanics of the complete IC test, the calculation of the upper and lower bounds, the adjustments that are made for demand effects, and the determination of efficient price increases for the US postal tariff. Our results are derived from USPS data and analyses reported to the PRC for the FY 2018 Annual Compliance Report (ACR) and the annual USPS econometric demand model.[5] Our results demonstrate that the complete IC test can be applied to inform pricing decisions across the entire spectrum of rates constituting the US postal tariff.

Overall, we find that the price increases that would have been needed ex post to correct the cross-subsidies caused by the FY 2018 tariff are more numerous and

[2] The procedure will reliably terminate with sufficient information to determine the price increases only in cases where the cost function is separable by product.

[3] Sub-modularity is a mathematical property analogous to concavity for real-valued functions defined over a lattice. Let Ω be the set of all possible combinations of postal services (a lattice). For given output levels, the postal cost function is a real-valued set function defined over Ω. The cost function is sub-modular if $C(X \cup Y) + C(X \cap Y) \leq C(X) + C(Y)$ for every $X, Y \in \Omega$. When the cost function is sub-modular, the incremental costs of disjoint subsets of products are super-additive, i.e., $IC(X + Y) \geq IC(X) + IC(Y)$ for the disjoint subsets X and Y (Pearsall 2009 and 2019).

[4] Subset-specific fixed costs are avoided when none of the products in the subset are produced.

[5] Some of the data used in this paper are nonpublic.

moderately higher than expected. Altogether, these increases could have eliminated a maximum cross-subsidy of $1913 million and, with demand effects, reduced USPS's FY 2018 losses by approximately the same amount.

In Section 2 we briefly review the relevant FY 2018 US postal data from the ACR and our postal cost model. In Section 3 we show how the myopic algorithm identifies the prices that cause cross-subsidies. In Section 4, using the information available at the termination of the complete IC test, we calculate upper and lower bounds for price increases needed to eliminate the cross-subsidies, modify the bounds to account for demand effects, and exhibit the Ramsey-Boiteux increases. In Section 5 we provide a brief review of the reasons for eliminating the cross-subsidies our research has revealed, and discuss the barriers to their elimination presented by current US postal law. Section 6 concludes the paper. A technical appendix (Pearsall 2019), deriving and analyzing the single-driver cost model and explaining the calculation of the Ramsey-Boiteux price increases, is available from the authors.

2 The USPS Data and the Single-Driver Model

Testing a tariff for cross-subsidies and computing bounds for price increases requires prices, volumes, and costs over a specified period of time for a predefined list of products. USPS compiles volume, revenue, and cost data, conducts special studies, and fits econometric demand models using common product definitions. USPS employs the same framework to annually report cost accounting data to the PRC by cost components, which are aggregated into cost segments. Each cost component is further divided into elements corresponding to discrete activities, so that components are groupings of distinct activities, e.g., city carrier street delivery activities or equipment depreciation.[6]

USPS determines total, attributable, volume-variable, product-specific, inframarginal, and institutional (other) costs by each cost component.[7] Volume-variable, product-specific, and some inframarginal costs are then attributed to products. Volume-variable costs are defined as the product of volume and marginal cost at current levels of output, which will not be the same as variable costs. Calculating the volume-variable costs employs predetermined parameters called "volume variabilities" that are used to calculate marginal costs for various levels of outputs. A volume variability is the elasticity of a component's cost with respect to a cost

[6] *See* PRC, Rule 39 C.F.R. Section 3050.60(f) Report for FY 2017 (Summary Descriptions), July 2, 2018 (FY 2017 Summary Descriptions Report). In the current paper, we have employed the USPS cost data at the greatest level of detail found in the FY 2018 Cost Segments and Components (CS&C) report filed with the FY 2018 ACR.

[7] For a description of the specialized terminology employed in the US postal cost models and accounting practices, see Panzar (2015). The USPS costing methodology employs definitions that are different from the standard economic cost concepts that divide costs into fixed and variable categories.

driver. We assume that these cost drivers are linear homogenous functions of postal volumes. For example, the cost driver for many transportation components is cubic-foot-miles. The volume-variable costs of these transportation components are distributed to product categories according to the cubic-foot-miles transported.[8] The cost drivers are not included in USPS's data sets but are typically explanatory variables in the models that USPS has developed within special studies to estimate the volume variabilities. Product-specific costs represent costs for certain products that are not volume variable but are directly or indirectly caused by those products.[9]

We assembled statistics for 112 detailed product categories using data reported to the PRC by USPS within the FY 2018 ACR.[10] Revenues and volumes were extracted individually for the product categories and used to distribute fees,[11] which were mostly available as class aggregates. Revenue for USPS's own mail is set equal to the volume-variable cost of this mail as would be the case if USPS had transfer-priced its own mail at marginal cost. The volumes and revenues (with the fees apportioned) are shown in Table 1.

Volume-variable costs are not always found in the ACR files at the level of product detail shown in Table 1. Instead, the files sometimes contained cost data for several aggregated categories. Where this occurred, we had little choice but to apportion volume-variable costs between categories according to some more-or-less arbitrary rule.[12] We have most often apportioned the costs using proportions taken directly from the volume data. In cases involving a worksharing discount, such as presort and dropship categories, rates are set as discounts from the non-workshared rate. The discounts are determined through the use of cost avoidance models. Consequently, we refined the allocation for these categories using estimates of cost avoided.[13] The FY 2018 ACR report provides data on USPS annual costs by 155 cost components.

[8] For a description of how this distribution key is developed, see FY 2018 Transportation Cost System (TRACS) documentation, Library Reference USPS-FY18-36.

[9] USPS Public Cost and Revenue Analysis, FY 2018 at 6

[10] Data for competitive categories of mail and services are kept under seal by the PRC and have been omitted from Tables 1 and 2 as detailed in the table notes.

[11] Revenues excludes mailing fees for various non-postage items such as certificates of mailing, address correction, application, and mailing permits. However, these fees are apportioned to services for purposes of assessing IC coverage.

[12] A better procedure would be to recompile the USPS cost accounts using a finer set of product categories. However, these data are not routinely made available to the PRC as part of the ACR filings.

[13] The formula for apportioning volume-variable costs while preserving differences in the cost avoided per piece is $C_i = \left(\left(\frac{C}{Q}\right) + \sum_j \frac{A_j Q_j}{Q} - A_i\right) Q_i \forall i$. C_i is the cost apportioned to product category i; Q_i is the category's volume; and A_i is the cost avoided per piece versus the cost per piece of a base category. C is the total volume-variable cost to be apportioned, and Q is the corresponding total volume. The summation in the formula is taken over all of the product categories included in the apportionment.

Table 1 The complete incremental cost test FY 2018

	Revenue with fees distributed	Volume variable and product specific costs	Volume pieces or transactions	Myopic algorithm process														Single-Svc. incremental cost (IC)	Max. subset incremental cost (IC)
				Backward cross-subsidy (Y)							Forward no cross-sub. (N)								
Postal mail or service category	(*millions*)	costs (*millions*)	(*thousands*)	*0*	*1*	*2*	*3*	*4*	*5*	*6*	*0*	*1*	*2*	*3*	*4*	*5*	*6*	(*millions*)	(*millions*)
Single-Piece First-Class Letters	$8400.68	$5048.68	16,830,360										N	N	N	N	N	$5164.81	$5409.03
Single-Piece First-Class Cards	$224.63	$182.87	630,117												N	N	N	$183.02	$191.10
Nonautomation Presort First-Class Letters	$280.19	$143.04	610,066										N	N	N	N	N	$143.12	$149.21
Automation Presort First-Class Letters	$13,495.40	$4253.19	35,185,624								N	N	N	N	N	N	N	$4323.70	$4521.16
Nonautomation Presort First-Class Cards	$34.36	$12.58	122,222									N	N	N	N	N	N	$12.58	$13.21
Automation Presort First-Class Cards	$505.70	$157.87	1,953,288									N	N	N	N	N	N	$158.03	$165.91
Single-Piece First-Class Flats	$1361.08	$1039.42	826,649											N	N	N	N	$1042.15	$1081.20
Nonautomation Presort First-Class Flats	$19.54	$18.51	15,658													N	N	$18.51	$19.19
Automation Presort First-Class Flats	$529.26	$493.28	539,557													N	N	$493.89	$512.23
Standard Regular H-D & Sat. Letters	$1109.62	$513.93	6,712,467										N	N	N	N	N	$495.11	$523.26
Standard Nonprofit H-D & Sat. Letters	$42.74	$42.48	503,908			Y	Y	Y	Y	Y								$40.89	$43.15
Standard Regular H-D & Sat. Flts/Pcls	$1948.47	$1325.88	10,889,925											N	N	N	N	$1376.58	$1470.22
Standard Nonprofit H-D & Sat. Flts/Pcls	$80.12	$73.82	732,847				Y	Y	Y	Y								$75.44	$80.13

(continued)

Table 1 (continued)

	Revenue with fees distributed	Volume variable and product specific	Volume pieces or transactions	Myopic algorithm process														Single-Svc. incremental	Max. subset incremental
				Backward cross-subsidy (Y)							Forward no cross-sub. (N)							cost (IC)	cost (IC)
Postal mail or service category	(*millions*)	costs (*millions*)	(*thousands*)	*0*	*1*	*2*	*3*	*4*	*5*	*6*	*0*	*1*	*2*	*3*	*4*	*5*	*6*	(*millions*)	(*millions*)
Standard Regular Car-Rte Letters	$1709.48	$1456.29	6146.460												N	N	N	$1468.11	$1545.25
Standard Regular Car-Rte Flts/Pcls	$65.84	$129.70	461,418		Y	Y	Y	Y	Y	Y								$129.79	$136.18
Standard Nonprofit Car-Rte Letters	$70.12	$108.61	416,644		Y	Y	Y	Y	Y	Y								$108.68	$114.04
Standard Nonprofit Car-Rte Flts/Pcls	$2.88	$8.55	28,038		Y	Y	Y	Y	Y	Y								$8.55	$8.98
Standard Regular Auto Letters	$8405.17	$3769.49	36,811,530									N	N	N	N	N	N	$3841.21	$4034.20
Standard Regular Nonauto Letters	$149.44	$68.42	520,804										N	N	N	N	N	$68.44	$71.64
Standard Nonprofit Auto Letters	$1037.22	$963.20	8,805,471													N	N	$967.71	$1013.84
Standard Nonprofit Nonauto Letters	$64.53	$51.94	379,362												N	N	N	$51.96	$54.39
Standard Regular Auto Flats	$1271.90	$1639.12	2,870,035		Y	Y	Y	Y	Y	Y								$1646.84	$1695.93
Standard Regular Nonauto Flats	$77.23	$94.12	141,843		Y	Y	Y	Y	Y	Y								$94.14	$97.89
Standard Nonprofit Auto Flats	$284.42	$632.55	1,023,813		Y	Y	Y	Y	Y	Y								$633.69	$656.72
Standard Nonprofit Nonauto Flats	$15.83	$30.97	43,076		Y	Y	Y	Y	Y	Y								$30.97	$32.22
Standard Regular Parcels	$0.00	$0.00	0									N	N	N	N	N	N	$0.00	$0.00
Standard Regular Marketing Parcels	$22.13	$37.80	21,081		Y	Y	Y	Y	Y	Y								$37.80	$39.28
Standard Nonprofit Parcels	$18.87	$33.15	12,561		Y	Y	Y	Y	Y	Y								$33.15	$34.46

Standard Nonprofit Marketing Parcels	$1.24	$2.47	1007		Y	Y	Y	Y	Y	Y								$2.47	$2.57
Every Door Direct Mail Retail	$126.63	$47.39	712,621										N	N	N	N	N	$47.43	$50.26
In County Periodicals	$55.92	$83.27	510,334		Y	Y	Y	Y	Y	Y								$83.32	$87.70
Outside County Classroom Periodicals	$10.57	$13.11	32,631		Y	Y	Y	Y	Y	Y								$13.11	$13.69
Outside County Nonprofit Periodicals	$262.33	$498.85	1,241,548		Y	Y	Y	Y	Y	Y								$499.69	$520.00
Outside County Regular Rate Periodicals	$941.50	$1289.28	3208.817		Y	Y	Y	Y	Y	Y								$1294.99	$1339.67
Alaska Bypass Service	$32.91	$18.72	1258		Y	Y	Y	Y	Y	Y								$42.94	$43.59
Single-Piece BPM Flats	$5.01	$2.42	2371										N	N	N	N	N	$2.42	$2.53
Presort BPM Flats	$192.66	$130.58	263,034											N	N	N	N	$130.64	$136.37
Single-Piece BPM Parcels	$15.31	$8.01	4839										N	N	N	N	N	$8.01	$8.40
Presort BPM Parcels	$302.93	$284.04	289,961													N	N	$284.46	$298.47
Single-Piece Media Mail	$243.50	$314.96	68,832		Y	Y	Y	Y	Y	Y								$315.54	$328.21
Presort Media Mail	$20.36	$27.44	6374		Y	Y	Y	Y	Y	Y								$27.44	$28.65
Single-Piece Library Mail	$11.71	$16.11	3521		Y	Y	Y	Y	Y	Y								$16.11	$16.83
Presort Library Mail	$0.74	$1.02	236		Y	Y	Y	Y	Y	Y								$1.02	$1.06
U.S. Postal Service	$331.53	$331.53	290,423		Y	Y	Y	Y	Y	Y								$332.16	$343.65
Free Mail	$60.53	$34.08	42,115										N	N	N	N	N	$34.08	$35.35
Certified Mail	$613.64	$521.77	178,689												N	N	N	$527.35	$563.35
COD	$3.97	$2.86	360												N	N	N	$2.86	$3.03
Insurance	$79.14	$48.45	17,619											N	N	N	N	$48.47	$49.66
Registered Mail	$29.14	$18.13	1,832											N	N	N	N	$18.13	$18.91
Stamped Envelopes	$11.16	$12.04	na		Y	Y	Y	Y	Y	Y								$13.45	$14.03
Stamped Cards	$0.59	$0.21	na									N	N	N	N	N	N	$0.21	$0.21

(continued)

Table 1 (continued)

Postal mail or service category	Revenue with fees distributed (*millions*)	Volume variable and product specific costs (*millions*)	Volume pieces or transactions (*thousands*)	Myopic algorithm process														Single-Svc. incremental cost (IC) (*millions*)	Max. subset incremental cost (IC) (*millions*)
				Backward cross-subsidy (Y)							Forward no cross-sub. (N)								
Postal mail or service category				*0*	*1*	*2*	*3*	*4*	*5*	*6*	*0*	*1*	*2*	*3*	*4*	*5*	*6*		
Other Ancillary Services	$401.65	$227.62	5,506,624											N	N	N	N	$228.02	$239.87
Address Management Services	$16.09	$5.44	na											N	N	N	N	$11.59	$12.00
Caller Service	$88.51	$26.30	na										N	N	N	N	N	$26.34	$27.61
Credit Card Authentication	$17.69	$2.20	na										N	N	N	N	N	$2.19	$2.31
Customized Postage	$0.07	$0.07	na			Y	Y	Y	Y	Y								$0.07	$0.08
Money Orders	$158.54	$145.07	83,390													N	N	$147.26	$153.61
Stamp Fulfillment Services	$3.87	$4.43	na		Y	Y	Y	Y	Y	Y								$4.41	$4.64

Notes: The Table omits all mail and service categories for which data is held under seal by the PRC at the request of USPS

This includes all competitive categories of domestic mail, all categories of International mail both inbound and outbound, all international services, all categories of negotiated service agreements (NSAs), and two categories of Post Office Box services

Altogether, 54 categories of mail and services have been omitted form Table 1 in order to avoid disclosing data held under seal

The apportionment of volume-variable and product-specific fixed costs to product categories was performed as described for every component. The attribution of these costs to product categories is also displayed in Table 1. All product and group-specific costs were fully distributed to individual products. Wherever these costs applied to multiple products, the costs were distributed to the product categories according to volumes. This procedure ignores the joint nature of some of these costs but turns out to apply to less than 0.5% of USPS's total costs. Most of USPS's fixed costs are included in the ACR data as "other" costs and are not product-specific. Product-specific costs were included in the total cost for a subset of postal services only for the products in the subset.

The USPS cost accounting system supports a "single-driver" cost model that makes the cost function sub-modular (Pearsall 2019). Sub-modularity is necessary for performing the complete IC test using the myopic algorithm. The parameters of the single-driver model are calculated directly from the assembled USPS data. Volume variabilities were estimated individually for the cost components by dividing the sum of volume-variable costs taken over all product categories by the total cost for the component given in the cost reporting for the FY 2018 ACR. The volume variability estimates are all less than or equal to one. The contribution of a category's volume to a component's driver is represented by a distribution key share. The distribution key shares for a cost component are estimated by dividing the volume-variable cost for each product by the total volume-variable cost for the component.

Total postal costs are the sum of costs taken over all cost components. This includes common fixed costs that can be avoided only if USPS ceases operations. The IC for a subset of omitted services is the difference between the total cost to USPS of providing all mail products and services and the cost of producing just the mail and services not included in the omitted subset. To apply the myopic algorithm, it is frequently necessary to compute an IC for the addition or deletion of a single product from a stipulated subset of products. These calculations are easily made using the single-driver model as the difference between the ICs for two subsets that differ by a single product.

Calculations of IC made with our single-driver cost model do not exactly replicate USPS's estimates of single-product IC found in the ACR files but are close. We have implemented the model at the finest level of detail permitted by the ACR data; however, USPS may have employed a finer differentiation of costs in its calculations. Also, we have estimated volume variabilities indirectly at the component level from the USPS's reported volume-variable and total costs. USPS uses volume variabilities taken directly from its various special studies. Finally, to estimate product-specific and group-specific costs, we distribute group-specific costs to products and services based on volumes. Any observed differences between cost estimates provided by USPS and calculated within our single-driver model are not substantial enough to alter either the analysis performed in the paper or our conclusions.

3 The Complete Incremental Cost Test

The complete IC test is applied as described in Pearsall (2009); we identify the smallest proper subset of product categories with the maximum cross-subsidy. When the cost function is sub-modular, the prices of these postal services are solely responsible for all of the cross-subsidies resulting from the tariff.

The maximizing subset is found using Pearsall's myopic algorithm. This algorithm is an iterative process with three stages named the "backward" process, the "forward" process, and the "final" process. The backward process identifies products that *must* be included in the maximizing subset. The forward process identifies products that *must not* be included in the maximizing subset. The final process, if necessary, resolves the differences.

Table 1 tracks the progress of the myopic algorithm. The columns labelled "0" to "6" for the backward process show the progressive identification of included products by designating them with a "Y." The process begins at column "0" with no products in the maximizing subset. Single-product ICs are computed as the difference in cost between producing all products and all-but-one product. These ICs are listed in the second column from the right in Table 1. Wherever IC exceeds revenue with fees distributed, we have a mail or service category that must be cross-subsidized. These services are marked with a "Y" in column "1." The algorithm now redoes the calculations of single-product IC but with all of the products designated as cross-subsidized in column "1" omitted. That is, the ICs are recomputed as the difference in cost between producing all products except those omitted plus one more omitted product. The resultant single-product ICs (not shown) are all somewhat higher (or remain unchanged) because of the omissions.[14] Several additional categories now have single-product ICs that exceed revenue and are added to the maximizing subset in column "2," for example, standard nonprofit H-D and saturation letters. The algorithm repeats six times which is sufficient to ensure that no new additions are made to the maximizing subset. Column "6" shows the final list of products that the backward process reveals must be included in the maximizing subset.

The forward process works in the opposite direction. It begins with a single product, automation presort first-class letters, which is assumed not to be cross-subsidized.[15] This category of mail is marked with an "N" in column "0" to indicate that it is not included in the maximizing subset. Single-product IC is now computed as the difference in cost between adding a product to the excluded subset and the

[14] This occurs because the postal cost function is sub-modular. Therefore, excluding a service increases (or leaves unchanged) the IC of any subset of services that remain.

[15] For reasons explained in Pearsall (2019), costs cannot be reliably calculated as the driver approaches zero using the single-driver model. Consequently, it is necessary to begin the forward process at a point on the cost function that is above the origin by assuming that a major category of mail is not cross-subsidized. Automation presort first-class letters with revenue of $13,495 million and volume-variable and product-specific costs of $4253 million are a good candidate. This assumption also excludes the set of all products being identified as the maximizing subset.

cost of producing just the excluded subset. We then proceed product-by-product to identify those products whose revenue covers their single-product IC. These are added to the subset that cannot be cross-subsidized and are marked with an "N" in column "1." Next, we recalculate the single-product ICs under the assumption that all of the products flagged "N" in column "1" are produced and repeat the comparisons with revenue to add more products to the subset that cannot be cross-subsidized. These additions appear in column "2." The steps are repeated until no new additions are made. All of the mail and service categories that the forward process finds cannot be included in the maximizing subset are marked with an "N" in column "6." These products have revenues that exceed single-product IC when only the maximizing subset of categories is produced. The ICs for this final comparison are shown in the right-hand column of Table 1.

The final process of the myopic algorithm is unnecessary when the subset of products that must be included in the maximizing subset is complementary to the subset of products that are not included. As shown in Table 1, the maximizing subset is fully determined by the backward and forward processes.

The complete IC test reveals that there are 32 USPS mail and service categories that contributed to cross-subsidies in FY 2018. They are the members of the maximizing subset.

The cross-subsidy for the maximizing subset is a general index of the cross-subsidies created by the postal tariff (Pearsall 2009). In a somewhat cruder application of the complete IC test to the FY 2007 tariff, it was found that the maximizing subset left a cross-subsidy of $1354 million (Fenster et al. 2008). After applying the complete IC test to the FY 2018 data, we have identified a cross-subsidy of $1913 million for a somewhat larger maximizing subset.[16] In FY 2018 USPS reported total revenue from all sources of $70,783 million and total costs of $74,696 million.[17] Therefore, the cross-subsidies caused by the postal tariff account for about half of USPS's losses for the year.

4 Bounds for the Price Increases Needed to Correct Cross-Subsidies

The myopic algorithm is an iterative process that terminates with information that can be used to establish bounds for the price increases needed to eliminate cross-subsidies. This is the same information contained in the two right-hand columns of Table 1.

---

[16] This estimate does not include the $332 million we have reassigned to US Postal Service mail as revenue. Fenster et al. did not make such a reassignment.

[17] ACR 2018, Library Reference USPS-FY18-1—FY 2018 Public Cost and Revenue Analysis, available at https://www.prc.gov/dockets/document/107642

A lower bound is simply the price increase needed to obtain enough additional revenue to cover the IC of a single cross-subsidized service category. Every product category in the maximizing subset has a single-product IC that is less than the product's revenue. For example, to cover the IC of single-piece media mail, the revenue of $243 million must be raised by 25.59% to cover the single-service IC of $316 million. Assuming that volumes are fixed, this would be the smallest price increase needed to eliminate the single-product cross-subsidy. In fact, the lower bound increase is just barely sufficient in the extreme case when all other cross-subsidies have been corrected. Lower bound price increases that are calculated in this way without considering demand effects are displayed for 25 of the 32 product categories of the maximizing subset in Table 2. A lower bound of zero means that it may not be necessary to raise a product's price at all.

An upper bound, still assuming inelastic demand, is computed in the same way using single-product IC calculated using the maximizing subset. To increase the revenue for single-piece media mail to $328 million requires a price increase of 34.79%. This is the largest price increase that would ever be needed to eliminate this price category as a cause of cross-subsidies under the assumption that mail volumes are fixed. This increase is sufficient to remove single-piece media mail from the maximizing subset even when no other cross-subsidies are corrected. All of the upper bound increases calculated without considering demand effects are shown for cross-subsidized product categories in Table 2.

Price increases within the upper and lower bounds computed under the assumption of perfectly inelastic demand might cause substantial losses in postal volumes, affecting both revenues and ICs. In turn, when the complete IC test is re-performed with lower volumes for any products, the price increases needed to eliminate cross-subsidies are all higher. Adjustment of the bounds for these demand effects would provide more accurate guidance to the price increases needed to eliminate cross-subsidies.

To illustrate how to make such adjustments, we use the USPS econometric estimates of own-price elasticities of demand shown in Table 2.[18] The upper and lower bounds are adjusted product-by-product. First, the price change for the unadjusted upper or lower bound is used along with the own-price demand elasticity to recalculate volume, revenue, and single-service IC. The ICs are recalculated by adjusting the product's distribution key share proportionately to mirror the decrease in the product's volume due to the effect of increasing the price to the bound. For example, if a price increase causes a 20% reduction in demand, then the product's distribution key share is reduced by 20% in all calculations of postal cost with the single-driver model. The new ICs for the lower bounds replace the single-service ICs shown in

[18] We use these elasticities because they are conveniently available as part of the USPS's annual demand model filings. Unfortunately, they are known to be defective in several respects as discussed by Bzhilyanskaya et al. (2015). In particular, these estimates omit cross-product effects and presume that average revenues are unit-elastic with respect to prices. These defects could affect the adjustments made to the bounds and, later, the calculation of Ramsey-Boiteux price increases (see Sect. 5).

Table 2 Price adjustments to correct cross-sibsidies in FY 2018

Cross-subsidized category	Revenue per Piece w/fees dist'd (*$/Pc*)	USPS estimated own-price *elasticity*	Lower bound increase w/o demand (*percent*)	Lower bound increase w demand (*percent*)	Bounded Ramsey increase (*percent*)	Upper bound increase w/o demand (*percent*)	Upper bound increase w demand (*percent*)
Standard Nonprofit H-D & Sat. Letters	0.0848	−0.8658	0.00%	0.00%	0.00%	0.97%	0.97%
Standard Nonprofit H-D & Sat. Flts/Pcls	0.1093	−1.2365	0.00%	0.00%	0.00%	0.01%	0.01%
Standard Regular Car-Rte Flts/Pcls	0.1427	−0.8502	97.13%	97.39%	102.10%	106.83%	107.12%
Standard Nonprofit Car-Rte Letters	0.1683	−0.6725	54.99%	55.09%	59.72%	62.64%	62.77%
Standard Nonprofit Car-Rte Flts/Pcls	0.1028	−0.6725	196.46%	196.87%	205.73%	211.47%	211.91%
Standard Regular Auto Flats	0.4432	−0.6725	29.48%	29.59%	32.81%	33.34%	33.48%
Standard Regular Nonauto Flats	0.5445	−0.6725	21.91%	21.92%	25.61%	26.76%	26.78%
Standard Nonprofit Auto Flats	0.2778	−0.8502	122.80%	123.13%	127.99%	130.90%	131.29%
Standard Nonprofit Nonauto Flats	0.3674	−0.8502	95.66%	95.75%	100.58%	103.54%	103.64%
Standard Regular Marketing Parcels	1.0497	−0.8493	70.82%	70.84%	75.13%	77.52%	77.54%
Standard Nonprofit Parcels	1.5024	−0.8493	75.69%	75.70%	80.13%	82.58%	82.61%

(continued)

Table 2 (continued)

Cross-subsidized category	Revenue per Piece w/fees dist'd (*$/Pc*)	USPS estimated own-price *elasticity*	Lower bound increase w/o demand (*percent*)	Lower bound increase w demand (*percent*)	Bounded Ramsey increase (*percent*)	Upper bound increase w/o demand (*percent*)	Upper bound increase w demand (*percent*)
Standard Nonprofit Marketing Parcels	1.2331	−0.8493	99.09%	99.12%	104.14%	106.95%	106.97%
In County Periodicals	0.1096	−0.1589	49.00%	49.01%	56.84%	56.82%	56.84%
Outside County Classroom Periodicals	0.3241	−0.2258	23.99%	23.99%	29.50%	29.49%	29.50%
Outside County Nonprofit Periodicals	0.2113	−0.2258	90.48%	90.53%	98.28%	98.22%	98.28%
Outside County Regular Rate Periodicals	0.2934	−0.0853	37.55%	37.56%	42.31%	42.29%	42.31%
Alaska Bypass Service	26.1668	−0.2303	30.48%	35.71%	35.71%	32.45%	38.13%
Single-Piece Media Mail	3.5375	−0.5980	29.59%	29.64%	33.69%	34.79%	34.87%
Presort Media Mail	3.1946	−0.5980	34.77%	34.80%	39.26%	40.70%	40.74%
Single-Piece Library Mail	3.3267	−0.5980	37.56%	37.60%	42.16%	43.64%	43.68%
Presort Library Mail	3.1480	−0.5980	36.81%	36.84%	41.39%	42.88%	42.92%
U.S. Postal Service	1.1415	0.0000	0.19%	0.19%	0.19%	3.66%	3.66%
Stamped Envelopes	na	−1.0000	20.47%	20.51%	22.85%	25.66%	25.71%
Customized Postage	na	−1.0000	0.00%	0.00%	1.81%	4.80%	4.80%
Stamp Fulfillment Services	na	−1.0000	13.81%	13.81%	16.47%	19.88%	19.88%

Notes: Seven categories of cross-subsidized mail and services are omitted from Table 2 to avoid disclosing data held under seal by the PRC at the request of USPS. The omitted categories are Inbound Single-Piece First-Class mail, Marketing mail NSAs, Post Office Box service (market dominant), USPS ground Alaska LOR, International Priority Airmail (IPA), International Surface Airlift (ISAL), and International Special Services the second column from the right of Table 1. The new ICs for the upper bound replace the ICs for the maximizing subset shown in the right-hand column of Table 1. The price increases for the bounds are then changed so that the recalculated revenues cover the recalculated ICs. The sequence of steps is repeated three times, assuming constant demand elasticity, by which time the recalculations yield negligible changes.

The adjusted upper and lower bounds, following the third iteration, appear in Table 2. We can see that adjusting for own-price elasticity demand effects raises the bounds; however, the increases are all quite small.

A more important observation is that the spreads between the upper and lower bounds are fairly narrow. For example, single-piece media mail has an adjusted lower bound of 29.64% and an adjusted upper bound of 34.87%. The spread is only 5.23%. Narrow spreads such as this leave little discretion in the selection of price increases to correct cross-subsidies. Therefore, if followed, the bounds would be quite effective as a guide to repricing the cross-subsidized categories.

5 On the Elimination of Cross-Subsidies in Practice

The cross-subsidies caused by the US postal tariff in FY 2018 were numerous and large overall. Out of 112 inclusive mail categories, there were 32 service categories which had prices causing cross-subsidies. The combined cross-subsidy for the maximizing subset was \$1913 million. The bounded Ramsey-Boiteux price changes would have made a contribution of \$1911 million toward reducing the USPS losses in FY 2018. This is composed of added revenues of \$944 million and reduced costs due to volume losses from the price increases of \$967 million.

In US regulatory practice, postal products are divided into market-dominant and competitive categories. The market-dominant mail consists of products for which USPS exercises sufficient market power that it can set prices substantially above costs, decrease quality of service, or restrict output. Competitive products consist of all other products (US Title 39, Section 3642). A key regulatory concern is that USPS does not compete unfairly by inappropriately leveraging its market-dominant products. Therefore, US postal law (US Title 39, Section 3633) prohibits subsidization of competitive mail products by market-dominant products. The PRC performs an annual IC test to ensure that this prohibition is not violated.[19]

The list of cross-subsidized mail and service categories exhibits a number of distinct patterns. First, almost all of the products with cross-subsidies are market-dominant mail categories. Second, all mail categories with preferential rates are cross-subsidized and, in total, constitute about half of the cross-subsidized categories.

---

[19] The test that the PRC employs to identify cross-subsidies is somewhat different from the complete IC test. See Pearsall (2018) for a discussion of cross-subsidy testing under the Postal Accountability and Enhancement Act (PAEA 2006).

Third, categories for flats and parcels tend to be heavily cross-subsidized regardless of how this mail is workshared to obtain a discount.

Also noteworthy are the products that are not cross-subsidized. These include virtually all competitive products; the only exceptions are minor: USPS Ground Alaska LOR and three small competitive international mail services. Mail that receives expedited service such as first-class, priority, and express mail is also almost completely absent from the list of cross-subsidized categories. Only inbound international mail that becomes part of the first-class mail stream is cross-subsidized. Finally, we note that several categories of mail popularly suspected to be cross-subsidized did not make the list. These include competitive parcel delivery services, including categories specifically for negotiated service agreements (NSAs) and inbound international mail other than first class.

These results confirm many previous findings by the PRC. Flat-shaped mail has long been recognized as not generating revenue sufficient to cover costs. In the FY 2018 Annual Compliance Determination (ACD) Report, the Commission found that the loss from marketing mail flats was $752 million and the loss from Periodicals was $614 million.[20] Given that nonprofit mail is required by statute to be priced below comparable regular rate mail, it is not surprising that all nonprofit mail is cross-subsidized.

One of the benefits of eliminating cross-subsidies is the correction of the inequitable distribution of the cost burden. Simply put, a cross-subsidy is an attributable cost that is not paid for by the consumers of the cross-subsidized subset of services. When a US postal tariff fails the IC test, the costs not covered by revenues must be covered by other customers overpaying for their services and/or by losses (or reduced profits). When a public enterprise such as USPS loses money, that loss is exactly offset by a decline in that enterprise's net worth. As the sole owner of that public enterprise, treasury takes the loss.[21]

The results shown in Table 2 confirm the findings of the PRC that USPS rates largely comply with US law intended to deter inefficient entry by USPS into competitive markets. Competitive products are mostly not cross-subsidized. The competitive products that are cross-subsidized are international mail services that have terminal dues set by the Universal Postal Union. The system for establishing terminal dues rates generally tends to set them at levels below domestic rates for comparable services (Pearsall 2016).

The price caps imposed by PAEA largely prevent the rapid elimination of the cross-subsidies caused by the tariff. Most of the increases indicated in Table 2 apply to market-dominant categories of mail and greatly exceed the increases permitted of

[20] PRC, FY 2018 ACD, pp. 41 and 49, available at https://www.prc.gov/docs/108/108781/2018_acd.pdf

[21] When prices are set under a profit constraint, such as a break-even condition, a cross-subsidy may be regarded as being borne entirely by other customers (Faulhaber 1975, p. 966). Prior to the Postal Accountability and Enhancement Act (PAEA 2006), US postal rates were set under such a constraint in the form of a net revenue condition which applied to a future test year. However, PAEA dropped this condition, and USPS does not currently set prices under a profit constraint.

such mail by PAEA's price caps. PAEA's price caps limit the annual rate of increase in the price of each class of market-dominant mail to the annual rate of increase in the Urban Consumer Price Index, typically only 2–3%. Therefore, the increases needed to eliminate cross-subsidies in a single year are not possible for any but the lowest volume categories without significant decreases in related categories. For example, the range of increases for standard mail carrier route flats and parcels is between 97 and 107%. A price increase in this range would not be permissible under PAEA's price cap without large offsetting price decreases in related categories of standard mail.

Even without the price caps, PAEA does not legally mandate the reduction of cross-subsidies at levels of product detail that are now possible with the complete IC test.

6 Conclusion

Our findings are derived from the application of the complete IC test to the USPS FY 2018 tariff at an unprecedented level of detail. The research demonstrates that the complete IC test with the myopic algorithm is feasible at almost any category level for which reliable cost data is available. For instance, USPS, if it chooses, can easily employ the method to identify cross-subsidies among mail categories that distinguish for worksharing such as presortation and destination entry, for hedonic properties such as weight and distance transported, and for preparation such as standardized packaging and palletization.

We have shown how to calculate upper and lower bounds for the price increases needed to correct the cross-subsidies. Further, we show how these bounds may be refined to account for the demand effects of the increased prices. In general, the bounds indicate that USPS does not have much discretion in how it would have to raise rates to eliminate cross-subsidies. Next, we show how the bounds may play a role in the derivation of price increases to efficiently and simultaneously correct all of the cross-subsidies identified by the complete IC test. These Ramsey-Boiteux increases are more numerous and somewhat higher than might be expected. Finally, we discuss the public benefits and legal obstacles under current law to eliminating the cross-subsidies presently caused by the US postal tariff.

References

Bzhilyanskaya, L. Y., Cigno, M. M., & Pearsall, E. S. (2015). A branching AIDS model for estimating U.S. postal price elasticities. In M. A. Crew & T. Brennan (Eds.), *Postal and delivery innovation in the digital economy*. Cham: Springer International Publishing.

Faulhaber, G. R. (1975). Cross subsidization: Pricing in public enterprises. *American Economic Review, 65*, 966–977.

Fenster, L., Monaco, D., Pearsall, E. S., Waller, J., Willette, G., & Xenakis, S. (2008). A complete test of U.S. postal rates for cross-subsidies. In presented at the 16th Conference on Postal and Delivery Economics, CRRI, Albufeira, Algarve, Portugal, May 28–31, 2008.

Panzar, J. C. (2015). The role of costs for postal regulation. In white paper prepared for the U.S. Postal Regulatory Commission, January 14, 2015, available at www.prc.gov

Pearsall, E. S. (2009). The complete incremental cost test for cross-subsidies with a sub-modular cost function. *Journal of Regulatory Economics, 36*, 274–285.

Pearsall, E. S. (2016). A game-theoretic model of the market for international mail. In M. A. Crew & T. Brennan (Eds.), *The future of the postal sector in a digital world.* Cham: Springer International Publishing.

Pearsall, E. S. (2018). PAEA's take on regulatory economics. In T. Brennan, V. Glass, & P. L. Parcu (Eds.), *The contribution of the postal and delivery sector*. Cham: Springer International Publishing.

Pearsall, E. S. (2019). Technical appendix: On correcting the cross-subsidies caused by the U.S. postal tariff. In manuscript available from the author at espearsall@verizon.net

Funding the USO: Cross-Subsidization and Net Cost Balancing

Andreas Haller, Christian Jaag, and Urs Trinkner

1 Introduction

With increasing digitalization, traditional universal service obligations (USO) such as daily universal delivery become less profitable, because revenues are declining, while costs cannot be reduced accordingly. Therefore, financing the USO has become more relevant than ever in many countries. The main funding options are well-known and include service provision under monopoly, compensation funds, and government subsidies. Ultimately, the first two are financed by the consumers and the latter by the taxpayer. To increase the economic utilization of the postal networks, many postal universal service providers (USP) are active in related business segments, thereby decreasing the financing needs as long as the related businesses earn more than their incremental (postal) network costs. In this case, part of the USO is financed by consumers in other markets.

In such an environment, different potential sources of (cross) subsidization are a competitive concern, e.g., over- or under-compensation of the USP, or contributions imposed on competitive operators if compensation funds are in place. In case the USP is being active in related markets, cross-subsidization can be an issue. Consequently, various kinds of price regulations and accounting rules are in place, affecting costing and pricing of (universal) services. If pricing is affected, overall welfare is too.

In this paper, we analyze the competitive and welfare properties of the Swiss net cost balancing mechanism (NCB), applied since 2013, and compare it to the traditional fully distributed cost approach based on activities (activity-based costing,

A. Haller · U. Trinkner (✉)
Swiss Economics and University of Zurich, Zürich, Switzerland
e-mail: andreas.haller@swiss-economics.ch; urs.trinkner@swiss-economics.ch

C. Jaag
Swiss Economics and EPFL, Zürich, Switzerland
e-mail: christian.jaag@swiss-economics.ch

P. L. Parcu et al. (eds.), *The Changing Postal Environment*, Topics in Regulatory Economics and Policy, https://doi.org/10.1007/978-3-030-34532-7_10

ABC). For the welfare properties, we refer to Haller et al. (2014). We find that NCB resolves the relevant competitive concerns while having superior welfare properties.

The remainder of this paper is structured as follows: Section 2 discusses the competitive properties of NCB as opposed to ABC. Section 3 compares the two cost allocation mechanisms in terms of overall welfare based on a stylized calibrated model. Section 4 concludes.

2 USO Funding and Cross-Subsidization

Medium-term sustainability of the Swiss USO financed by the residual monopoly is jeopardized by the increasingly intensive competition from electronic means of communication. At the same time, there is strong price regulation of Swiss Post's services (see Jaag and Maegli 2015). For the reserved area, the Postal Act authorizes the Federal Council to define and approve the adaptation of regulated prices for individual services. Outside of the reserved service, another (non-sector-specific) authority, the Price Supervisor, is responsible, provided that the prices are not the result of effective competition. This price regulation is cost-based, which prevents services arising that generate a significant surplus to Swiss Post. However, it also prevents these services from covering losses from unprofitable services due to the USO.

Jaag and Maegli (2015) show that the ordinance on the new Postal Act resolves this conflict by means of a specific financing instrument, net cost balancing. Swiss Post is allowed to reallocate the net cost of the USO through transfer payments between its units and subsidiaries. It can charge these costs to the services for which it is able to generate high prices in order to relieve unprofitable services. By shifting costs to the more profitable services, it increases its costs and can therefore opt for higher prices under the cost-based price regulation. Hence, the legislation made cost-based pricing consistent with USO funding by allocating USO net costs to profitable services and including that in the "cost" used to set prices. Hence, the monopoly for letter mail contributes to financing the USO, but it is also a potential source for cross-subsidies of competitive services.[1]

The European Commission applied a modified form of the Faulhaber rule (Faulhaber 1975), stating that cross-subsidization occurs where "the earnings from a given service do not suffice to cover the incremental costs of providing that service and where there is another service or bundle of services from which exceed the stand-alone costs" (OJ L 125 of 5.5.2001, p. 29, para 6, Deutsche Post AG. COMP/35.141). Also, according to Swiss postal legislation, problematic cross-subsidization is present if there is a product that does not cover its incremental cost, while the earnings of another product or product bundle (in the reserved area) exceed its stand-alone costs.

[1]For more details on the implementation in the Swiss Postal market, see Jaag and Maegli (2015).

Consequently, this implementation of the Faulhaber rule consists of two tests:

(i) The *incremental cost test* is satisfied if the revenue from any quantity of service (or service bundle) of a multiproduct firm is greater than or equal to the change in total cost caused by not producing the service (or service bundle). The increment in cost is the difference in total cost with and without this quantity of service (or service bundle). If incremental costs are covered by revenues, it is considered that the service does not receive a cross-subsidy.
(ii) The *stand-alone cost test* is satisfied if the revenue of a product or product group in the reserved area does not exceed its stand-alone cost. This test is about whether revenues from the reserved area are cross-subsidizing services outside the reserved area.

If the incremental cost test is satisfied, there is no cross-subsidization. If it is not satisfied, the service can still be considered to not receive a cross-subsidy from reserved area revenues if the stand-alone cost test is satisfied (see Parsons 1998). Cross-subsidization according to Faulhaber is present if both tests are not satisfied.

We now investigate how NCB relates with the Faulhaber rule and highlight under what conditions NCB satisfies the Faulhaber rule. Under NCB, a regulated USP is allowed to reallocate the net cost of the USO through internal transfer payments.[2] The net costs are the difference in profits of the USP with and without the USO (Jaag and Trinkner 2011). In this way, the USP can charge the services for which it is able to generate a surplus on the market and support unprofitable (USO) services. This interplay between the financing of the USO and price regulation facilitates in providing universal services without external financing (with a USP inhibiting significant market power, SMP). Alternatively, if the USO is granted a legal monopoly over a subset of services to finance the USO, a net cost balancing mechanism will cap prices in the monopoly area such that the additional return will not exceed the net cost of the USO.

NCB has the following economic properties: Compared to the same amount of external funding of the net cost of the USO, the USP is strictly worse off under NCB. With external funds, net costs are fully compensated. Under NCB, however, allowed price increases of services with market power are mirrored by price decreases of other USO services. (NCB aims at a better allocating the burden of the USO to products, not at compensating the USP for net costs.) NCB however has a positive effect on overall profits of the USP (compared to a situation without NCB or external funding) if the USP allocates net costs to products with comparably lower price elasticities. These additional profits are however strictly lower than external funding of net costs, i.e., with NCB as the only financing mechanism, the USP is systematically exposed to an "underfunded" situation as compared to an external funding of the net cost.

---

[2] As a side effect, net cost balancing makes it possible for a USP to separate operational accounting from regulatory accounting: In a first step, cost can be allocated according to regular accounting principles (business accounting); in a second step, the net cost balancing is carried out in the form of transfer payments (regulatory accounting).

In addition, under NCB, cost-regulated services with significant market power (SMP) can at most be surcharged to cover the USO net costs, i.e., the disadvantage the USP has in the market because of the USO. Again, no net advantage to the USP arises. Under reasonable cost regulation, stand-alone costs of such SMP services are likely to be substantially higher than regulated earnings, as regulators, following EGRP accounting standards, tend to apply ABC accounting standards which do not allow allocating common costs to SMP services entirely. If net costs are accepted as costs,[3] the Faulhaber stand-alone test is passed in general. However, if the cost of services outside the USO after NCB payments does not exceed their incremental costs, then Faulhaber's incremental cost test is not passed for these services.

Combining these observations suggest that the Faulhaber rule will be fulfilled under NCB because NCB transfer payments are generally free of cross-subsidization. If competitive concerns related to cross-subsidization of non-USO services are considered more important than public policy objectives related to financing the USO, then general competition law might apply. Such a regulatory setting would be stricter than the Faulhaber rule. In either case, the USP is systematically underfunded under NCB.

We conclude that NCB is as least as strict as the standard Faulhaber (1975) rule. If general competition law applies to nonuniversal services, NCB can be considered stricter and puts the USP at a net disadvantage compared to external funding of the net cost. NCB can therefore be seen as an implementation of the Faulhaber rule, because NCB restricts pricing of SMP USO services in a way consistent with the rule.

3 Cost Allocation Rules and Impact on Welfare

Most incumbent postal operators are active in business segments outside the universal service obligation (USO). Often, price regulation is cost-oriented and differentiated between USO and non-USO products. Hence, regulatory rules on cost allocation impact regulated prices and overall welfare.

In this section we analyze the effects of cost allocation based on NCB on pricing and welfare relative to fully distributed cost based on activities (activity-based costing, ABC),[4] assuming profit regulation in place. We use a stylized model with a set of products characterized by different price elasticities perceived by the USP. As a benchmark, we derive a welfare optimal allocation of costs based on Ramsey prices such that the incumbent USP breaks even. We then compare this result to ABC and NCB cost accounting.

---

[3] If net costs are not compensated (see a), they are a real opportunity cost and should be accepted.

[4] ABC is tandard method and is most widely used in the postal sector (ERGP 2012). Its key principle is the following: cost objects (products, customers...) consume activities which in turn consume resources (ERGP 2013).

We consider a postal operator that is active in a set of I markets. In each market $i \in I$, the postal operator can set its price p_i and faces a demand function $x(p_i)$. The supply of goods in market i causes variable cost, denoted by $C_i(x_i(p_i))$, and fixed cost, denoted by F_i. Moreover, the USO is assumed to cause a fixed cost independent of serving a specific market, denoted by F_G. We interpret this fixed cost to be the net cost of the USO.

The profit function of the postal operator is given by

$$\pi = \sum_{i \in I} p_i x_i(p_i) - \sum_{i \in I} C_i(x_i(p_i)) - \sum_{i \in I} F_i - F_G$$

and welfare (measured by consumer surplus and assuming independent demands) is given by

$$W = \sum_{i \in I} \int_{p_i}^{\infty} x_i\left(\tilde{p}_i\right) d\tilde{p}_i .$$

We study three different regulatory frameworks: Ramsey pricing (RP), net cost balancing (NCB), and activity-based cost allocation (ABC). In our setup, they correspond to a zero-profit condition to the following maximization problems:

$$(RP): \max_{p_i} W\, s.t. \pi = 0 (NCB): \max_{p_i} W\, s.t. p_i x_i(p_i) - C_i(x_i(p_i))$$
$$-F_i - \alpha_i F_g = 0 \forall i \in I, \sum_{i \in I} \alpha_i = 1, 0 \leq \alpha_i \leq 1 \forall i \in I$$

$$(ABC): \max_{p_i} W\, s.t. p_i x_i(p_i) - C_i(x_i(p_i)) - F_i - \frac{x_i(p_i)}{\sum_i x_i(p_i)} F_g = 0 \forall i \in I$$

The following welfare ordering arises $W_{AC} \leq W_{NC} \leq W_{RP}$, because the constraints in RP are less strict than NCB, and the NCB constraints related to the distribution of F_g are less strict than in ABC, where the weights are predefined. Intuitively, the NCB regime allows more flexibility in allocating costs and hence in determining prices which results in higher welfare under the assumption that the postal operator's objective function is indeed welfare.

The zero-profit condition and the postal operator maximizing welfare may not be realistic. Therefore, we also study the case of a profit regulation instead of a zero-profit condition. Additionally, a Faulhaber rule is imposed as a constraint in the sense that the price of a product must at least cover its incremental costs.[5] The postal

[5] Formally, Faulhaber's incremental cost test is to be applied to individual services and to all possible groups of services. In a two-product company with break-even constraint, this translates to the restriction that $p_i x_i \geq c_i x_i + F_i$. If there are no product-specific fixed costs ($F_i = 0$), the restriction simplifies to $p_i \geq c_i$, i.e., prices must exceed variable cost. For analytical convenience, the latter is assumed in the formal part of the analysis (Sect. 2). The results are nevertheless in line with the numerical findings in Sect. 3 (which assume $F_i > 0$).

operator is allowed to make profits of at most β percent of total revenues ("profit regulation"). Formally, the three regimes then correspond to the following maximization problems:

$$(RP): \max_{p_i} W \, s.t. \beta \sum_i p_i x_i(p_i) \leq \pi, p_i \geq c_i \forall i$$

$$(NCB): \max_{p_i} \pi \, s.t. (1-\beta) p_i x_i(p_i) \leq C_i(x_i(p_i))$$
$$+F_i + \alpha_i F_g \forall i \in I, \sum_{i \in I} \alpha_i = 1, 0 \leq \alpha_i \leq 1 \forall i \in I, p_i \geq c_i \forall i$$

$$(ABC): \max_{p_i} \pi \, s.t. (1-\beta) p_i x_i(p_i) \leq C_i(x_i(p_i)) + F_i + \frac{x_i(p_i)}{\sum_i x_i(p_i)} F_g \forall i \in I, p_i \geq c_i \forall i$$

We can derive the prices of these regimes and do comparative statics. However, in this general specification, it is not possible to make a statement about whether the NCB or ABC regime is superior in terms of welfare and, more importantly, how large the differences are. Therefore, we calibrate the model for a scenario representing the postal market in industrialized countries. We assume that the postal operator is active in two markets. One market has a higher price elasticity of demand, whereas the other market has a lower price elasticity of demand for a given price and quantity. The demand function for the two markets is assumed to be linear and of the form

$$x_i(p_i) = A_i - \theta_i * p_i \, \text{where} \, i \in \{h, l\}.$$

For the numerical simulations, we set the following parameters $\beta = 0.05$, $C_i = 0.5$. Demand parameters A_i, θ_i are then calibrated to satisfy the following three equalities for a price set to unity, i.e., $p_l = p_h = 1$: (i) $x_h = x_l = 1{,}000{,}000{,}000$, (ii) $e_l = -0.5 = \frac{\partial x_l}{\partial p_l} \frac{p_l}{x_l}$, and (iii) $e_h = \frac{\partial x_h}{\partial p_h} \frac{p_h}{x_h}$, where the elasticity of demand e_h is varied from −0.75 to −3 (at $p_l = p_h = 1$ and $x_h = x_l = 1{,}000{,}000{,}000$). In our base case, we set $e_h = -1.5$. This value corresponds to empirical estimates of postal price elasticities (see, e.g., Nikali 2011). Moreover, we set $F_h = F_l = (CHF\ 1'000'000'000 - F_g)/2$ and let the net costs F_g vary from CHF 10 million up to CHF 500 million. In the base case, we set F_g = CHF 200 million. This calibration setup mirrors the cost and demand structure in the Swiss postal market.

In the base case, the optimal prices as shown in Table 1 emerge in the different regimes. The regime "monopolist" is the case with an unconstrained monopolist

Table 1 Simulation results base case calibration

	RP	Monopolist	NCB	ABC	Elasticity at RP prices
Price *h* (in CHF)	0.87	1.08	0.89	1.11	−1.09
Price *l* (in CHF)	1.27	1.75	1.25	1.08	−0.73
Welfare	1226.62	645.83	1225.76	1148.22	

Table 2 Sensitivity analysis welfare difference

F_g(Mio. CHF)\Elasticity	−0.75	−1.00	−1.25	−1.50	−2.00
100	7.34	11.01	13.21	14.68	16.51
300	36.68	55.03	66.03	73.37	82.54
500	71.19	106.92	128.14	142.38	160.18

Table 3 Summary statistics sensitivity analysis

	Mean	Median	Min	Max
Welfare differential NCB-ABC (%)	4.29%	3.41%	0.07%	12.46%
Welfare differential NCB-ABC (Mio. CHF)	61.75	48.86	1.14	174.87

charging the monopoly price in both market segments. Relative to an unconstrained monopoly, the prices in NCB are closer to the welfare optimal prices in RP than the prices under ABC, as indicated also by higher welfare in NCB compared to ABC in the last row of the table.

To check the robustness of this result in our base calibration, we let e_h vary from −0.75 to −3 in incremental steps of 0.25 and let F_g vary from 10 million up to 500 million in incremental steps of 10 million. Tables 2 und 3 summarize the results of this computation. Table 2 reports the welfare difference between NCB and ABC for different parameter constellations. For example, with an elasticity of −0.75 and net costs of CHF 100 million, welfare with NCB is CHF 7.3 higher than with ABC. Table 3 contains the descriptive statistics of the sensitivity analysis. In all our parameter constellations, NCB is always better than ABC in terms of welfare. On average NCB offers a welfare surplus of 4.29% compared to ABC which corresponds to an absolute difference of CHF 61.75 million.

Table 3 shows that the welfare difference between NCB and ABC increases with a larger difference between the two elasticities and a higher level of net cost F_g. This makes intuitive sense, as NCB allows for pricing closer to the Ramsey solution: With a higher the difference between the two elasticities, welfare losses under ABC are higher, which are then partially offset under NCB; if net costs are higher, more costs can be allocated to services with low elasticities, which increases welfare.

4 Conclusions

Incumbent operators providing universal services are increasingly active in competitive markets. Prices of USO products are often regulated. The traditional solution is to regulate the USO products by separating accounts between USO and non-USO products and imposing a product-specific rate-of-return regulation on US products with fully allocated cost based on activities (activity-based costing, ABC) as a point of reference.

In this paper we have analyzed the competitive and welfare effects of the Swiss net cost balancing mechanism (NCB). NCB is applied since 2013 and allows the regulated USP to reallocate its net cost of the USO through internal transfer payments. The analysis in Section 2 leads to the conclusion that NCB is as least as strict as the standard Faulhaber (1975) rule. If general competition law applies to nonuniversal services, NCB can be considered stricter. NCB can therefore be seen as an implementation of the Faulhaber rule. The main reason is that NCB restricts pricing of SMP USO services consistently with the Faulhaber rule.

The welfare analysis in Section 3 compares NCB to ACB. As an economic benchmark, a welfare-maximizing regulation regime is derived resulting in Ramsey prices. All three scenarios are held cross-subsidy free in the sense of Faulhaber (1975). The formal analysis reveals that with all mechanisms, optimal prices depend (negatively) on demand elasticity. Because the constraints in RP are less strict than NCB and the NCB constraints are less strict than the predefined weights of ABC, generally welfare of NCB will be between RP (optimal) and ABC (lowest).

A numerical analysis based on a stylized calibrated model reflecting an industrialized postal market confirms that Ramsey prices result in the highest welfare. An unconstrained monopolist results in a clear welfare loss as compared to all three regulated regimes. Interestingly, the NCB regime leads to results that almost replicate the Ramsey optimum. As expected, the NCB regime is generally superior to ABC costing, because in comparison it is less restricted by the amount of the net cost which is allowed to be reallocated. With the chosen calibration, on average, NCB increases welfare by 4% compared to ABC costing. The welfare difference between NCB and ABC is large if the difference in elasticities of products is high or net costs are high.

In summary, a net cost balancing mechanism increases welfare as compared to ABC costing clearly. In relative terms, ABC costing decreases overall welfare consistently. The welfare increases are induced by a more market-oriented but cross-subsidy free pricing by the USP. A net cost balancing mechanism may hence reduce external compensation for the USO.[6] The results indicate that a net cost balancing mechanism can be applied to effectively and optimally constrain a universal service provider with a legal monopoly that is active in other markets as well. By analogy, an NCB regime could be imposed on a USP with significant market power (SMP) that is active in other markets as well. A NCB-kind approach may be an alternative to regulate SMP.

References

ERGP (2012). *ERGP Report on common cost allocation.*

ERGP (2013). *ERGP common position on cost allocation rules.*

Faulhaber, G. (1975). Cross-subsidization: Pricing in public enterprises. *American Economics Review, 65*(5), 966–977.

[6] Price regulation can represent a means for (partial) financing of the USO; see Jaag (2013).

Haller, A., Jaag, C., & Trinkner, U. (2014). *USO cost allocation rules and welfare*. Swiss Economics Working Paper 0049.

Jaag, C. (2013). Price regulation and the financing of universal services in network industries. *Review of Law and Economics, 9*(1), 125–150.

Jaag, C., & Maegli, M. (2015). Market regulations and USO in the revised Swiss postal act: Provisions and authorities. In M. Crew & T. Brennan (Eds.), *Postal and delivery innovation in the digital economy. Topics in regulatory economics and policy* (Vol. 50). Cham: Springer.

Jaag, C., & Trinkner, U. (2011). The interaction between universal service costing and financing in the postal sector: a calibrated approach. *Journal of Regulatory Economics, 39*(1), 89–110.

Nikali, H. (2011). Does the level of price elasticity change with the progression of substitution? In M. Crew & P. Kleindorfer (Eds.), *Reinventing the postal sector in an electronic Age* (pp. 36–46). Cheltenham: Edward Elgar.

Parsons, S. (1998). Cross-subsidization in telecommunications. *Journal of Regulatory Economics, 13*, 157–182.

The Compensation Fund on the Postal Market: The Polish Case

Mateusz Chołodecki

1 Introduction

In 2008, the EU adopted the third postal directive. This legislation introduced the legal basis for gradual market opening. It set a deadline of 31 December 2010 for full market opening for 16 member states and 31 December 2012 for the remaining 11 member states, mostly from the Central and Eastern European countries (Crew and Kleindorfer 2008, p. 3; Snażyk 2015, p. 13). The third postal directive also changed the method, in which the universal postal service could be provided and financed. Additionally, the directive required the EU Commission to provide assistance to member states on its implementation, including the calculation of any net cost of the universal service (Bailly and Meidinger 2011).

Similar to other postal markets in Europe, the Polish postal market was monopolized until the end of the twentieth century. The monopolized postal market contained one state owned postal operator Poczta Polska S.A. (PP),[1] which used to be a part of the government. Liberalization of the postal market in Poland came after its accession to the EU in 2004, which began a long process of demonopolization. On 1 January 2013, a newly adopted Postal Law Act,[2] which had implemented the third EU postal directive, overturned the last exclusive rights held by PP Poland which was one of the last countries to fully open its postal market in EU (Snażyk 2015, p. 13).

[1] PP is a joint-stock company solely owned by the state.

[2] Act of 1 January 2013 Postal Law, consolidated text Journal of Laws of 2012, item 1529, as amended.

M. Chołodecki (✉)
Faculty of Law and Administration at Adam Mickiewicz University in Poznan, Poznań, Poland
e-mail: mateusz.cholodecki@amu.edu.pl

P. L. Parcu et al. (eds.), *The Changing Postal Environment*, Topics in Regulatory Economics and Policy, https://doi.org/10.1007/978-3-030-34532-7_11

Based on the third EU postal directive, the Polish Postal Law Act required that the net cost of universal service obligations be shared between providers of services (Art. 108 Postal Law Act), establishing a compensation fund. The compensation fund is to be financed by all the service providers that offer universal services, including the designated postal operator. In 2017, there were 54 postal operators in Poland.[3] From 2013, PP has been the designated universal services provider (until 2025). However, PP has only once declared the net cost of the universal service obligations, that is, for 2013. At the same time, PP market share has been constantly decreasing, in terms of both volume and revenues. Such a situation raises questions about why PP does not declare a revised net cost.

The aim of this paper is to characterize the legal aspects of the Polish compensation fund and examine whether it can create an entry barrier to the services falling within the scope of universal service for postal operators. In the paper the key legal elements of the compensation fund are shown. Section 2 presents the scope of the universal postal service under the EU and Polish law. Section 3 describes the institution of the designated operator on the postal market and tariff setting for universal service. Section 4 demonstrates the net cost calculation. Section 5 characterizes the compensation fund on the postal market and presents the legal procedure in which the designated operator can receive the subsidy from the fund. Section 6 describes and discusses the methods of financing the universal service in the telecommunication market in Poland. Postal and telecommunication markets have almost the same universal service obligation regulations. Moreover, this two markets share the same regulatory authority. Section 6 concludes the paper.

2 The Universal Postal Service

Universal postal service can be characterized by its commercial nature and specific mission (Szydło 2006, p. 119). Crew and Kleindorfer proposed the definition of a universal service obligation as the "provision of a ubiquitous service at a uniform price and quality" (Crew and Kleindorfer 2000, p. 5). Legal sources of universal service can be found in the international law, the EU law[4] and in the Polish law (Rowsell 2016, p. 33–35).[5] In EU postal regulation, the universal service plays a key role. Thus, guaranteeing universal service for users is the primary obligation of the EU member states.

The most important basis for current legislation in Poland is the third EU postal directive, which obligates all member states to ensure the right to a universal service

[3] Source: UKE. (2018). Report on the state of the postal market in 2017.

[4] Basically: Art. 36 of the Charter of Fundamental Rights of the EU (CFR) and Art. 14, the Treaty on the Functioning of the EU (TFEU).

[5] There are constitutional sources of universal service in Poland: Art. 20 of the Constitution of the Republic of Poland (CRP), Art. 32 CRP (prohibition of discrimination), or Art. 69 CRP (special assistance for the disabled).

for all users. The third EU postal directive defines very detailed requirements for universal service. EU law obligates that the universal service must involve the permanent provision of a postal service of specified quality at all points in their territory at affordable prices for all users (Art. 3).

Art. 12 of the third EU postal directive also requires that tariffs for each part of the universal service must be affordable, cost-oriented, transparent, and non-discriminatory and give incentives for an efficient universal service provision. A uniform tariff shall not prevent a universal service provider to conclude individual agreements on prices with users, but in doing so shall apply the principles of transparency and non-discrimination with regard both to the tariffs and to the associated conditions.

Responsibility of these principles rests with the postal regulator. Member states must provide adequate legal instruments for postal regulators to enforce these principles. Most of the legal instruments held by the postal regulator in Poland – the President of the Office of Electronic Communications (the President of UKE) – are related to the universal service (Chołodecki and Popowska 2018, p. 18–19).

Polish documents emphasized that universal service must be of good quality and affordable (Snażyk 2015, p. 72, 82).

According to the Article 45 (a) of the Postal Law Act, universal service includes postal services provided in domestic and cross-border traffic, covering clearance, sorting, transport, and delivery of letter items including items for the blind and postal parcels. Sorting, transport, and delivery of postal parcels sent from abroad are part of universal service as well. Article 46 (2) of the Postal Law Act defines that the universal service must be provided in uniform manner under comparable circumstances. Designated operator must provide universal service throughout the whole of the national territory, comply with the routing time indicators, offer affordable prices, ensure frequency of service, and provide sender a document confirming the receipt of a recorded item.

For the end users, liberalization of the postal market hardly changed under the universal service provision. PP is still the universal service provider, and the scope of universal service has remained almost the same. This is particularly noticeable, in legal proceedings in Poland. Article 17 of the Postal Law Act states that only a recorded item issued by PP has the power of an official document. Thus, a letter, being a part of universal service, sanded only by the designated operator is tantamount to bringing it to court or public institution. This exclusive right of the designated operator must be seen as a near-monopoly because alternative postal operators cannot compete with the designated operator on this important segment of the postal market.

3 The Designated Operator

According to the EU postal regulations, member states may designate one or more entities as universal service providers. Member states may designate different entities to provide different elements of universal service and/or to cover different parts of the national territory (Art. 4.2 of the third EU postal directive). In the EU, only Germany does not formally designate a universal service provider.[6]

The Polish legislature declared that only a single postal operator can provide universal service. Polish postal regulation has designated PP to be this provider. At the same time, the universal service provider has the right to subcontract some of their activities within a universal service. PP makes use of this right and subcontracts part of their activities.

The designated operator must be appointed for the period of 10 years by the President of UKE by administrative decision[7] from among postal operators selected in the course of a contest. Postal law contains detailed requirements for the contest. According to Art. 71 (2) of the Postal Law Act, the postal operator must have a network of postal points of contact and dispatch centers, means of transport, and financial liquidity. Presently only PP could satisfy these requirements. For the first 3 years after the Postal Law Act entered into force, PP became the designated operator by law (from 2013 to 2015). In 2015, the postal regulator was obligated to select a new designated operator to provide universal service for the next 10 years (2015–2025). Only two postal operators took part in the contest for the designated operator that was judged by postal regulators: PP and an alternative operator, InPost, which led to a strong competition between them. Nevertheless, PP won the contest. Additionally, InPost lost other important contest (public tender) for providing mail service for common courts in Poland in 2015.[8]Shortly after, InPost announced termination of its activity in the letter segment of the postal market.

To understand the net cost of universal service provision, it is essential to demonstrate the legal mechanism for establishing tariffs. Tariffs set by the designated operator must comply with annual price caps for universal service set by the President of UKE (Poland's postal regulator) for 3-year periods. The postal regulator should set the price cap with regard to the costs of universal service provision, ensuring price affordability as well as market and economic conditions. In fact, the minister responsible for communications, in agreement with the minister responsible for public finances, lays down by ordinance a method for setting the annual price caps for universal service tariffs.[9] The price cap may be set for a particular universal service or for those services grouped together due to their similarity. The postal regulator has power to change its decision and determine the annual price caps for universal service tariffs at any time (Chołodecki and Popowska 2018, p. 16).

[6]Deutsche Post DHL is a designated operator in terms of international postal regulations, i.e., for the Universal Postal Union.

[7]Party may appeal against the President UKE administrative decision to the administrative courts [Administrative Voivodeship Court in Warsaw]. The judicial control exercised by the administrative courts against the decisions is performed on the basis of the legality (model of cassation).

[8]The public tender for providing mail service for common courts in Poland in 2016–2018 was won by PP and 2019–2022.

[9]Ordinance of the Minister of Administration and Digitization of 6 May 2013 on the methodology for setting maximum annual levels of fees for universal services, Journal of Laws of 2013, item 543.

Table 1 Prices of register letters and normal letters 2013–2019, tariffs of the PP

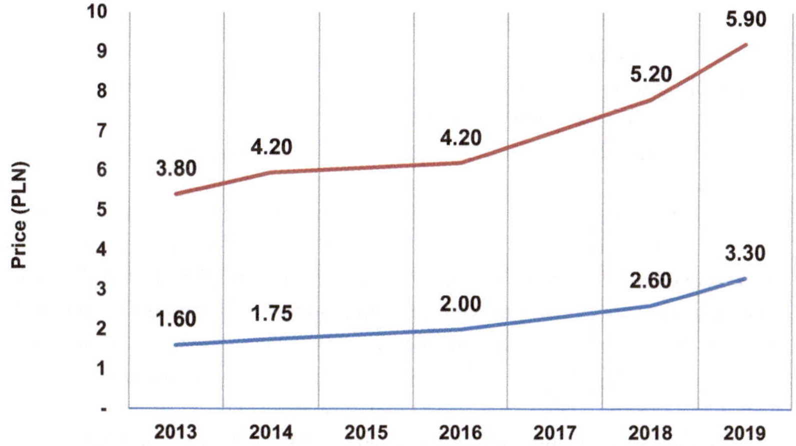

	01-05-2013	01-02-2014	07-04-2014	01-03-2016	01-04-2018	01-04-2019
Registered letter	3.80	4.20	4.20	4.20	5.20	5.90
Letter	1.60	1.75	1.75	2.00	2.60	3.30

Source: The President of UKE decisions available on www.uke.gov.pl

Since 2013, when the Postal Law Act came into force, PP has changed the universal service tariffs six times. Table 1 shows that the price for most common services has increased:[10] 64% for domestic registered letters[11] and 48% for domestic normal letters.[12] At the same time, PP has delivered approximately 98% of letter items in the universal service category.[13] In 2017, PP has had PLN 564.7 million of turnover in universal services and reported PLN 2778.7 million of revenue. The letter market is the most important part of PP activity as designated operator in terms of both volume and revenues. Constantly declining letter market is an essential financial issue for PP. Thus, PP can maintain price tariffs for universal service and record the net cost or increase the price tariffs. The second option is much more convenient for PP since Postal Law Act does not give appropriate legal instruments for price regulation to the postal regulator. That is one of the reasons why PP has not declared net cost on universal service since 2014.

[10]Yearly price indices of consumer goods and services in Poland were 2013, 0,9%; 2014, 0%; 2015, −0,9%; 2016, −0,6%; 2017, 2,0%; and 2018, 1,6%. [https://stat.gov.pl/en/topics/prices-trade/price-indices/price-indices-of-consumer-goods-and-services/yearly-price-indices-of-consumer-goods-and-services-from-1950/].

[11]According to the Postal Law Act, registered item is a letter item which is a recorded item, transported and delivered in a manner that protects it against loss, partial loss of its contents, or damage.

[12]According to the Postal Law Act, letter item is an item of correspondence or a printed form, excluding direct mail.

[13]Source: The UKE Report on the state of the postal market in 2016

4 Calculating the Net Cost

The EU postal directive contains a legal definition of the "net cost" of universal service obligations. According to this definition, the net cost is any cost related to, and necessary for, the operation of the universal service provision (Annex I Postal Directive). This legal definition does not reflect the appropriate sense of the "net" cost, since this is the definition of the gross cost, which does not take into account revenue. The Postal Law Act contains the appropriate definition, which states that the net cost of the universal service obligation shall constitute the difference between the net cost for a designated operator for operating with the universal service obligations and the same postal service provider operating without the universal service obligations, decreased by intangible benefits related to the provision of universal services and the benefits resulting from special or exclusive rights granted to the designated operator (Art. 106 the Postal Law Act). The designated operator in calculating the net cost must take into account costs related to universal service provision, revenues from universal service provision, intangible benefits related to universal service provision, and benefits resulting from special or exclusive rights granted to the designated operator that can take into account reasonable profit based on the rate of weighted average cost of capital. There is a net cost for financing only if the provision of universal service led to a loss.

The net cost in Poland is financed by some of the postal operators and by the state budget, if the sum of shares in the subsidy is insufficient to finance the net cost. Only those postal operators that provide the universal service or services within the scope of universal service are obliged to contribute to cover the net cost.[14] Additionally, a contributing operator's revenue from those services must exceed one million PLN. The amount of the postal operator's contribution to the subsidy may not be higher than 2% of its revenues from services within the scope of universal service.

Participation to the compensation fund is a form of tax for obliged postal operators. A tax is generally considered as a compulsory financial contribution in order to fund public expenditures. There is no doubt that the universal service is a public duty. Thus, postal operators providing services falling within the scope of universal service must pay extra contribution (tax) to the state via postal regulator. Such a charge is an entry barrier for new postal operators and thus can limit the competition on the universal service market (Fee et al. 2004).[15]

[14] The segment of the services falling within the scope of universal service includes letter items and postal parcels of the weight and dimensions specified for universal service and items for the blind, not provided by the designated operator to offer universal service. Services falling within the scope of universal service do not include postal services consisting in clearance, sorting, transport, and delivery of courier items.

[15] Economists have not yet been able to reach a broad consensus over the definition of an entry barrier, although I acknowledged the entry barrier as proposed by Fee, Preston, R., Hugo M. Mialon, and Michael A. Williams that "an economic barrier to entry is a cost that must be incurred by a new entrant and that incumbents do not or have not had to incur."

The Table 2 below shows a simulation of the prediction of the net cost of universal service obligation for PP in 2013. The last time the PP declared the net cost of the universal service was for 2013. So far, the postal regulator responsible for the compensation fund did not pass the final decision (see Section 5).

Official data provided by the postal regulator shows that, at the end of 2016, 291 entities were registered as postal operators in Poland. Only 151 postal operators carried on actual business activities in the field of postal services. In the segment of services falling within the scope of universal service, 53 postal operators operated in 2017. The total share of the four largest operators (excluding the PP) providing services in the segment of services falling within the scope of universal service amounted to approximately 99% in revenues and in the volume of services in this segment. To summarize, the net cost is financed mainly by the designated operator. Currently, besides PP, only four of the postal operators are large enough to be required to contribute to cover PP net cost.

Table 2 Simulation of the prediction of the net cost of universal service obligation for PP in 2013

	Analytical position	**Amount in PLN** (million)		**Comments**
1.	Revenues from the universal service	3 252,3		
2.	Cost of the universal service	3 347,4		
3.	Elements of the net cost	322,3		elimination of unprofitable postal points, reduction of delivery of postal items in rural areas, cost of capital
4.	Indirect benefits for PP as designated operator	182,8		
5.	The net cost of the universal service obligation in 2013	139,5		Difference from point 3 and 4
6.	The amount of redress	**95,1**	**100%**	The amount of loss
7.	PP participation in the compensation fund	84,6	**89%**	2% revenues from the universal postal service
8.	The amount for PP	10,5		Difference from point 6 and 7
9.	Alternative operators	4,4	**4,6%**	2% revenues from alternative operators
10.	State Budget	6,1	**6,4%**	the sum of shares by alternative operators is insufficient to finance the net cost

Source: Borowiec 2017, p. 46

5 The Compensation Fund

The EU postal directive contains four basic methods for financing universal service. Two involve public funding either directly or through procurement. It also allows, and Poland has adopted, the compensation fund financed by service providers as described above. This is similar to that established for telecommunications (as described in the next section). The compensation fund is administered by the postal regulator, which issues a decision comprising the verified net cost, loss on universal service, and the level of contribution to the compensation fund, with a 30-day time limit for paying the contribution to the subsidy.

Prices of the universal service provision are set by the minister in the ordinance. The postal regulator does not have any legal instrument against the tariffs set by the designated operator, if they are set within the limits of a price cap. Moreover, more than 90% of the subsidy to the compensation fund is paid by the designated operator and the state budget. For the designated operator, it is better to increase prices for the universal services rather than incur a financial loss on the universal service, particularly in case, when the designated operator does not have any competitors on the letter market. Such a situation is contrary to Art. 108 of the Postal Law Act.

According to the Postal Law Act, in order to receive subsidy from the compensation fund, several actions must be taken. It is complex proceedings, which involves several entities. Though, only the designated operator is entitled to initiate the compensation fund. The President of UKE decides on the final subsidy. Diagram 1 shows the procedure of the compensation fund according to the Postal Law Act.

6 The Compensation Fund on the Telecommunication Market in Poland

Postal and telecommunication sectors have the same obligation to provide universal service for users (Fratini 2016, p. 154). Additionally, the universal service in the EU telecommunication sector was regulated prior to the postal one (Eccles 2011 p. 152–162). In Poland, these two markets share the same regulator – the President of UKE. The method of financing universal service on the telecommunication market in Poland is very similar to the method described in the Polish postal law. Thus, I will show only the major differences between the regulations on both markets.

Article 3 (1) of the Universal Service Directive[16] obligates the EU member states to ensure that the universal services are available with the quality specified to all end users in their territory, independently of geographical location, in the light of spe-

[16] Directive 2002/22/EC of the European Parliament and of the Council of 7 March 2002 on universal service and users' rights relating to electronic communications networks and services (Universal Service Directive) (OJ L 108 24.4.2002, p. 51). Similar regulation is in Art. 84 Directive (EU) 2018/1972 of the European Parliament and of the Council of 11 December 2018 establishing the European Electronic Communications Code (Recast), (OJ L 321, 17.12.2018, p. 36–214).

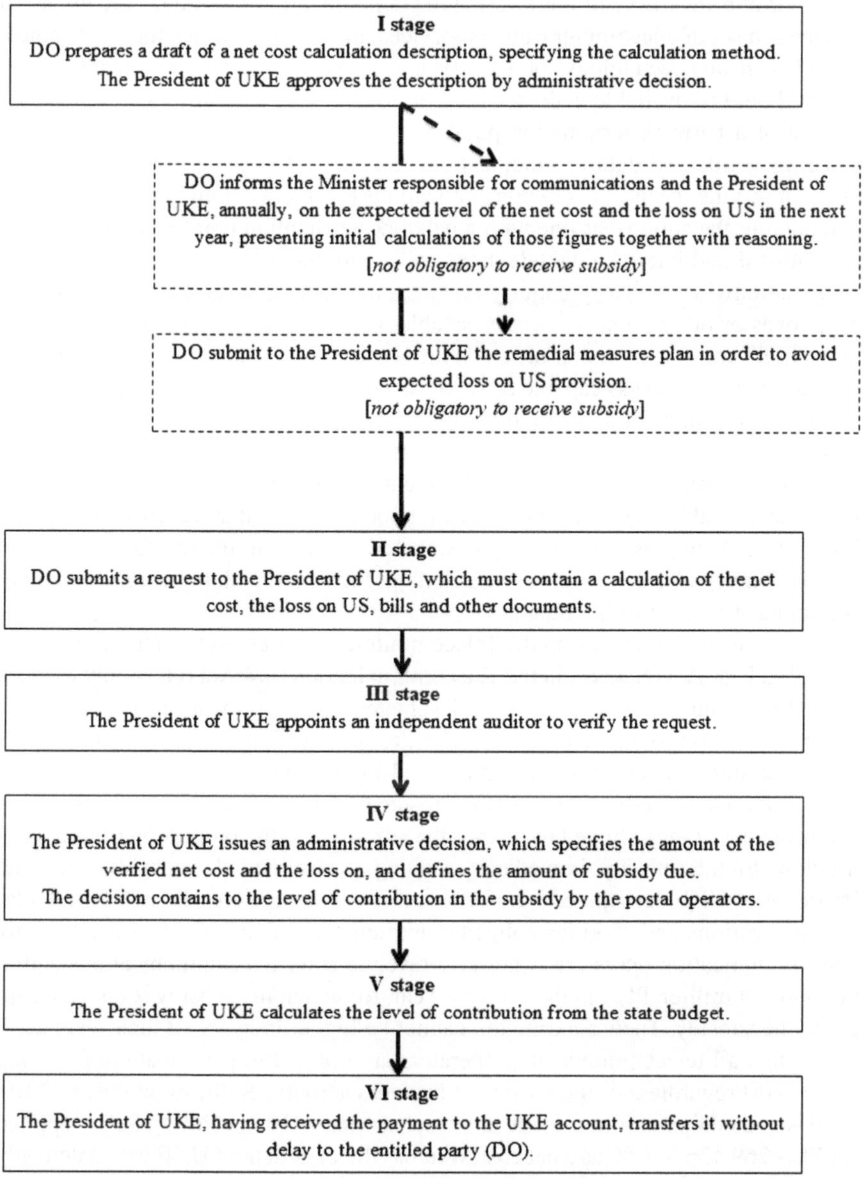

Diagram 1 Procedure of the compensation fund according to the Postal Law Act

cific national conditions, and at an affordable price. Similar to the postal market, the price of the universal service is one of the most important factors in EU electronic communications regulations. Available methods of financing universal telecommunication service are fairly similar to the postal regulations. It can be a mechanism to compensate from public funds or to have providers of electronic communications networks and services share the net cost of universal service obligations.

According to Art. 81 of the Polish Telecommunication Law Act,[17] the universal service is a set of telecommunications services, including facilities for the disabled, provided in any technology, preserving good quality and at a reasonable price, which should be available in the territory of Poland. This set includes services: connection of a network termination point at a fixed location, capable of supporting voice, facsimile and data communications, including functional Internet access at rates supporting the use of common applications to handle current daily life matters, maintaining the subscriber line with a network termination point ready for providing national and international telephone calls, national and international telephone calls, nationwide directory enquiry services, available also to the users of public payphones or other points of access capable of voice communications, nationwide directories, and the provision of telephone services by means of public payphones or other points of access capable of voice communications.

The telecommunication law does not allow the unilateral designation of the undertaking for the universal service provision. Designation is made only if the results of consultations made by the President of UKE show that any universal service is unavailable or is not provided with good quality and at the affordable price. Since 2011, there has not been any designated operator in the telecommunication market. Universal service has been carried out fully by the highly competitive telecommunication market in Poland.

The definition of net cost in the Telecommunication Law Act differs from that in the Postal Law Act. Net cost in the Telecommunication Law Act refers only to those costs that would not be incurred by a designated service provider if it did not have an obligation to provide that service. The President of UKE in calculating the net cost takes into account costs, revenues, and indirect benefits related to universal service provision. In the next step, the President of UKE determines telecommunications undertakings obliged to finance the subsidy and the proportion of their contribution to the subsidy immediately having determined the subsidy due. The President of UKE determines a uniform rate of percentage contribution for all telecommunications undertakings obliged to participate in financing the subsidy. Only telecommunication operators, who have revenue from telecommunications activities above 4 million PLN in the calendar year, for which the subsidy is due, contribute to the subsidy. Their contribution cannot be higher than 1% of their revenue. It means that all telecommunication operators are obliged to participate in financing the net cost regardless of their scope of business activity. To illustrate this, in 2010, the designated operator to provide universal service – Orange Polska S.A. – applied for PLN 269 436 354.80 as a net cost, whereas the President of UKE calculated only PLN 51 410 495.71. There were 117 telecommunication entities obligated by the President of UKE to pay 0.12% of their total revenue. The subsidy from the compensation fund for 2010 was paid to the designated operator in 2018. Such a long

[17] Act of 16 July 2004 Telecommunications Law, consolidated text Journal of Laws of 2018, item 1954, uniform text.

period was caused by the ongoing administrative and court-administrative procedure related to determining the final amount of the subsidy.

The compensation fund from the Telecommunication Law Act does not create entry barrier for the telecommunication market compared to the compensation fund from the Postal Law Act since all telecommunications entities are obliged to participate in financing the subsidy. Moreover, an administrative procedure that takes almost 10 years must be seen as inefficient. A similar situation exists in the postal market in Poland with net cost from the 2013.

7 Conclusions

The key component of the universal postal service is its affordable price. Together with other requirements such as postal points of contact and delivery frequency across the whole national territory, universal service can generate financial losses for the service provider. The Polish Postal Law Act determines the scope of the universal service very precisely and does not give the designated operator any freedom to modify it. Thus, financing of the universal service must be ensured by law.

The EU postal regulation provides several possible methods of financing universal postal service. One of the methods is the compensation fund. The mechanisms of the compensation fund can differ from each other as is illustrated in the postal and telecommunication markets. The differences between the regulations are not significant; however, they can have a strong impact on the market situation. Two important factors are the entities participating in the compensation fund and participation in the compensation fund by the state budget.

My analyses conducted in this paper show that the compensation fund regulation in the Polish Postal Law Act creates an entry barrier for new postal operators and thus can limit the competition on the universal service market. The entry barriers are the special contribution (tax) paid by postal operators providing services within the scope of universal service to the compensation fund and the privileged position of the PP as designated operator. Moreover, the PP is the biggest participant in the compensation fund, and thus, it is not interested in updating the net cost of the universal service obligations. L. Borowiec presented prediction of net cost for 2013, where the designated operator – PP – shall participate in approx. 89%, alternative postal operator in approx. 5%, and state budget in approx. 6% (Borowiec 2017, p. 46). PP is a fully state-owned company. The last time PP declared a net cost of the universal service obligation was in 2013. Contrary to the Postal Law Act, the costs of the universal service obligation have been paid by the end users since the price of the registered letters has increased for approx. 67% in the last 6 years. Summarizing, the Postal Law Act creates an entry barrier by the compensation fund and does not regulate tariffs of the universal service provision, which give the designated operator a favored position on the market. Thus, financing universal service from the state budget should be considered as the most efficient solution for the market (Visco-Comandini 2018, p. 117; Chołodecki 2019, p. 40).

Maintaining the compensation fund requires essential changes similar to those pursued in the telecommunication market in Poland. Most of all, all postal operators should participate in the compensation fund. Such a change can potentially decrease the prices of universal postal service in Poland and, thus, make it more affordable and contribute to consumer welfare.

References

Bailly, D., & Meidinger, M. (2011). The dual tend towards operational efficiencies and social regulation in European postal service. In M. A. Crew & P. R. Kleindorfer (Eds.), *Reinventing the postal sector in an electronic age*. Cheltenham: Edward Elgar.

Borowiec, L. (2017). Fundusz kompensacyjny jako metoda finansowania powszechnych usług pocztowych. *Annales Universitatis Mariae Curie-Skłodowska, sectio H – Oeconomia, LI*(5), 41–49.

Chołodecki, M. (2019). Fundusz kompensacyjny na rynku telekomunikacyjnym i pocztowym. *iKAR, 3*(8), 31–41.

Chołodecki, M., & Popowska, B. (2018). Instrumenty prawne Prezesa UKE na rynku pocztowym. *iKAR, 1*(7), 8–22.

Crew, M. A., & Kleindorfer, P. R. (2000). Liberalization and the universal service obligation in postal service. In M. A. Crew & P. R. Kleindorfer (Eds.), *Current directions in postal reform*. Boston: Kluwer.

Crew, M. A., & Kleindorfer, P. R. (2008). Regulation and the USO under entry. In M. A. Crew & P. R. Kleindorfer (Eds.), *Competition and regulation in the postal and delivery sector*. Cheltenham, Northampton: Edward Elgar.

Eccles, R. (2011). State funding and cost sharing of the USO under the 2008 EU postal services directive. In M. Crew & P. Kleindorfer (Eds.), *Reinventing the postal sector in an electronic age*. Cheltenham: Edward Elgar.

Fee, P. R., Mialon, H. M., & Williams, M. A. (2004). What is a barrier to entry? *American Economic Review, 94*(2), 461–465.

Fratini, A. (2016). Compensation fund under EU law: A suitable solution for the postal market? In M. L. A. Crew & T. J. Brennan (Eds.), *The future of the postal sector in a digital world*. Cham: Springer.

Rowsell, C. (2016). Origins of "universal service". In M. L. A. Crew & T. J. Brennan (Eds.), *The future of the postal sector in a digital world*. Cham: Springer.

Snażyk, Z. (2015). *Świadczenie pocztowej usługi powszechnej w warunkach liberalizacji rynku*. Warszawa: C.H. Beck.

Szydło, M. (2006). Usługa powszechna w telekomunikacji jako instytucja prawa Wspólnoty Europejskiej. *Przegląd Sądowy, 16*(5), 107–128.

UKE. (2018). *Report on the state of the postal market in 2017* https://uke.gov.pl/download/gfx/uke/en/defaultaktualnosci/36/96/1/report_on_the_state_of_the_postal_market_in_2017.pdf.

Visco-Comandini, V. (2018). Is the compensation fund an appropriate tool for financing universal postal service obligations? In P. Parcu, T. Brennan, & V. Glass (Eds.), *New business and regulatory strategies in the postal sector. Topics in regulatory economics and policy*. Cham: Springer.

Blockchain and Postal Digital Services: Opportunities and Drawbacks

Blandine Eggrickx, Marine Lefort, and Alain Roset

1 Introduction

Blockchain is a technology that allows information or value to be transferred over the Internet on a peer-to-peer network without intermediaries and without the use of a trusted third party. Blockchain makes decentralized and secure exchanges possible, at low cost with anonymization of the parties involved. This technology is being used to develop services in various sectors such as finance, logistics, and health care. Regarding digital public services, in particular those provided by postal operators (POs), we consider blockchain to be an opportunity. Because of its unique characteristics (traceability, immutability, transparency, and decentralization), it is a way to efficiently redesign these services.

This technology is often seen as disruptive, since it is associated with a new mode of governance of distributed trust. Even two-sided platforms may be weakened by this new technology, opening a window of opportunities for new actors. However, new fully efficient blockchain services cannot work without taking into account current legislation. Crucial issues include the definition of roles and

This paper represents the personal views of the authors and should not be taken to represent the position of La Poste.

B. Eggrickx
In charge of European Affairs, European and International Relations Division – Groupe La Poste, Paris, France

M. Lefort (✉)
Economist in the Department "Doctrine et Modélisation", Direction of Institutional Affairs and Regulation – Groupe La Poste, Paris, France
e-mail: marine.lefort@laposte.fr

A. Roset
Blockchain Expert, Digital Division – Groupe La Poste, Paris, France

P. L. Parcu et al. (eds.), *The Changing Postal Environment*, Topics in Regulatory Economics and Policy, https://doi.org/10.1007/978-3-030-34532-7_12

responsibilities, the protection of personal data, and, above all, compatibility with data protection rules and the control of anti-competitive behavior.

This article focuses on the opportunity for POs to offer digital services through blockchain and on the main regulatory challenges they will face to do it. Blockchain applications for POs have been discussed (Bach and Jaag 2016; OIG 2016), but this article extends previous analysis and focuses mainly on regulation issues. After this introduction, Sect. 2 will present the blockchain technology and its disruptive characteristics. Section 3 will attempt to demonstrate that blockchain is an opportunity for POs to develop trusted digital services as e-identity or e-voting and to diversify their activities. Section 4 presents the main challenges blockchain faces with regard to existing legislation, while Sect. 5 concludes.

2 Blockchain: A Disruptive Technology

2.1 What Is Blockchain? A Brief Description

Blockchain is a type of distributed ledger technology (DLT) "[…] that can record—manually or automatically—all sorts of transactions between users. Once they are recorded, these transactions are permanent and can be seen by all users, which is one of the reasons why blockchain can be trusted" (Schrepel 2018). Transactions refer to information and more generally to any "operation." No intermediary is needed to manage the blockchain because it is a decentralized public ledger that is distributed in all servers of the network of participants, called "nodes." The nodes of the network are able to communicate with each other. Each addition of information to the database is done through a decentralized "consensus mechanism" allowing some users (called "miners") to validate new "blocks" that will be transmitted to the nodes of the network. This validation is necessary to ensure the security, the integrity, and the consistency of the blockchain (and also the unicity of each block added). In the famous example of the Bitcoin, the consensus mechanism is called a "proof of work," because it implies for miners to resolve a cryptographic puzzle – this action is called "mining." The miners are motivated to solve this puzzle because they obtain a reward: some Bitcoins. The block validated is transmitted to each node but only after a control of transaction rules compliance. Then the validated block is added to the blockchain. It should be noted that other forms of consensus exist, with different rewards for the miners, but they do not guarantee at this time the same level of security and resilience.

Originally used to exchange cryptocurrencies, the decentralized technology of blockchain can be extended to many different kinds of services like financial services, execution of contracts, or authentication services. All individual data are stored and grouped by blocks to form a blockchain. The blockchain grows with every new data stored. Each of the verifiers of the network retains a copy of the ledger, which makes blockchain a secure and decentralized way to share data and record transactions. All operations and information in the chain are immutable since they are written in the ledger, which means that all the nodes in the network conserve an identical copy of the whole blockchain.

Finally, traceability is ensured by cryptographic electronic time-stamping process. Each block containing a set of information is linked to another block. Each piece of information is checked chronologically and then added to the blockchain. Therefore, the blockchain does not use a trusted third party to validate the exchange, as is currently the case during an exchange over the Internet, examples including banking, notary, and insurance. This technology is often associated with a new, leaner mode of governance. This challenges the existence of intermediaries and the platforms' business models within the current digital economy. For POs, it means that they can use blockchain as an underlying technology to provide new services (cf. Section 3).

Three types of blockchains coexist. A first is public or "permissionless" blockchains, where the architecture is open and anyone can continue the ledger, perform transactions, or participate in the validation process. Transactions are publicly available for anyone to read. Permissionless blockchains are expected to contain a large number of nodes, as any of them are allowed to join. A second type is private or "permissioned" blockchains, for which access and use are only possible for authorized agents. There are restrictions on who in the network can validate operations and who can perform operations. Private blockchains are closed ecosystems where users are not freely able to join the network. In between are hybrid or consortium blockchains, with a preselection of the number of nodes that validate the different transaction blocks. Access to the third type can be permissionless or permissioned. Governance rules are defined to control the way the blockchain is used by all the participants.

2.2 A New Challenge to Two-Sided Platforms?

An interesting feature of blockchain decentralized structure is that it may challenge and even transform the business model of two-sided platforms existing since the golden age of the web technologies around the 2000s as studied in the economic literature (Rochet and Tirole 2003). Some blockchain projects or new start-ups try to challenge well-established two-sided platforms with cheaper services, less hidden costs, or without personal data exploitation.

Meanwhile, POs themselves have been compared to two-sided platforms in order to segment markets and customers and define new pricing strategies. If a PO's behavior is deemed to be similar to two-sided platforms (by performing transactions as the delivery of a registered letter, the scan of a parcel or any banking operation), the emergence of blockchain technology should be of great interest to POs. They must carefully observe and analyze the emergence of the blockchain technologies. It is crucial for them not only to avoid to be disrupted by new stakeholders but also to determine the relevance of this technology to provide some of their traditional services such as registered mail.

The blockchain technology may indeed impact two-sided platforms and potentially improve the global efficiency of their related markets, by questioning their structure and essential characteristics. Parker and Van Alstyne (2005, 2009) represent the structure of two-sided platforms by the interaction of a sponsor who develops platform technologies and is responsible for the design of the platform. The sponsor is normally the platform provider, which interacts directly with two types of end users (representing demand and supply). A new market structure, allowed by the blockchain, may be built without a central provider, based on the interconnection of the nodes of users mainly from the providers' side. The role of the platform sponsor may be reduced to only launch the group, organize the rules of governance, define the interfaces, and attract new users.

Two-sided platforms typical characteristics are a pricing policy with potential cross-subsidies, a strong network effect with a "winner takes all" consequence once a critical mass of users has been reached, and a strategy to attract a critical mass of targeted users.

Blockchain applications may challenge most of the previous characteristics of platforms listed above. First, blockchain algorithms could be seen by all the participants since they are present in all the nodes of the network.[1] This avoids the implementation of hidden algorithms under the control of a unique actor. In other words the "business model" (or governance) is known by all the participants in the blockchain. Second, the value of data is not captured by a single actor, because data transparency within a blockchain may be limited by cryptographic methods. This allows customers to exchange data with only relevant providers of services. Thus the intermediation service will not be the only one capturing the value created, and the value may be shared with the data owner.

Moreover, with digital platforms, those with the largest network effects are more attractive than smaller platforms. In other words, network effects are a powerful source of market power. With blockchain, though, the benefits from adoption are shared among stakeholders (users, developers of complementary applications, and providers of key resources). That is a way to prevent a network effect from harming consumers and competition.

The first blockchain implementations indicate that trust emerges from the consensus mechanism, eliminating any intermediary. But trust providers are not completely eliminated by the technology, but the role of these providers shifts in two ways. They provide trust in the information uploaded in the blockchain and build easily understandable interfaces for users. Indeed, this technology has the potential to benefit individuals while being rather obscure for most of them. It is therefore crucial that trusted third parties provide clear and consistent interfaces for users.

[1] Even if the transparency of the data exchanged between users of a blockchain may be limited by cryptographic functions.

3 Blockchain Applications for Digital Services: A Future Opportunity for Posts

Even if it remains associated with virtual currencies, the blockchain technology can be used to provide many other digital services. This article particularly refers to public digital services, i.e., services offered by governments or public administrations in order to improve the relationship between administrations, citizens, and businesses, such as e-voting or e-identity. The governments providing these services and adopting technologies are often referred as "e-governments" or "digital governments." Blockchain really seems to be the relevant technology to use to provide services to citizens to securely navigate online while protecting their privacy.

3.1 Why Use Blockchain to Provide Digital Services?

The EU Blockchain Observatory (2018a) well explains why governments might be interested in using blockchain for digital public services. Blockchain technology is a way to create "trust in information and processes in situations where there are large, heterogeneous sets of stakeholders or users" (EU Blockchain Observatory 2018a p. 10). Blockchain is also a tool "making it simple to create platforms to track when and where data was entered, what it has been used for, who has accessed it, and so on. This can greatly increase transparency in terms of data handling and processes" (EU Blockchain Observatory 2018a p. 10). Then, blockchain "makes it relatively easy to keep data both private and easily shareable. [...] Administrators can develop complex permissioning schemes to control who has access to what kinds of information, what can be shared by whom." And blockchain-distributed systems bring efficiency: "They can be used to design efficient, inexpensive platforms, potentially leading to significant cost savings in data processing while increasing the robustness of the system." All these advantages apply to digital services, being public or private. By using blockchain for implementing digital services, many positive characteristics of blockchain can be relied upon: traceability, immutability, and transparency.

For example, using blockchain for digital identities is a way to secure personal data by a decentralized storage, while they remain traceable and unforgeable. This is also a way for public and private actors to have access to data and add more information in citizens' digital identities. For example, schools could store the proof of diplomas on the digital identity blockchain of a citizen in such a way that they are accessible to firms when hiring. Blockchain gives also citizens more power to maintain control over their data, which is an important factor in the acceptance and adoption of national digital identity systems.

Blockchain technology has a real added value compared to nowadays public databases. In the medical or educational field, for example, records are often kept separately from an institution to another, making it difficult, costly, and sometimes unsecured to share them between public agencies and other third parties. Furthermore, as the (EU Blockchain Observatory 2018a p.10) argues "unlike traditional, centralized databases, where a single entity is generally responsible for collecting, securing and sharing information, blockchain platforms are based on decentralized, shared databases that are updated and verified by the community of users. With "smart contracts[2]", users can also pre-agree on processes for how to use the data, which can then be automated in the knowledge that they will be carried out as agreed." Blockchain is therefore an interesting tool when it comes to cost and timesaving for administrations.

Finally, it is worth noting that EU governments already recognized the potential of blockchain for digital services when they signed in April 2018 a declaration establishing the "European Blockchain Partnership." Its aim is in particular to cooperate in the establishment of a European Blockchain Services Infrastructure (EBSI) and use this infrastructure to provide cross-border digital public services.

3.2 POs' Opportunities to Use Blockchain

3.2.1 Why POs Could Seize the Opportunities?

Eggrickx et al. (2018) studied the role of POs as providers of digital services. POs are playing a significant role in digitalized countries because they provide key digital services for e-government. Borsenberger et al. (2017) also studied POs' role in digital identification. Being user-centric, privacy-by-design in their historical role, and able to manage data and identities at a large scale, POs can naturally handle digital identity registration and verification and are already engaged in these frameworks in various ways.

Secrecy of correspondence is a fundamental legal principle enshrined in the constitutions of many democratic countries. Consequently, respect of confidentiality, data protection, and privacy are logically associated with postal brands (Borsenberger et al. 2016). POs also are generally considered as safe, trusted, reliable institutions. They often provide services of general economic interest (SGEI) on behalf of the state; some are still public administration or state-owned companies, increasing the feeling of trust and security of these institutions.

When it comes to using blockchain to provide digital services, the difference relies only within the technology used. The qualities of POs remain as relevant as they were before. The only difference is that blockchain is taking the main parameters of trust, security, and transparency to a next level, which constitutes a natural

[2] Smart contracts are tools to automatically execute actions when the necessary, preset conditions have been met.

additional step for POs to make on their way to consolidate their place as digital service providers. In this context, POs would not act as intermediaries but as trusted third party ensuring that the data shared is fair and to empower citizen with a still unknown technology.

3.2.2 POs and Blockchain: Some Examples of Initiatives Related to Digital Services

Projects for digital services using blockchain technology from POs are already blooming, and the opportunity for POs has been identified by the POs themselves or other stakeholders. Bach and Jaag (2016) identified different opportunities for POs arising from blockchain, including financial applications, identity verification, or improvement of supply chain management.

In 2016, it was announced that Australia Post was exploring the option to use blockchain technology for electronic transactions and digital identity projects. Using blockchain technology in this case would allow people to verify their identity quickly for simple online services but also for important administrative services. Indeed, the robustness of the technology would ensure the security of the service.

In that same year, Australia Post mentioned[3] that blockchain technology would be relevant for e-voting, suggesting the possibility of handling elections online using blockchain. Indeed, blockchain could guarantee all the requirements a proper voting system absolutely needs: an inviolable, traceable, resilient system that cannot be manipulated. Regarding data privacy, blockchain could also allow anonymity, as the information would be cryptographically kept in the blockchain. A possibility could be to experiment with corporate elections, for example, to be able to later scale up to regional or national elections. The fact that Australia Post is keeping open the option of blockchain for digital services like digital identity or voting indicates that the technology will develop.

Furthermore, the United States Postal Service (USPS) filed a patent in 2017 titled "Methods and Systems for a Digital Trust Architecture."[4] USPS emphasizes that users cannot always be sure about the security of online operations. Its architecture would address this issue by verifying a user's account with his identity information and providing an electronic signature with a private key. This would be built on a blockchain configured to receive records of any mail or of any data exchanged from the user, and add them to the blockchain. This architecture would also be built on an in-person verification system, probably using the physical network of the postal operator, and would provide public directories of all the members of the network.

In mid-2017 Docaposte, a subsidiary of the La Poste Group (France), launched a blockchain archiving solution for businesses. This new service allows each actor in

[3] https://www.zdnet.com/article/australia-post-details-plan-to-use-blockchain-for-voting/

[4] appft.uspto.gov/netacgi/nph-Parser?Sect1=PTO2&Sect2=HITOFF&u=%2Fnetahtml%2FPTO%2Fsearch-adv.html&r=1&p=1&f=G&l=50&d=PG01&S1=20180083771.PGNR.&OS=dn/20180083771&RS=DN/20180083771

the blockchain ecosystem to reinforce the value of their service with a solution for storing documents associated with transactions with a trusted third party. It can be used to prove the existence of a contract between two parties involving driving or tenant insurance or a real estate transaction. In May 2019, Docaposte along with different partners – French energy suppliers, Caisse des dépôts et consignation – have presented a new project called "Archipels[5]." Archipels is a certification blockchain aiming to certify information related to their clients and fighting fraud.

At the end of 2018, Swiss Post and Swisscom officially announced that they are building a blockchain infrastructure for Swiss applications. This infrastructure will allow them to develop their own blockchain-based services. Moreover, this private blockchain can be operated jointly with other partners. Companies as well as public authorities handling sensitive data (as it is the case for digital services), or operating sensible businesses, can use this secured infrastructure to develop safe applications based on blockchain.

On another perspective, in countries where POs are not (yet) using blockchain to offer digital services, other stakeholders themselves found that it could prove to be a great opportunity. For example, the Office of the Inspector General (OIG) of the USPS has published a report in May 2016 called "Blockchain Technology: Possibilities for the U.S. Postal Service." This report describes the opportunities for the use of blockchain technology by USPS, including "identity verification services" (p. 16). This service of digital identity would also be built on in person verifications at post office.

Similarly, at the end of 2016, the Standing Committee on Government Operations and Estimates (Canadian House of Commons 2016) published a report on the way forward for Canada Post. This report promotes the role that Canada Post could play for authentication services for Canadian citizens. For the Committee, a free digital infrastructure is indeed needed for trusted communication between citizens and government or between themselves. This could be done using blockchain.

4 Is Blockchain Challenged by Legislation and Competition Rules?

If an entity chooses to use blockchain technology to provide a digital service, it will be confronted with existing regulations. This is particularly the case for applications launched by POs. Notably, blockchain presents challenges to current legislation as much as legislation challenges technological applications based on blockchain. Even if some of the legislative developments described here are rather recent, they do not address specific features of the blockchain technology, which makes it challenging to apply them. The use of blockchain technology to provide services like digital services is a change of paradigm. It questions the way supervision and trust

[5]Archipels is a project in the process of being notified to the relevant competition authorities.

have been conceived. This does not necessarily mean that the use of blockchain technology would be incompatible with existing legislation, but it poses strategic questions from the very beginning of any project.

4.1 Governance Is the Keystone for Solutions Based on Blockchain

Governance of the blockchain is a crucial, preliminary element necessary for the implementation of any solution using this technology. According to Caprioli (2017), it would be the creation of an organization, endowed with the status of a legal person that will make it possible to establish a legal, technical, and secured framework for decentralized management. The operating rules of the entity would be specified in the internal regulations of the organization, covering decision-making and management, modification of the rules of the organization, access procedures, verification of operations, and other processes. These documents would establish the rights and obligations of each stakeholder in the blockchain.

Indeed, it is necessary to have a person liable and who would pay damages, otherwise no trust would be possible. It is especially important as current European regulations rely on a strict and clear distribution of roles. It is better to use blockchains only when a clear framework and allocation of roles are established. Governance of blockchain should therefore be examined with respect to data protection and e-identification.

4.1.1 Roles and Responsibilities in the GDPR

Rules regarding data protection, especially the ones laid down in the famous GDPR regulation,[6] essentially concern the allocation of roles and responsibilities. To use blockchain to provide digital services, providers will have to collect and process considerable amounts and special categories of personal data such as health or biometric data. In this respect, the "controller[7]" or "joint controllers" and the eventual "processors[8]" have to be identified beforehand.

[6] Regulation (EU) 2016/679 of 27 April 2016 on the protection of natural persons with regard to the processing of personal data and on the free movement of such data.

[7] "Controller" means the natural or legal person, public authority, agency, or other body which, alone or jointly with others, determines the purposes and means of the processing of personal data; where the purposes and means of such processing are determined by Union or Member State law, the controller or the specific criteria for its nomination may be provided for by Union or Member State law (Article 4 of the GDPR).

[8] "Processor" means a natural or legal person, public authority, agency, or other body which processes personal data on behalf of the controller (Article 4 of the GDPR).

It is necessary to differentiate between public and private blockchains. Regarding public blockchains, the French Data Protection Authority's initial analysis (CNIL 2018) confirms the difficulty: "The GDPR, and more generally the traditional principles of data protection, were designed in a world where data management is centralized within specific entities." In the case of blockchain, "the multiplicity of actors involved in data processing complicate the definition of each other's roles."

For the CNIL, participants in a blockchain are controllers because they determine the objectives pursued by the processing and the means implemented, including data format. "Miners" are not controllers, as their actions are restricted to the validations of the operations submitted to them by the participants and they do not determine the purpose of the processing. It is therefore possible in some cases to consider miners as processors within the meaning of the GDPR as they execute the instructions of the controller.[9] Consequently, when a group of participants decides to implement a processing operation with a common purpose, the CNIL recommends that the controller be identified beforehand. This means identifying a participant who makes the decisions for the group and designating him or her as the controller.

4.1.2 Blockchain and Digital Services

For digital services, the application of the so-called eIDAS Regulation[10] is a major statement with regard to governance. This Regulation defines digital "trusted services" and establishes supervision by trusted third parties[11] of these types of services, regardless of the provider. According to Article 19 of the Regulation, Trusted Service Providers must take adequate security measures, whether technical or organizational. As Caprioli (2017) affirms, it is not enough to claim that blockchain is infallible or unfalsifiable to guarantee its safety. It is necessary to carry out a specific risk analysis.

In addition, one may question the scope of the security rules imposed on these providers in the case of public blockchains. Indeed, as explained in the Sect. 2.1 in permissionless blockchains, the architecture is open, and anyone can perform an operation or participate in the validation process; it is therefore difficult to identify who is responsible to implement security measures. The Regulation however specifies that it does not apply to the provision of trusted services[12] used

[9] In its report CNIL states: "Aware of certain practical difficulties that may arise from the qualification of minors as processors in the public blockchain (in particular with regard to the obligation to contract relations with the controller), the CNIL is currently conducting an in-depth study on this issue."

[10] Regulation (EU) No. 910/2014 of 23 July 2014 on electronic identification and trust services for electronic transactions in the internal market.

[11] Article 17 of eIDAS.

[12] Article 2 of eIDAS.

exclusively in closed systems resulting from national law or agreements within a defined set of participants, a situation which appears to be that of a private/consortium blockchain.

4.2 *Is Blockchain Compatible with Data Protection Rules?*

The most often mentioned difficulties between the regulatory framework and blockchain technology is its potential conflict with GDPR. We have already mentioned governance issues relating to GDPR, but other difficulties exist regarding the exercise of rights of data subjects and the protection of personal data.

4.2.1 Is Blockchain Contrary to the Main Principles Laid Down in the GDPR?

Some principles laid down in the GDPR could seem incompatible with blockchain, including data minimization, storage limitation, and confidentiality. The principle of data minimization requires that data collected are relevant and limited to what is necessary for the purposes for which they are processed. In addition, personal data cannot be stored indefinitely; a storage period must therefore be determined according to the purpose of the data processing. However, one of the characteristics of the blockchain is that the data recorded in it cannot be technically modified or deleted.

EU Blockchain Observatory (2018b) describes data obfuscation, irreversible encryption, and aggregation techniques that can potentially be used to anonymize personal data. The CNIL (2018) acknowledges that some encryption techniques for anonymizing data could be evaluated. This subject is one of the issues to be better discussed at the European level, particularly in the European Data Protection Board to give more certainty to the undertakings wanting to use the blockchain technology.

4.2.2 Exercise of Data Subjects' Rights and Transparency

The GDPR poses other challenges to the blockchain especially regarding data subjects' rights: rights of access[13] to and rectification or erasure[14] of personal data. It is technically impossible to grant a data subject's request for erasure when data are entered in the blockchain. However, it is technologically possible for the controller to make the data almost inaccessible in the blockchain. Indeed, it is the case when

[13] Article 15 of GDPR.

[14] Article 17 of GDPR.

data are entered in the blockchain in a way that they are stored in the blockchain but at the same time impossible to find or recognize. Indeed only the information proving the existence of the data is truly stored. It can be done using cryptographic primitives like a commitment scheme. Other techniques exist such as registering the data as a fingerprint from a key hash function[15] or an encrypted fingerprint using a state-of-the-art algorithm and keys. For the CNIL, this approach would have the effects of an erasure of the data. This idea is still being debated.

With regard to a right to rectification, according to CNIL (2018), the absence of any possibility of modifying the data entered in a block must lead the controller to enter the updated data in a new block. Indeed, a subsequent operation can always cancel the first operation, even if the first operation will always remain in the chain. The same solution as in the case of a request to delete personal data could be applied to the erroneous data that must be deleted.

4.2.3 How to Protect Personal Data in the Blockchain?

One of the main controversial issues identified is how to protect personal data in the blockchain. It should be noted that the GDPR applies to any information relating to an identified or identifiable natural person. The CNIL (2018) observed that identifiers of participants and minors and other additional data are stored in the blockchain. The CNIL recognizes that it is not possible to further minimize identifiers and that their retention is, in essence, determined by the blockchain's lifetime. As for other data stored, the CNIL finds that personal data should be recorded in the blockchain using one of the techniques available to make the data almost inaccessible. If this is not possible, registration in the form of a fingerprint obtained with a key hash function, or at least an encrypted one, should be employed to ensure a high level of confidentiality.

A preliminary conclusion regarding the compatibility of blockchain with the GDPR is that an entity must consider, in advance, the relevance of the choice of this technology for the implementation of its processing. Indeed, blockchain is not necessarily the most appropriate technology for all kind of data processing. Nevertheless, if an entity early identifies the precise challenges regarding compatibility with the GDPR or other data protection rules and conducts a specific assessment to find a balanced solution that complies with the substance of the GDPR, the Regulation could not constitute an unsurmountable obstacle.

[15] According to note n°4 "Comprendre les blockchains (chaînes de blocs)" (April 2018), the "Office parlementaire d'évaluation des choix scientifiques et technologiques" specified that, in the blockchain, "each block has an identifier that takes the form of a "hash" to connect the blocks to each other. In computing, "hashing" makes it possible to convert any set of digital data into a hash, i.e. a short binary sequence of its own. The encryption algorithm used for this purpose is called the cryptographic hash function" [unofficial translation].

4.3 *Can Blockchain Create Competition Risks?*

Blockchain technology is used to create new business models and new services. Blockchains and especially private (or consortium) blockchains are ways to gather a restricted number of people or firms. Therefore, they are controlled by a limited number of actors with specific rules. This new governance of private blockchain has raised many concerns in the literature regarding competition risks (Catalini and Tucker 2018; Nazzini 2018; Schrepel 2018; Tucker 2018). It should be noted that the distinction between public and private blockchain is crucial when talking about possible antitrust behaviors with blockchain (Schrepel 2018). This is because public blockchains are free to join and accessible to an unlimited number of people and therefore anticompetitive practices seems less likely. For the moment there are no case law regarding antitrust and blockchain, but competition authorities could be interested in these new business models. When launching new services using these technologies, POs as other actors have to keep in mind this question.

Some competition risks may be associated with blockchain (OECD 2018). Blockchain technology could be used for price monitoring or to facilitate collusive behavior, in particular for private and consortium blockchains. With a single platform, actors can exchange more easily information and agree to collude on prices and other terms. Moreover, the transparency of blockchain can help identify any deviation by blockchain participants. Smart contracts could be used to monitor markets and to apply specific punishments in case of deviation. Consortium blockchain can create barriers to entry. In a consortium blockchain, access is controlled by the members. Access can become an essential input to compete in the market. Refusal to access can be used to exclude competitors and new entrants.

Moreover, traditionally antitrust law is used in context where there are clearly defined firms and consumers. Antitrust law has been designed to tackle cases where market power is centralized. For Catalini and Tucker (2018), the decentralization of blockchain could be a challenge for antitrust enforcement: "The decentralized nature of the technology means that identifying an entity to prosecute or hold responsible for any degree of market power (or its abuse) is impossible, and that collusion and price setting between competitors may be harder to detect." The question of intent is also more difficult to prove since authorities cannot rely on internal documents and identify participants. Actually, data are encrypted, and it might have no way to recovering the original information if the encryption keys have been destroyed.

5 Conclusions

Our discussion on the interactions between regulation and blockchain, as well as of the impact of blockchain technologies on two-sided platforms, points to the role of the governance of blockchain as the key element to determine the compliance with existing rules. The technology by itself does not imply any deterministic response to these challenges, as the collaborative and cooperative structure of any blockchain system is mainly defined by the on-chain and off-chain governance of the system. Blockchain technology offers new tools to implement distributed governance, but all the stakeholders of a system must accept these distributed rules.

Decentralization and centralization are therefore two options of governance for a given ecosystem. The two models have their own underlying IT structures and relevance depending on the market, user needs, and the regulatory framework. In the future development of blockchain applications, it will be necessary to demonstrate that the distributed management of blockchain technology is more efficient than the centralized management of platforms. POs must analyze how blockchain can disrupt the provision of some of their traditional services currently provided in two-sided markets.

In both cases, postal operators have a key role to play as trusted third parties. Regarding blockchain, this role is less about the intermediation than to guarantee the integrity of the information stored in the blockchain and making this technology accessible for all users.

The blockchain technology is an opportunity to reaffirm POs as trusted providers and to in new digital services based on a cooperative approach with a large panel of different new stakeholders. They have to learn how to implement this new and always evolving technology, and they have to organize groups of interest with a balanced and well-suited governance to address and develop new businesses.

References

Bach, C., & Jaag, C. (2016). *Blockchain technology and cryptocurrencies: Opportunities for postal financial services*, Swiss Economics working paper 0056.

Borsenberger, C., Klargaard, O., & Régnard, P. (2016). Personal data and privacy issues and postal operators stand. In M. A. Crew & T. J. Brennan (Eds.), *The future of the postal sector in a digital world* (pp. 261–270). Cham: Springer International Publishing Switzerland.

Borsenberger, C., Klargaard, O., & Régnard, P. (2017). Digital identities: A good move for postal operators. In B. Crew & Parcu (Eds.), *The changing postal and delivery sector* (pp. 223–332). Cham: Springer International Publishing Switzerland.

Canadian House of Commons. (2016). The way forward for Canada Post – Report of the Standing Committee on Government Operations and Estimates, 42nd Parliament, 1st Session.

Caprioli, E. (2017). *Les enjeux juridiques et sécurité des blockchains, Cahiers de droit de l'entreprise n°3, mai/juin 2017.*

Catalini, C., & Tucker, C. (2018). *Antitrust and costless verification: An optimistic and a pessimistic view of the implications of blockchain technology*. MIT Sloan Research Paper No. 5523-18.

CNIL – Commission Nationale de l'Informatique et des Libertés. (2018). *Premiers éléments d'analyses de la CNIL – Blockchain, September 2018.*

Eggrickx, B., Klargaard, O., Lefort, M., & Régnard, P. (2018). E-government: A curse or an opportunity for posts? In P. L. Parcu et al. (Eds.), *New business and regulatory strategies in the postal sector* (pp. 235–249). Cham: Springer International Publishing Switzerland.

European Blockchain Observatory. (2018a). *Blockchain for government and public services*, Thematic report, December.

European Blockchain Observatory. (2018b). *Blockchain and the GDPR*, Thematic report, October.

Nazzini, R. (2018). *The Blockchain (R)evolution and the role of Antitrust*. Available at SSRN: https://ssrn.com/abstract=3256728 or https://doi.org/10.2139/ssrn.3256728

OECD. (2018). Blockchain Technology and Competition Policy. Issues paper by the Secretariat. Directorate for financial and enterprise affairs, Competition Committee, DAF/COMP/WD(2018)47.

OIG. (2016). *Blockchain technology: Possibilities for the US postal service*, RARC Report.

Parker, G., & Van Alstyne, M. (2005). Two-sided network effects: A theory of information product design. *Management Science, 51*(10), 1494.

Parker, G., & Van Alstyne, M. (2009). Six challenges in platform innovation and open licensing. *Communications and Strategies, 74*(2nd quarter), 17–36.

Rochet, J. C., & Tirole, J. (2003). Platform competition in two-sided markets. *Journal of the European Economic Association, 1*(4), 990.

Schrepel, T. (2018). Is blockchain, the death of antitrust law? The blockchain anitrust paradox. *3 Georgetown Law Technology Review, 281*, 59. (Forthcoming).

Tucker, C. (2018). *Blockchain, economics, and litigation*, Q&A Analysis Group. https://www.analysisgroup.com/Insights/ag-feature/q-and-a/blockchain-economics-and-litigation/

E-Commerce Growth: Competition and Regulatory Implications for the Postal Sector

Roberto Alimonti, Leonardo Mautino, and Luigi Stammati

1 Introduction

Business-to-consumer (B2C) e-commerce has shown considerable growth in Europe in recent years, generating a turnover in excess of €300bn in the largest European countries (i.e., France, Germany, Italy, Spain, and the UK) in 2018.[1] With the emergence of B2C e-commerce, marketplaces have grown significantly, expanding in different parts of the supply chain: from providing an ecosystem[2] to online merchants and e-shoppers to offering logistics and cloud services.

There are a number of studies that have looked at the possible impacts of online platforms.[3] In the postal and delivery sector, Borsenberger et al. (2019) show that, under certain conditions, vertical integration between a marketplace[4] and the provision of logistics and delivery services to online merchants could harm welfare

The content of this article does not reflect the opinion of Oxera Consulting LLP. Responsibility for the information and views expressed therein lies entirely with the authors.

[1] Politecnico di Milano e osservatori.net (2018).

[2] The term ecosystem is used to encompass the various groups of economic agents linked to a given marketplace. These include online merchants, final consumers, and postal operators and express couriers.

[3] See, e.g., Crémer et al. (2019).

[4] The terms online platforms and marketplaces are used as synonyms.

R. Alimonti (✉) · L. Stammati
Oxera Consulting LLP, Oxford, UK

Oxera Consulting LLP, Rome, Italy
e-mail: Roberto.Alimonti@oxera.com

L. Mautino
Oxera Consulting LLP, Oxford, UK

P. L. Parcu et al. (eds.), *The Changing Postal Environment*, Topics in Regulatory Economics and Policy, https://doi.org/10.1007/978-3-030-34532-7_13

compared to a situation where the marketplace is not vertically integrated. Borsenberger (2015) points out that although the two-sided online platform sales model offers a number of benefits to both consumers and sellers, it also has the potential of making small online merchants economically dependent on the marketplace. The notion of economic dependence has also been discussed by Raco (2018), in relation to rival retailers and traditional delivery operators. In addition, Borsenberger et al. (2016) show that when the bargaining power of the marketplace increases, there could be negative consequences for the delivery operator, who may not be able to cover its fixed costs due to the reduction in the delivery fees charged to the marketplace.

This paper builds on these studies to account for the effects of possible anticompetitive practices of online sales platforms on the logistics and delivery part of the supply chain and considers a number of potential regulatory remedies.

Section 2 discusses two theories of harm that are being explored in the context of e-commerce by national and supranational competition authorities in Europe. Section 3 considers whether any adjustments to the tools used by competition authorities to assess whether there is a breach of competition law, while Sect. 4 examines whether specific ex ante regulation (in addition to ex post antitrust intervention) would be warranted to ensure a level playing field in this dynamic area of the economy. Section 5 concludes.

2 Marketplaces: Positive Effects and Possible Theories of Harm

A marketplace is an example of a multi-sided platform—i.e., an ecosystem in which a multiplicity of economic agents interact through the mediation offered by the marketplace itself.[5] Multi-sided platforms can create value by bringing together groups of economic agents and by facilitating interactions between them. Greater involvement by agents of at least one group increases the value of the platform to agents of another group. Such network effects resemble the features of economies of scale, albeit on the demand side.[6]

By virtue of these network effects, economic agents may have an incentive to use of fewer platforms—in some cases, only one ("market tipping"). Without aiming at providing an exhaustive list, economic theory suggests that the use of a single marketplace by consumers could give rise to a number of positive effects, including[7]

[5] In the context of this paper, a marketplace is a platform for the online sale of tangible products (as opposed to intangible services) to consumers.

[6] See Evans and Schmalensee (2014).

[7] See Crémer et al. (2019) for a detailed discussion.

lower search costs and prices for consumers,[8,9] lower market power and entry barriers for online merchants, and lower transaction costs for postal and delivery operators.

However, under certain circumstances, the rise of marketplaces may give rise to potential competition and consumer protection concerns.[10] The rest of this section considers two possible theories of harm that are currently explored by national and supranational competition authorities in Europe.

2.1 *Abuse of Dominance by Vertically Integrated Online Platforms: The Case of Tying*

Bundling and tying[11] are common commercial practices and not always harmful to competition. Indeed, they can give rise to a number of efficiencies. On the supply side, bundling practices can reduce production and distribution costs by leveraging economies of scale, purpose, and density. Also, bundling strategies can be aimed at protecting a company's reputation.

On the demand side, consumers benefit from product and service bundles that reduce transaction costs. Furthermore, by exploiting the heterogeneity of consumer preferences, bundling practices facilitate price discrimination.[12]

However, under certain circumstances, bundling and tying strategies can be used for anticompetitive purposes. For example, a vertically integrated operator could leverage its market power in a given geographical area and/or product to strengthen its position in a more competitive market.

Although we recognize that in principle a tying strategy might be put in place also to allow the marketplace to ensure the quality of the delivery phase, in what follows, we set out the possible anticompetitive consequences that can arise if a dominant marketplace links the access to its marketplace to its logistics and distribution services.

With regard to rival online platforms, a tying strategy could increase barriers to entry for competing marketplaces in the same or adjacent markets. In relation to delivery operators and the USO provider, tying could give rise to cream skimming and hold-up problems described below.

---

[8] Oxera (2015a).

[9] See, e.g., European Commission (2017), Brynjolfsson and Smith (2000) and Scott Morton et al. (2001).

[10] See, e.g., Competition and Markets Authority (2015).

[11] See, e.g., Niels et al. (2016).

[12] The effect of price discrimination on consumers and total welfare depends on the characteristics of the market, such as the intensity of competition and consumers' sensitivity to price. See Oxera (2015b).

Cream skimming The dominant marketplace could decide to distribute products directly (e.g., via its vertically integrated delivery company) only in the most profitable geographical areas and/or at the most profitable delivery frequencies, relegating other delivery operators and the USO provider to the less profitable areas and/or frequencies. Indeed, the USO provider has an obligation to serve both profitable and less profitable areas, as well as to meet certain standards in terms of frequency of delivery. This, of course, requires a widespread network with significant fixed costs. To saturate the network and to recover part of its fixed costs, the USO provider could have an incentive to offer additional services that rely (in part or in full) on the same network. However, a cream skimming strategy pursued by the dominant marketplace could make the USO provider unable to capitalize on its USO network in the more profitable areas. Under the condition that the USO provider is not able to reprice upward its products in the less profitable areas (possibly because the willingness to pay in said areas is too low), such a tying strategy may have important repercussions on the ability of the USO provider to keep its business sustainable in a declining traditional mail market. In the long run, because of the vertical tying strategy and cream skimming practices adopted by dominant marketplace, the USO provider could be faced with two possible choices: (i) stop delivering e-commerce parcels in less profitable areas given that it cannot recover the costs of serving these areas with the profits deriving from the more profitable ones or (ii) provide e-commerce parcel delivery in less profitable areas at higher prices, with a negative impact on vulnerable consumers.

Hold-up[13] Due to the aforementioned cream skimming strategy, delivery operators and the USO provider may not be able to cover the costs of investing in and developing their distribution network in order to absorb the B2C parcel volumes received from the dominant marketplace. This could generate a hold-up problem. If delivery operators foresee it, they might decide to underinvest, generating repercussions on the development of the e-commerce. In contrast, if they do not foresee it, they might have to accept lower prices from the dominant online sales platforms than expected when making the investment.

With regard to online merchants, although, in the short-term, some online merchants could benefit from the tying strategy (because the marketplace may be willing to offer benefits to online merchants who rely solely on its bundle of services in order to effectively implement its tying strategy), in the long run, such a strategy might force online merchants into a state of economic dependence.

With regard to consumers, a tying strategy that leads, in the long run, to a weakening of the delivery operators could generate a worsening of the delivery choices offered by the marketplace to e-shoppers. Furthermore, as discussed above, e-shoppers living in less profitable areas may no longer benefit from e-commerce

[13] Hold-up refers to a situation where two parties are about to make a transaction that requires specific investments on one side or the other. Hold-up problems occur when one of the two parties risks not benefiting from the investment due to the possible opportunistic behavior of the other party after the transaction.

or receive a suboptimal level of service if the dominant marketplace and the USO provider do not find an agreement for delivering parcels in those areas or strike a suboptimal deal for consumers.[14]

The possible issues set out above are supported by ongoing antitrust investigations. Indeed, in April 2019, the Italian Competition Authority (AGCM)[15] launched an antitrust investigation against Amazon for an alleged abuse of dominance in relation to the advantages conferred by Amazon to online merchants subscribing to the so-called "Fulfilled by Amazon" service, whereby Amazon bundles together access to its marketplace and the delivery of the product to e-shoppers. According to the AGCM, Amazon's allegedly abusive strategy would have repercussions on the logistics market and potentially on marketplaces.

2.2 *Abuse of Economic Dependence of Online Merchants by Marketplaces*

While competition law is not meant to protect competitors but rather consumer welfare, several EU Member States have put in place-specific legal provisions regarding the notion of abuse of economic dependence (e.g., French,[16] German, Italian, Portuguese, and Greek national competition laws).[17] For example, in Italian legislation, a "state of economic dependence exists when a business finds itself in a position to bring about excessive imbalances in the rights and obligations pertaining to its commercial relations with another business."[18]

To understand whether an abuse of economic dependence is feasible in the e-commerce market and its possible effects, it would be necessary to assess whether there are strong imbalances in the bargaining power between the marketplace and the online merchants. This exercise would involve providing an answer to three questions, as discussed below.

Firstly, it should be assessed whether the market structure creates the conditions for commercial relationships characterized by a strong imbalance between the rights and obligations of marketplaces and those of other economic agents in the value chain, such as online merchants.

We note that the European retail sales sector, which includes the B2C online market, is particularly fragmented. According to Eurostat, in France, Germany, Italy, Spain, and the UK between 81% and 96% of retail and wholesale enterprises

[14] This would also apply to consumers in need of particular services (e.g., in terms of delivery frequencies) that only the USO provider would be able to supply at reasonable prices.

[15] AGCM (2019), Procedimento A528.

[16] Code de Commerce, Article L420–2.

[17] See, e.g., Bougette et al. (2018).

[18] Articolo 9, legge 18 giugno 1998, n. 192, "Disciplina della subfornitura nelle attività produttive".

have fewer than 10 employees.[19] With specific reference to online merchants, there are more than 135,000 sellers only on the Amazon marketplace in Italy.[20] In 2017, the number of sellers on Amazon UK was more than 280,000.[21] This evidence seems to support the idea that a dominant marketplace would have the ability, in principle, to use its negotiating power against a very large number of atomized online merchants.

Secondly, the contractual conditions offered by marketplaces for access to online merchants should be analyzed in order to understand whether they point to the existence of market power.

According to the European Commission, a large number of businesses experience problems in the course of their platform-to-business relationships. These range from sudden unexplained changes in the terms and conditions imposed unilaterally by platforms without prior notice to the delisting of products without clear statements of reasons, from ranking of business users or their offers to issues related to data access and use, and from discrimination of businesses to favoring of online platforms' own competing services.[22]

Finally, one should explore whether online merchants are "forced" to use the services offered by a dominant marketplace (as the latter is the only one capable of accessing a critical mass of consumers) or whether online merchants actually have different choices (outside options).[23] It should also be assessed whether it is reasonable to talk about "inside options" for online merchants.[24] Similarly, one should understand what are the "outside options" available to the dominant marketplace and what can we say about its "inside options."

Apart from the possibility to sell via the traditional offline channel, online merchants have the outside option of continuing to sell online either through their own website/application or through a competing marketplace. However, smaller online merchants could encounter difficulties in resorting to their own channel(s). As shown in Fig. 1, smaller companies exhibit a higher propensity to use marketplaces, possibly because they lack the know-how necessary to create their own online sales channel or simply because they value the benefit of accessing a large audience of consumers through a marketplace.

Finally, given the high degree of market concentration of marketplaces,[25] the possibility of online merchants using (or threatening to use) one or more competing

[19] Eurostat (2016), SMEs annual enterprises statistics by size and class (distributive trade).

[20] See https://algopix.com/amazon/italy

[21] See https://tamebay.com/2017/09/uk-sellers-registered-amazon-ebay.html

[22] European Parliament and Council (2019).

[23] In the framework of bargaining theory, the outside option is the opportunity cost for bargaining of each player, i.e., the utility each would receive if negotiations were terminated.

[24] Inside option refers to the payoff that a player obtains during the bargaining process, i.e., while the parties to the negotiations are in temporary disagreement.

[25] In the USA, Amazon had a market share of 56% in the fourth quarter of 2018, while Ebay 20%. See Statista (2018), Leading online marketplace websites in the United States as of 4th quarter 2018, based on share of visits. In Europe, the situation is similar: the two main online sales platforms are Amazon and eBay, with a market share, in 2015, of 90.2% (up from 88.5% in 2006). See AGCM (2019), Procedimento A528.

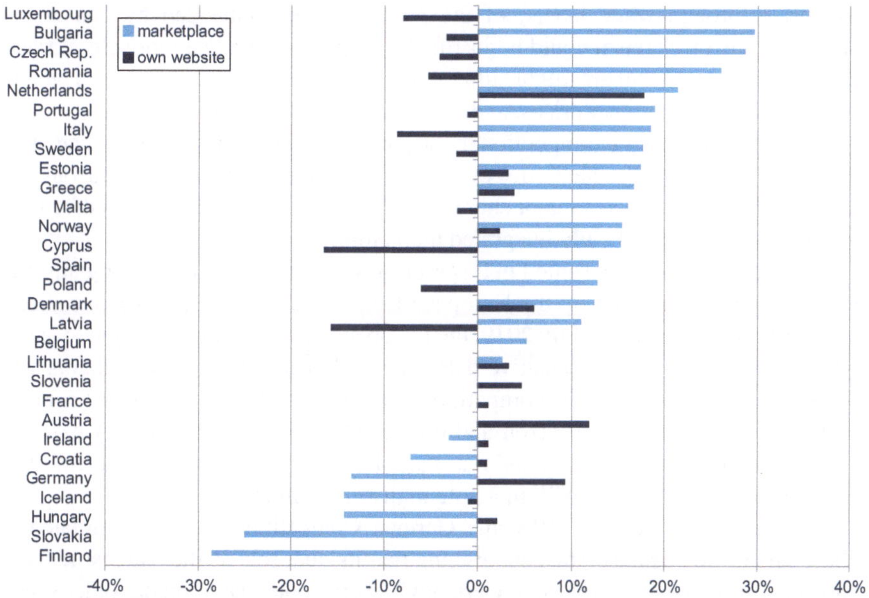

Source: Eurostat.

Fig. 1 Change in the number of enterprises selling via a marketplace or their own website or app as a percentage of all enterprises with web sales between 2017 and 2018 (%). (Source: Eurostat)

platforms, under certain conditions and/or for certain retailers, is severely limited. This could be explained by the presence of network effects: online merchants may prefer to use the dominant marketplace, as that can attract the largest number of consumers.

As for marketplaces, these are faced with a large number of outside options (i.e., online merchants potentially interested in accessing their marketplace). This means that if the negotiations between a marketplace and a single online merchant are terminated, the marketplace can still negotiate deals with a large number of alternative merchants. With the exception of the larger online merchants that might have a certain degree of negotiating power, the terms and conditions imposed by the main online platforms seem to suggest that marketplaces face a highly atomized market of online merchants.

The discussion set out above would suggest that, under certain conditions, dominant marketplaces may be able to abuse the economic dependence of online merchants. If this were the case, the effects of such abuse would be that in the short-term, vertically integrated marketplaces would have the incentive to attract as many online merchants as possible to achieve higher revenues and, in light of the network effects, attract a large number of consumers (which in turn will encourage more online merchants to use the platform). However, once online merchants have been attracted to the marketplace, the latter could have the ability and incentive to use the data and information on third-party sellers' products to vertically integrate into the production (or resale through white labels) of the products most demanded by consumers. Although this mechanism could be justified by a pro-competitive rationale, it raises the concern that consumers might suffer due to the lower range of products available on the marketplace, higher prices, and lower service quality.[26] Similarly, this strategy could reduce the level of competition in the parcel delivery market and have negative repercussions on the sustainability of the USO provider (for the same reasons discussed in Sect. 2.1), once a major share of the products available on the platform are sold directly by the vertically integrated marketplace.

The theory of harm presented in this section seems in line with ongoing antitrust investigations carried out by the European Commission and a number of national competition authorities. In July 2019, the EC opened a formal investigation to assess whether Amazon's use of sensitive data from independent online merchants who sell on its marketplace affects competition, by analyzing both the standard contractual agreements between Amazon and online merchants (which allow Amazon to analyze and use online merchants' data) and how this data affects the selection of the winners of the "Buy Box"[27] in a potentially anticompetitive way.[28]

Similarly, in November 2018, the German Competition Authority initiated an abuse proceeding against Amazon, arguing that its dual role as the "largest retailer" and "largest online marketplace in Germany" has the potential to hinder other sellers on its platform.[29] In a similar way, in February 2019, the Austrian Federal Competition Authority has begun investigating whether Amazon is exploiting its market dominance in relation to other retailers that use its website as a marketplace.[30]

3 Are Traditional Competition Policy Tools Fit for Purpose?

At the time of writing this paper, it is unclear what the findings of the abovementioned antitrust inquiries will be. With that in mind, the paper considers whether any adjustments should be made to the traditional competition policy tools

[26] When dealing with large merchants, a vertically integrated marketplace may be a more effective bargaining partner than dedicated distribution networks and hence enhance consumer welfare. Moreover, if there were a monopoly both at the level of the marketplace and the online merchants, vertical integration would be welfare enhancing as it would prevent the so-called double marginalization. However, since in reality, a large number of online merchants are highly atomised, vertical integration might simply reduce competition at the level of online merchants through the foreclosure of competing online merchants by the dominant and vertically integrated marketplace.

[27] The "Buy Box" refers to the white box on the right side of the Amazon product detail page, which allows customers to add items from a specific online merchant directly into their shopping carts.

[28] European Commission (2019), "Antitrust: Commission opens investigation into possible anticompetitive conduct of Amazon – Press release," 17 July.

[29] Bundeskartellamt (2018), "Bundeskartellamt initiates abuse proceeding against Amazon".

[30] Austrian Federal Competition Authority (2019), "Austrian Federal Competition Authority initiates investigation proceedings against Amazon".

employed by competition authorities and practitioners to assess whether there is a breach of competition law.

While standard antitrust provisions continue to be relevant for many (if not most) of the competition theories of harm being raised, and so will be a case-by-case assessment of the effects of these alleged anticompetitive conduct, certain approaches may need updating or adapting to reflect the specificities of highly dynamic online markets.

3.1 *Defining the Relevant Market*

Typically, the first exercise carried out by competition authorities is to define the so-called relevant market. We note that its application to online markets and multi-sided markets has become quite controversial.[31] In particular, the use of the SSNIP test is complicated, for example, by the fact that price is not the only or main factor platforms compete on.

In addition, dynamic markets are typically characterized by a "leap frog" competition. As such, markets defined by considering only a snapshot of the market at the time when the inquiry is conducted can lead to a narrow market definition, with a possible risk of over-enforcement.

Given the difficulties of defining the relevant market by looking at consumer behavior, an alternative approach in cases relating to digital platforms such as marketplaces could be to focus, rather than on consumers, on the other side of the market and consider which platforms businesses and advertisers see as reasonable substitutes.[32] To date, this approach does not seem to have been considered by competition authorities.[33,34]

3.2 *Assessing Market Power*

Assessing market power in digital industries can also be a complex exercise due to a combination of rapidly evolving consumer trends, the role of data, the presence of strong network effects, as well as the ability of a platform to leverage its market power from one market to where its degree of market power is lower.

---

[31] See Wismer and Rasek (2018) and Crémer et al. (2019).

[32] Ibid.

[33] See Commission Decision of 27.6.2017 relating to proceedings under Article 102 of the Treaty on the

Functioning of the European Union and Article 54 of the Agreement on the European Economic Area (Case

AT.39740 Google Search (Shopping)).

[34] AGCM (2019), Procedimento A528.

In order to take into account the rapidly evolving consumer trends, a dynamic assessment of market shares, as well as other relevant variables, such as consumer switching, multi-homing, intensity of commercial activities (e.g., new product launch, advertisement campaigns), prices, quality of service, and customer satisfaction, just to name a few, can be useful.

In addition, as noted earlier, the use of a bargaining framework for the assessment of market power would be crucial. A shift to a bargaining framework can be seen in recent and ongoing cases (e.g., the AGCM case previously mentioned).[35]

Finally, competition authorities should carefully consider the countervailing role of efficiencies by paying attention to both the short-term and the long-term effects of the anticompetitive practices of online platforms.

In this framework, in order to protect consumer welfare in digital markets in the long run, it may be necessary to ensure that other competitors can enter the market without being acquired by incumbents during their start-up phase. The role of competitors in protecting the competitive process and the interests of consumers has been recognized also by the European Court of Justice with respect to Art. 102 TFUE.[36]

3.3 *Assessing the Use of Data*

Competition authorities should fully recognize that access to data is a key input in the matching processes offered by marketplaces to provide benefits to consumers. Partially, competition authorities are already recognizing the crucial role of data in relation to e-commerce marketplaces (e.g., the AGCM in its case against Amazon).[37]

However, as underlined by Oxera (2018a), a more complete framework of the impact of data on competition should consider the extent to which different firms are able to access similar data. This framework should recognize that there are two dimensions to consider when determining whether—and the extent to which—data can provide market power to a firm: (i) the cost of acquiring the data and (ii) the rate at which the value of data depreciates.[38] Concurrently with the analysis of the market power given by the ownership of data, it is also important to place appropriate weight on factors like network effects, which in the context of online platforms are capable of creating entry barriers and/or market tipping (as recognized by the AGCM).

---

[35] Ibid.

[36] European Commission (1975), Case C-6/72 Europemballage Corporation and Continental Can Company v Commission [1975] ECR I-00495.

[37] AGCM (2019), Procedimento A528.

[38] Data that is cheap to obtain and that does not erode quickly in value is likely to be easily acquired by many firms, suggesting that they can compete effectively; meanwhile, data that does not erode quickly in value, but is costly to obtain, may enable a longer-term advantage in a specific data segment.

4 Is ex Ante Regulation Better Placed?

In this section, we briefly consider some of the types of regulatory interventions that have been discussed in the competition and regulatory arena thus far in relation to marketplaces.

In light of the challenges of antitrust tools in the context of the analysis of marketplaces discussed in Sect. 3 and the need to minimize the risk of over or under-enforcement, it is reasonable to ask whether competition policy in general is indeed the only tool to ensure a level playing field and maximize consumer welfare in the medium to long term.

Depending on the specific context, the implementation of ex ante regulatory remedies may be a complementary policy option, which, without excluding the need for competition policy interventions, may be more suitable to deal with some of the issues generated by the development of e-commerce, in particular to (i) ensure that the evolving needs and preferences of consumers are met; (ii) solve any existing market failures or prevent the onset of new ones; and (iii) promote a level playing field for economic agents active in the e-commerce ecosystem and avoid "social dumping."[39]

When comparing ex ante regulation with ex post antitrust intervention, one would need to carefully account for the intrinsic costs that the former might generate. Remedies should be proportionate to the issues identified and based on a thorough ex ante assessment of the costs and benefits that each remedy would bring about.[40]

Also, the application of ex ante remedies should be linked to the existence or risk of one of the theories of harm discussed in Sects. 2.1 and 2.2 and thus ensure a level playing field in the market, with regard to (*i*) postal operators and express couriers (especially the possibility that cream skimming practices hinder the sustainability of the USO provider and the provision of e-commerce services in less profitable, rural areas) and (*ii*) online merchants (especially in relation to any possible contractual imbalances imposed and the alleged anticompetitive use of data by a dominant marketplace).

The following possible remedies affecting the postal sector could help address some of the potential concerns identified above.

Reconsider the perimeter of the universal service obligation to encompass certain parcel delivery services typical of the e-commerce. This remedy would ensure that all consumers—including those who live in less profitable areas—have access to e-commerce parcel delivery services at reasonable prices and with minimum delivery standards, notwithstanding the cream skimming strategy followed by other

[39] The notion of social dumping refers to the practice whereby an employer uses cheaper labor compared to what is usually available and employed in a given sector. A company engaging in social dumping typically aims at gaining an economic advantage over competitors using more expensive labour.

[40] Oxera (2018b).

parcel delivery service providers, including vertically integrated marketplaces. In Italy, for example, a recently adopted law goes in this direction, providing that from 2020 the USO may also include "the activities of collection, transport, sorting and distribution of postal items up to 5 kg."[41] This remedy would be in line with the declining trend of traditional mail and consistent with the EU Postal Services Directive, which provides that[42]:

> Each Member State shall take steps to ensure that universal service provision meets the following requirements [...] — it shall evolve in response to the technical, economic and social environment and to the needs of users.

Activate, where available, the compensation fund to cover the share of the net cost of the universal service obligation that is not covered with State resources One of the objectives of the compensation fund is to reduce the risk of distortions to competition possibly arising when only one operator in the market is charged with the financing of the USO. It might be argued that providers of parcel delivery services that carry out B2C deliveries, including the delivery arms of vertically integrated marketplaces, should participate in the financing of the compensation fund. This could help to prevent the negative effects potentially arising from the cream skimming practices of vertically integrated marketplaces, which would relegate the USO provider to the less profitable rural areas/services.

Ensure that vertically integrated marketplaces comply with the regulatory and legal obligations of postal operators (e.g., employment terms and conditions) Views from the industry suggest that this remedy would allow the achievement of two fundamental objectives: (*i*) ensuring a level playing field for B2C parcel delivery service providers and limit "social dumping" by vertically integrated marketplaces, alternative postal operators, and express couriers and (*ii*) limiting the use of anticompetitive bundling strategies driven by the fact that dominant and vertically integrated marketplaces could instrumentally use the absence of regulatory obligations in order to achieve levels of efficiency artificially higher than those of competing B2C parcel delivery service providers.

As for the possible remedies affecting marketplaces, it must be acknowledged that significant steps ahead have recently been made at the European level in a number of areas. These include:

The need to regulate the contractual conditions imposed by marketplaces to online merchants[43] To avoid the risk of marketplaces abusing any economic dependence of online merchants, it could be necessary to consider regulating the terms and conditions imposed by marketplaces to online merchants. Since

[41] Legge 27 dicembre 2017, n. 205, art. 1(462).

[42] Directive 2008/6/EC.

[43] An example is that of the remedies imposed the Competition Commission in the UK in the context of the market investigation conducted in the supermarket sector. Competition Commission (2008), "The supply of groceries in the UK market investigation – Final Report".

marketplaces reduce transaction costs for consumers, especially in highly atomized markets such as that of online merchants, the centralized bargaining mechanism typical of marketplaces should not be discouraged. However, in order to ensure that online merchants have the possibility of entering into contracts that truly give them a fair access to marketplaces, terms, and conditions offered by marketplaces could include general opt-out clauses. The European Parliament and the Council have recently reached an agreement on the proposed regulation on promoting fairness and transparency for business users of online intermediation services, although the regulation has not entered into force yet at the time of writing.[44] Before considering whether further intervention is necessary, it will still need to be seen whether the regulation will be sufficient to achieve its objectives.

The need to regulate how data on online merchants' metrics is used by online platforms The abovementioned EU regulation on fairness and transparency encompasses specific provisions that aim to address also the possibility that the dual role of vertically integrated marketplaces (both as aggregators of products marketed by third parties and as resellers of in-house products) could encourage a dominant marketplace to give less visibility to products of third-party online merchants to limit cannibalization[45] of its own in-house products (as discussed earlier also in relation to the EC, German, and Austrian antitrust investigations).

5 Conclusions

B2C e-commerce has shown considerable growth, and, in most European countries, online merchants, especially SMEs, are increasingly relying on online marketplaces.

National and supranational competition authorities in Europe are currently looking into the possible anticompetitive practices of large marketplaces. At the time of writing, these investigations are still ongoing. As such, it is premature to reach a conclusion as to whether and how competition authorities will find an abuse. Nevertheless, many academics and practitioners have started to question the effectiveness of standard competition policy tools, calling for changes and, in parallel, for more regulatory intervention.

We believe that while standard antitrust provisions continue to be relevant for many (if not most) of the competition theories of harm being raised, and so will be a case-by-case assessment of the effects of these alleged anticompetitive conducts, certain approaches may need some updating or adapting to reflect the specificities of highly dynamic online markets.

[44] Regulation (EU) 2019/1150 of the European Parliament and of the Council of 20 June 2019 on promoting fairness and transparency for business users of online intermediation services.

[45] Cannibalisation refers to a reduction in volumes, revenues, or market shares of one product as a result of the introduction of a new product by the same company.

At the same time, we acknowledged that significant ex ante regulatory steps have been taken to alleviate some of the concerns currently explored by competition authorities. The recent EU regulation on promoting fairness and transparency for business users of online intermediation services seems to be a valid example, although it remains to be seen how effective it will be.

Nevertheless, there remain a number of areas where further ad hoc regulatory intervention might be necessary. However, if further remedies are deemed necessary, it is important to steer away from a "one-size-fits-all" approach. Regulatory intervention should be carefully assessed through an evidence-based evaluation of the costs and benefits it would entail to ensure it can be expected to unambiguously improve consumer outcomes. Policymakers should also avoid adopting a one-size-fits-all approach, unable to distinguish between different digital platforms, which could limit many of the benefits that such companies offer.

References

AGCM. (2019). *Procedimento A528.*

Borsenberger, C. (2015). The concentration phenomenon in e-commerce. In M. A. Crew & T. J. Brennan (Eds.), *Postal and delivery innovation in the digital economy*. Cheltenham: Edward Elgar.

Borsenberger C., Cremer H., Joram D., & Lozachmeur, J. M. (2016). *Pricing of delivery services and the emergence of marketplace platforms*, Working Paper TSE 686, August, Toulouse School of Economics.

Borsenberger, C., Cremer, H., Joram, D., & Lozachmeur, J. M. (2019). Vertical integration in the E-commerce sector. In P. Parcu, T. Brennan, & V. Glass (Eds.), *New business and regulatory strategies in the postal sector*. Cham: Topics in Regulatory Economics and Policy, Springer.

Bougette, P., Budzinski, O., & Marty, F.M. (2018). *Exploitative abuse and abuse of economic dependence: What can we learn from the industrial organization approach?*, Ilmenau Economics Discussion Papers, No. 119.

Brynjolfsson, E., & Smith, M. D. (2000). Frictionless commerce? A comparison of internet and conventional retailers. *Management Science, 46*(4), 563–585.

Competition and Markets Authority (2015). *Written evidence sent to the House of Lords in the context of the EU Internal Market Sub-Committee inquiry into online platforms in the EU Digital Single Market.* http://data.parliament.uk/writtenevidence/committeeevidence.svc/evidencedocument/eu-internal-market-subcommittee/online-platforms-and-the-eu-digital-singlemarket/written/23391.html

Crémer, J., de Montjoye, Y.-A., & Schweitzer, H. (2019). *Competition policy for the digital era', European Commission*. Luxembourg: Publications Office of the European Union.

European Commission. (2017). *Report from the Commission to the Council and the European Parliament*. Final report on the sectoral survey on e-commerce.

European Parliament and European Union Council. (2019). *Regulation (EU) 2019/1150 of the European Parliament and of the Council of 20 June 2019 on promoting fairness and transparency for business users of online intermediation services.* 20 June. https://ec.europa.eu/competition/antitrust/sector_inquiry_final_report_it.pdf

Eurostat. (2016). *SMEs annual enterprises statistics by size and class (distributive trade).*

Evans, D. S., & Schmalensee, R. (2014). The Antitrust analysis of multi-sided platform businesses. In R. Blair & D. Sokol (Eds.), *Oxford handbook on international antitrust economics*. New York: Oxford University Press.

Niels, G., Jenkins, H., & Kavanagh, J. (2016). *Economics for competition lawyers* (2nd ed.). Oxford: Oxford University Press.

Oxera (2015a). *Benefits of online platforms, prepared for Google, October.* https://www.oxera.com/wp-content/uploads/2018/07/The-benefits-of-online-platforms-main-findings-October-2015.pdf.pdf

Oxera (2015b). *The Cloud, or a silver lining? Differentiated pricing in online markets, Agenda, May.* https://www.oxera.com/agenda/the-cloud-or-a-silver-lining-differentiated-pricing-in-online-markets/

Oxera (2018a). *Data in digital markets: Prepared for the European Commission, Agenda, September.* https://www.oxera.com/wp-content/uploads/2018/10/Data-in-digital-markets.pdf

Oxera (2018b). *It's what you know about who you know: Market power in digital platforms, Agenda, December.* https://www.oxera.com/agenda/its-what-you-know-about-who-you-know-market-power-in-digital-platforms/

Politecnico di Milano e osservatori.net. (2018). *eCommerce B2c in Italia: aumenta il mercato, ma cresce il valore?* https://www.osservatori.net/it_it/osservatori/comunicati-stampa/ecommerce-b2c-crescita-mercato-2018

Raco, M. (2018). *The reassessment of the postal service regulation.* A view on e-commerce and the online platforms role, paper presented at the 26th Conference on Postal and Delivery Economics, Split.

Scott Morton, F., Zettelmeyer, F., & Silva-Risso, J. (2001). Internet car retailing. *Journal of Industrial Economics, 49*(4), 501–519.

Statista (2018). *Leading online marketplace websites in the United States as of 4th quarter 2018, based on share of visits.* Database.

Wismer, S., & Rasek, A. (2018). Market definition in multi-sided markets, pp. 55–68 in OECD (2018) *Rethinking antitrust tools for multi-sided platforms.* http://www.oecd.org/competition/rethinking-antitrust-toolsfor-multi-sided-platforms.htm

“Gravity” and the Packaging of B2C Cross-Border Ecommerce

Tim Walsh

1 Introduction

World trade in physical goods increased 7.7%, from \$18.1 to \$19.5 trillion between 2012 and 2018. Cross-border business-to-consumer (B2C) ecommerce trade stands at an estimated \$500 bn and grew by 224% in volume over the same period, the fastest-growing segment in world trade. The individualization of trade through ecommerce promises increased consumer welfare through greater choice, better prices, and enhanced efficiency. However, the packaging of trade in an estimated 2.87 billion annually of unique, small, lightweight, and low-value packets, arriving one-by-one, is testing inbound sorting and delivery networks and challenging extant logistic and trade rules designed for a previous, less connected age of traditional trade flows.

An enduring finding in the international economics literature is that bilateral trade flows are subject to “gravity”; a country trades more with large and nearby countries than with those that are small and at a distance (Tinbergen 1962). Yet established patterns of cross-border ecommerce suggest that the sale of online physical goods may not be subject to “gravity” in the way that the standard model would suggest. China, in particular, is a major source of cross-border ecommerce volumes. There is a concern that its dominance might reflect price and policy distortions that weaken the distance deterrent and cause trade distorting, rather than trade-creating, bilateral flows (Navarro 2019).[1]

[1] Viner (1950) was first to distinguish between trade creation and trade diversion. Trade creation refers to trade between two countries based on comparative advantage determined by factor endowments, technology, and other genuine cost advantages. Trade diversion is exchange based on distortion such that flows from least-cost production countries are displaced by trade from higher-cost countries. Trade creation increases net global trade through welfare-promoting, optimal resource allocation between trading pairs.

T. Walsh (✉)
Independent Postal and Ecommerce Consultant, London, UK

P. L. Parcu et al. (eds.), *The Changing Postal Environment*, Topics in Regulatory Economics and Policy, https://doi.org/10.1007/978-3-030-34532-7_14

This chapter reviews trade-related policy aspects that might explain patterns of cross-border ecommerce. The next section examines the fundamentals of cross-border ecommerce, compared to the standard trade model. Section 3 reviews economists' gravity model and explores the geography of flows. Section 4 considers the role of illicit trade through small packets, while Sects. 5 and 6 review tax aspects of ecommerce. Section 7 discusses logistic-related issues, including terminal dues (TDs), as explanations for the apparent suspension of "gravity." Sect. 8 concludes the chapter.

2 The Fundamentals of Cross-Border Ecommerce Trade

Cross-border B2C ecommerce can be defined as the use of the internet by businesses to sell goods across national borders to consumers using digital platforms and physical networks. Access to supply-side platforms (marketplaces, retailers, and brands) and demand-side integrators (such as Facebook and Amazon Prime) supported by transaction enablers (payment solutions, software specialists, and delivery companies) integrates digital and physical components of a transaction in cross-border B2C sales.

Table 1 provides an estimate (Apex Insight 2019) that total cross-border ecommerce grew to 2.87 billion items between 2012 and 2018, a rise of 224%. China's outbound volumes increased even more, 430% to over 1 billion items, increasing its share of global outbound volumes from 22.9% to 37.5% over the period.

The top four global marketplaces (Amazon, Alibaba, eBay, and Wish) accounted for 63% of B2C cross-border ecommerce items. Such packets are typically small and lightweight, with 80% arriving without having paid taxes or duties (delivery-duty-unpaid). Eighty-four percent of items are below 2 kg, and 50% weigh less than 500 g. Average order values are also low. Eighteen percent of items are

Table 1 Cross-border ecommerce, 2012 and 2018 million parcels

	2012	2018	Percentage change
Cross-border (outbound)			
China	203	1076	430
Rest of the world	683	1793	162
Global cross-border total	**886**	**2870**	**224**
Total domestic and cross-border			
China	3411	36,939	983
Rest of the world	7946	17,050	115
Global total	**11,357**	**53,988**	**375**

Source: Estimates based on Apex Insight, 2019
Notes: Based on data for the 16 largest countries, covering about 88% of all volumes
Smaller countries estimated based on their global share of online retail, population, and/or GDP
Parcel upper weight limit varies by carrier

valued below €9, and 40% are valued at less than €24 (IPC 2019). The quantities, growth, and the characteristics of these singular item flows challenge the capacities of border authorities compared to conventional, high-value, bulk commercial trade streams.

Two-sided platforms facilitate cross-border exchange of a vast assortment of goods from digitized merchant catalogues, by aggregating and organizing information from beyond national frontiers. Search, transaction, and contract enforcement costs, which otherwise typically grow as distance increases, are radically reduced. Web shops represent global showrooms deploying user data and intangible marketing assets (such as brand, design rights, intellectual property, and customer relationships) to create value. In GATS terminology, the provision of services shifts from the commercial presence of a locally established affiliate (Mode 3) to cross-border supply through telecommunications and postal services (Mode 1).

In this way, online retailers with only a limited physical presence in consumption jurisdictions can develop a large customer base and know more about their needs, willingness to pay, and preferences than a physical, local business in situ. The fear, however, is that digital trading can more easily displace revenues toward low corporation tax centers than conventional trade. Ecommerce certainly fosters the ability to build cross-jurisdictional economic scale without physical mass in users' countries, breaking the link between the location in which value is created and where the profits are taxed.

While trade through individual consumers, acting as the principal importing agents, has the potential to promote economic welfare, the fragmentation of trade into millions of small packets raises "health, safety and security challenges that governments need to address" (OECD 2018, 110). New classes of sellers and buyers (including occasional and seasonal shippers and shoppers) are empowered. This brings risks associated with the limited knowledge of diverse exporters and multiple shipments to many individual consignee importers.

These risks are increased due to the fluid and diverse way ecommerce consignments are fulfilled, distributed, and delivered. B2C cross-border ecommerce can be conducted through posts' internationally brokered networks, including postal customs clearance and UPU documentation. B2C exchange might also take place through integrated, end-to-end networks of the kind provided by express carriers with cargo clearance and commercial airway bills. Alternatively, a consolidator model involves commercial customs clearance through the EU's low-value bulk import schemes (in the USA through Section 321 clearance) which allows traders to declare, in simplified format, multiple low-value consignments as a single customs import entry with a reduced data set while remaining below tax and duty de minimis thresholds. Finally, based on predictive analytics, bonded warehouse operations in destination markets hold high-demand stock for release and delivery on order.

Alternative distribution models support a range of services for reliability, price, and value-added features to cater for both the low-value and higher average order value segments of the market. However, discontinuity in regulatory burdens, and therefore trade costs between the various operational models, can create an incentive for opportunistic behavior and a challenge for market surveillance authorities.

3 Ecommerce and the Gravity Effect

The gravity equation is "the workhorse model" to explain international trade flows (Möhlmann et al. 2010, 226). Inspired by Newtonian physics in which gravitational forces between two bodies depend on their mass and distance, the gravity model relates bilateral trade flows to the GDP levels of the countries and their distance, including regulatory, cultural, and legal differences as well as propinquity. Despite the long-term decline in transport and communication costs, the impact of distance on the geography of traditional trade remains significant.[2]

Consumer data show that cross-border ecommerce interactions are fostered by "the positive effect of adjacency" (Head and Mayer 2010, 190) with bilateral flows shaped by large and geographically close clusters of countries. In Belgium, 49% of ecommerce purchases are from France, in Ireland, 58% of purchases are from UK websites, and in Austria 68% of purchases are from Germany (WIK-Consult 2019). Outside Europe, too, the gravitational pull of adjacency is present. For example, 53% of Canadians' most recent purchase come from the USA (IPC 2019).

China, however, is a significant source country for virtually all EU states. In Hungary, as many as 67% of B2C purchases are from China (compared, based on 2018 IMF trade statistics, to just 5.3% of Hungary's total imports coming from China). In the UK, Europe's largest ecommerce market, fully one-third of purchases are from China, far higher than might be predicted with a "gravity" view of the world (and three times greater than overall UK imports from China at 11.7%). For Germany, too, whereas 41% of ecommerce purchases are from China (WIK-Consult 2019), just 7% of its total imports are from China. IPC data confirm China's dominance, with, for example, 57% of US cross-border purchases coming from China (compared to 29.3% of total US imports). Overall, China's share of total ecommerce export volumes has risen from 26% to 36% between 2016 and 2018, the same share as the next three countries, Germany, the UK, and the USA, combined (IPC 2019).

We would expect that distance had a smaller effect on the online trade due to lower search costs,[3] the erosion of "intangible barriers to trade" (laws, language, and culture), and reduction in the mental distance between exporters and importers (Möhlmann et al. 2010, 226), for example, through website localization and local payment options. To the extent, too, that distance proxies for taste, geography might shrink as consumer tastes converge, particularly for standard products with a higher elasticity of substitution between imported and domestic goods (Blum and Goldfarb 2006, 385). China's growing cross-border dominance might additionally

---

[2] Krugman and Obstfeld (2006) found a strong negative effect of distance on trade in physical goods: each 1% increase in distance between two countries is associated with a fall of between 0.7% and 1.0% in trade.

[3] One study, comparing the distance effect on eBay and for total trade for 40 product categories across 61 counties between 2004 and 2009, found that the coefficient of distance is on average 65% smaller on eBay than offline. This difference is explained in most part by a reduction in search costs and reduced information frictions due to eBay's consumer ratings (Lendle et al. 2016).

be understood by the innovation and strength of its domestic ecommerce sector, including the Chinese government's support for the industry to internationalize, for example, through its Belt and Road Initiative, such that single-piece Chinese ecommerce packets now arrive in Europe consolidated in containers on trains.

However, the gravity model explains bilateral trade flows not just in relation to GDP but also by policies and prices which affect exchange costs and frictions. Thus, an explanation for China's seemingly disproportionate share of total cross-border ecommerce should include institutional arrangements such as the scope for illicit trade in small packets, differential application of fiscal and non-fiscal rules at borders, and differences in delivery costs. Where costs are not reflected in ecommerce exchange between bilateral pairs, "gravity" is likely to be suspended, resulting in trade diversion where product origin shifts from a domestic producer, whose resource costs are otherwise lower, to an overseas producer whose costs are higher.

4 Illicit Trade in Small Packets

Trade based on Ricardian comparative advantage requires clear rules and effective enforcement such that illicit flows are constrained. Illicit flows violate the laws of exporting or importing countries, by infringing trademarks, patents, and design rights or by breaching product safety rules and other prohibitions. Illicit merchandise represents "free-riding" on the intellectual property rights of others and undermines trade creation based on innovation, creativity, and design. Such flows unfairly disadvantage legitimate domestic and overseas retailers, threaten consumers' health and safety, and reduce domestic tax revenues. In so doing, the weight of "gravity" is reduced, and trade diversion is promoted.

Counterfeit and pirated goods are increasing in international trade, rising from 2.5% to 3.3% of world trade between 2013 and 2016, the main cause of which is corruption and failure to enforce in provenance countries (OECD 2018). Most counterfeits are traded in bulk imports, with container ships dominating, 56%; compared to mail, 11%; and express, 8% (OECD/EUIPO 2019:2).

That said, ecommerce can swell illicit flows. On the demand side, availability and low shipping fees drive greater consumer complicity, with 7% of online shoppers having bought counterfeit goods, rising to 15% among 15–24 year olds. On the supply-side, trading online affords greater scope for anonymity and allows easy access 24/7 to multiple market. China is the largest source country for illicit goods including the key ecommerce categories of apparel, electronics, and cosmetics as well as synthetic drugs, such as fentanyl, whose primary mode of shipment is through postal and express streams often in quantities below 1 kg (OECD 2018).[4]

[4] China is acting against illicit trade in ecommerce. Article 42 of China's new Ecommerce Law, January 2019, requires platforms to take all necessary measures against IP violation, with fines of up to 500,000 RMB.

The wave of anonymous, small packets poses a particular challenge for postal flows, where the amount of information on items is limited and often not received before arrival. This lack of data makes it difficult to assess, target, and interdict "on a granular scale" (OECD 2018, 110) with the risk that illicit, trade-diverting ecommerce packets will provoke a policy reaction that impedes licit, trade-creating flows.

Hitherto, while third-party (eBay, Alibaba, Etsy, and Rakuten) and vertically integrated marketplaces (Amazon) allow users to transact, unless they have taken title of the goods as the merchant of record, it is the suppliers of merchandise who retain control of the goods as well as of any liabilities toward consumers, for example, as in respect of product safety and VAT. Such is the growth in small packet volumes, however, that border agencies are beginning to hold marketplaces and carriers responsible for import liabilities, rather than the seller or the consumer as the merchant of record, because authorities neither have the jurisdiction to enforce against overseas sellers nor the resources to apply rules on millions of individual buyers.

Additionally, many jurisdictions are requiring electronic data ahead of the goods' arrival, including country of origin and item data on ecommerce flows. Advanced security data allows authorities to "push the border out" (OECD 2018, 95) and is an important factor in reducing the volume of illicit shipments.[5] Data sharing across the value chain may simultaneously enhance facilitation, with packets from low-risk trusted traders handled speedily through "green lanes" while customs dedicate resource to more challenging, trade diverted shipments. Nonetheless, additional costs from new liabilities and data requirements will impact the volume and character of flows and assist in bearing down on distortions which undermine the efficiency of trade.

5 Physical Presence and Taxation

Under Article 7 of the OECD Model Tax Convention, countries may tax the profits from commercial activity carried out within its borders by a foreign entity if the latter has a substantial physical presence. This permanent establishment test provides not only clear rules for ascertaining the tax due from companies operating overseas but also an equitable basis for sharing the taxation benefits arising from cross-border commerce. The reach of ecommerce, however, allows firms to be involved in the economic activity of multiple nations without any physical presence. The basis for international profits taxation is thus increasingly out of touch with modern commerce. The physical presence rule creates an increasingly artificial distinction

[5]Article 17.2.16 of the UPU's Regulations and the EU's Union Customs Code, 952/2013, obliges all posts to provide electronic advance data on all small packets containing goods by 1 January 2021.Since 1 January 2019, the USA's STOP Act requires that advanced electronic security data is provided on 100% of inbound items by 31 December 2020. China's 2019 Ecommerce Act also incentivizes the provision of item-level advance data.

between traders and results in profits base erosion which the OECD aims to address by 2020. Divergent and less onerous direct tax treatment of remote sellers compared to local traders with physical presence distorts the geography of ecommerce.

The European concept of permanent establishment is comparable to the US physical nexus test, whereby a US state is entitled to impose state and local sales taxes on an enterprise of another US state, if that business maintains a substantial physical presence within the state in which it trades. Before the advent of ecommerce, the US Supreme Court had determined (in 1967 and in 1992) that the "mere shipment" of catalogue ordered goods did not satisfy the physical presence requirement" (South Dakota v Wayfair Inc., 585 U.S. ___, 138 S. Ct. 2080 (2018), 1, hereafter Wayfair).

However, in its 2018 Wayfair decision, the US Supreme Court overturned the need for a physical presence as the basis for out-of-state sellers to collect and remit sales tax. The Court ruled that "it is an inescapable fact" of the modern economy that business can be transacted without any physical presence. Besides, the majority opined that a pure-play online retailer might be said to have a physical presence by virtue of its customers' computers, cookies saved to their hard drives, or apps on their mobile devices and that a business with "substantial virtual connections" did not need to be present in the traditional sense of that term (South Dakota v Wayfair Inc 2018, 15).

The potential for indirect tax to reduce market distortions ran through the Supreme Court's judgment. It argued that to treat a business with a small warehouse within a state differently to an out-of-state company with a pervasive online presence would be "arbitrary," "anachronistic," and "unfair and unjust" that it simply made "no sense" to create a tax shelter for businesses that limit their physical presence and permit the "tax-free solicitation of customers" (South Dakota v Wayfair Inc 2018, 14–17. The Court implicitly recognized that the incidence of tax will fall in part at least on consumers and that this is likely to restrain growth of domestic and cross-border ecommerce.[6]

6 Customs and De Minimis

While Wayfair did not explicitly refer to inbound cross-border items, international sellers who are the merchant-of-record and whose volumes reach state threshold levels have become liable to collect and remit US state and municipal taxes, effectively circumventing the USA's federal $800 de minimis introduced as a facilitation measure in 2016. Outside the USA, too, a growing number of countries are seeking to collect indirect taxes on what the New Zealand legislation refers to as

[6] Drawing on US household data and matching these to local sales tax rates, one study found that "internet sales are highly sensitive to local taxation" and that a 10% increase in the after-tax price of a good was likely to induce a 20–40% decrease in sales from web-based firms (Goolsbee 2000).

"distantly taxable goods" contained within all small packets through the removal of de minimis tax exemptions (New Zealand 2018, Section 4b).[7]

The removal of low-value de minimis exemptions may reflect a shift in border priorities from trade facilitation to revenue collection, fair trade, and control. When de minimis levels were introduced, there were few individual purchases of low-value imported goods. Compliance and administrative costs involved in taxing such imports outweighed tax revenues collected. However, the growth in cross-border ecommerce has meant that the revenues foregone are increasingly significant and domestic businesses are disadvantaged compared with offshore firms whose prices exclude indirect taxes. The EU, for example, estimated that the foregone VAT on inbound ecommerce packets below its de minimis level (€22), plus non-compliance and fraud (mis-declaration of goods, including items presented as consumer-to-consumer "gifts," undervaluation, and split entries) amounted to a loss of €4.2 billion annually (Deloitte 2016, 21).

One result of this realignment of border priorities is a fundamental change in liabilities which has hitherto underpinned ecommerce sales. For example, since July 2018, it is mandatory for offshore sellers to Australia to register with the tax authorities. They are deemed for GST purposes to be the supplier of goods (merchant of record) sold to Australian consumers. In the EU, while not compulsory, sellers are encouraged to register with the EU's import one-stop-shop and will be liable to collect VAT at the point of sale and remit these funds to destination member states without any de minimis exemptions. VAT liability will also apply on the sale of goods stored by non-EU companies in EU-based fulfillment centers, even if payments are processed from an address outside the EU. This is based on the observation that Chinese warehouses in the UK were fulfilling goods "but processing payments from addresses outside the UK," thus avoiding VAT and gaining competitive advantage (EY 2015, 79).

Where small packets arrive in the EU with VAT unpaid, the tax will be collected from consumers by the customs declarant, typically the postal operator, courier, or customs agent. Copenhagen Economics estimated that this VAT fallback liability would cause "major and disproportionate costs" for declarants, estimated at between €0.7 and €1.9 bn (2017, 1). To avoid such additional costs ultimately flowing to buyers, platforms selling into the EU are likely to be incentivized to remove the option of a delivery duty unpaid service from their websites.[8]

---

[7] The GST Offshore Supplier Registration Bill (2018) requires offshore websites with annual sales to New Zealanders above NZ$60,000 to register and collect GST (15%) on imported goods valued up to NZ$1000 from 1 October 2019. The explicit goal is to improve and ensure competitive neutrality for domestic retailers. Many countries are introducing similar schemes including Sweden (March 2018), Australia (July 2018), Switzerland (January 2019), and the EU (January 2021).

[8] The costs of policing the border are becoming visible in other ways. The South Africa Post Office charges recipients 25 Rand on each inbound packet, revenue which they share with customs; and Australia's Home Affairs department are considering an AUS $5–7 tax on inbound low-value packets to cover the costs of biosecurity screening. Other external costs such as relating to carbon emissions, packaging, and the environment may also not be reflected in prices, especially the pricing of ecommerce returns.

For example, under pressure from domestic retailers, PostNord Sweden was required to collect VAT (25%) and duties on inbound packets with a value below €150 from 1 March 2018. To defray collection costs, a fee of up to 125 SEK (≈ €12.5) was added. As a consequence, inbound shipments fell by 90%, from 150,000 to 15,000 per day, with much of this decline occurring in the low-value, trade-diverted segment. Volumes have begun to return, including through new delivery duty paid solutions offered by websites targeting Swedish consumers and by the rerouting of flows for free circulation clearance in neighboring EU states where VAT on low-value consignments is not yet a requirement. The application of VAT to outbound Jersey Post packets in 2012 saw a similar collapse in volumes from 60 to 5 million per annum, and early data from Australia suggests that the levying of GST (10%) from 1 July 2018 may have reduced inbound volumes in excess of 20% over prior year, with perhaps still higher reductions on low average order value packets.[9]

We might deduce from these changes that the individualization of trade, and pace of its growth, is changing the balance of border priorities in the USA, Europe, and elsewhere.[10] There is greater focus on revenue generation (and its fair distribution), security control, and the removal of competitive distortions that promote trade-diverting ecommerce. The move toward taxing the profits on digital sales of physical goods, the removal of de minimis indirect tax exemptions on low-value inbound consignments, and the externalization of other border costs will restore somewhat the force of "gravity" and the competitiveness of local, in-market sales over foreign ecommerce trade.

7 Terminal Dues

The seemingly weak pull of "gravity" in cross-border ecommerce may be further explained by small packet shipping rates. Distribution and delivery represent some 60% of total costs (excluding merchandise) and strongly affect B2C imports. The critical inbound delivery rate that posts pay each other for the delivery of cross-border packets below 2 kg is terminal dues (TDs), and these rates are set on a one-country, one-vote basis within the Universal Postal Union (UPU). While TD rates are only available to each national designated post, TDs are the reference rate against

---

[9] These negative volume impacts differ significantly from EY's review of price and import elasticities for typical ecommerce categories. EY concluded somewhat confusingly that the demand for ecommerce goods is "largely inelastic" but that data limitations meant that the impact of VAT on consumers' purchasing decisions could be "significant" (EY 2015, 111–112).

[10] Perhaps reflecting a valorization of trade facilitation over control and revenue collection, the USA increased its postal and express de minimis in 2016 from $200 to $800 (US Trade Facilitation and Trade Enforcement Act 2015). However, under the terms of the facilitation chapter of the 2019 US, Mexico, and Canadian Agreement, the USA reserved the right to impose a lower, "reciprocal amount" equal to Mexico and Canada's agreed threshold levels which, if exercised, would take the US de minimis threshold below the $200 amount that had existed prior to 2016 (Footnote 3 to Article 7.8 (1) (f) of the USMCA).

which bilateral and commercial rates are negotiated. They thus indirectly affect all inbound rates, even constraining prices that can be achieved for value-added elements (such as tracking) in the higher order value segments of the market.

TDs are based on a complex per item and per kg formula based on the capping of delivery costs to high-cost destinations and the protection of developing countries by cost floors below which their revenue cannot fall. The system includes separate rates payable by posts in industrialized (Group I), advanced developing (II), mid-level developing (III), and the least developed (Group IV) countries. As a result, TDs are not related to destination country domestic delivery costs and distort trade patterns. Campbell (2016, 313) commented that a structurally unreformed TD system represented "a signal failure in modern international trade policy."

Changes to the TDs system were introduced at the 2016 Istanbul Congress for the period 2018–2022, including the move of China to a higher-cost category (Group III) and annual, but differentiated, increases in caps rates across all countries, with China's Group III rates rising 13% per annum compared to least developed country increases of 2% per kg per annum. Higher supplementary terminal due rates were also established for the UPU's signature-on-delivery product, which some posts had been accessing for ecommerce packets in the absence of affordable, tracked UPU packet service. These reforms reduced the discount to equivalent domestic rates between many bilateral pairs and will have a volume impact, though such is the scale of cross-border ecommerce growth that net financial transfers between low cost and net exporter posts and high cost and net importers will continue to increase (Okholm et al. 2017, 85).

From a trade perspective, below cost inbound delivery prices weaken the distance deterrent and incentivize producers and consumers to move industrial country sales offshore. As a memorandum from the US President put it, TDs "distorts the flow of small packets around the world by incentivizing the shipping of goods from foreign countries that benefit from artificially low reimbursement rates" (US Presidential Memorandum 2018, 3). The USA thus declared that the United States Postal Service (USPS) would adopt self-declared inbound packets rates, at 100% of domestic rates for comparable services no later than 1 January 2020 and gave 1-year notice of withdrawal from the UPU in order to bring pressure to bear for structural reform (US White House 2018).

Whatever the outcome of TDs discussions among the world's posts, ecommerce delivery prices (inbound to the USA and, in consequence, to all other markets) will increase significantly. The USA may not be able to secure agreement for TD rates to be based on 100% of domestic tariffs, but a move toward 70% of domestic rates does have precedence in regional postal remuneration systems. Increased TDs will test the findings of existing postal gravity studies that suggest the absence of search costs alone explains the pattern of online ecommerce. The eBay transactional data study, for example, concluded that adding shipping costs to the model barely affects the distance coefficient on all country pairs and that therefore the "death of distance" on eBay flows is "most-likely not due to a reduction or different distribution of shipping costs" (Lendle et al. 2016, 418). Similar studies have found that the distance coefficients are "well below" the −0.9 average elasticity of distance, suggesting packets volumes were less sensitive to transport and related costs (Anson and Helble 2013, 42).

An alternative hypothesis might be that at such low rates for postal cross-border delivery, "gravity" and the impact of shipping costs on bilateral trade volumes are switched-off. While low online search costs, a rich assortment of products on Chinese marketplaces, convenience, and local payment solutions, will continue to support online cross-border shopping, higher delivery costs, in addition to direct and indirect taxes and controls at borders, is likely to increase gravity's power on such trade.

The basis of advantage, too, between cross-border operational models will change. Below-cost TDs may have incentivized UPU members to forge competitiveness on cost alone, rather than by though improved quality, reliability and service features. If the mix of cross-border volumes shifts from trade-distorted, low-value delivery-duty-unpaid packets to higher-value duty-paid items, improved network reliability, digital support for the physical flows, and greater integration between actors across the global value-chain will be necessary, both as a competitive differentiator and to address the needs of border authorities as they rebalance control with facilitation through advanced electronic security data.

TDs are only available to designated operators, not to other carriers, nor to posts' extraterritorial offices of exchange (ETOEs).[11] ETOEs are a significant part of the market, with some 150 facilities competing against national posts and other carriers in major outbound ecommerce delivery markets. While such competition supports efficiency and quality improvement in cross-border ecommerce, some ETOEs surreptitiously access favorable TD rates, rather than the inbound post's domestic delivery rates, thus amplifying distortions. There is evidence, too, that in "a growing number of cases" (Portugal 2019) commercial companies use "the postal indicia of group IV" posts for the remailing of items (New Zealand 2019). These practices intensify price-based competition from an industry weaned on below-cost TDs and distort flows toward imports from countries paying artificially low TDs.

Greater TD cost coverage will be consequential in terms of volume, geography, and networks. Progressively higher inbound delivery rates are likely to restrain growth rates witnessed over recent years with perhaps the low-value segment of the market disappearing entirely or shifting from a B2C postal model to bonded warehouse operations for popular stock categories in destination markets. Further changes toward more cost-reflective inbound rates will reduce trade distortions by changing online buying patterns, and the flow of packets between origin and destination pairs, to the benefit of domestic retailers and local fulfillment.

[11] An ETOE is defined as a commercial processing facility operated by, or in connection with, a postal operator on the territory of another (ecommerce origin) country. Under the UPU Convention, ETOE volumes cannot use UPU documentation nor access TDs.

8 Conclusion

Though still a relatively small proportion of total trade, huge flows of individualized, small, lightweight, low-value packets are transforming the fundamentals of commerce. Cross-border ecommerce increases the heterogeneity of traders and brings benefits to consumers worldwide. However, the packaging of trade for personal use on the scale and at the growth rates of recent years was never anticipated. While consistency with the gravity principle can be observed in bilateral pair flows between neighboring countries, China's share is far higher than the level that might be predicted by a "gravity" view of trade.

The rapid growth of digitally ordered, direct-to-consumer packets has raised concerns as to whether policy and border practices are properly aligned to the new trade realities. To the extent that the institutional environment for cross-border packets may not have sufficiently protected property rights, nor treated domestic and overseas merchants equitably in terms of indirect taxation, buying decisions would have been skewed in favor of the overseas rather than the domestic supplier. Equally, if the costs of cross-border ecommerce, such as external or delivery costs, are not properly reflected in prices, excessive demand for cross-border over local purchases will result, undermining the welfare benefits of trade.

As a result, there is a reordering of border authorities' priorities as between security and fiscal control, fair trade and trade facilitation, and a shift in the treatment third-party marketplaces and carriers in respect of importer-of-record liabilities. Reordered border priorities will not be without consequences for volume, value and product mix (delivery duty paid), bilateral pair flows, and the competitive basis of cross-border ecommerce operational models. The challenge for policymakers will be to design controls on trade-diverted flows while fostering legitimate, trade-creating, and welfare-enhancing volumes.

References

Anson, J., & Helble, M. (2013). A gravity model of international postal exchanges. In M. A. Crew & P. R. Kleindorfer (Eds.), *Reforming the postal sector in the face of electronic competition.* Cheltenham: Edward Elgar.

Apex-Insight. (2019). *Global parcels insight report, March, London.*

Blum, B. S., & Goldfarb, A. (2006). Does the Internet defy the law of gravity? *Journal of International Economics, 70*(2), 384–405, Elsevier.

Campbell, J. I. (2016). Quantifying the distortive effects of UPU terminal dues. In M. A. Crew & T. J. Brennan (Eds.), *The future of the postal sector in a digital worlds*. Heidelberg: Springer.

Copenhagen Economics. (2017). *Effects of removing the VAT De Minimis on ecommerce imports,* 11th October, Copenhagen.

Deloitte. (2016). VAT aspects of cross-border E-commerce, March, DG Taxation and Customs Union, Brussels.

EY. (2015). *Assessment of the application and impact of VAT exemption and importation of small consignments*, Report to the European Commission.

Goolsbee, A. (2000). In a world without borders: The impact of taxes on internet commerce. *Quarterly Journal of Economics, 115*(2), 561–576.
Head, K., & Mayer, T. (2010). Illusory border effects. In A. G. Van Bergeijk & S. Brakman (Eds.), *The gravity model of international trade*. Cambridge: Cambridge University Press.
IPC. (2019). *Cross-border E-commerce shopper survey, 2018, January, Brussels.*
Krugman, Paul R. and Maurice Obstfeld (2006), *International economics, Longman.*
Lendle, A., Olareaga, M., Schropp, S., & Venzina, P.-L. (2016). There goes gravity: eBay and the death of distance. *Economic Journal, 126*(591), 406–441.
Möhlmann, L. J., Ederveen, S., de Groot, H. L. F., & Linders, G.-J. M. (2010). Intangible barriers to international trade. In A. G. Van Bergeijk & S. Brakman (Eds.), *The gravity model of international trade*. Cambridge: CUP.
Navarro, P. (2019). *Trump has a plan to stop fake goods, Wall Street Journal, April 3rd.*
New Zealand. (2018). *Taxation (annual rates for 2019–20) GST offshore supplier registration and remedial matters bill, 114–3, December 2019.*
New Zealand. (2019). *UPU international bureau circular, 25 19 February.*
OECD. (2018). *Governance frameworks to counter illicit trade, March, Paris.*
OECD/EUIPO. (2019). *Trends in trade in counterfeit and pirated goods, Paris.*
Okholm, H. B., Basalisco, B., Gårdebrink, J., & Boive, A. M. (2017). An economic perspective on terminal dues. In M. Crew, P. L. Parcu, & T. J. Brennan (Eds.), *The changing postal and delivery sector*. Heidelberg: Springer.
Portugal. (2019). *UPU international bureau circular 14,* 4 February 2019.
South Dakota v Wayfair Inc. (2018). 585 U.S. _ No 17–494 2018, 15, June 21st.
The Taxation (Annual Rates for 2019–20, GST Offshore Supplier Registration, and Remedial Matters) Bill (2018), New Zeland
Tinbergen, J. (1962). *Shaping the world economy*. New York: The Twentieth Century Fund.
U.S. Presidential Memorandum. (2018). *Modernizing the monetary reimbursement model for the delivery of goods through the international postal system and enhancing the security and safety of international mail,* August 23, Washington DC.
U.S. Trade Facilitation and Trade Enforcement Act, (2015). U.S. Congress, Washington DC.
U.S. White House. (2018). *Statement from the press secretary,* October 17th, Washington DC.
Viner, J. (1950). *The custom union issue*. London: Stevens and Son.
WIK-Consult. (2019). Development of cross-border E-commerce through parcel delivery. In *A study for the European Commission*. Brussels: DG GROW.

Postal Traffic in Portugal: Applying Time Series Modeling

Carla Machado and Filipa Silva

1 Introduction

The postal sector is adapting to the Internet technology (IT) revolution. Short message service (SMS) or email competes with correspondences (e-substitution). On the other hand, the purchase of physical products over the Internet (e-commerce) affects positively the volume of parcels delivered, a phenomenon expected to grow, spurred in part by digital single market goals.[1] Because parcel growth is an e-commerce phenomenon, fixed broadband penetration appears more correlated with postal traffic than gross domestic product (GDP) (EGIDE et al. 2015).

This paper aims to present models that fit and forecast postal traffic and parcels postal traffic. The two are estimated and forecasted separately because of their different tendencies over the period of the analysis. The estimation methods used are ARIMA, ARIMAX, decomposition, and multiple linear regressions. The dataset used for estimations is quarterly traffic of postal mail in Portugal (domestic and outgoing international), beginning in the first quarter of 2005 (1Q2005) and ending in the second quarter of 2018 (2Q2018), from postal operators, collected by ANACOM.

After this introduction, Sect. 2 provides a literature review. Section 3 presents the Portuguese data considered and its sources, as well as the analysis of the postal traffic in Portugal, for both correspondences and parcels, and analysis of their drivers. Section 4 explores the methodological framework and compares the main results of

[1] https://ec.europa.eu/digital-single-market/en/new-eu-rules-e-commerce

ANACOM. The opinions expressed are those of the author and do not necessarily reflect the views of ANACOM.

C. Machado (✉) · F. Silva
ANACOM, Lisbon, Portugal
e-mail: carla.machado@anacom.pt

P. L. Parcu et al. (eds.), *The Changing Postal Environment*, Topics in Regulatory Economics and Policy, https://doi.org/10.1007/978-3-030-34532-7_15

the estimated models under different approaches. The best model is then applied to forecast the short-term evolution of correspondence and parcels traffic in Portugal. Conclusions are discussed in Sect. 5.

2 Literature Review

The postal sector is a pillar of socioeconomic development, and historically, according to UPU (2014) until the year 2000, letter-post volume per capita grew at a similar pace as GDP per capita in industrialized countries. However, after that year, there was a decoupling of the two trends: GDP per capita continued to grow, while the number of letters per capita declined noticeably.

In Portugal, EGIDE et al. (2015) mention that GDP lost its main power to explain postal traffic since 2005, although ANACOM (2011) refers that the main senders of postal traffic (big enterprises) remain very sensitive to the price of the postal services. With the development of IT, there was a decrease of the traditional letter mail volumes (because of e-substitution and changes in interpersonal communication) and an increase of parcels volumes, especially cross-borders (due to the adoption of e-commerce) – UPU (2019), Wik (2019), Copenhagen Economics (2018), and EGIDE et al. (2015), among others, all document this result.

EGIDE et al. (2015) explained that postal traffic in European countries was decreasing because of five main forces: economic growth,[2] population, digitalization, costs for the clients,[3] and legal provisions,[4] although digitalization, in general, is the main driver of the decline.

On the other hand, the authors mention that parcels traffic is increasing in every European country. UPU (2018) mentions economic growth, trade, and connectivity as the factors that mostly affect postal traffic – GDP and exports create demand for postal services, while connectivity (measured as the rate of Internet penetration) and digitization encourage the increase of e-commerce. However, Wik (2019) warns that available data on cross-border parcels are limited and underestimate the actual volumes, namely, because they do not consider small packets delivered through the letter-post stream.

Wik (2019) and ERGP (2019) also alert that there might be a problem in the definition of what is a postal service or a postal operator (for instance, what are the boundaries between postal and transport services), in addition to the fact that different countries have different definitions of postal services and operators.

---

[2] Namely, GDP.

[3] Increases of the costs have impact on the traffic volumes because these are the drivers for digitalization.

[4] This last, especially where e-government policies have been adopted, is the case in Portugal.

ERGP (2019) includes the environment impact of postal delivery (ecological footprint) and labor conditions in the drivers of the postal traffic (e.g., temporary employment, subcontracted workers, and the need for more flexible deliveries, at night, extra work during peak periods). In addition, they refer that the postal market is becoming more receiver-oriented, than sender-oriented, due to the increase of the power of postal receivers to influence the quality characteristics of the deliveries (for instance, requiring efficient track and trace).

3 Postal Traffic in Portugal

3.1 Data Source and Samples

In this article, the demand for postal services is described as outgoing international volumes of correspondences, and parcels, from the quarterly statistical indicators of ANACOM, the Portuguese postal regulator, collected from the postal service providers.[5]

The time span of the data is from 1Q2005 to 2Q2018. In 2012, the full competition regime was adopted on national territory, as well as of international services to or from national territory, due to the legal regime (Law no. 17/2012, of 26 April[6]) that governs the provision of postal services. That regime also changed some of the postal definitions, namely, new types of postal items[7] related to postal services (prior to that, information about editorial mail and direct mail was not clearly separated), and the maximum weight limit for postal parcels (previously, 20 kg) was removed from the definition, affecting the data collected by ANACOM from postal operators. As a result, from 4Q2012 onward, ANACOM adopted the definitions of postal services indicated in the new law and started collecting information with these new criteria.

With the new law, certain providers considered that (at least) some of their services were not anymore within the definition of postal services; therefore, they stopped reporting statistical information since 2014, according to ANACOM

[5] Statistical indicators include data on traffic, revenues, postal network, and human and material resources. Data is subject to changes with revised or updated new quarterly information. More information is available at https://www.anacom.pt/render.jsp?categoryId=337756.

[6] Transposes the national legal system Directive 2008/6/EC of 20 February 2008. More information is available at https://www.anacom.pt/render.jsp?contentId=1127982.

[7] According to the definition, a postal item is an item addressed in the final form, which observes the physical and technical specifications that allows it to be sorted by a postal network, as well as delivered at the address indicated on the object itself or on its wrapping, namely, (a) correspondence, which consists of a communication in written form on any kind of physical medium, including direct mail; (b) editorial mail as books, catalogues, newspapers, and other periodicals; and (c) postal parcel, which is a package containing merchandise or objects with or without commercial value.

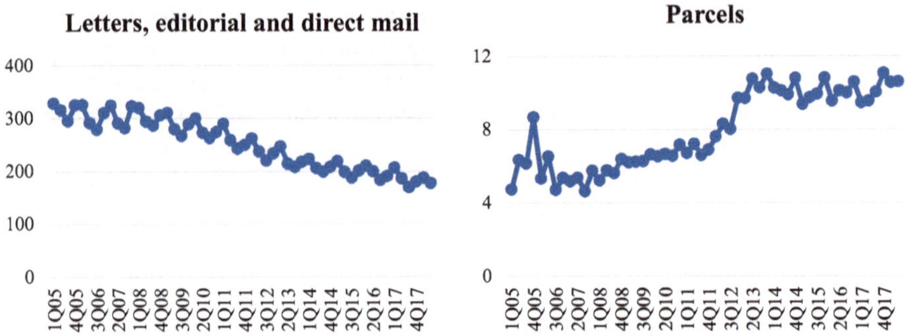

Fig. 1 Evolution of the postal traffic by item (domestic and outgoing international), Portugal. Unit: Millions of objects. (Source: Authors, with data from ANACOM)

(2018). Wik (2019) and ERGP (2019) also note a similar development for other countries.

3.2 *The Evolution of Postal Traffic*

Portugal observed a drop in postal traffic over the last few years, with a decrease of the total traffic of 4.4% per year, in the last 10 years, mainly due to the decrease of the letters sent. By type of item, considering data from the 1Q2005 to the 2Q2018, there is a negative trend in letters, editorial mail, and direct mail and a positive trend in parcels.

Figure 1 presents the postal evolution by type of item, gathered according to these common trends.

The volume of correspondences (letters, editorial mail, and direct mail) has a negative trend at least since the 1Q2005, with a higher decrease between the end of 2007 and the end of 2011 and an eased negative trend from then on.[8] The volume of parcels had a positive but slow increasing trend from 2008 to the end of 2011, in 2012 it took a leap, and from 2013 on, it stabilized around the 10 million objects.[9]

In the 2Q2018, the volume of parcels represented only 6% of the total postal traffic (domestic and outgoing international,), while around 80% were letters, 7% editorial mail, and 8% direct mail, a distribution that is slowly changing since 2012 – in the 2Q2012 parcels represented 3% of the total postal traffic in Portugal.

[8]The structural break analysis identified two breaks (4Q2007 and 4Q2011) in the time series of correspondence traffic.

[9]The structural break analysis identified one break in the time series of correspondence traffic (4Q2012).

3.3 *Postal Traffic Determinants*

This report considers data to capture the effect of digitalization (fixed broadband penetration[10]) and e-commerce (exports) on postal traffic, together with data to capture the economic evolution in Portugal (GDP, consumer price index, exports, unemployment rate, economic sentiment indicator, and consumer confidence indicator).[11]

3.3.1 Correspondence (Letters, Editorial Mail, and Direct Mail) Determinants

The SIMPLEX program, adopted by the Portuguese Government in 2006 to simplify administrative and legislative procedures using, among others, electronic channels (e-government), explains partially the postal traffic decline between 2007 and 2011. Among other government initiatives were the promotion of the access to Internet and to computers at a small price to young and adult people (e-initiatives program, launched in 2007)[12] and the availability of electronic forms to citizens and companies and the dematerialization of some acts of registration, making it possible to request them without physical relocation to conservatoires. Between 2007 and 2018, according to Eurostat data, the Internet usage in Portugal increased notoriously (from 40% to 75%), especially in people with ages between 25 and 44.

After the initial phase of the SIMPLEX program, the decrease of postal traffic started to ease.

The financial crisis between 2010 and 2014 in Portugal may have helped to delay the process of dematerialization of the invoices of the Portuguese companies and, as a consequence, to slow down the correspondence decrease.

Considering the explanatory variables initially mentioned, from the 1Q2005 to the 2Q2018, the variable with the highest correlation with the volume of correspondences is fixed broadband penetration (−94%[13]). This correlation is strongly negative, acting as a proxy for digitalization (e-substitution, e-government, and e-invoice). The second main variable related with the volume of correspondences is exports (−92%), also with a negative relation. If one considers the evolution in time of the correlations, instead of just the correlation in one specific period, Fig. 2 shows that the correlation between postal correspondence and fixed broadband penetration growth in time, during the

[10] Fixed broadband accesses per 100 inhabitants. Data from ANACOM, Portugal.

[11] Data from Instituto Nacional de Estatística, Portugal (www.ine.pt).

[12] E-initiatives (e-opportunities, e-school, and e-teachers) was launched by the Portuguese Government, in September 15, 2007, in order to promote the information and communication technologies, which permitted to students (young and adult) and teachers to receive a laptop and access to the Internet at a symbolic price, with training classes to explain how to work with the equipment. In 2 years, 852 thousands individuals took part in this program, 1/3 were less than 16 years old, 1/3 between 17 and 35 and the other 1/3 more than 35 years (15% with more than 45 years).

[13] The Pearson correlation coefficient was considered in correlation analysis.

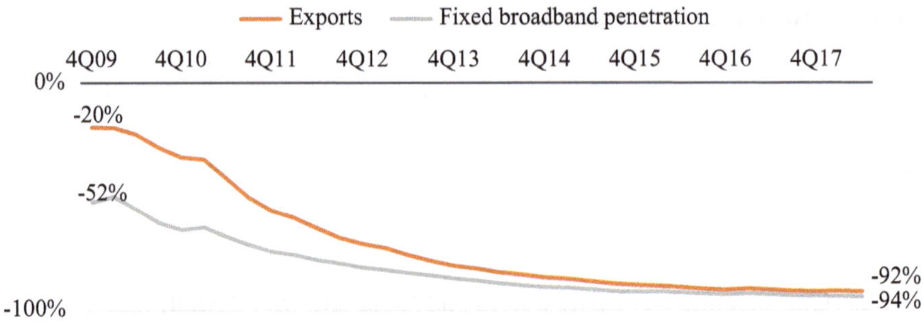

Fig. 2 Correlation between correspondence traffic (letters, editorial mail, and direct mail) exports and fixed broadband penetration, between the 1Q2005 and the date mentioned in horizontal line, Portugal. (Source: Authors, with data from ANACOM)

1Q2005 and until the 4Q2009, was −52%, but if we extend the data until the 2Q2018, the negative correlation was −94%. A similar trend holds for the correlation between postal correspondence and exports.

3.3.2 Parcels Determinants

The growth of parcels traffic in 2012, compared with previous years, might be explained by the new legal regime that governs the provision of postal services under a full competition regime, on national territory, as well as of international services to or from national territory,[14] layed down in 2012.

However, according to ANACOM (2018), from 2014 on, certain providers started considering that (at least) some of their services were not falling anymore in the definition of postal service; therefore, they stopped reporting statistical information or providing statistical information to ANACOM using a new reclassification of object type. ANACOM (2018) mentions that this might be a move to escape the legal regime, and its fees, applicable to all postal service providers. As for the parcels traffic evolution, this lack of data reporting may help explain why from 2014 parcels traffic has stabilized around 10 million objects.

Using the explanatory variables already mentioned for correspondences, fixed broadband penetration results again as the variable with the higher relation with parcels' volumes, exhibiting a strong positive correlation (+86%) between 1Q2005 and 2Q2018, probably due to the effect of e-commerce. Exports is the second important variable, with a high correlation with parcels (+83%), but slightly lower than with correspondences.

[14] Law no. 17/2012, of 26 April, that transposes the national legal system Directive 2008/6/EC of 20 February 2008. More information is available at https://www.anacom.pt/render.jsp?contentId=1127982.

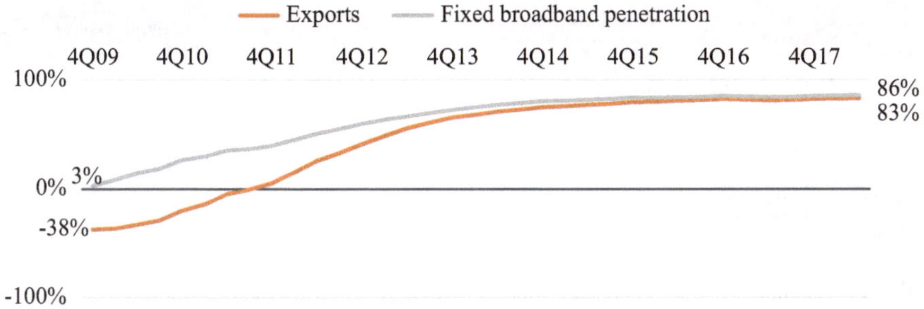

Fig. 3 Correlation between parcels traffic and Internet penetration, between the 1Q05 and the date mentioned in horizontal line, Portugal. (Source: Authors, with data from ANACOM)

The evolution of the correlations shows that while until about the end of 2011, exports were negatively related with the volume of parcels, recently they are highly positively correlated (+83%), potentially because, on the one hand, it creates demand for postal traffic but also associates with the growth of the e-commerce conditions in the last years (Fig. 3).

4 Time Series Modeling

4.1 Methodological Framework

To model the time series of postal traffic, we consider three methodological approaches: (1) ARIMA (autoregressive integrated moving average) and ARIMAX (extend ARIMA models through the inclusion of exogenous variables) models, (2) decomposition models, and (3) multiple linear regressions.

ARIMA models are based on the Box-Jenkins approach (Box and Jenkins 1970). They include two nonseasonal components in time: the autoregressive (AR) component, related with the effect of the time series in itself, and the moving average (MA) component, related with the effect of the error in the time series. If the time series has seasonality, this becomes a SARIMA model, and the seasonal AR and MA components are considered.

The extended ARIMA models through the inclusion of exogenous variables (*ARIMAX models*) were also analyzed and discussed in Sect. 3.3.

Decomposition models are based on the splitting of the time series in three different components: (a) tendency, (b) seasonality, and (c) other oscillating movements. These models include exponential smoothing models, in particular, Holt (1957) developed the approach with the tendency and Winters (1960) developed the approach with seasonality. These are now known as Holt-Winters (HW) models. They can be additive or multiplicative, depending on the relation between the three previous components of the model. Forecasts derived from exponential smoothing are weighted averages of

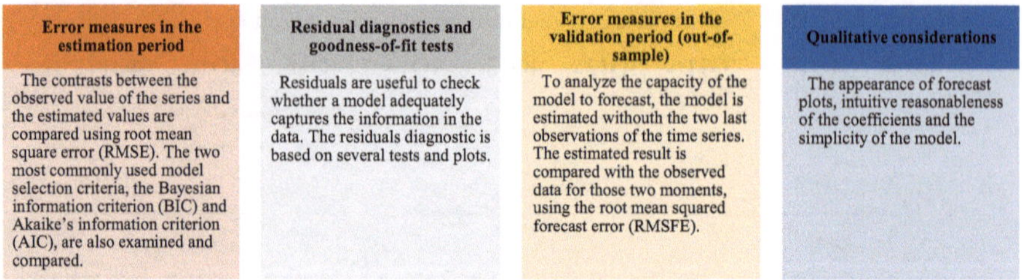

Fig. 4 Criteria to compare the results after estimation. (Source: Authors)

past observations, with the weights decaying exponentially as the observations get older, so the more recent observations have a higher weight in the predictions.

The *multiple linear regression (MLR) method* also expresses the long-term trend in which a common linear regression model is established between the incidence studied and time t. These models may also include dummies for seasonality and for structural breaks (to identify when a time series abruptly changes at a point in time).

The MLR models enable to include exogenous variables in the estimation, in our case those discussed in Sect. 3.3.

The objective of the estimations is to determine which of the candidate models best explain the postal traffic, considering the available data, which involves minimizing the loss of information. To compare the results after the estimation, different criteria are used (Fig. 4).

4.2 *Estimation, Goodness-of-Fit and Forecast*

4.2.1 Correspondence (Letters, Editorial, and Direct Mail)

The traffic of the postal correspondence, available quarterly for the 1Q2005 to the 2Q2018 (54 observations), is a nonstationary[15] time series, with negative trend and seasonal effects. The log transformation stabilizes its variance.

According to the ACF and PACF functions and to the residuals diagnostic, it was selected an ARIMA model, with seasonality (seasonal order is 4, due to quarterly data) denoted as $SARIMA(p, d, q)(P, D, Q)_s$.[16] This is a seasonal exponential smoothing

[15] Verified by the Augmented Dickey-Fuller test and Phillips-Perron test for unit root.

[16] An ARIMA with seasonality is denoted as SARIMA (p, d, q) $(P, D, Q)_s$ and is given by $\Pi(B^s)\Phi(B)\Delta^D_s\Delta^d Y_t = \Theta(B^s)\theta(B)\varepsilon_t$. The nonseasonal AR and MA components are represented by polynomials $\Phi(B)$ and $\theta(B)$ of orders p and q, respectively, and the seasonal AR and MA components by $\Pi(B^s)$ and $\Theta(B^s)$ of orders P and Q. Nonseasonal and seasonal difference components by $\Delta^d=(1\text{-}B)^d$ and $\Delta^D_s=(1\text{-}B^S)^D$, where, p, d, and q are the orders of nonseasonal AR, differencing, and MA, respectively; P, D, and Q are the orders of seasonal AR, differencing, and MA, respectively, and s represents seasonal order ($s = 4$ for quarterly data).

Table 1 Estimated results Box-Jenkins approach (compared SARIMA and ARIMAX model) for postal correspondence traffic

Variable	(1.1) SARIMA
ln_Correspondence	
_cons	−0,001
ARMA ar	
L1.	−0,408*
Sigma	
_cons	0,025***
ARMA4 ma	
L1.	−0,565***
Statistics	
RMSE	25,5
AIC	−213,7
BIC	−206,2
Skewness	−0,182
Pr(skewness)	0,564
Kurtosis	3,178
Pr(kurtosis)	0,485

Source: The authors
Legend: * $p < 0.05$; ** $p < 0.01$; *** $p < 0.001$

model, conceptually similar to the Winters model: (1.1) $SARIMA(p, d, q)(P, D, Q)_s = SARIMA(0, 1, 1)(0, 1, 1)_4$.

ARIMAX models[17] were developed using exogenous variables that were highly correlated with the time series for correspondence traffic, as presented in Sect. 3.3. If one considered the fixed broadband penetration, the residuals were not normal distributed, while in the case of exports, the model had certain misspecification problems (Table 1).

The results of the exponential smoothing models with seasonal effects (additive and multiplicative) show that, although the additive and multiplicative methods have similar goodness-of-fit, the multiplicative method (1.2) is slightly better (Table 2).

The last models to comparison are the *multiple linear regression method.* Two different models were considered to the comparison. The first multiple linear regression method[18] considers the linear trend (t), seasonal dummies (Q_1, Q_2, and Q_3),[19] a dummy for the structural break of 4Q2007 (B_{4Q2007}), and a dummy for the structural break of 4Q2011 ($t*B_{4Q2011}$). The time breaks were pre-identified with a structural break analysis. The first break is related with the beginning of the digitalization, and the last break may be explained by the end of the first stage of digitalization and with the financial crisis, as mentioned in Sect. 3.

[17] General model is given by $\Pi(B^S)\Phi(B)\Delta^D{}_S\Delta^d Y_t = \Psi(B)X_t + \Theta(B^S)\theta(B)\varepsilon_t$, where Xt are the exogenous variables.

[18] General model is given by $Yt = \beta_0 + \beta_1 X_{1t} + \beta_2 X_{2t} + \ldots + \beta_p X_{pt}$, where Xpt ($p = 1,\ldots,r$) are the independent variables, β_t are the parameters, and βr is the number of regressors.

[19] Q_4 was not included, to avoid multicollinearity problems.

Table 2 Exponential smoothing model parameters and model fit statistics for postal correspondence traffic

	Holt-Winters' additive (HWA) method		(1.2) Holt-Winters' multiplicative (HWM) method	
	Coefficients	SE	Coefficients	SE
Alpha (level – l)	0,548	*(0,117)*	0,553	*(0,117)*
Beta (trend – b)	0,001	*(0,016)*	0,002	*(0,016)*
Gamma (season – s)	0,811	*(0,264)*	0,807	*(0,266)*
R-squared	0,986		0,987	
RMSE	23,70		23,68	
MAPE	145,60		145,43	
MAE	18,08		18,06	
Normalized BIC	−7,263		−7,265	
Ljung-Box Q *Sig.*	*0,801*		*0,805*	

Source: The authors

$$\begin{aligned} \text{In\_corresp}_t = {} & 12,75 - 0,009t + 0,041Q_{1t} - 0,041Q_{2t} - 0,085Q_{3t} \\ & - 0,036B4Q2007t - 0,003t * B_{4Q2011t} \end{aligned} \quad (1.3)$$

(Adj *R*-squared = 0,986)

The second model was estimated including exogenous variables (fixed broadband penetration) to capture the trend of the time series, seasonal dummies, and a dummy for the structural break that happened in 4Q2011. The regressions diagnostic does not identify heteroscedasticity, misspecification, or multicollinearity problems, and the residuals follow a normal distribution.[20]

$$\begin{aligned} \text{In\_corresp}_t = {} & 13,19 + 0,041Q_{1t} - 0,043Q_{2t} - 0,087Q_{3t} - 0,348\,\text{ln\_penetBB}_t \\ & + 0,931B_{4Q2011t} - 0,213\ \text{ln\_penetBB}_t{}^{*}\text{B}_{4Q2011t} \end{aligned} \quad (1.4)$$

(Adj *R*-squared = 0,979)

The analysis of different indicators related to the goodness-of-fit and error measures (in the estimation period and validation period) identifies model (1.2) – Holt-Winters' multiplicative method – as the best model to fit and forecast correspondence traffic in Portugal, in the period from the 1Q2005 to the 2Q2018 (Table 3).

Figure 5 shows the forecast of the correspondence traffic for the third and fourth quarters of 2018, as well as the respectively confidence limits. According to the results, postal correspondence traffic is better explained by its own behavior than by the explanatory variables considered, eventual because some important variables that might explain postal correspondence are not available or may not be measured.

[20] Breusch-Pagan test and White's test, Ramsey RESET test, and Shapiro-Wilk W test for normal data

Table 3 Error measures in the estimation and validation period, for postal correspondence traffic

Models	(1.1) SARIMA $(0,1,1)(0,1,1)_4$	(1.2) Holt-Winters' multiplicative	(1.3) MLR	(1.4) MLR + lnPenetrationBB
RMSE	25,5	**23,0**	23,3	26,7
AIC	−213,7	(∗)	−243,3	−222,6
BIC	−206,1	(∗)	−229,4	−208,7
Predictive capacity (RMSFE)∗∗	24,5	**20,3**	21,0	25,3

Source: The authors

Notes: (∗) not comparable indicators; (∗∗) out-of-sample analysis – comparison between predicted values to real values of the time series. The set forecasts to start from the first quarter of 2018 to the end of the second quarter of 2018

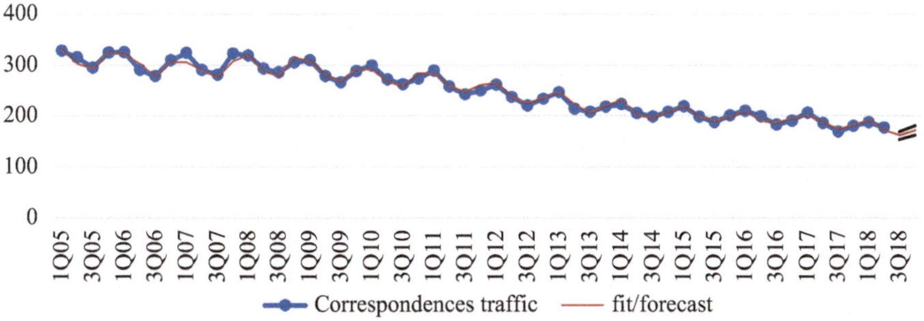

Fig. 5 Time series fit and forecast for postal correspondence traffic. Unit: Millions of objects. Note: Lower confidence limits (LCL) and upper confidence limits (UCL) for 95% confidence interval. (Source: Authors, with data from ANACOM)

4.2.2 Parcels

The time series of the parcels traffic starts in the 1Q2007 and goes to the 2Q2018 (46 observations). Although we have data since 2005, the first observations cannot be considered because of a strong variation in the results, explained by the break tests applied to the time series. The data is a nonstationary[21] time series, with a positive trend and a significant break that begins in the 1Q2012. This break is a consequence of digitalization and e-commerce, as well as the beginning of the new postal law and the lack of report of statistical information by some providers since 2014, as previously mentioned. The log transformation was applied to stabilize the variance of the time series and the first differences to obtain stationarity.

An *ARIMA model* was selected after residuals, ACF and PACF diagnostic,[22] and *ARIMAX models* were developed using the exogenous variables highly correlated

[21] Verified by the Augmented Dickey-Fuller test and Phillips-Perron test for unit root.

[22] General model is denoted as ARIMA (p, d, q) and given by $\Phi(B)\Delta^d y_t = \theta(B)\varepsilon_t$. The nonseasonal AR and MA components are represented by polynomials B and B of orders p and q, respectively, and d-difference components by $\Delta^d=(1-B)^d$; p, d, and q are the orders of nonseasonal AR, differentiation, and MA, respectively.

Table 4 Estimated results Box-Jenkins approach (compared ARIMA and ARIMAX model) for postal parcels traffic

Variable	(2.1) ARIMA	(2.2) ARIMAX I PenetrationBB
ln_Parcels		
ln_PenetraBB		
D1.		−2218**
_cons	0,016	0,058
ARMA		
ar		
L1.	−0,363*	
ARMA4		
ar		
L1.	0,514**	0,965***
ma		
L1.		−0,691***
Sigma		
_cons	0,059***	0,053***
Statistics		
rmse	61,9	57,7
aic	−116,9	−121,8
bic	−109,7	−112,8
Skewness	0,24	0,029
Pr(skewness)	0,46	0,928
Kurtosis	3,63	2,685
Pr(kurtosis)	0,21	0,901

Source: The authors
Legend: * $p < 0.05$; ** $p < 0.01$; *** $p < 0.001$

with the parcels traffic presented in Sect. 3.3. The estimated results of the best models are (2.1) *ARIMA*(4, 1, 0) and (2.2) *ARIMAX* (0,1,0) $(1,0,1)_4$ with fixed broadband penetration as exogenous variable.[23] The *ARIMAX model* with export as exogenous variable has misspecification problems (Table 4).

The results of the exponential smoothing model with seasonal effect show that the additive method (2.3) has the best goodness-of-fit, compared with the multiplicative method (Table 5).

Two different *multiple regression models* were considered for comparison.

The first considers a linear trend (t), seasonal dummies (Q_2, Q_3, Q_4),[24] a dummy for the structural break in the 4Q2012 (B4Q2012), and a dummy for the 1Q2014 related to missing report of statistical information (D1Q2014).

[23] General model is given by $\Phi(B)\Delta^d y_t = \Psi(B)X_t + \theta(B)\varepsilon_t$ where Xt are the exogenous variables.
[24] Q1 is excluded to avoid multicollinearity problems.

Table 5 Exponential smoothing model parameters and model fit statistics for postal parcels traffic

	(2.3) Holt-Winters' additive (HWA) method		Holt-Winters' multiplicative (HWM) method	
	Coefficients	SE	Coefficients	SE
Alpha (level – l)	0,899	*(0,156)*	0,700	*(0,136)*
Beta (trend – b)	0,000	*(0,055)*	0,000	*(0,057)*
Gamma (season – s)	0,000	*(0,375)*	1000	*(0,513)*
R-squared	0,959		0,955	
RMSE	0,053		0,056	
MAPE	0,438		0,515	
MAE	0,039		0,046	
Normalized BIC	−5,609		−5,504	
Ljung-Box *Q Sig.*	0,397		0,755	

Source: The authors

$$\begin{aligned} \text{In\_parcels}_t &= 8{,}5 - 0{,}002t * \left(1 - D_{1Q2014t}\right) + 0{,}038\text{Q}_{2t} + 0{,}065Q_{4t} \\ &+ 0{,}198B_{4Q2012t} + 0{,}500D_{1Q2014t} \end{aligned} \tag{2.4}$$

(Adj. *R*-squared = 0,971)

The second model was estimated including fixed broadband penetration. Since this variable has a positive trend, in this model the time trend was not included to avoid multicollinearity.

$$\begin{aligned} \text{In\_parcels}_t &= 6{,}166 + 0{,}891\text{ln\_penetBB} * \left(1 - D_{1Q2014t}\right) \\ &+ 0{,}052Q_{4t} + 0{,}236B4Q2012t + 2{,}81D_{1Q2014t} \end{aligned} \tag{2.5}$$

(Adj. *R*-squared = 0,9614)

The regressions diagnostic does not identify any problems related to heteroscedasticity, misspecification, multicollinearity, and normality of residuals.[25] The addition of exports as exogenous variable does not improve the model specification.

The results of the error measures return ARIMA as the best model if one considers the predictive capacity measure, while MRL model is the best model if one considers least RMSE measure (Table 6). Because parcels traffic presents an increase of its volume in the most recent data (1Q2018 and 2Q2018, when it had a constant trend since 2014), this affects negatively the estimation and forecast capabilities of the models. Since, at this time, we cannot determine if that growth is temporary or permanent, we assumed MRL model as the best model to fit parcels traffic in Portugal, in the period from the 1Q2007 to the 2Q2018.

[25] Breusch-Pagan test and White's test, Ramsey RESET test, and Shapiro-Wilk W test for normal data.

Table 6 Error measures in the estimation and validation period for postal parcels traffic

Models	(2.1) ARIMA	(2.2) ARIMAX (+lnPenetrationBB)	(2.3) Holt-Winters' additive	(2.4) MLR	(2.5) MLR (+lnPenetrationBB)
RMSE	61,69	57,70	50,27	**41,32**	48,06
AIC	−116,9	−121,8	(∗)	−150,61	−138,71
BIC	−109,7	−112,8	(∗)	−139,64	−129,57
Predictive capacity (RMSFE)∗∗	**20,55**	27,38	59,24	30,75	36,59

Source: The authors

Notes: (∗) not comparable indicators; (∗∗) out-of-sample analysis – comparison between predicted values to real values of the time series. The set forecasts to start from the first quarter of 2018 to the end of the second quarter of 2018

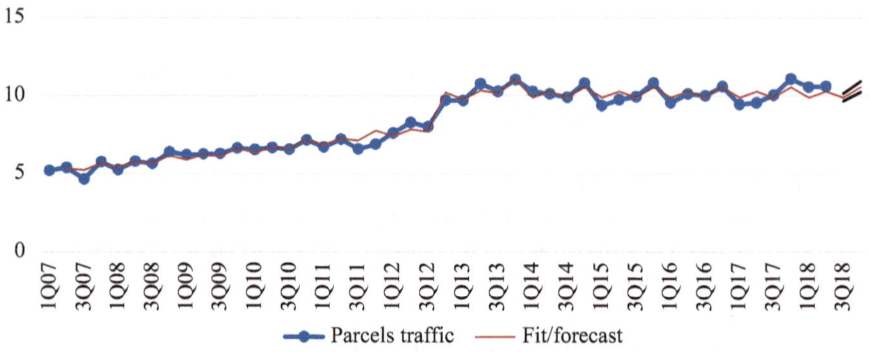

Fig. 6 Time series fit and forecast: Parcels traffic. Unit: Millions of objects. Note: Lower confidence limits (LCL) and upper confidence limits (UCL) for 95% confidence interval. (Source: the authors)

Figure 6 shows the forecast of the parcels traffic for the 3Q2018 and 4Q2018, considering MRL model (2.4).

5 Conclusions

The dynamics of the Internet technology sector has two different effects on the postal sector. On the one hand, digitalization, which includes e-government, e-substitution, and e-invoice, is a negative impact on the correspondence's postal traffic, and on the other hand, e-commerce helped the parcels traffic to grow, due to the delivery of physical product bought through the Internet. As a result, in Portugal, fixed broadband penetration and exports are highly correlated with the postal traffic, both in postal correspondences traffic and in parcels traffic (domestic and outgoing international), although with opposite effects.

At the time of the analysis, it was put in place by the law (Law no. 17/2012, of 26 April) that governs the provision of postal services under a full competition regime, on national territory, as well as of international services to or from national territory. Therefore, some definitions of some postal services changed. In particular, the maximum weight limit for postal parcels (previously, 20 kg) was removed.

In this study, three methodological approaches were compared: ARIMA and ARIMAX models, decomposition models, and multiple linear regressions.

The results show that, in the short run, postal traffic time series are better explained by their own behavior then when considering explanatory variables. Maybe that is because, apart from digitalization and e-commerce, other factors are affecting postal correspondences traffic, which are not being measured in this analysis (unavailability of the information, namely, variables that are more relevant than the trend itself, or inexistence of quarterly data).

With the digital single market goals, the decrease of the correspondence traffic is not expected to slow down soon, in Portugal. Regarding parcels traffic (domestic and outgoing international), the forecast models predict a stabilization of the series, even though the uncertainty related with the last two quarters of the time series, which might be explained by e-commerce but can also be the result of the use of different postal definition by some postal operators.

Some big questions remain not precisely answered, namely, what is the exact impact of digitalization on correspondences traffic and the direct effect of e-commerce on parcels traffic. For correspondence, data on big postal senders is necessary to understand the future evolution of the traffic. Concerning parcels, data from postal operators, disaggregated by origin (which traffic comes from e-commerce and which comes from other sources), would also be helpful to predict the future of parcels delivery.

Future works may concern the estimation of models with deseasonalized data, the consideration of relative values of the time series instead of absolute values, and the use of data regarding revenues, since they directly affect postal traffic. Considering that the causes affecting correspondences and parcels traffic are related, the estimation of a simultaneous equation models for correspondences and parcels traffic remains another promising possibility for future work.

References

ANACOM. (2011). *Challenges facing the postal sector as it moves to full liberalization.* https://www.anacom.pt/render.jsp?contentId=1092318

ANACOM. (2015). Study on the development of the postal sector. https://www.anacom.pt/render.jsp?contentId=1361251

ANACOM. (2018). *The communications sector 2017.* https://www.anacom.pt/render.jsp?categoryId=349440

Box, G. E. P., & Jenkins, G. M. (1970). *Time series analysis: Forecasting and control.* San Francisco: Holden-Day.

Box, G., Jenkins, G., & Reinsel, G. (1994). Time series analysis: Forecasting and control (3rd ed.). Hoboken: Prentice-Hall.

Brockwell, P., & Davis, R. (1991). Time series: Theory and methods (2nd ed.). New York: Springer.

Cazals, C., & Florens, J.-P. (2002). Econometrics of mail demand. In M. A. Crew & P. R. Kleindorfer (Eds.), Postal and delivery services (pp. 119–140). Boston: Kluwer Academic Publishers.

Cazals, C., Florens, J. P., Veruete-Mckay, L., Rodriguez, F., & Soteri, S. (2010). UK letter mail demand: A content based time series analysis using overlapping market survey statistical techniques. Available at https://www.tse-fr.eu/publications/uk-letter-mail-demand-content-based-time-series-analysis-using-overlapping-market-survey-statistical

Copenhagen Economics. (2018). *Main developments in the postal sector (2013–2016)*. Luxembourg: Publications Office of the European Union.

CTT. (2018). E-commerce report 2018.

EGIDE, IMR & ANACOM. (2015). *Study on the development of the postal sector*. https://www.anacom.pt/render.jsp?contentId=1361251

Enders, W. (1995). Applied econometric time series. New York: Wiley.

ERGP. (2019). *Developments in the postal sector and implications for regulation*. Available at https://ec.europa.eu/docsroom/documents/34881/attachments/1/translations/en/renditions/native

Holt, C. E. (1957). *Forecasting seasonals and trends by exponentially weighted averages (O.N.R. Memorandum No. 52)*. Pittsburgh: Carnegie Institute of Technology.

Jarosik, M., Nankervis, J., Pope, J., Soteri, S., & Veruete-McKay, L. (2002). Reforming the postal sector in the face of electronic competition. In M. A. Crew & P. R. Kleindorfer (Eds.), Postal and delivery services: delivering on competition (pp. 194–210). Boston: Springer.

Murteira, B., Muller, D., & Turkman, K. (1993). Análise de sucessões cronológicas. Lisboa: Mc Graw Hill.

Nikali, H., Mattila, J., Rintanen, I., & Huunhtanen, V. (2017). Demand and regulation for e-commerce in goods. In M. A. Crew & T. J. Brennan (Eds.), The future of the postal sector in a digital world (pp. 247–260). Cham: Springer Verlag.

StataCorp LLC. (2017). Stata time-series reference manual: Release 15 . Texas: College Station.

UPU. (2014). *Development strategies for the postal sector: an economic perspective*. Delft: Eburon Academic Publishers.

UPU. (2018). *Postal economic outlook 2018*. Universal postal union postal statistics. Available online in http://www.upu.int/en/resources/postal-statistics/latest-results.html

UPU. (2019). *Postal economic outlook 2019*. Universal postal union postal statistics. Available online in http://www.upu.int/en/resources/postal-statistics/latest-results.html

Wik. (2006). Main developments in the postal sector (2004–2006). New York: Springer.

Wik. (2009). The evolution of the European postal market since 1997. Available at https://ec.europa.eu/growth/sectors/postal-services/studies_en

Wik. (2019). *Development of cross-border e-commerce through parcel delivery*. Luxembourg: Publications Office of the European Union.

Winters, P. R. (1960). Forecasting sales by exponentially weighted moving averages. *Management Science, 6*, 324–342.

Yaffee, R., & McGee, R. (2000). Time series analysis and forecasting, with applications of SAS and SPSS . San Diego: Academic Press.

Demand Elasticities at the Intensive and Extensive Margins for Advertising Mail Traffic in the UK

Frédérique Fève, Thierry Magnac, and Soterios Soteri

1 Introduction

Advertising letter mail competes for marketing budgets against a range of different media types. Since the early 2000s, its share of total advertising expenditure in the UK declined by approximately half to account for less than a tenth by the end of 2018.[1] However, advertising mail remains an important component of UK letter volumes, accounting for over three billion items and around a third of addressed inland letters in 2018. A number of factors impact the demand for advertising letters, some outside the control of postal operators and decision-makers (such as economic conditions and advances in new technology), but price is a factor that can influence demand. Here we investigate advertising price elasticities using a rich source of UK customer data.

Senders of advertising mail in the UK tend to be large mailers who can choose among several types of advertising letter products that differ in format type, speed of delivery, and level of sortation.[2] Furthermore, customers can choose a Royal Mail end-to-end advertising retail product or a network access service offered by com-

[1] Estimates informed by figures from various World Advertising Research Center (WARC) Expenditure Reports.

[2] For example, to use a Royal Mail advertising mail product, a customer needs to mail a minimum of 1000 letters or parcels, and parcels or 250 large letters.

*The views expressed in this paper are those of the authors and do not necessarily reflect those of their affiliated organizations.

F. Fève · T. Magnac (✉)
Toulouse School of Economics, University of Toulouse, Toulouse, France
e-mail: thierry.magnac@tse-fr.eu

S. Soteri
Royal Mail Group, London, UK

P. L. Parcu et al. (eds.), *The Changing Postal Environment*, Topics in Regulatory Economics and Policy, https://doi.org/10.1007/978-3-030-34532-7_16

petitors that handle the upstream elements of a postal operation (in particular, collection, sortation, and trunking services) and then pay Royal Mail an access price per item to deliver letters to recipients.

Within such an environment, this study uses a large panel of Royal Mail retail customers to estimate advertising price elasticities and provide some new insights to the postal economics literature. In particular, this chapter extends our estimation of price elasticities reported in Fève et al. (2018) for advertising letters in the UK using a large panel of customers. In our previous paper, elasticities at the *intensive margin* were estimated by restricting data to effective customers of each product, i.e., those consuming a positive quantity of a product. There are many customers, however, who do not consume every type of product in each period (around 95% of observations are zero), and this likely affects the estimation of elasticities. In order to take this into account, this paper estimates price elasticities at the *extensive margin* by analyzing the customer's binary response to consume, or not, each product when prices change. Our model provides both own-price and cross-price elasticity estimates at the intensive margin and at the extensive margin. We use a data set covering Royal Mail addressed retail advertising customers over the period 2011–2017 to estimate price elasticities that take into account customer characteristics such as sector and firm size.

Section 2 describes the data and estimation methodology for modelling price elasticities at the intensive and the extensive margins. Section 3 contains results. Section 4 provides a summary and conclusion.

2 Modeling Demand for Advertising Traffic

The econometric analysis, whose results are reported in this chapter, uses a rich data set of Royal Mail retail customers, to estimate price elasticities for addressed letter advertising traffic. The individual customer data were grouped into eight product categories ($m = 8$), consisting of two sortation levels (low and high sort), and two speeds of delivery (second class and economy), for each of two letter format sizes (standard and large).[3] Information was available for 2640 ($= n$) retail addressed advertising customers, for the period July 2011 to September 2017, and the data were aggregated on a quarterly time period basis, t. The customers contained in this data set accounted for almost a quarter of all addressed advertising sent in the UK over the time period examined. We excluded customers solely sending advertising mail via access operators over the entire period of the analysis, as these customers

[3] It would have been possible to differentiate product categories further, for example, by machine-readable font type or eco-friendly paper envelopes. However, Royal Mail product managers, in the first instance, tend to differentiate addressed advertising letters by speed, sortation, and format level, and this product grouping categorization was adopted. A further point to note is that customers infrequently send a relatively very small number of First-Class sorted advertising letters which have been excluded from this analysis.

could not be identified. Furthermore, we do not have data on mail sent via access operators for the customers included in the database. Nonetheless, we condition the following analysis on the price of access products.

Price elasticities of letter demand are derived from the function relating letter traffic volumes, denoted by Q_{ijt}, sent by different customers, each denoted by i, for different types of letter mail products, denoted by j, during a quarter denoted by t, and the level of prices charged to send mail, denoted by p, and environmental exogenous variables denoted by X. Where data are available on these variables for n customers during T periods, the demand function is written as:

$$Q_{ijt} = f\left(P_{ijt}, X_{ijt}, u_{ijt}\right) \quad i = 1,\ldots,n, j = 1,\ldots,m \text{ and } t = 1,\ldots,T. \tag{1}$$

where u is a random error term

It is unlikely that customers use every product type at every time period. The set of observations for which demand, Q_{ijt}, is positive constitutes fewer than 4% of the total number of observations.[4] Note however that:

$$E\left(Q_{ijt} | p_{ijt,} X_{ijt}\right) = E\left(Q_{ijt} |, p_{ijt,} X_{ijt} |, Q_{ijt} > 0\right) \Pr\left(Q_{ijt} > 0 | p_{ijt,} X_{ijt}\right),$$

so that effects of prices are the composition of effects on expected demand when demand is positive and on the probability that demand is positive. Elasticities referring to the first term on the right-hand side are describing what happens at the *intensive margin*, while the effects referring to the second term are describing the *extensive margin.*

In our previous work (Fève et al. 2018), we estimated elasticities of demand at the intensive margin by considering only positive observations. In this paper, we first revisit the estimation of elasticities at the intensive margin and extend this analysis by estimating cross-price elasticities relative to a substitute, access products, to retail advertising letters.[5] We then turn to the estimation of elasticities at the extensive margin. Those elasticities reflect competition with access advertising mail, which is clearly a direct substitute, and competition with other media. Evidence on the latter comes from two sources: firstly, direct customer information on reallocating budgets to other media (mainly digital) and, secondly, via econometric studies; see, for example, Veruete-McKay et al. (2011). Note however that, for the extensive margin, our estimates refer to the population of customers, having at least one positive demand for one product category during this period. We nevertheless control for "entry" and "exit" of these customers from any of these product markets over this period.

[4] The main reason for the relatively low number of non-zero observations is that customers do not simultaneously consume all eight product categories at each point in time. That is, customers do not send addressed advertising mail containing all levels of sortation, all speeds of delivery, and all format types in every three months of the year.

[5] Access products are collected and sorted by upstream competitors to Royal Mail, as well as some very large customers, who then transport it to a Royal Mail inward mail center prior to Royal Mail delivering it to its final destination.

2.1 Intensive Margin

A traditional parametric econometric approach was used to estimate the demand function (1) using log-linear models in the 4% sample of observations with positive values, similar to Fève et al. (2018), and took the following form:

$$\ln\left(Q_{ijt}\right)=\alpha+\beta\ln\left(p_{ijt}\right)+\gamma_1\left(\ln\left(size_i\right)\ln\left(p_{ijt}\right)\right)+\gamma\left(\ln\left(size_i\right)\right)$$
$$+\delta_k\, dsector_k+\lambda_j dproduct_j+\mu_t dtime_t+v_{ijt} \quad (2)$$

Our enhanced specification introduces the price of access letter products (pa) in logs to estimate the cross-price elasticity of access and retail and takes the following form:

$$\ln\left(Q_{ijt}\right)=\alpha+\beta\ln\left(p_{ijt}\right)+\gamma_1\left(\ln\left(size_i\right)\ln\left(p_{ijt}\right)\right)+\gamma\left(\ln\left(size_i\right)\right)+\delta_k\, dsector_k$$
$$+\lambda_j dproduct_j+\mu_t dtime_t+\zeta\ln\left(pa_{jt}\right)+v_{ijt} \quad (3)$$

with some variables, such as letter mail volumes (Q), retail mail prices (p) access prices (pa), and customer size, are in logarithmic form denoted by ln( ). Other environment variables, X_{ijt}, comprise three sets of dummy variables that account for sectoral heterogeneity of senders – *dsector*, describing 10 (= k) sectors – for differences in products (*dproduct*), and time effects (*dtime*), to capture the impact of macroeconomic variables, e-substitution, and other external events. We do not allow for any dynamic impact of prices as the presence of adjustment costs or habit formation is unlikely or negligible.

We allow for heterogeneity in price responses of customers by including an interaction term between prices and customer size (*size*) in logarithms. This means that the own-price elasticity varies by customer size and is equal to $\beta + \gamma_1\ln(size)$ as derived from expression (3). For simplicity, variable *size* is measured by the deviation of the number of employees of the customer, with respect to the sample average, as the price elasticity for the mean customer can be thus read as β.

The coefficient of the logarithm of access price, ζ, directly reads as the cross-price elasticity for the mean customer. A note of caution is in order since this price is the compensation set by Royal Mail and does not include the relatively small mark-up added by access providers, as customer feedback on contracts lost to access operators indicate.

Furthermore, we use a logarithmic form for this equation for simplicity. This is the most common way of estimating elasticities in samples in which quantities are positive since the error term is unbounded from below.

There are still three technical issues. First, we assume that the error term is mean independent of regressors and therefore an absence of selection bias. Given the relatively small number of selected observations and the absence of any valid exclusion restrictions, it is difficult to envision how to deal with selection issues without strong functional form assumptions. We then assume away selection issues although this assumption could be questioned and potentially examined further in the light of a richer data as an extension to this chapter. This assumption can be justified by using the literature on the infrequency of purchases dealing with purchases of customers at (conditionally on regressors) infrequent times (see Deaton and Irish 1984).

Second, the technical appendix shows that the logarithmic specification does not affect the estimation of mean elasticities that would be obtained by modeling this equation in levels, provided that the error term, v_{ijt}, is independent of regressors instead of being mean independent only. The constant term, using a logarithmic form, might be biased but not mean elasticities as described by Eq. (1).

Third, ordinary least squares (OLS) estimates of Eq. (3) are likely to be biased, however, since customer prices for a specific letter product for each quarter, p_{ijt}, were derived by dividing customer revenue data, R_{ijt}, by the corresponding volume, Q_{ijt}. Measurement errors affecting volumes will impact prices and introduce a spurious correlation between the left-hand side variable and the right-hand side variables (see, for instance, Borjas 1980). Furthermore, Royal Mail used price discounts to incentivize customers to mail additional volumes (e.g., "incentive for growth schemes") that are also probably positively correlated with volumes. To correct for endogeneity, we use 2SLS estimation techniques and the standard rate card price, p_{ijt}^{0}, as an instrument. It affects prices p_{ijt} and is excluded from Eq. (3).

The estimation proceeded as follows. Firstly, an instrumental variable auxiliary equation was estimated by regressing the endogenous variable $\ln(p_{ijt})$, the price paid by firms; on the rate card, $\ln(p_{ijt}^{0})$; the Royal Mail pre-announced publicly published price[6]; and on any other variables appearing in model (3). Second, instead of replacing the endogenous variable by its predictor, derived from the instrumental equation, two-stage least squares (2SLS) estimates were obtained, by the equivalent procedure of including residuals from the instrumental variable equation (see Davidson and MacKinnon 2004). We estimate by OLS the augmented regressions:

$$\ln\left(Q_{ijt}\right)=\alpha+\beta\ln\left(p_{ijt}\right)+\gamma_1\left(\ln\left(size_i\right)\ln\left(p_{ijt}\right)\right)+\gamma\left(\ln\left(size_i\right)\right)+\delta_k\, dsector_k + \lambda_j dproduct_j + \mu_t dtime_t + \psi\,\hat{u}_{ijt} + \varphi\ln\left(size_i\right)\hat{u}_{ijt} + \zeta\ln\left(pa\right) + v_{ijt} \quad (4)$$

in which $\hat{u}_{ijt}$ is the residual constructed from the instrumental regressions in each sector with $\ln(p_{ijt})$ as the dependent variable, and as explanatory variables, all variables (except price) included in model (3).

2.2 *Extensive Margin*

The structure of the data is such that quantities are equal to zero and prices are missing whenever product *j* is not consumed by firm *i* during quarter *t*. There are many zeros in the data (more than 95%) and this is likely to affect the estimation of price elasticities.

---

[6] The price paid by large senders of advertising mail tends to be subject to competitive tenders and can differ to the standard rate card price publicly available at the time.

In this section, we take into account the effect that prices have on the binary variable, describing whether each firm reports consumption of product j at time t, or not. We consider the full sample of firm-product-quarter and we write:

$$\left.\begin{array}{ll} Q_{ijt} > 0 & \text{if } \ln p^0_{ijt} + z_{ijt}\,\gamma_z + v_{ijt} > 0, \\ Q_{ijt} = 0 & \text{if not,} \end{array}\right\} \tag{5}$$

in which, p^0_{ijt}, denotes again the rate card price, assumed to be exogenous to individual firm actions since it is determined in advance by Royal Mail at the market level. We use the same exogenous shift variables as in model (3) above. Such that variables z_{ijt} are dummies for products, sectors and time (quarters), as well as the logarithm of access prices, ln(*pa*), customer size, $\ln(size_i)$ and its interaction with log prices, $\left(\ln(size_i)\ln\left(p^0_{ijt}\right)\right)$. Errors, v_{ijt}, are assumed to be normally or logistically distributed so that parameters, γ and γ_z, are estimated by parametric methods such as Probit or Logit.

For Probit we can write:

$$\Pr\left(Q_{ijt} > 0 \mid \ln p^0_{ijt,}\, z_{ijt}\right) = \Phi\left(\gamma \ln p^0_{ijt} + z_{ijt}\gamma_z\right)$$

in which Φ is the cumulative distribution of the normal.

Taking a step back, note that the full average elasticity at both intensive and extensive margins is equal to:

$$\frac{1}{E\left(Q_{ijt} \mid \log p^0_{ijt,}\, z_{ijt}\right)} \frac{\partial E\left(Q_{ijt} \mid \log p^0_{ijt,}\, z_{ijt}\right)}{\partial \log p^0_{ijt,}},$$

which, in turn, is equal to the composition of elasticities at the intensive and extensive margins[7]:

$$\underbrace{\varepsilon_i}_{\text{Intensive margin}} + \gamma \underbrace{\frac{\varphi\left(\gamma \ln\ p^0_{ijt} + z_{ijt}\gamma_z\right)}{\phi\left(\gamma \ln\ p^0_{ijt} + z_{ijt}\gamma_z\right)}}_{\text{Extensive margin}} \tag{6}$$

In which ε_i is the estimated average own-price elasticity obtained using Eq. (3). To obtain this result, we assumed that the derivative of the true log prices underlying the observed log prices, $\ln(p_{ijt})$ with respect to $\ln(p^0_{ijt})$ is equal to 1. This is how we can make both elasticities at the intensive and extensive margin comparable. Hypotheses postulating other values of the elasticity of true prices to the rate card, set by Royal Mail, can also be considered.

[7]A technical appendix detailing these computations is available upon request from the authors.

Returning to the estimation of the elasticity at the extensive margin, we use generalized estimating equations in panels (Liang and Zeger 1986) and allows for different within-customer correlation structure over time. More specifically, we use the setting of Pan (2001), as updated by Hin and Wang (2009), for selecting the best covariance structure.

3 Estimated Price Elasticities for Retail Addressed Advertising Mail

In this section, we report estimation results on models (3) and (5) and in particular estimates of average elasticities at the intensive and extensive margins.

3.1 Intensive Margin

Table 1 reports the estimated coefficients for the price effects and their respective standard errors for models (2) and (3), and the appendix contains further information on estimates. Recall that model (2) was estimated by Fève et al. (2018), and results are reported for the purpose of comparing them to our new results when we estimate cross-price elasticities as well. We therefore focus on the estimates of model (3) which suggest that retail advertising customer price elasticities tend to increase in absolute terms with customer size and that the average elasticity is around −1.15 (95% confidence interval, [−0.76, −1.55]). It is a significantly larger elasticity than the one obtained when we omit the log-price of access products (e.g., model 2) even if the 95% confidence intervals overlap. A possible specification test

Table 1 Retail addressed advertising mail estimated price elasticities *at the intensive margin*

Model (2)		Model (3)	
Coefficient	Standard error	Coefficient	Standard error
Estimated aggregate own-price elasticity (β) varies by customer size (γ)		Estimated aggregate own-price elasticity (β) varies by customer size (γ) Estimated aggregated cross-price elasticity (ζ)	
$\beta = -0.71$***	(0.21)	$\beta = -1.15$***	(0.20)
$\gamma = -0.06$***	(0.01)	$\gamma = -0.06$***	(0.01)
		$\zeta = 1.50$**	(0.42)
No. of obs. 34,075	$F(45, 34{,}029) = 383.5$	No. of obs. 34,075	$F(47, 34{,}027) = 368.7$
$R^2 = 0.34$	Prob > $F = 0.0000$	$R^2 = 0.34$	Prob > $F = 0.0000$
Adjusted $R^2 = 0.34$	RMSE = 1.3191	Adjusted $R^2 = 0.34$	RMSE = 1.3182

Notes: *Denotes statistically significant at 10% level, **at 5% level, and ***at 1% level
Figures in parenthesis are standard errors for price coefficients

between the two models is obtained by testing the absence of significance of the latter price, and this hypothesis is strongly rejected – its Student t-statistic is equal to 3.57. The cross-price elasticity is significantly positive and quite large although the 95% confidence interval is quite wide ([0.66, 2.34]). The reason why the omitted variable bias in model 2 goes in the direction of a lower elasticity is likely to be that access and retail log-prices are positively correlated over time. The omission of the access log-price in model 2 therefore upward biases (i.e., makes it less negative) the coefficient of the retail log-price.

This colinearity issue, due to correlation of prices over time, also affects the estimated relative magnitude of the own- and cross-price elasticities. Note that since we estimate a single demand function for retail traffic, Slutsky cross-equation restriction with respect to access traffic cannot be estimated and tested.[8] However, the property that demand is homogeneous of degree zero in prices implies that the sum of the impact of own-price and cross-price elasticities on demand should be equal to zero. In our case, the estimated cross-price elasticity is larger, in absolute value, than the estimated own-price elasticity and with a different sign. The higher absolute cross-price elasticity is likely to reflect two factors: firstly, the much higher level of expenditure on access advertising letters relative to retail traffic and, secondly, the presence of multi-colinearity between access and retail prices. Formal testing does not reject the hypothesis that the combined impacts of the retail own- and cross-price elasticities are equal and opposite in magnitude at the mean point (Student statistic equal to 1.10). Furthermore, the homogeneity property applies to all prices that affect firm production, and not only retail and access prices, so that even if the property was rejected, the evidence would be fragile. Nonetheless, via Slutsky restrictions, we can say that the corresponding cross-price elasticity for access traffic – which is unobservable at the customer level in our data – could potentially be around a third of our estimated retail cross-price elasticity because of the higher level of expenditure in access traffic (approximately three times retail expenditure). If this were the case and this cross-price elasticity were, say, 0.5, then as long as the access own-price elasticity was ≤ -0.5, total advertising letter demand would not increase as access prices increased.

The results reported in Table 1 also indicate that, in general, larger firms tend to be more price sensitive than smaller firms. This may be due to the greater flexibility that larger firms have with respect to access to other media advertising channels, such as digital or television. The demand elasticity ε_i, at the intensive margin, is estimated to be a function of customer size (measured by the number of employees of the organization sending mail), and the formula is $\varepsilon_i = -1.15 - 0.06\ \ln(\text{size})$. On average, the estimated price elasticity for a relatively small company (say 20 employees) is equal to around -1.10 and for a very large firm (say, more than 2000 employees) around -1.38.

[8] Unfortunately, we do not have data on customers who switch from sending advertising mail via a Royal Mail retail product to an access operator service, and therefore we cannot directly estimate access customer cross-price elasticities.

3.2 Extensive Margin

We fit generalized estimated equations (Liang and Zeger 1986) to estimate Eq. (5). We specify different within-product and customer correlation structures over time although we always assume independence between groups – i.e., at the product-consumer level. More specifically, we allow for different flexible time-varying correlations (unstructured or stationary with 20 lags) and less flexible structures like an autoregression structure (ar 1) or full independence over time. All estimates are consistent (Avery et al., 1983). Detailed results are reported in Table 2.

Results vary considerably with the correlation structure adopted. In particular, own-price elasticities vary from around −0.5 to −1 for unstructured and stationary correlation; −1.6 to around −2 for the AR 1; and −3 to −5 under independence.

A model selection procedure is therefore required to choose among these different estimates. Pan (2001) proposed such a procedure by using a quasi-likelihood information criterion (QIC) generalizing Akaike's. Hin and Wang (2009) refined this procedure for covariance structure selection by proposing another criterion, dominating QIC that they named, correlation information criteria (CIC). This statistic is reported in Table 2.

Unambiguously, minimizing CIC favors the selection of the results in the first column of Table 2 and indicates that the best estimates are obtained under a general unstructured correlation structure. However, it is noticeable that the standard errors for the own-price elasticities are quite large, and the estimated coefficients for the own-price elasticities are not statistically significant for either the Probit or Logit estimates. These large standard errors are related to the flatness of the CIC values which indicates that selecting the best model – across which elasticities vary – may be a close call. Cross-price elasticities are positive as expected, given the large substitutability between retail and access products. They are of the same magnitude as the own-price elasticities but they are highly significantly different from zero. Given the strong correlation between rate card and access prices, it is not unlikely that multi-colinearity is impacting the identification and precision of estimates for both elasticities.

3.3 Full Price Elasticities: Adding Margins

As shown by Eq. (6), the full elasticity is the sum of elasticities at the intensive and extensive margins. The elasticity at the intensive margin is estimated using a conditional model, while the elasticity at the extensive margin is estimated using a marginal model; these two estimates are independent and can be easily composed. Nonetheless, as mentioned above, we use different prices when computing elasticities at the intensive margin (the price effectively paid by the customer) and elasticities at the extensive margin (the rate cards set by Royal Mail). The relationship between these two prices is likely to vary on a near one-to-one basis such that the

Table 2 Retail addressed advertising mail estimated price elasticities *at the extensive margin*

	Unstructured		Ar 1		Stationary 20		Independence	
	Coefficient	Standard error	Coefficient	Standard error	Coefficient	Standard error	Coefficient	Standard error
Logit								
Own-price	−1.11	(0.92)	−2.18	(1.15)	−0.46	(0.89)	−5.09	(0.94)
Cross-price	2.47	(0.52)	2.62	(0.52)	2.30	(0.51)	3.69	(0.36)
CIC	201,73		203,97		203,93		206,67	
pcard	−1.25*	(0.99)	−2.37*	(1.29)	−0.55	(0.95)	−5.49***	(1.01)
pcard*psize	−0.28***	(0.05)	−0.18***	(0.03)	−0.27***	(0.05)	−0.17***	(0.02)
pa	2.64***	(0.53)	2.81***	(0.53)	2.47***	(0.53)	3.96 ***	(0.37)
Probit								
Own-price	−0.91	(1.00)	−1.61	(1.24	−0.54	(0.96)	−3.32	(1.00)
Cross-price	2.20	(0.44)	2.42	(0.43)	1.95	(0.44)	3.60	(0.28)
CIC	197,32		201,10		199,31		204,38	
pcard	−0.98**	(0.49)	−1.66**	(0.55)	−0.61*	(−1.28)	−3.36***	(0.50)
pcard*psize	−0.15***	(0.02)	−0.10***	(0.02)	−0.15***	(0.02)	0.09***	(0.09)
pa	1.09***	(0.25)	1.20***	(0.25)	0.97***	(0.03)	1.79***	(0.17)

Notes: *Denotes statistically significant at 10% level, ** at 5% level, and *** at 1% level. Number of observations: 485,776
The three rows starting from "pcard" report the estimated coefficients for Probit and Logit. Own- and cross-price elasticities derived from Logit and Probit estimates. CIC is the correlation information criterion defined in Hin and Wang (2009)
Figures in parenthesis are standard errors for price coefficients

Table 3 Full price elasticities

	Elasticity	Standard error
Logit		
Own-price	−2.26	(0.94)
Cross-price	3.96	(0.67)
Probit		
Own-price	−2.06	(1.02)
Cross-price	3.69	(0.61)

Figures in parenthesis are standard errors for price elasticities

full elasticity can be approximated by adding up the two-price terms (the intensive and extensive margins) as in Eq. (6).

Under this assumption, Table 3 reports the full own-price elasticity to be around −2 for Probit and Logit with a standard error around 1 and therefore significant at the 5% level. This estimate is somewhat higher in absolute terms than those estimated in some other studies. In particular, Veruete-McKay et al. (2011) estimate own-price elasticities for direct mail in the UK to be in a range from −0.7 to −1.4 and Bzhilyanskaya et al. (2015) estimate USPS advertising own-price elasticities to be around −0.9.

The full-cross-price elasticity is estimated to be approximately around 3.4 with a standard error equal to 0.45, which makes it highly significant, and suggests that Royal Mail retail advertising products and competitor access products are intensively competing against each other. It is difficult to assess whether the extent of this competition is greater or less than in elsewhere as we are not aware of any other studies to directly compare our estimated cross-price elasticity effects. For example, Bzhilyanskaya et al. (2015) estimate much smaller advertising cross-price elasticities for competing product ranges, but it is not clear if these are for similarly close substitutes.[9]

4 Conclusion

In this paper, we have advanced and improved upon the conclusions of Fève et al. (2018) concerning the estimation of own-price elasticities of advertising letter traffic, in two directions. We first assessed the importance of including substitutable letter products, in particular access products. We found that, indeed, cross-price elasticities are significant, and the omission of such prices of substitutes biases downward own-price elasticities. Second, we estimated elasticities at the extensive

[9] For example, advertising cross-price elasticity estimates with respect to First-Class Mail and Periodical lie in the range 0.1–0.2 and are substantially lower than estimates reported in Table 2, possibly reflecting the fact that the USPS product groups contain mails that, in general, are used for different purposes.

margin by using the binary decisions of all customers to consume or not each product over the entire sample period. Our results showed that these elasticities are sizeable but somewhat imprecisely estimated. An avenue for further research, which may help to improve on these results, is to examine the potential implications of any customer selection bias using, if possible, a richer data set.

In conclusion, we leave postal operators and policy makers with the following thoughts to help guide and inform future decision-making with respect to advertising mail: when taking into account factors impacting customers effective purchases (i.e., their intensive margin price elasticity impact) and assessing whether to purchase or not (their extensive margin price elasticity impact), advertising mail own-price elasticities are likely to be high (possibly around −2 in the UK) and competition with respect to close substitutes intense.

References

Avery, R. B., Hansen, L. P., & Hotz, V. J. (1983). Multiperiod probit models and orthogonality condition estimation. *International Economic Review, 24*(1), 21–35.

Borjas, G. J. (1980). The relationship between wages and weekly hours of work: The role of division bias. *The Journal of Human Resources, 15*(3), 409–423.

Bzhilyanskaya, L. Y., Cigno, M., & Pearsall, E. S. (2015). A branching AIDS model for estimating U.S. postal price elasticities. In M. A. Crew & T. J. Brennan (Eds.), *Postal and delivery innovation in the digital economy* (pp. 91–113). Cham: Springer International Publishing.

Davidson, R., & MacKinnon, J. (2004). *Econometric theory and methods*. New York: Oxford University Press.

Deaton, A., & Irish, M. (1984). Statistical models for zero expenditures in household budgets. *Journal of Public Economics, 23*, 59–80.

Fève, F., Magnac, T., Soteri, S., & Veruete-McKay, L. (2018). How price sensitive is letter advertising mail in the UK. In P. L. Parcu, T. Brennan, & V. Glass (Eds.), *New business and regulatory strategies in the postal sector* (pp. 207–217). Cham: Springer International Publishing.

Hin, L. Y., & Wang, Y. G. (2009). Working-correlation structure identification in generalized estimating equations. *Statistics in Medicine, 28*(4), 642–658.

Liang, K. Y., & Zeger, S. L. (1986). Longitudinal data analysis using generalized linear models. *Biometrika, 73*(1), 13–22.

Pan, W. (2001). Akaike's information criterion in generalized estimating equations. *Biometrics, 57*(1), 120–125.

Veruete-McKay, L., Soteri, S., Nankervis, J., & Rodriguez, F. (2011). Letter traffic demand in the UK: An analysis by product and envelope content type. *Review of Network Economics, 10*(3), 1–28.

Platform Competition: Market Structure and Pricing

Claire Borsenberger, Helmuth Cremer, Denis Joram, Jean-Marie Lozachmeur, and Estelle Malavolti

1 Introduction

The significant development of e-commerce and Internet marketplaces has provided numerous benefits to both retailers and customers. In addition, it has been a boon for delivery operators, allowing postal services to compensate at least in part revenue losses due to declining mail volumes. However, increasing concentration in e-commerce and the worry that market power may be extended into adjacent markets has turned into a major concern of policy makers and competition authorities. While many argue that traditional regulatory or competition policy may have to be amended within the context of platforms, there are so far few rigorous studies that can provide guidance.

In this paper we propose a step in this direction. We consider an e-commerce sector with two retailers (which may themselves be marketplaces) and two delivery operators. Products are differentiated according to the retailer and the mode of delivery. Consequently there are four variants of the product. Integration and/or delivery restrictions reduce product variety, leading to some of the four variants no longer being available. The representation of product differentiation is inspired by

We thank Tim Brennan, Yassin Lefouilli, Per Luigi Parcu, and Ed Pearsall for their insightful remarks and suggestions. We thank all the participants of the 27th Conference on Postal and Delivery Economics for their comments.

C. Borsenberger · D. Joram
Direction of Regulation and Economic Studies – Le Groupe La Poste, Paris, France

H. Cremer (✉) · J.-M. Lozachmeur
Toulouse School of Economics, University of Toulouse Capitole, Toulouse, France
e-mail: helmuth.cremer@tse-fr.eu

E. Malavolti
Toulouse School of Economics, ENAC, Toulouse, France

P. L. Parcu et al. (eds.), *The Changing Postal Environment*, Topics in Regulatory Economics and Policy, https://doi.org/10.1007/978-3-030-34532-7_17

the Anderson et al. (1992) discrete choice model. While there is an extensive literature on vertical integration and restraints (see, for instance, Rey and Tirole (2007) for an overview), to our knowledge the issues have not been studied with such a discrete choice model. This is rather surprising for the model has otherwise been widely used in the IO literature and particularly in empirical applications.

We study several scenarios, starting with a reference case without integration or delivery restrictions. Then, we examine how the equilibrium is affected by the vertical integration of a retailer/delivery operator pair.[1] Next, vertical restraints like bundling and/or foreclosure are considered on top of the integration.[2] Vertical integration in itself eliminates double marginalization for the concerned products. This enhances consumers' welfare. On the other hand, it reduces product variety, and the market power it conveys is likely to reduce profits of the remaining firms. Bundling or foreclosure can be expected to further exacerbate these negative effects. A major lesson that emerges from our study is that the discrete choice approach points to effects that have otherwise been neglected (in particular the impact on product variety).[3]

Profits, prices, and consumer welfare in these scenarios demonstrate the (anti) competitive effects of integration and strategies like bundling and foreclosure. The most remarkable result we obtain is that vertical integration of a single retailer/operator pair will lead to bundling and foreclosure and possibly the complete exit of the remaining retailers and operators. This is true even when no explicit bundling or foreclosure is put in place on an a priori basis or even when such strategies are put in place with no particular anticompetitive goal. The restraints emerge spontaneously as profit maximizing strategies in a Nash equilibrium.

These results lead to the following policy recommendations. When the regulating authority is concerned with total welfare, the initial merger should not be allowed. If, however, a vertical integration has already taken place, competition authorities should also eventually give their clearance to the merger between the two remaining independent entities. This is better for consumers as well as the rest of the sector.

Section 2 presents the model. Section 3 examines the game under various strategies implemented by the economic actors. Section 4 presents some numerical results. Section 5 concludes.

[1] In France, for instance, Amazon bought a share of Colis Privé's capital in 2014.

[2] In the economic literature, foreclosure is defined as the dominant firm's denial of proper access to an essential good it produces, with the intent of extending monopoly from that segment to an adjacent segment (Rey and Tirole 2007).

[3] Ordover et al. (1990) study issues that are similar to ours and some of their intuitions also apply in our model. However, within their setting the input supplied in the upstream market is homogenous. In other words even absent of integration in their setting, there are only two variants of the product; consumers do not care about which upstream firm provides the input. This turns out to have a drastic impact on the result for in their setting mergers emerge only under commitment (see their Section C), while in our setting no commitment is necessary.

2 The Model

We consider an e-commerce sector with two retailers, which may be marketplaces, and two delivery operators. Products are differentiated according to the retailer and the mode of delivery. Consequently there are four variants of the product. In our model, any integration and/or delivery restrictions will reduce product variety; some of the four variants will no longer be available.

Product differentiation is represented by the Anderson et al. (1992) discrete choice model. This approach is widely used in the industrial organization literature to model product differentiation.[4] However, it has not been used to study vertical relationships (integration, bundling, or foreclosure).

A differentiated product is sold by downstream sellers A and B (indexed by j) with marginal cost normalized to 0 and shipped via differentiated upstream postal operators 1 and 2 (indexed by i) with marginal costs of c. Consequently there are potentially four different variants of the product.

There is a mass 1 of consumers. Consumer l derives utility

$$U_{ij}^{l} = b - p_{ij} + \varepsilon_{ij}^{l}$$

from consuming good ij where $j = A, B$ and $i = 1, 2$. The random variables ε_{ij}^{l} are identically and independently distributed across consumers and products with double exponential distribution over R with scale parameter σ.[5]

The parameter σ reflects the degree of product differentiation. When σ is small, the different variants are close substitutes and competition is intense.[6] When σ is large, each variant has roughly speaking a local monopoly and competition is not very intense.

Consumers buy their preferred variant of the product if any. Consequently, consumer l buys product ij when

$$U_{ij}^{l} \geq \max_{mn \neq ij} \{U_{mn}\}$$

It can be shown that the demand for good ij is then given by

$$D_{ij}(\mathrm{p}) = \frac{\exp\left(-\frac{p_{ij}}{\sigma}\right)}{\sum_{i=1,2} \sum_{j=A,B} \exp\left(-\frac{p_{ij}}{\sigma}\right)} \tag{1}$$

[4] Which occurs when different variants of a product or service are offered to accommodate differences in tastes

[5] The distribution function of the double exponential distribution is $F(x) = \exp\left(-\exp\left(-\frac{x}{\sigma}\right)\right)$.

[6] When the distribution of x is given by $F(x) = \exp\left(-\exp\left(-\frac{x}{\sigma}\right)\right)$, a smaller σ means that there is a larger probability of x exceeding a given threshold. This can be interpreted as the products supplied being closer substitutes.

where p = $(p_{1A}, p_{1B}, p_{2A}, p_{2B})$ is the vector of consumer prices.

When there is an outside option this expression has to be amended as shown below. The impact of prices on demand levels are expressed by

$$\frac{\partial D_{ij}(\mathrm{p})}{\partial p_{ij}} = \frac{-\frac{1}{\sigma}\exp\left(-\frac{p_{ij}}{\sigma}\right)\left(\sum_{i=1,2}\sum_{j=A,B}\exp\left(-\frac{p_{ij}}{\sigma}\right)\right)+\frac{1}{\sigma}\exp\left(\frac{p_{ij}}{\sigma}\right)\exp\left(-\frac{p_{ij}}{\sigma}\right)}{\left(\sum_{i=1,2}\sum_{j=A,B}\exp\left(-\frac{p_{ij}}{\sigma}\right)\right)^2}$$

$$=\frac{1}{\sigma}\left(-D_{ij}+D_{ij}^2\right)$$

$$=\frac{1}{\sigma}D_{ij}\left(D_{ij}-1\right)<0,$$

so that a variant's market share is, not surprisingly, a decreasing function of its price.

Further we have

$$\frac{\partial D_{ij}(p)}{\partial p_{mn}} = \frac{\frac{1}{\sigma}\exp\left(-\frac{p_{ij}}{\sigma}\right)\exp\left(-\frac{p_{mn}}{\sigma}\right)}{\left(\sum_{i=1,2}\sum_{j=A,B}\exp\left(-\frac{p_{ij}}{\sigma}\right)\right)^2}$$

$$=\frac{1}{\sigma}D_{ij}D_{mn}>0,$$

so that demand for any variant increases if the price of one of the other variants increases. This shows that the variants are indeed substitutes and also illustrates the role of the parameter σ. In particular the cross price effect is the larger the smaller is σ.

Expected consumer surplus is given by

$$CS=\sigma\ln\left(\sum_{i=1,2}\sum_{j=A,B}\exp\left(\frac{b-p_{ij}}{\sigma}\right)\right),$$

see Ben-Akiva and Lerman (1979), p.114.

In the simplest version of this model the market is fully covered. Each consumer buys one of the variants. This is convenient and often used in industrial economics models, but it has the disadvantage that absolute price levels do not matter. Relative prices are important because they affect the allocation of consumers across variants, but multiplying all prices by a positive constant has no impact on the outcome (at least as far as total surplus and demand levels are concerned). To introduce adjustments at the extensive margin, we can introduce an outside option as a fifth variant with a given price p_0.[7] Then the levels of prices also matter and welfare measures are more meaningful.

[7] In that case expression (1) becomes

Numerical results for both cases are reported separately, the ones without outside option are in appendix. We consider different scenarios with or without integration and/or exclusion or bundling. We state the problem and define the underlying game and specifically its timing. We start with the unrestricted case where retailers and operators are independent, and there are no vertical restraints. Then we define the different scenarios. For the sake of interpretation, note that within this model, integration and vertical restraints affect prices but also product variety. Restraints will reduce the number of variants available to consumers, which decreases welfare unless compensated by a sufficient decrease in prices.

In the symmetric case, the model can be solved analytically, but the expressions are not very telling; see Anderson et al. (1992). In the asymmetric cases, obtaining analytical closed form solutions would be at best very tedious. However, the model has essentially only one or two parameters, depending on whether we consider an outside option. When there is no outside option, the only relevant parameter is σ. Cost c plays no role and can be normalized to any (strictly positive) level. When there is an outside option, the relevant parameters are σ and p_0. To be more precise, the crucial second parameter is not the absolute level of p_0 but the ratio p_0/c.

Consequently numerical solutions are just as informative as analytical expressions and with one or two parameters only, their robustness is easy to verify. Comparing the scenarios tells out how integration, foreclosure, or bundling affect profits and thus entry as well as consumer surplus and overall welfare.

3 Equilibrium Under Various Scenarios

We now describe the specification of the game in each of the considered scenarios. In each case the solution determines the equilibrium consumer prices p and delivery rates t. Equilibrium profits are obtained by substituting these values into the relevant profit functions. Similarly consumer surplus can be determined by using the expression for CS provided above (while restricting the summation to the variants which exist under the considered scenario).

3.1 The Game Without Integration or Restrictions

We start with a reference scenario with no integration or delivery restrictions, see Fig. 1. Upstream, the delivery operators compete and set their linear delivery rates for each retailer. Retailers compete for the final customers for whom variants of the

---

$$D_{ij}(\mathrm{p}) = \frac{\exp\left(-\frac{p_{ij}}{\sigma}\right)}{\sum_{i=1,2}\sum_{j=A,B}\exp\left(-\frac{p_{ij}}{\sigma}\right)+\exp\left(-\frac{p_0}{\sigma}\right)}$$

and the subsequent expressions have to be amended in a straightforward way.

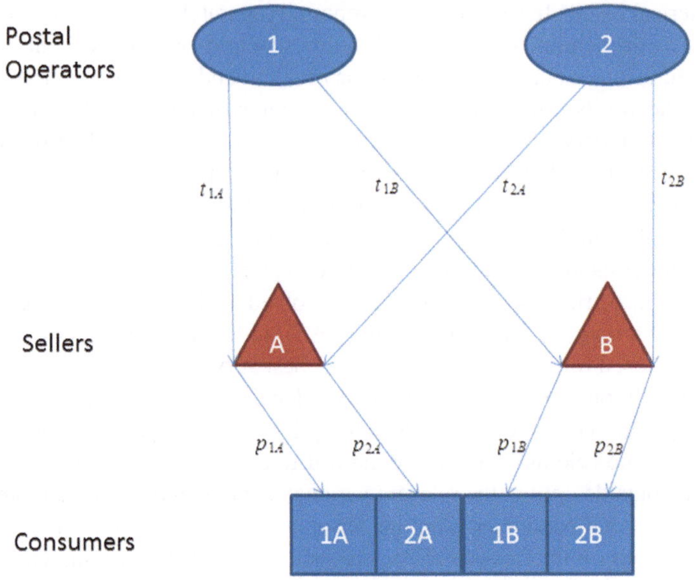

Fig. 1 Reference scenario

product are differentiated according to the retailer and the delivery operator. Each retailer can use both delivery operators.

The timing of the game is as follows. In a first stage delivery operators $i = 1, 2$ simultaneously set delivery rates t_{iA} and t_{iB} for retailers A and B, respectively, given their expectation of how those rates will affect the prices chosen by the retailers. Their profit is given by

$$\Pi_i = \sum_j \left(t_{ij} - c\right) D_{ij}\left(.\right), i = 1,2.$$

In stage 2, retailers $j = A, B$ simultaneously set their prices p_{1j} and p_{2j} by taking as given the delivery rates. Their profit is given by

$$\pi_j = \sum_i \left(p_{ij} - t_{ij}\right) D_{ij}\left(.\right), j = 1,2.$$

Note that a game with the opposite sequence would not be well defined and doesn't make sense.[8] We determine the subgame perfect equilibrium of the game which, as usual, is solved by backward induction. We briefly explain the main steps for this scenario. To avoid repetitions we skip this part for the subsequent scenarios.

[8] When retailers move first, consumer price are given; demand does not depend on delivery rates; and the operator's problem is not well defined.

3.1.1 Stage 2

The problem of retailer *j* is given by

$$\max_{p_{1j},p_{2j}} \pi_j = \sum_i \left(p_{ij} - t_{ij}\right) D_{ij}\left(\mathrm{p}\right),$$

with first order conditions

$$D_{1j} + \left(p_{1j} - t_{1j}\right)\frac{\partial D_{1j}}{p_{1j}} = 0,$$

$$D_{2j} + \left(p_{2j} - t_{2j}\right)\frac{\partial D_{2j}}{p_{2j}} = 0,$$

which yields for $j = A, B$

$$1 - \left(p_{1j} - t_{1j}\right)\frac{1}{\sigma}\left(1 - D_{1j}\left(\mathrm{p}\right)\right) = 0, \tag{2}$$

$$1 - \left(p_{2j} - t_{2j}\right)\frac{1}{\sigma}\left(1 - D_{2j}\left(\mathrm{p}\right)\right) = 0. \tag{3}$$

This defines the second stage equilibrium prices $\mathrm{p(t)} = (p_{1A}(\mathrm{t}), p_{1B}(\mathrm{t}), p_{2A}(\mathrm{t}), p_{2B}(\mathrm{t}))$ as functions of $\mathrm{t} = (t_{1A}, t_{1B}, t_{2A}, t_{2B})$, the vector of delivery rates.

3.1.2 Stage 1

In this stage, operators anticipate the equilibrium induced in stage 2. Problem of operator $i = 1, 2$ is

$$\max_{t_{iA},t_{iB}} \Pi_i = \sum_j \left(t_{ij} - c\right) D_{ij}\left(\mathrm{p}\left(\mathrm{t}\right)\right), i = 1,2$$

with first order condition

$$D_{iA} + \left(t_{iA} - c\right)\sum_{l=1,2}\sum_{j=A,B}\frac{\partial D_{iA}}{\partial p_{lj}}\frac{\partial p_{lj}}{\partial t_{iA}} + \left(t_{iB} - c\right)\sum_{l=1,2}\sum_{j=A,B}\frac{\partial D_{iB}}{\partial p_{lj}}\frac{\partial p_{lj}}{\partial t_{iA}} = 0,$$

$$D_{iB} + \left(t_{iB} - c\right)\sum_{l=1,2}\sum_{j=A,B}\frac{\partial D_{iB}}{\partial p_{lj}}\frac{\partial p_{lj}}{\partial t_{iB}} + \left(t_{iA} - c\right)\sum_{l=1,2}\sum_{j=A,B}\frac{\partial D_{iA}}{\partial p_{lj}}\frac{\partial p_{lj}}{\partial t_{iB}} = 0.$$

Solving this system of equations for $i = 1, 2$ yields the vector of equilibrium delivery rates, which in turn determine the equilibrium retail prices p(t) in the first stage.

3.2 Integration Without Delivery Restrictions

Assume now that retailer A and operator 1 are integrated. The integrated firm sells and delivers good A, the marginal cost of which is c. The integrated firm can also deliver good B in quantity D_{1B} at a rate t_{1B} and may have good A delivered by firm 2 at rate t_{2A} and in quantity D_{2A}. This scenario is represented in Fig. 2.

The timing of the game is as follows by. In stage 1, the integrated firm chooses t_{1B} such that it maximizes

$$\Pi_1^I = (p_{1A} - c) D_{1A}(\mathrm{p}) + (p_{2A} - t_{2A}) D_{2A}(\mathrm{p}) + (t_{1B} - c) D_{1B}(\mathrm{p})$$

and delivery operator 2 chooses t_{2A} and t_{2B} to maximize

$$\Pi_2 = \sum_j (t_{2j} - c) D_{2j}(\mathrm{p}).$$

In stage 2, retailers once again simultaneously choose their prices. For firm B, the problem is exactly the same as in the previous scenario; it sets prices p_{1B} and p_{2B} to maximize

$$\pi_B = \sum_{i=1,2} (p_{iB} - t_{iB}) D_{iB}(\mathrm{p}).$$

The problem of the integrated firm, on the other hand, is different as it maximizes total profits from its upstream and downstream activities. Formally, it chooses p_{1A} and p_{2A} to maximize

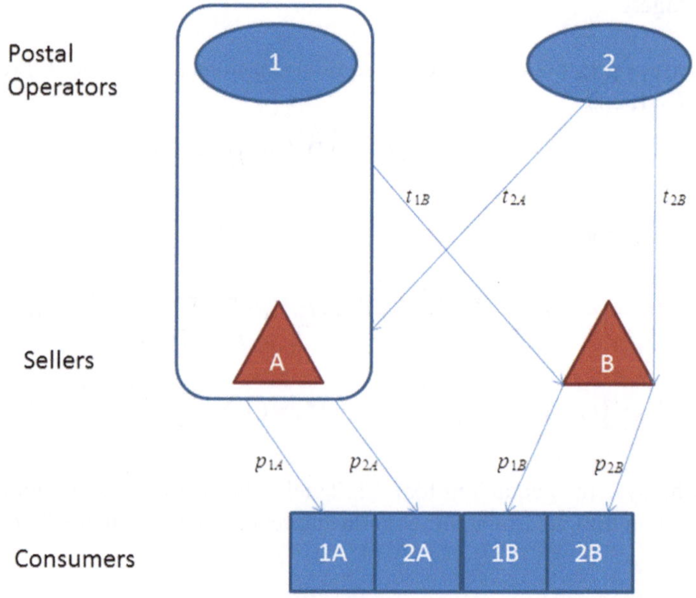

Fig. 2 Integration without delivery restrictions

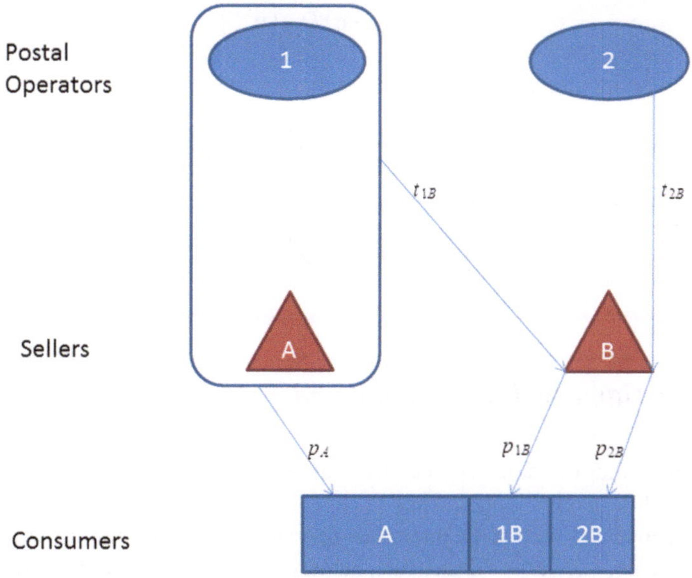

Fig. 3 Integration and bundling

$$\Pi_1^I = (p_{1A} - c) D_{1A}(\mathrm{p}) + (p_{2A} - t_{2A}) D_{2A}(\mathrm{p}) + (t_{1B} - c) D_{1B}(\mathrm{p}).$$

3.3 *The Game with Integration and Bundling*

Compared to the previous scenario, we add the extra constraint that there is bundling in the sense that the product sold by firm A *must* be delivered by the integrated operator 1. Variant $2A$ of the product thus no longer exists. Let $\mathrm{p}^{FA} = (p_A, p_{1B}, p_{2B})$ the prices of the remaining variants. The demand functions for these variants follow directly from Eq. (1).[9] This scenario is represented in Fig. 3.

The timing of the game is as follows. In stage 1, the integrated firm chooses t_{1B} to maximize

$$\Pi_1^I = (p_A - c) D_A(\mathrm{p}^{FA}) + (t_{1B} - c) D_{1B}(\mathrm{p}^{FA}),$$

while delivery operator 2 chooses t_{2B} to maximize

[9]We have $D_A(\mathrm{p}^{FA}) = \dfrac{\exp\left(-\frac{p_A}{\sigma}\right)}{\exp\left(-\frac{p_A}{\sigma}\right) + \sum_{i=1,2} \exp\left(-\frac{p_{iB}}{\sigma}\right)}$, and $D_{iB}(\mathrm{p}^{FA}) = \dfrac{\exp\left(-\frac{p_{iB}}{\sigma}\right)}{\exp\left(-\frac{p_A}{\sigma}\right) + \sum_{i=1,2} \exp\left(-\frac{p_{iB}}{\sigma}\right)}$ for $i = 1, 2$.

$$\Pi_2 = (t_{2B} - c) D_{2B}(\mathrm{p}^{FA}).$$

In stage 2, the integrated firm sets p_A in order to maximize

$$\Pi_1^I = (p_A - c) D_A(\mathrm{p}^{FA}) + (t_{1B} - c) D_{1B}(\mathrm{p}^{FA}),$$

while retailer B sets its prices p_{1B} and p_{2B} to maximize

$$\pi_B = \sum_{i=1,2} (p_{iB} - t_{iB}) D_{iB}(\mathrm{p}).$$

3.4 *The Game with Integration and Foreclosure*

Assume now that the delivery operator that is part of the integrated firm does not deliver good B. In other words, when the integrated retailer is seen as a marketplace, its affiliate must deliver via the integrated operator. This yields the scenario depicted in Fig. 4. Again, one variety disappears, namely, $1B$, and we define $\mathrm{p}^{FB} = (p_{A1}, p_{A2}, p_B)$ as the vector of prices of the remaining variants. The derivation of the demand functions $D_{iA}(\mathrm{p}^{FA})$ and $D_B(\mathrm{p}^{FA})$ is straightforward.[10]

The timing of the game is as follows by. In the first stage, delivery operator 2 is the sole active player and chooses t_{2A} and t_2 to maximize

$$\Pi_2 = (t_{2A} - c) D_{2A}(\mathrm{p}^{FB}) + (t_{2B} - c) D_B(\mathrm{p}^{FB}).$$

In stage 2, retailer B chooses its price p_B like in the previous scenarios, that is, to maximize

$$\pi_B = (p_B - t_{2B}) D_B(\mathrm{p}^{FB}).$$

The integrated firm simultaneously sets p_{1A} and p_{2A} and to maximize the sum of upstream and downstream profits given by

$$\Pi_1^I = (p_{1A} - c) D_{1A}(\mathrm{p}^{FB}) + (p_{2A} - t_{2A}) D_{2A}(\mathrm{p}^{FB}).$$

---

[10] We have $D_{iA}(\mathrm{p}^{FA}) = \dfrac{\exp\left(-\frac{p_{iA}}{\sigma}\right)}{\exp\left(-\frac{p_B}{\sigma}\right) + \sum_{i=1,2} \exp\left(-\frac{p_{iA}}{\sigma}\right)}$ and $D_B(\mathrm{p}^{FA}) = \dfrac{\exp\left(-\frac{p_B}{\sigma}\right)}{\exp\left(-\frac{p_B}{\sigma}\right) + \sum_{i=1,2} \exp\left(-\frac{p_{iA}}{\sigma}\right)}$.

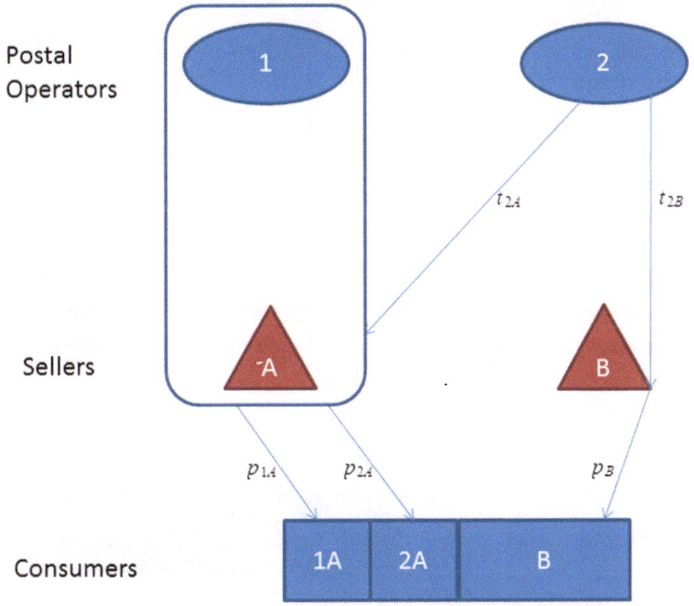

Fig. 4 Integration and foreclosure

3.5 *The Game with Integration and Total Bundling/ Foreclosure*

Assume now that the integrated retailer delivers good A only via its own operator and that the integrated delivery operator does not deliver good B; see Fig. 5. We are now left with two variants with prices $\mathrm{p}^F = (p_A, p_B)$.[11]

The timing follows the same logic as in the previous scenarios. In the first stage, delivery operator 2 is the only active player and chooses t_2 to maximize

$$\Pi_2 = (t_2 - c) D_A(\mathrm{p}^F).$$

In stage 2, the integrated firm chooses p_A to maximize

$$\Pi_1^I = (p_A - c) D_A(\mathrm{p}^F),$$

[11] Demand functions are given by $D_A(\mathrm{p}^F) = \dfrac{\exp\left(-\frac{p_A}{\sigma}\right)}{\exp\left(-\frac{p_A}{\sigma}\right) + \exp\left(-\frac{p_B}{\sigma}\right)}$, and $D_B(\mathrm{p}^F) = \dfrac{\exp\left(-\frac{p_B}{\sigma}\right)}{\exp\left(-\frac{p_A}{\sigma}\right) + \exp\left(-\frac{p_B}{\sigma}\right)}$.

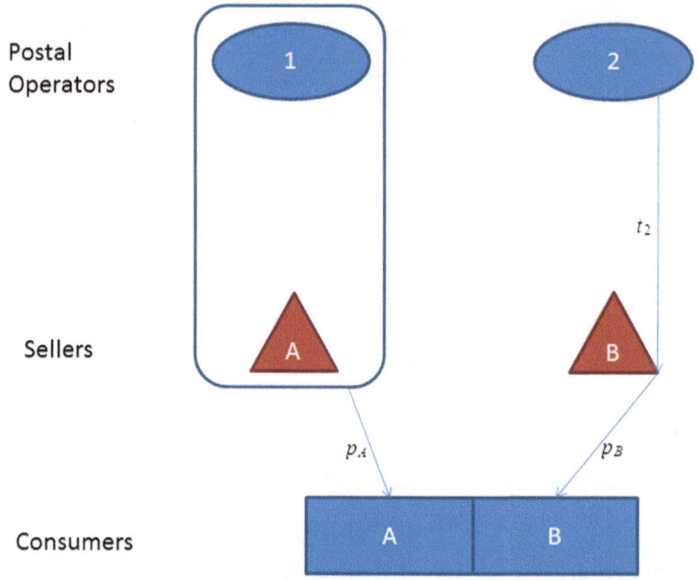

Fig. 5 Integration with bundling and foreclosure

while the problem of retailer B continues to be the same as in the previous scenarios; it simultaneously chooses its price p_B to maximize

$$\pi_B = (p_B - t_2) D_B(\mathrm{p}^F).$$

3.6 Double Integration

Finally, we consider the case where both retailer/operator pairs integrate: retailer A with operator 1 and retailer B with operator 2. This scenario is not directly relevant for studying the issues of bundling and foreclosure. However, it is interesting to draw a complete picture of the implications of vertical integration. Furthermore this scenario is useful for comparing the results obtained in this setting with product differentiation to those obtained in a homogenous product model by Borsenberger et al. (2018).

We skip the formal definition of this game which follows in a straightforward way from the previous scenarios. Like in sub-section 3.5 there are only two variants left, and demand functions are as specified in Footnote 6. Roughly speaking the game now reduces to a single stage, where the integrated firms choose p_{1A} and p_{2B} to maximize their respective profits and we calculate the Nash equilibrium of this game.

4 Numerical Results

The equilibria in the scenarios with outside option are reported in Tables 1 and 2.[12] The tables for the most are self-explanatory. The first column is the equilibrium without integration. The second represents integration without restrictions. The third is integration plus bundling, the fourth integration plus foreclosure, the fifth integration with foreclosure and bundling—all as defined above. The last column is the double integration scenario. For each scenario we report all the relevant equilibrium prices, delivery rates, profits of retailers and delivery operators, demand levels, as well as consumer surplus (*CS*) and total surplus (*TS*). The symbol – in a cell means that the corresponding variable is not relevant. The symbol $*$ (for prices or delivery rates) means that there is a "corner solution": demand drops to zero (the price is then not uniquely determined—all levels sufficiently large to yield zero demand are equivalent). In all simulations c is set to 1; this is essentially just a normalization.

We consider two main cases: low σ, variants are relatively close substitutes on the one hand, and large σ, variants are not as easily substitutable on the other hand. While the overall picture is the same, some specific results differ according to

Table 1 Outside option such that $p_0 = 3c$; low $\sigma = 0.5$

	No Int.	Int. no restr.	Int. bundling	Int. for.	Int. for. and b.	Double Int.
p_{1A}	2.92	2.60	2.86	2.60	2.60	1.94
p_{2A}	2.92	$*$	–	$*$	–	–
p_{1B}	2.92	$*$	2.63	$*$	–	–
p_{2B}	2.92	$*$	2.94	–	$*$	1.94
t_{1A}	2.08	–	–	–	–	–
t_{2A}	2.08	$*$	–	$*$	–	–
t_{1B}	2.08	$*$	1.61	–	–	–
t_{2B}	2.08	$*$	1.98	$*$	$*$	–
π_1	0.44	1.10	0.67	1.10	1.10	0.44
π_2	0.44	0	0.19	0	0	0.44
π_A	0.34	–	–	–	–	–
π_B	0.34	0	0.58	0	0	–
D_{1A}	0.20	0.68	0.23	0.68	0.68	0.47
D_{2A}	0.20	0	–	0	–	–
D_{1B}	0.20	0	0.37	–	–	–
D_{2B}	0.20	0	0.20	0	0	0.47
CS	7.86	7.58	7.85	7.58	7.58	8.43
TS	9.44	8.68	9.30	8.68	8.68	9.32

[12] As mentioned above, the scenarios without outside option yielding a fully covered market are not suitable to study welfare effects. Due to space constraints, we omit them but they can be found in an earlier working paper version; see Borsenberger et al. (2019).

Table 2 Outside option with $p_0 = 8c$; large $\sigma = 1$

	No Int.	Int. no restr.	Int. bundling	Int. for.	Int. for. and b.	Double Int.
p_{1A}	8.31	5.65	8.06	5.98	5.65	4.68
p_{2A}	8.31	*	–	8.44	–	–
p_{1B}	8.31	*	7.12	7.36	–	–
p_{2B}	8.31	7.27	8.38	–	7.27	4.68
t_{1A}	5.05	–	–	–	–	–
t_{2A}	5.05	*	–	3.45	–	–
t_{1B}	5.05	*	3.23	–	–	–
t_{2B}	5.05	4.59	4.68	4.76	4.59	–
π_1	1.56	2.65	2.37	2.98	2.65	1.68
π_2	1.56	0.91	0.69	1.20	0.91	1.68
π_A	1.26	–	–	–	–	–
π_B	1.26	0.67	2.09	0.60	0.67	–
D_{1A}	0.19	0.57	0.22	0.46	0.57	0.45
D_{2A}	0.19	0	–	0.13	–	0.45
D_{1B}	0.19	0	0.35	–	–	–
D_{2B}	0.19	0.25	0.18	0.23	0.25	–
CS	4.97	5.47	4.93	5.55	5.47	6.88
TS	10.63	9.71	10.09	10.34	9.71	10.24

whether an outside option is available or not. We concentrate on the cases where an outside option is available because welfare measures are more meaningful in this case. Table 1 presents the results with a low σ ($\sigma = 0.5$), while Table 2 considers a larger level of σ ($\sigma = 1$). The counterparts to these results for the case without outside option are presented in the appendix. Within each of the two cases that emerge, different levels of σ and p_0 appear to yield the same pattern of results.

The first remarkable property is that when retailer A integrates, foreclosure and bundling appear "spontaneously" (in equilibrium) even when they are not imposed ex ante. In other words, even when the retailer does not commit to such a policy (say in stage 0), as in the following scenarios, the relevant markets disappear in the Nash equilibrium. Consequently columns 2 and 5 are essentially identical. In particular, the consumer surplus is identical: such spontaneous vertical restraints are not detrimental to consumers. They cannot be considered and condemned as anticompetitive practices when in a first step, merger between upstream and downstream entities has been authorized.

Intuitively, the integrated firm increases the delivery rate applied to the other retailer because this increases the competitor's cost. This increase is so significant that the other retailer no longer uses this delivery option so that we effectively have foreclosure in equilibrium. Note that since variety $1B$ is no longer available, the integrated operator foregoes some revenues, but it also reduces competition in the downstream market, and this effect dominates. As to the bundling, the integrated firm prefers using its own delivery operator which is cheaper. Once again it foregoes a variety in the process (viz., $2A$), but the cost effect dominates.

When σ is small so that the products are relatively close substitutes, these forces are so significant that when A and 1 integrate, the remaining retailer and delivery operator exit the market in equilibrium (their demands drop to zero). As the last column shows, they can, however, avoid this outcome by forming their own vertical chain (which would realize a positive profit of 0.44).

When σ is sufficiently large, on the other hand, retailer B will be able to preserve a positive market share (and profit) in equilibrium and use operator 2's delivery services. Intuitively, products are then sufficiently differentiated to that retailer A cannot capture the entire market. Still integration leads to an equilibrium with both foreclosure and bundling (D_{1B} and D_{2A} drop to zero). Furthermore, like for smaller levels of σ it remains true that B and 2 would be better off by forming their own vertical chain.

So far we have considered the cases where the integrated firm does not a priori commit to any vertical restraint. When it commits to both policies, we get exactly the same outcome. With a low σ this is also true when it only commits to foreclosure. Interestingly, however, when it commits to bundling only, there will be no foreclosure in equilibrium, and the independent actors remain in the market, irrespective of the level of σ. To understand these results, consider first the case where the integrated firm *commits to foreclose*. In other words, it foregoes some delivery activity, namely, that of the good sold by retailer B. In this case, it is in its interest to bundle its own product with delivery by its parcel delivery business unit in order to maximize its delivery activity. This is achieved because under bundling consumers of good A no longer have the option of receiving delivery by operator 2.

Next consider the case where the integrated firm *commits to bundle* its good and delivery service. In this case, it is not in its interest to practice foreclosure. Quite the opposite, it maximizes the activity of its retailing division by allowing consumers to be delivered by the independent delivery operator. This is reminiscent of a result obtained by Reisinger and Tarantino (2015) who show that when an upstream monopolist integrates with a (inefficient) retailer, the monopolist would prefer maintaining the distribution of its goods through the other retailer. We do not consider differences in retailers' efficiency, but like in their setting, we have an output-shifting effect as the efficient retailer helps him expand the output on the final market. Furthermore, when the integration is associated with commitment to bundling only, the remaining firms no longer gain by forming a second vertical chain.

Turning to welfare, our results show that integration of any kind, with or without extra restraints, decreases welfare. Consumer surplus, on the other hand, is highest in the double integration scenario. This is because the absence of double marginalization leads to a drastic decrease in prices which more than outweighs the reduction of product differentiation. However, the increase in consumer surplus is not sufficiently significant to compensate the decrease in producer surplus.

To sum up, vertical integration of a single retailer/operator pair will lead to bundling and foreclosure and possibly the complete exit of the remaining retailers and operators. This is true even when no explicit bundling or foreclosure is put in place on an a priori basis. The restraints emerge spontaneously as profit maximizing strategies in a Nash equilibrium.

5 Concluding Comments

From a competition policy perspective, this is an example of a situation where market power in one market segment may spill over to others. This is in line with the results of Rey and Tirole (2007) who show that the anticompetitive effects of exclusionary practices are more important if the market power is in the downstream market. This is because the exclusive practices enhance its monopoly power as it extracts all the profits from the upstream firms and charges monopoly price to final consumers. In EU, the treatment of these restraints, initially based on the Block Exemption Regulation of 1999, is now essentially relying on Regulation 330/2010 and some more recent guidelines. The main evolution, following the growth of massive retailers in Europe and the rise of Internet distribution, has been to move toward a more "effect-based" approach. This means that the crucial issue is to determine whether a vertical agreement (or part of it) has actual or potential anticompetitive effects that are not outweighed by procompetitive effects (or objective justifications); see Petit and Henry (2010).

When the negative effects of the exclusionary practice outweigh the positive effects, some remedies are recommended to restore an outcome that enhances social welfare. The remedies can be either structural ones like the divestiture of the property rights or the prohibition of the vertical merger. There could be behavioral remedies that would consist in imposing unbundling or nondiscriminatory practices.

In the case we studied, the following policy recommendations could be made: based on the maximization of total welfare criteria, the initial merger should not be allowed. If, however, a vertical integration has already taken place, competition authorities should also give their clearance to the merger between the two remaining independent entities. This is better for consumers as well as the collectivity as a whole.

References

Anderson, S., De Palma, A., & Thisse, J. F. (1992). *Discrete choice theory of product differentiation*. Cambridge, MA: MIT Press.

Ben-Akiva, M., & Lerman, S. (1979). Disaggregate travel and mobility choice models and measures of accessibility. In D. A. Hensher & P. R. Stopher (Eds.), *Behavioral travel modelling* (pp. 654–679). London: Croon Helm.

Borsenberger, C., Cremer, H., Joram, D., & Lozachmeur, J.-M. (2018). Vertical integration in the e-commerce sector. In P. Parcu, T. Brennan, & V. Glass (Eds.), *New business and regulatory strategies in the postal sector*. Cham: Springer International Publishing.

Borsenberger, C., Cremer, H., Joram, D., Lozachmeur, J.-M., & Malavolti, E. (2019). *Platform competition: Market structure and pricing*, TSE WP 1010. https://www.tse-fr.eu/sites/default/files/TSE/documents/doc/wp/2019/wp_tse_1010.pdf

Ordover, J. A., Saloner, G., & Salop, S. (1990). Equilibrium vertical restraints. *The American Economic Review, 80*, 127–142.

Petit, N., & Henry, D. (2010). Vertical restraints under EU competition law: Conceptual foundations and practical framework. https://doi.org/10.2139/ssrn.1724891.

Reisinger, M., & Tarantino, E. (2015). Vertical integration, foreclosure, and productive efficiency. *The Rand Journal of Economics, 46*(3), 461–479.

Rey, P., & Tirole, J. (2007). A primer in foreclosure. In *Handbook of industrial organization* (vol. 3, pp. 2145–2220).

Ex Ante and Ex Post Access Regime in the Postal Sector: A Revival of Margin Squeeze?

Pier Luigi Parcu and Anna Renata Pisarkiewicz

1 Introduction

Third-party access is one of the key tools used by regulators to stimulate competition in network industries. However, in the postal sector, incumbent operators could refuse to provide access to their networks on competitive terms. As the experience from the electronic communications sectors shows, constructive refusals to deal,[1] caused by unreasonable or onerous terms, are far more frequent than outright refusals. These could be implemented through a *margin squeeze*, where a dominant firm offers wholesale access at a price greater than the difference between its retail price and its wholesale cost. Such combination of retail and wholesale prices allows the dominant firm to leverage its upstream position and to make downstream competitors unprofitable. Only a vertically integrated company can engage in a price squeeze as it needs to be able to influence prices, or better the margin between the prices, in two related markets. Without a simultaneous presence in two vertically integrated markets, a company can still engage in predatory or excessive pricing, discrimination, or refusal to deal, but only in one market.

Margin squeeze as an abuse of dominant position has primarily occurred in electronic communications markets, where the national regulatory authorities (NRAs) had already granted mandatory access to legacy networks under sectorial regulation. However, in the last few years, a number of national competition authorities (NCAs) have started to investigate margin squeeze cases in major European postal markets where mandatory access had not always been required

[1]Constructive refusal to deal, in the Commission's 2009 Enforcement Guidance on ex-Article 82 EC, means a proposal of access to a competitor at terms technically and economically so unacceptable to correspond to an effective refusal.

P. L. Parcu · A. R. Pisarkiewicz (✉)
European University Institute, Fiesole, Italy
e-mail: pierluigi.parcu@eui.eu

P. L. Parcu et al. (eds.), *The Changing Postal Environment*, Topics in Regulatory Economics and Policy, https://doi.org/10.1007/978-3-030-34532-7_18

under sectorial regulations. These include AGCM (Italy) in 2017, Bundeskartellamt (Germany) in 2015, CNMC (Spain) in 2014, and Ofcom (UK) in 2018.[2] In any case, the standing of margin squeeze as an independent form of abuse is now well-settled in the EU.[3] Only a few academics have expressed concern that margin squeeze could compromise the internal coherence of competition law by providing a rule that seems to respond specifically to the problems and needs of the electronic communications sector or, at most, the regulated network industries.[4] Precisely because of their general applicability, provisions of competition law have to be sufficiently flexible so as to encompass a whole spectrum of anticompetitive practices, independently of the features of the industry in which they may take place. On the other hand, even the US Supreme Court pointed out in its *Trinko* decision that "antitrust analysis must sensitively recognize and reflect the distinctive economic and legal setting of the regulated industry to which it applies."[5]

In light of the different economic features of the telecommunications and postal sectors, the related diversity of the respective access regimes, and the digitalization and the emergence of new business models, we wish to explore whether recent margin squeeze investigations in the postal sector reflect its distinctive economic and legal setting. To address this question, the paper examines recent margin squeeze investigations in the postal sector under existing national regulatory frameworks, and, where useful, compares them with landmark European margin squeeze cases in the telecoms sector.

In terms of the structure, the paper is divided in five sections. Following the introduction, which explained the timely relevance of the topic, Section 2 discusses access to the postal and the telecoms networks in light of the technical and economic features that distinguish these sectors. Section 3 reviews margin squeeze cases in the postal sector, and Section 4 compares them with Article 102 TFEU margin squeeze cases in the telecoms sector. Section 5 briefly concludes.

---

[2] Ofcom has actually investigated Royal Mail for discriminatory pricing, and not for margin squeeze, but even if it explicitly stated that the case at hand was not an example of margin squeeze, in Section 4 we discuss the arguments that led Ofcom to consider discriminatory pricing and not margin squeeze to be the more appropriate analytical framework in a relatively similar context.

[3] See, for example, Case C-280/08P, *Deutsche Telekom v. Commission*, ECLI:EU:C:2010:603; Case C-52/09, *TeliaSonera*, ECLI:EU:C:2011:83; Case C-295/12P, *Telefónica and Telefónica de España v. Commission*, ECLI:EU:C:2014:2062.

[4] This allegation is, in particular, grounded in the distinction that the Commission made in its Enforcement Priorities Guidance between situation where indispensability has to be proven or not. The Commission indicated that it is discharged from the burden of proving indispensability of the upstream input on the condition that at least one of the following is true: (i) there is a regulatory obligation to supply, and the balancing of incentives has already been carried out by the national regulator; and/or (ii) the upstream market position has been established under the protection of special or exclusive rights or has been financed by state resources.

[5] *Verizon Communications v Law Offices of Curtis Trinko*, LLP, 540 U.S. 398 (2004).

2 Access to the Postal and the Telecom Networks in Light of the Respective Technical and Economic Features

The existence of sector-specific regulation, and in particular the imposition of access requirements on incumbents, is typically justified by the existence of a bottleneck that cannot reasonably be replicated and is necessary for entrants. In telecommunications, for example, the existence of the bottleneck (local loop) necessary to access end users involved substantial sunk costs, which made the duplication of the existing network, at least for the so-called last mile, unfeasible in economic terms. The postal sector, in contrast, does not require a high last-mile sunk costs that would involve extensive civil works and high fixed costs. Instead, most costs are labor-related since mail delivery is a very labor-intensive business (Okholm et al. 2015). This makes the postal network more easily replicable, allowing alternative postal operators to bypass the legacy network to a significant, albeit not full, extent.[6] The possibility of bypass implies that end-to-end operators could offer more significant price reductions than access-based operators, whose ability to reduce prices is determined, among others, by the point of access they use (Copenhagen Economics 2013). Moreover, "postal infrastructures are somewhat different from other network infrastructures in that much of the transmission is made up of common means of transportation, with no dedicated physical infrastructure" (Parcu and Silvestri 2017).

This difference concerning sunk costs has important implications. In particular, the fact that the postal network is unlikely to be seen as a "sunk cost bottleneck," since labor costs are not sunk, weakens traditionally invoked justifications for mandatory access (Geradin 2015:528). Lower last-mile sunk costs for the postal network are to be considered a good explanation for the differences between the respective regulatory frameworks of posts and telecoms. Article 11a of the Postal Directive refers to the Member States' right, but not an obligation, to "adopt measures to ensure access to the postal network under transparent, proportional and non-discriminatory conditions."[7] In contrast, the importance of effective access in telecoms was such that before the Access Directive 2002/19/EC was adopted, the European Parliament and the Council decided that it was necessary to lay down conditions for mandatory access already in Regulation 2887/2000.[8]

Revenues in the postal and the telecoms sector are shaped differently due to a different demand structure. In the postal sector, demand is more concentrated and comes primarily from a limited number of large business customers (Okholm et al. 2015). As Geradin (2015) explained, even a small reduction in price could allow competing operators to convince a large mailer to switch away from the incumbent.

---

[6] In the telecoms sector, such kind of extensive bypass is economically impossible, which renders access necessary.

[7] Still, 20 countries decided to impose mandatory access, whereas only 7 are without (Austria, Denmark, France, Italy, Poland, Slovakia, and Sweden), ERGP (2017).

[8] Regulation (EC) No. 2887/2000 of the European Parliament and of the Council of 18 December 2000 on unbundled access to the local loop, O.J. [2000] L 336/4.

Such a concentrated demand has another important implication: the inability to compete in the market for bulk mail may have a negative impact on the overall level of competition. This is because large customers are important for alternative postal operators as, due to their size, they help them achieve economies of scale, which are necessary to operate in a sustained and competitive manner.

Also, the traditional distinction between wholesale and retail services differs from that in telecommunications. In the telecommunications sector, competitors mostly seek access to incumbents' networks, and incumbents have an incentive to discriminate between them and their own retail arm. Also, discrimination is likely to be implied, and not overt, and detecting it in the prevailing context of vertical integration may be difficult as long as wholesale and retail activities are not fully separated. In the postal sector, on the other hand, there are two main different types of access seekers, competing postal operators and large postal users. Postal incumbents may have a clear incentive to discriminate between the two groups, favoring the latter, which makes discrimination easier to detect. To the extent that services provided by these two groups may be equivalent, there is a strong possibility that such a discrimination could violate Article 102 TFEU.

As we will see in the next section, in all analyzed cases, national incumbent postal operators effectively discriminated between competing postal operators and large postal users or between end-to-end and access-only operators. Only the UK examined the conduct of its incumbent as a case of discrimination, whereas Germany, Italy, and Spain decided to frame their cases as margin squeeze violations. To the extent that all cases concerned similar scenarios, the question arises whether it makes any true difference which analytical framework (discrimination or margin squeeze) a national competition authority decides to use.

3 Margin Squeeze Abuses in the Postal Sector

Commercial strategies and the propensity of a given sector to a particular type of abusive behavior depend on economic features of the sector and the sectorial regulation that reflects them. Margin squeeze has become widely known as an independent type of abuse mostly due to the Commission's Article 102 cases in the telecoms sector, but also the fact that its approach was in a stark contrast with the US Supreme Court's ruling in the 2009 *linkLine* case.[9] The telecommunications sector provided fertile ground for such behavior, as it satisfied the conditions necessary to make margin squeeze feasible and profitable. A vertically integrated incumbent, strongly

[9] The US Supreme Court, instead of focusing on the margin, analyzed separately the lawfulness of the upstream and downstream prices of AT&T. It then held that "if both the wholesale price and the retail price are independently lawful, there is no basis for imposing antitrust liability simply because a vertically integrated firm's wholesale price happens to be greater than or equal to its retail prices." *Pacific Bell Tel. Co. v linkLine Comm'ns, Inc.* (*linkLine*), 555 U.S. 438 (2009). For arguments against recognizing margin squeeze as an independent abuse, see Sidak (2008).

dominant in an upstream market, faced limited downstream competition[10] that depends on access to the incumbent's upstream bottleneck (even if a given bottleneck fell short of an essential facility, as it was defined in *Bronner*). Also, despite regulation, incumbents retained the ability to manipulate the margin between wholesale and retail prices.

The postal sector seems to satisfy these conditions necessary to implement a margin squeeze. Yet, abuse of dominant position in the postal sector is typically associated with violations regarding discriminatory pricing and anticompetitive rebates.[11] Copenhagen Economics (2013:186), based on responses from NRAs and NCAs to a survey covering a 10-year period up to 2011, identified 17 cases concerning discriminatory pricing and 11 concerning conditional rebates, but only 1 margin squeeze.[12] Still, as mentioned earlier, in the last few years, a number of NCAs started to investigate margin squeeze allegations in the postal sector. All of these cases concerned the market for bulk mail delivery, in which the demand for services comes from business clients – postal operators' final customers, who send large volumes of mail to their own customers – and from competing postal operators.

Let us start with the 2014 margin squeeze decision of the Spanish CNMC. In the downstream market, the Spanish postal incumbent, Correos, held approximately a 90% market share measured in terms of revenue and 84% in terms of volume, whereas its main competitor, Unipost, held, respectively, 8% and 11%. Correos enjoyed a monopoly as the only provider of wholesale access services. Unipost filed a complaint alleging that Correos offered discounts to its large customers far higher than those it offered to Unipost and other similar competitors for using its postal network. The discounts, based on the volume of consignments, savings, and regularity, were approved by the then existing National Postal Sector Commission. They could reach 16% when granted to alternative postal operators, but went up to 57% when offered to large customers.[13]

According to the CNMC, this difference prevented alternative operators from competing with Correos for the large customer segment. Unipost complained that

[10] With no downstream competition, margin squeeze could not take place, whereas in a perfectly competitive downstream market, it would no longer be feasible.

[11] The reason we see more rebates in posts but not telecoms can be explained by the different nature of the demand for postal and telecommunications services. As we explained earlier, the former tends to be highly concentrated as a rather small number of large users accounts for a significant share of total demand. In the latter, on the other hand, demand from residential consumers is more important. Only with concentrated demand fidelity rebates can have a significant economic appeal for a dominant company.

[12] Lack of reported margin squeeze cases in Copenhagen Economics' study (2013) may also be due to the fact that it covers the period up to 2011, while the postal market was fully liberalized only in 2012. Most margin squeeze cases also in the telecoms sector took place after its full liberalization in 1998, when mandatory access facilitated downstream competition, which has to be present, as otherwise margin squeeze could not even take place.

[13] This significant difference in rebates existed even though the eligibility criteria to obtain different types of discounts laid down in Correos' contracts with large customers and with competing operators appeared as formally equivalent.

these discounts were so high that it could never offer its services to those customers without incurring losses, and this according to the authority amounted to an abusive margin squeeze. The CNMC agreed and imposed on Correos a fine of nearly 8.2 million EUR, which Correos appealed before the National Court (*Audiencia Nacional*). The Court annulled the decision and the fine on the grounds that even though the CNMC had proven the existence of a margin squeeze, it failed to establish abuse as it had not demonstrated that the conduct in question led, "even in a presumed or potential manner" (Audiencia Nacional 2015, p. 6), to the exclusion of competitors.

While an abuse of a dominant position consisting of a margin squeeze does not require the competition authority to demonstrate intent to exclude nor the existence of effective consequences, the authority should prove that exclusionary effects are, at least, possible (Audiencia Nacional, Spain 2015). The ruling of Audiencia Nacional was upheld by the Supreme Court, which dismissed the cassation appeal filed by the State Attorney.[14] The Supreme Court clarified that, in the present case, the possible existence of exclusionary effects had not been proven, since, as the CNMC itself had acknowledged, Unipost had the capacity to counteract the margin squeeze carried out by Correos, which is why the finding of abuse of dominant position could not be made. In particular, the CNMC found that Unipost had a network that allows it to access 90% of consignments and 70% of the population and that its market share had apparently been increasing. This led the CNMC to the following important conclusion, which was often cited and debated by both Audiencia Nacional and the Supreme Court (2018:7):

> Unipost could use its own capacity to reach the target population without resorting to Correos' network. In these circumstances, Correos' refusal to sell the use of its network at a price equal to that offered to large customers, in no way prevented it from competing for those customers. It cannot therefore be said that Correos, with its discount policy, prevented its main competitor, an alternative operator, from competing for the large customers' business in its entirety.

Another margin squeeze decision was handed down in December 2017 in Italy where, following a complaint filed by Nexive, Poste Italiane's main competitor, the AGCM found that Poste Italiane abused its dominant position in the Italian bulk mail delivery market through several behaviors that together amounted to a single exclusionary strategy (AGCM 2017). These included, in particular, technical non-replicability of the incumbent's offers, margin squeeze, as well as various types of rebates. According to the AGCM, Poste Italiane prevented its competitors from entering the downstream market for deliveries of bulk mail in extra-urban areas, where only Poste Italiane had the infrastructure to deliver the mail, by charging them wholesale prices for bulk mail delivery services that were higher than the retail prices it offered to its business customers for the same service. As a result, even competitors as efficient as the incumbent could not match prices that it was able to offer to its final customers. The AGCM imposed on the incumbent operator a fine of 23.1 million EUR.

[14] Tribunal Supremo (2018), STS 254/2018, ECLI:ES:TS:2018:254.

In 2015, the BKartA found that Deutsche Post, holding well above 80% market share for licensed postal services, abused its dominant position by granting four large customers (Deutsche Telekom, Vodafone, Telefónica, and Freenet), through so-called target price agreements, discounts below the prices its competitors had to pay for access to its mail delivery network (Bundeskartellamt 2015). The BKartA, just as the CNMC and the AGCM, found that this conduct constituted an abusive margin squeeze. It hindered alternative operators from competing with Deutsche Post as they were impeded to compete for the large customers in question.

In contrast to the BKartA, the CNMC, and the AGCM, Ofcom investigated certain behaviors by Royal Mail as price discrimination in the first abuse of dominance decision that Ofcom issued against Royal Mail (Ofcom 2018). It concerned the market for bulk mail delivery in the UK, where the incumbent operators had a market share in excess of 98%. Whistl, a subsidiary of the Dutch postal incumbent, TNT, was the "first ever delivery competitor to pose a serious challenge to Royal Mail's effective monopoly in the delivery of letters." In its complaint to Ofcom, Whistl argued that in January 2014 Royal Mail proposed a number of changes to the terms and conditions of its price plans Contract Chance Notices (CCN) that would inhibit its ability to compete, requiring it to cease its own delivery operations should it wish to use a lower priced access service (Ofcom 2018, p. 1.14). Ofcom was careful to stress that it was not a case of "a potential example of margin squeeze involving the relationship between Royal Mail's upstream and downstream prices and costs" and that it was "not seeking to establish whether the prices charged to all customers by a dominant undertaking make it impossible for a competitor at the same level of the dominant undertaking to compete on price" (Ofcom 2018, p. 7.196).

To properly understand the case, it is necessary to consider ex ante regulation and in particular Ofcom's 2014 consultation on a possible modification of the regulatory access regime. During that consultation, Ofcom found that Royal Mail's "zonal tilt"[15] and "price differential"[16] could discourage entry (Ofcom 2014). To address these concerns, Ofcom put forward some proposals. However, as Whistl ceased its operations in the delivery market in June 2015, Ofcom chose not to move forward with these proposals as it considered them inappropriate and disproportionate given that the entry of "another end-to-end entrant of sufficient scale and scope to provide a significant level of letter delivery competition to Royal Mail in the foreseeable future" was unlikely (Ofcom 2017, p. 5.12). Yet, Ofcom's abuse of dominant position investigation carried out shortly after the consultation revolved around just one of the two issues, namely, the price differential. It is thus striking that while both the zonal tilt and price differential were considered inimical to entry from ex ante perspective, only the latter was examined ex post in the abuse of dominance case.

---

[15] Royal Mail aggregated together different areas on the basis of common characteristics concerning different delivery costs. Zonal prices were calculated by reference to NPP1, APP2, and ZPP3 prices. The "zonal tilt" refers to a set of percentage-based adjustments that were applied to the uniform APP2 prices to produce different prices for each of the four Royal Mail zones. Ofcom (2018:40, p. 3.60).

[16] Price differential refers to the difference in price introduced by the CCNs between APP2/ZPP3 and NPP1.

In its decision, Ofcom committed itself to demonstrating that Royal Mail intentionally hampered Whistl's entry in to the bulk delivery market. Although proof of intent is not necessary for establishing an abuse of a dominant position, it can nonetheless be relevant. In the postal sector, incumbent operators will likely invoke intent as a defense, arguing that the conduct in question was motivated by the need to ensure delivery under the Universal Service Obligation (USO). Royal Mail made this argument, as has Poste Italiane.[17] In both cases, NCAs disagreed. In rejecting Royal Mail's argument, Ofcom relied on the incumbent's internal document, which indicated that Royal Mail opted for a strategy that, if implemented, would have led to a lower loss of market share (just 1.4%). While this strategy involved both the zonal tilt and price differential, only the price differential was analyzed by Ofcom in its investigation.[18]

4 What Do Comparisons of Margin Squeeze in the Postal and the Telecoms Sectors Tell Us?

In light of the outcomes of these cases, we would like to concentrate the rest of the analysis on two important issues – essentiality of the incumbent's network and the difference and relationship between margin squeeze and discriminatory pricing. These are directly relevant for understanding the different way in which Ofcom framed its analysis of Royal Mail's conduct compared to the other NCAs postal margin squeeze cases.

4.1 *Is the Legacy Postal Network an Essential Facility or Just an Important Input?*

This is clearly a topical question. If Unipost could rely on its own capacity to reach 90% of consignments and 70% of the population, then another part of the CNMC's decision that seems to consider Correos' network to be an essential facility, without explicitly stating so, is perplexing. CNMC, for example, notes that "the postal network managed by Correos *is difficult to replicate*, since private operators do not enjoy sufficient economies of scale to bear the costs of deploying their own network that could replicate the coverage and capillarity of the Correos' network" (emphasis added, CNMC 2014). If there was any doubt that "difficult to replicate" may still not mean impossible, in another paragraph, CNMC explicitly states that "it is not economically viable for competitors to replicate the coverage and capillarity of Correos' postal network."

---

[17] Ofcom (2018), p. 1.25–1.26; AGCM (2017), p. 172–173.

[18] Ofcom acknowledged "that other changes introduced by the CCNs, which are not subject of this decision, would also have had an adverse impact on Whistl's profitability" (Ofcom 2018), p. 7.159.

In Europe, many commentators supported including essentiality of the input into the margin squeeze test (Crocioni and Veljanovski 2003; Gerardin and O'Donoghue 2005). Also, ERG's *Guidelines on the application of the margin squeeze test to bundles*, as well as various passages from *Deutsche Telekom* and *Telefónica* decisions, imply that even if the Commission's telecoms decisions, confirmed by the Courts, do not require the upstream input to be strictly essential, that characteristic may nevertheless play an important role in margin squeeze cases.

The argument re-emerged in the national margin squeeze cases. The Bundeskartellamt's (BKartA) decision issued in 2015 against Deutsche Post and AGCM's decision from 2017 are other cases in point. Deutsche Post and Poste Italiane, just as Telefónica, disputed the existence of the abuse arguing that access to their networks is not indispensable, as network can be replicated, and that some competitors had their own delivery networks. Poste Italiane, for example, went so far as to assert, erroneously according to the AGCM, that its network could be duplicated in 99.8% of the cases. As the AGCM (2017, p. 234) pointed out:

> the development of alternative networks throughout the national territory, and in particular in the extra-urban areas, have a structural limit which is caused by their non-profitability. In fact, both the geomorphic characteristics and the lack of demand for postal services due to low population density make the development of an additional network economically unsustainable compared to that of Poste Italiane which, in fact, ensures 100% coverage of the postal codes and population only inasmuch as it benefits from public contributions aimed at covering the losses deriving from the provision of postal services in situations of market failure.

Moreover, even the most innovative and efficient competitors, such as Nexive and Fulmine, which have heavily invested in the development of alternative end-to-end networks, covering, respectively, 80% and 75% of the population, cannot develop them further. This led the authority to conclude that "the Poste Italiane's service is an essential input for competitors to complete their offer. In other words [...], Poste Italiane's services to competitors constitute the 'indispensable service' referred to by the law on margin squeeze" (AGCM 2017, p. 234). Despite these observations, the AGCM, just as the BKartA, formally followed the Commission's position and found that the indispensability of a wholesale product is not required in order to prove potentially anticompetitive effects of a margin squeeze.

However, Advocate General Mazák in its opinion in *TeliaSonera* argued that when other inputs are available, and therefore a given input is not essential, margin squeeze cannot be implemented simply because a dominant firm's competitors are no longer dependent on its upstream input.[19] Such view is consistent with the analysis applied in vertical mergers, where competition authorities have to consider, among others, the ability to substantially foreclose access to input. If alternative operators do not need access to a wholesale product to provide their own service on the retail market, then in case of margin squeeze, they would simply bypass the wholesale product in question. This means that the incumbent's ability to foreclose access would be just theoretical, and not effective, which is what ultimately matters if foreclosure is to have a significant detrimental effect on downstream competition.

[19] Case C-52/09, *TeliaSonera*, Opinion of Advocate General Mazák, p. 11.

Although the CJEU in its decision did not follow AG Mazák's position, it has nonetheless acknowledged that "the question whether the wholesale input is indispensable may be relevant when assessing the effects of the margin squeeze."[20] Arguably, paragraphs 70–72 of the *TeliaSonera* ruling imply that if an input is indispensable, and competitors suffer a competitive disadvantage from the squeeze, an anticompetitive effect can be presumed. On the other hand, if an input is not indispensable, the competent authority has to consider whether a margin squeeze is capable of producing anticompetitive effects, as it would seem that such effects would be less likely.

For the CJEU, indispensability is not a prerequisite in margin squeeze cases. Rather, just as in the EU *Non-Horizontal Merger Guidelines*, it becomes relevant only to the extent it can inform the analysis of the likelihood of foreclosure (Pisarkiewicz 2018). In any event, the concept of essentiality, as defined in *Bronner*, may be too stringent to be meaningfully applied in continuously evolving telecommunications and postal markets. New business models may change the modes of competition, while technology could allow the bypass of existing bottleneck and drastically change the demand for core services.

4.2 *Margin Squeeze and Discriminatory Pricing*

As we mentioned earlier, the AGCM, BKartA, and CNMC investigated the conduct of their respective postal incumbents primarily as a margin squeeze, but Ofcom opted for price discrimination. According to Ofcom (2018, p. 7.139(c)), "given the nature of the discrimination in issue, the type of foreclosure effect [...], and the prevailing conditions of competition in the market at the time [the] conduct took place, it [was] neither necessary nor appropriate [...] to carry out an AEC test (or any other type of price-cost test) in assessing the likely effect of the price differential."

Margin squeeze may itself be a by-product of price discrimination, which could violate Article 102 TFEU. When it is possible to subsume a particular abuse under different legal labels, competition authorities have to choose the category that in their view will capture best its potential anticompetitive effects. In margin squeeze cases, authorities are mainly concerned about the insufficient profit margin that would inhibit existing and potential competitors from successfully challenging the incumbent's position. In case of a discriminatory squeeze, discrimination would exist between the incumbent's own downstream arm and its competitor. In case of the postal sector, however, discrimination may affect just a specific category of the

[20] However, instead of explaining with more precision and clarity when indispensability would be relevant, the Court mentioned in a rather convoluted manner that "the possibility cannot be ruled out that, by reason simply of the fact that the wholesale product is not indispensable for the supply of the retail product, a pricing practice which causes margin squeeze may not be able to produce any anticompetitive effect, even potentially", p. 72.

incumbent's customers, and this is precisely what happened in the *Royal Mail* case. According to Ofcom, the prevailing concern was that price differential amounted in effect to a penalty on access customers seeking to compete in bulk mail on end-to-end delivery. In the case of Whistl, an end-to-end operator that sought to expand its entry in the bulk delivery mail beyond a very limited number of standard selection codes (SSCs) would no longer be able to rely on a lower nationally priced NNP1, but would have to switch to higher APP2/ZPP3 zonal charges.

According to Ofcom, the impact of the price differential would have been material. In a market such as that of bulk mail delivery, not only competition was already limited, but growth would have to be achieved in the context of a declining market, which makes entry and expansion increasingly difficult over time (Ofcom 2018, p. 7.162). If achieved, however, competition in delivery services could trigger significant benefits as it accounts for the major part of the value chain, in contrast to the much more competitive segment of collection and initial sortation services, which accounts approximately for only 10%. This is why Ofcom saw discrimination by Royal Mail as an attempt to penalize any growth in bulk mail delivery competition beyond a limited scale as a central competition issue.

According to the Revised ERG *Common Position on Remedies*, which concerned the telecoms sector, margin squeeze, rather than as potentially anticompetitive conduct, can be seen as an anticompetitive effect that can arise in a vertical leveraging context through price-based as well as non-price-based abuses.[21] The European Regulators Group states that "although margin squeeze also has a behavioral aspect, it is classified as an effect here, as it can be the result of different behaviors of the dominant undertaking" (ERG 2006). This distinction becomes particularly important when the authority has to design remedies, as it will make a difference which particular behavior has led to margin squeeze. If potential harm to competition is clearly related to discrimination, it may be more effective to frame the behavior as such rather than as margin squeeze as the finding of a violation would also imply the obligation to cease anticompetitive discrimination.

As Ofcom's Royal Mail Access Pricing Review reveals, Ofcom has for a long time been concerned about the impact of discrimination. Although "the USPA Condition […] prohibits undue discrimination in relation to matters connected with access […] this condition would not necessarily prevent Royal Mail from seeking to […] differentiate between operators of varying sizes and mailing profile […] which could result in different prices being available as between access-only and end-to-end operators" (Ofcom 2014, p. 4.48). Ofcom believed that uncertainty faced by an end-to-end competitor as to whether they were likely to be able to rely on access prices on similar terms as access-only operator required urgent intervention. Seen from this perspective, the choice of discriminatory pricing rather than margin squeeze as an analytical framework for assessing the impact of Royal Mail's behavior is clearly more understandable and justified.

[21] According to the ERG Common Remedies, margin squeeze can result from bundling/tying, price discrimination, cross-subsidization, and predatory pricing.

5 Conclusions

Over the years, margin squeeze has become a frequently alleged and analyzed type of abuse in the EU. However, it has been associated mostly with the electronic communications sector, where landmark cases have been investigated at the European level by the DG Competition of the Commission. In contrast, recent major margin squeeze cases in the postal sector were investigated only by national competition authorities. Their decisions show that in the postal sector, margin squeeze was often coupled with, or resulted from, other practices and in particular from price rebates or discrimination. In contrast, in the telecoms sector, margin squeeze was mostly examined on its own. Comparing the decisions of national competition authorities in similar cases confirms that, where it is possible to subsume a particular abuse under different legal labels, competition authorities choose the category that in their view captures best the potential anticompetitive effects of a given conduct considering its nature, the type of foreclosure, and the prevailing conditions of competition in the market. As for the debate about a requirement of essentiality of the incumbent's input for the competitors, we have noted that while NCAs formally follow the Commission's stance and do not require it in margin squeeze cases, they nonetheless seem to recognize that legacy postal network often provide incumbents with the kind of advantage which in other contexts has led to the very definition of essentiality.

References

AGCM. (2017). Delibera A493 – *Poste Italiane/Prezzi Recapito*.

Audiencia Nacional Spain. (2015). SAN 2759/2015, ECLI:ES:AN:2015:2759.

Bundeskartellamt. (2015). *Decision B9-128/12*.

CNMC. (2014). *Resolución expediente S/0373/11*, Correos 2.

Copenhagen Economics. (2013). *Pricing behavior of postal operators*.

Crocioni, P., & Veljanovski, C. (2003). Price squeezes, foreclosure and competition law. *Journal of Network Industries, 4*(1), 28–60.

ERG. (2006). Revised ERG Common Position on the approach to appropriate remedies in the ECNS regulatory framework. *ERG*, (06), 33.

ERGP PL. (2017). 38, *Report on recommendations and best practices in regulation for access to the postal network of the incumbent operator* (in terms of competition, prices and quality of service).

Geradin, D. (2015). Is mandatory access to the postal network desirable and if so at what terms? *European Competition Journal, 11*(2–3), 520–556.

Gerardin, D., & O'Donoghue, R. (2005). The concurrent application of competition law and regulation: The case of margin squeeze abuses in the telecommunications sector. *Journal of Competition Law and Economics, 1*(2), 355–425.

Ofcom. (2014). *Royal Mail Access Pricing Review – Proposed amendments to the regulatory framework*.

Ofcom. (2017). *Review of regulation of royal mail*.

Ofcom. (2018). *Discriminatory pricing in relation to the supply of bulk delivery services in the UK*, CW/01122/01/14.

Okholm, H. B., Möller, A., & Basalisco, B. (2015). Regulatory developments in post and telecommunications: A tale of two industries. In *Postal and delivery innovation in the digital economy* (pp. 169–181). Cham: Springer.
Parcu, P. L., & Silvestri, V. (2017). Lessons from the postal sector to telecommunications and vice versa. In M. Crew et al. (Eds.), *The changing postal and delivery sector*. Cham: Springer International Publishing.
Pisarkiewicz, A. R. (2018). *Margin squeeze in the electronic communications sector: Critical analysis of the decisional practice and case law*. Alphen aan den Rijn: Wolters Kluwer.
Sidak, G. J. (2008). Abolishing the price squeeze as a theory of antitrust liability. *Journal of Competition Law and Economics, 4*(2), 279–309.

Competition Law in the Postal Sector: Trends and Analyses of Competition Cases in Europe

Olga Bohorquez Suarez and Jade Neveu

1 Introduction

The opening of the European postal sector to competition has taken place in a gradual and controlled way. Over the last three decades, the European Commission (EC) has set the regulatory landscape with three Directives. In the meantime, continuing technological developments, in particular, in electronic communication and electronic commerce, have decreased mail demand and increased parcels demands. Postal operators have accelerated their diversification into new activities.

Today, the postal sector is characterized by the coexistence of universal service obligations and activities open to competition after liberalization. In addition, the state monopoly incumbents continue to have predominant market shares. Those specific features of the postal sector make its analysis interesting from a competition law point of view.

The topic of competition law in the postal sector in Europe has already been addressed by diverse researches.[1] But those studies have mainly focused on a case-by-case assessment of the EC decisional practice in the postal sector. We want to tackle the subject in another way. Our objective is to describe the trend in competition case law in the postal sector and identify and understand any link between the

[1] See, for instance, Kjolbye and Malamataris (2016), Gerardin and Malamataris (2013), and Valentiny (2015).

This paper represents the personal views of the authors and do not necessarily reflect those of La Poste.

O. Bohorquez Suarez (✉)
Institutional Affairs and Regulation—Groupe La Poste, Paris, France
e-mail: olga.bohorquez-suarez@laposte.fr

J. Neveu
Regulated Activities and Consumption—Groupe La Poste, Paris, France

P. L. Parcu et al. (eds.), *The Changing Postal Environment*, Topics in Regulatory Economics and Policy, https://doi.org/10.1007/978-3-030-34532-7_19

competition law trend and regulatory changes in the sector. For this purpose, the authors constructed a database on the EC's competition decisions in the postal sector, from 1990 to the current day.

The paper is organized as follows. After this introduction, Section 2 sums up the main regulatory changes and market trends observed in the postal sector. Section 3 explains the analytical framework used by the EC to deal with state aid, mergers and antitrust cases. Section 4 describes the methodology used to answer the research question. Section 5 describes the trend in competition case law in the postal sector and its link to regulatory changes on the sector. Finally, Section 6 presents the main conclusions that can be drawn of competition decisions in the postal sector, as well as possible developments for future research.

2 Regulatory Evolution and Market Trends in the Postal Sector

As explained in the introduction, the specific features of the postal sector in the European Union—recent full liberalization coexisting with a universal service obligation and market trend changes—could affect competition regulation in the postal sector. To understand this influence, this section recalls the main regulatory changes and market trends observed in Europe in the postal sector during the last decades.

2.1 The Regulatory Landscape in the Postal Sector in Europe

2.1.1 Green Paper

The EC's Green paper on the development of the single market for postal services was adopted in 1992. Its objectives were, first, to provide a thorough-going analysis of the situation of the sector at the time; second, to discuss what should be the Community objectives for its postal sector; and third, to discuss how these objectives could be achieved. The guiding principle of the Green paper was the maintenance and the development of a universal postal service which would provide collection and delivery facilities throughout the Community at affordable prices and with a satisfactory quality of services.

The Green paper highlighted a major concern on the sector: the lack of harmonization. At the time when the Green paper was published, each Member State already reserved certain services in order to pursue some universal service objectives. But the scope of such services was usually larger than what was required to meet the objective. Considering this context, the option chosen by the Commission to further open of the market and strengthen the universal service was to implement liberalization and harmonization measures in a gradual manner. The Commission would remove certain services from the reserved area and define the universal service that should be provided in a coordinate manner throughout the Community.

2.1.2 First Directive (Directive 97/67/EC)

The first Postal Directive, adopted in December 1997, established a regulatory framework for European postal services. In line with the conclusions of the Green paper, the first Directive defined the minimum criteria for universal postal services[2] to be guaranteed by each Member and the conditions governing the provision of non-reserved services. The Directive also established common rules concerning tariff principles, quality and technical standards, and creation of independent national regulatory authorities. According to Hearn (2017), a major legal effect of the Postal Directive was to put in place exceptions from competition law to protect incumbents from the full rigor of the provisions of the Treaty of Rome for a transitional period of gradual and controlled liberalization of the market. The Directive stated that Member States should translate those provisions into national law no later than 12 months after the date of its entry into force (20 December 1997).

2.1.3 Second Directive (Directive 2002/39/EC)

The second Postal Directive, adopted in June 2002, amended the Directive 97/67/EC with regard to the further opening to competition of Community postal services. The Directive provided a timetable for a gradual and controlled opening to competition. The scope of the reserved area was therefore modified. The Directive stated that Member States should bring into force those provisions no later than 31 December 2002.

2.1.4 Third Directive (Directive 2008/6/EC)

The third Postal Directive, adopted in February 2008, amended again Directive 97/67/EC, with regard to the full accomplishment of the rules for governing internal market for Community postal services. This Directive set a deadline for full market opening of 31 December 2010 for 16 Member States,[3] and an exemption was granted to the (then) remaining 11 Member States.[4] The third Directive did not change the scope of the Universal Services Obligation (USO). All Member States must continue to ensure affordable universal postal services throughout the entire territory.

---

[2] Recital 2 of Directive 97/67 considered postal services as an essential instrument of communication and trade. The concept of universal service is not a particularity of the postal sector, but it applies to all Services of General Economic Interest (SGEI) (services provided in the public interest, where the market may not have sufficient incentives to do it, EC's communication 2001/C 17/04).

[3] Austria, Belgium, Bulgaria, Denmark, Estonia, Finland, France, Germany, Ireland, Italy, Netherlands, Portugal, Slovenia, Spain, Sweden, and United Kingdom.

[4] Cyprus, Czech Republic, Greece, Hungary, Latvia, Lithuania, Luxembourg, Malta, Poland, Romania, and Slovakia. Although Croatia formally joined the EU on 1 July 2013, its postal market was fully liberalized from 1 January 2013.

Full liberalization implied that maintaining a reserved area closed to competition is no longer an option. Member States could no longer grant or maintain exclusive or special rights for the establishment and provision of postal services. Consequently, Member States were provided with different possibilities to ensure the provision of the universal service, e.g., designation of one or several companies, different undertakings providing different elements of the universal service, and/or covering different parts of the national territory. Regarding financing of the universal service, the third Postal Directive provided a flexible and non-exhaustive list of financing possibilities: state aid, compensation funds, tendering procedures, or the establishment of a universal service fund.

2.2 *Market Trends in the Postal Sector in Europe*

At the beginning of the 1990s, mail services were provided in the reserved area (letters) and in the non-reserved area (parcels and express services). Those non-reserved areas were more profitable. Private operators were present mainly in parcels and express and in some cross-border letter services.

Since the beginning of the first decade of the year 2000, the postal sector has experienced a slowdown in the growth of mail sector. Each year, postal operators have seen their volume decrease, with an acceleration of the downward trend after the 2008 financial crisis. This decrease is mainly due to the development of new digital forms of communication.

In contrast to the letter volume decline, the postal sector is experiencing growth in parcels and express services. This growth is mainly due to the development of e-commerce, which has created new opportunities for the postal sector. In Europe, e-commerce turnover in 2017 amounted to €540 billion, 12.8% more than in 2016. In France, e-commerce growth in 2017 was 14.4%, with revenues of €81.7 billion. In 2017, there were 505 billion packages, 10.5% more than in 2016 (FEVAD 2018).

In the majority of postal markets, the Universal Service Providers' (USPs') profitability margin has been declining. With the structural changes in the postal sector, postal operators are developing new diversification strategies in other areas, mainly express services, logistics and freight services, and financial services. In France, La Poste has also chosen to focus its diversification strategy on personal services.

3 The EC Analytical Framework for Competition Decisions in the Postal Sector

The EC, as a competition authority at EU level, shall ensure the application of the principles laid down in the Treaty, particularly the competition rules. With regard to the postal sector, the objective is to promote and safeguard effective competition in the areas of antitrust and cartels, mergers, and state aid. In 1998, a notice set out the Commission's interpretation of the competition rules of the Treaty to the postal sector (European Commission 1998).

This section provides a brief description of how the Commission deals with each type of procedure. A prerequisite to elaborate, treat, and interpret the EC's decisions is to understand how procedures work: what triggers a new investigation, what are the different steps of the investigations, is there a maximum length for those steps, and what could be the possible outcomes of a procedure.

3.1 Antitrust and Cartels Procedure

The antitrust policy is developed from two articles in the Treaty on the Functioning of the European Union (TFEU). Article 101 prohibits agreements between two or more independent market operators that restrict competition. Article 102 prohibits firms that hold a dominant position in a given market from abusing that position. The Commission and the national competition authorities shall apply the provisions on anti-competitive practices in cooperation.

Cases under Article 101 and 102 TFEU can begin with a complaint, an own-initiative investigation, an information reported by individuals, or a leniency application from one of the participants to a cartel. Even if the procedure for anti-competitive practices is not precisely structured in the time by specific deadlines, there are two phases: an initial investigation and an in-depth investigation. The Commission and the national competition authorities may sanction and impose fines on companies found guilty, but may also set up a commitment procedure enabling undertakings to advance and implement specific proposals aimed at solving the competition issues.

3.2 Merger Control Procedure

The legal basis for EU merger control is Council Regulation (EC) n°139/2004. According to this regulation, only concentrations that do not impede effective competition in the common market or in a substantial part of it, in particular as a result of the creation or strengthening of a dominant position, shall be allowed.

Authority for merger control is shared by the Commission and the national competition authorities. Parties must notify the Commission of a proposed merger prior to its implementation when it has an EU dimension, if the annual turnover of the combined businesses exceeds specified thresholds in terms of global and European sales. Below these thresholds, the national competition authorities may review the merger. After notification, the Commission analyses the deal during the phase 1 investigation. An in-depth analysis can be opened if the merger raises important competition concerns. The Commission can decide to authorize, authorize under conditions, or forbid the merger.

3.3 State Aid Control Procedure

The postal sector is subject to general provisions on state aid (Art. 107 TFEU) and to specific provisions for undertakings entrusted with the operation of services of general economic interest (SGEI) (Art. 106 TFEU). Under the provisions specific to SGEI, Member States can compensate a USP for the net cost of the public service, but they cannot overcompensate it. The control of state aid falls within the exclusive competence of the Commission. Case law begins in different ways: a formal notification by a Member State, a complaint (e.g., from a competing operator), or a self-referral to the Commission.

EC's merger and state aid procedures are very time-bound. The Commission has the possibility of closing cases through simplified procedures. This is why the duration of those types of procedures can be very brief. On the contrary, procedures relating to anti-competitive practices can last longer because of the complexity of investigations, many related exchanges between the competition authorities and the companies concerned, and, sometimes, even the need to undertake public consultations.

4 Postal Competition Analysis Data

As explained in Section 2, the postal sector is characterized by the coexistence between universal service obligations and activities left to free competition. According to Valentiny (2015):

> [T]he completion of market opening in network services proved that the role of competition rules increase following a full market opening. The new entrants into the market attempt to avert the market-protection steps of the incumbent service providers by using the prohibition on restrictions of competition. (p. 55)

Given specificities and developments in the postal sector as well as the competition rules applying to it, the question arises as how the competition case law has evolved in the sector in Europe, particularly regarding the link with regulatory developments observed. This question has been previously addressed by other researches,[5] mainly using a case-by-case assessment of the EC decisional practice in the postal sector. We aim to tackle this subject by using a different method of analysis. Our purpose is to focus on the trend in competition case law in the postal sector and identify and understand—if it exists—the link between the competition law trend and regulatory changes and market trends in the sector. To do so, we constructed a database of the EC's competition decisions in the postal sector using the EC's research tool for competition cases available on their website. This database contains general information on the investigations including the date the complaint was filed, the name of

[5] Kjolbye and Malamataris (2016), Gerardin and Malamataris (2013), and Valentiny (2015).

the complainant, the dates of notification, adoption of the statement of objections and initiation of an in-depth investigation (if relevant), the country related to the case (either if it is the complainant on an antitrust case, the country providing the aid for an state aid decision or the country were a merging company locates), the relevant market, the amount of state aid approved, the final decision, the amount of the fine imposed (for antitrust decisions), the adoption of commitments, and the appeals related to each case (if applicable).[6]

In the EC's website, the postal sector was identified by choosing cases in the "H.53 – Postal and courier activities" category. For this analysis, the postal sector was restricted to those activities related to collection, sorting, transportation, and delivering of postal items—addressed mail, unaddressed mail, catalogues, newspapers, and parcels—including all express and cross-border services related to those items. This study therefore excludes some of the cases under the code H.53, either because they were misclassified and corresponded to another sector or because there were decisions concerning sectors where postal operators may be present but that are not directly related with postal activities (e.g., decisions on the banking sector).[7]

All decisions on state aid, mergers, and antitrust concerning the postal sector and available on the EC's website were listed and analyzed. The EC's advance research tool contains cases that have been the object of a Commission decision since 1 January 2000 for state aid cases, 21 September 1990 for merger cases and 1 January 1999 for antitrust cases. The final dataset covers all the competition cases in the postal sector available on the EC's website and initiated from 1990 to today. In summary, 96 competition cases in the postal sector were listed, corresponding to initiations of new competition cases on state aid, antitrust (including abuse of dominance), and mergers.

5 Analysis of the Trend in Competition Case Law in the Postal Sector and Link with Regulatory Changes and Market Trends

This section analyses the competition cases in the postal sector in Europe since 1990 as previously classified. The number of competition cases reported by the EC has been much less prolific in the postal sector than in other infrastructure sectors. When filtering on the sector "H.53 Postal and courier activities," 153 cases were reported. Doing the same exercise on other sectors provides a much large number of

[6] Because of lack of data availability and limited time, the database produced by this tool does not include decisions of national competitions authorities—a very interesting extension for future research.

[7] The research using the code H.53 resulted in 153 cases (94 for state aid, 50 for merger, and 13 for antitrust). After refining the perimeter, authors retained 96 cases (47 for state aid, 38 for merger, and 11 for antitrust).

cases: 1054 cases for sector "D.35, electricity, gas, steam and air conditioning supply," and 671 cases for sector "J.61, telecommunications." This difference can be explained by different reasons. First, the telecommunications and energy sectors are larger sectors that have opened up to competition earlier and faster than the postal sector. Indeed, the telecommunications sector has been open since 1998 and the energy sector since 2007. Secondly, the energy and telecommunications sectors are dynamic sectors with many growth drivers and innovations. This dynamism attracts many players capable of competing with the incumbent. In contrast, the opening up of the postal sector to competition was completed at a time when mail volumes were falling. The postal sector, with the exception of parcels, is a less dynamic sector. This reduces the incentive for players to enter this market and thus reduces competitive activity of the sector. The importance of competition in a sector will therefore have an impact on the number of competition cases in that sector.

The first step in the research was to elaborate descriptive statistics with this data and extract some conclusions. A second step consisted in studying the trend in competition case law in the postal sector and comparing it to the market trends and regulatory changes in the postal sector. Figure 1 presents the evolution of the number of initiations of new competition cases in the postal sector in the EU between 1990 and 2017, disaggregated by policy areas. Among the 96 cases that were covered, 49% corresponded to state aid cases, 40% were merger cases, and 11% were antitrust investigations. Antitrust investigations were less frequent during the period, but their average duration from the initiation until the termination date was the longest: 40 months for antitrust, against 21 months for state aid cases, and 1.5 months for merger cases.

We observe a variation in the number of cases along the three decades. During the 1990s, the average number of initiations per year was 2.7, whereas in the decade 2000–2010, this number increased to 4.5 initiations per year. After 2010, the average number of initiations has decreased to 4.13.

An increase in the number of initiations of state aid cases has been observed since 2002, which coincides with the date of adoption of the second Postal Directive.

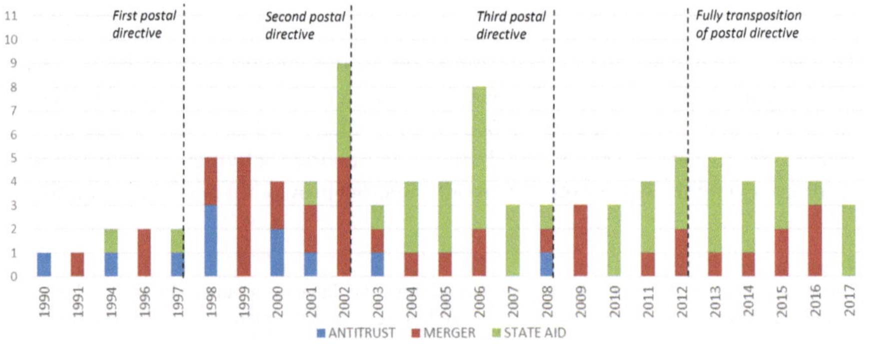

Fig. 1 Number of initiations of new competition cases in the postal sector by type of policy area, 1990–2017

In fact, this Directive provided for the reduction of the scope of reserved area, which was brought into force in 2003, and then further reduced in 2006. Reducing the reserved area may have had a negative impact on the financial sustainability of the USOs, so that Member States started to grant more compensations to Universal Service Providers (USPs).

The number of initiations in merger cases increased during 1998–2002, with an average of 3.2 decisions per year. But it has decreased since 2002, and it is more or less remained stable in the range of 1–3 cases per year, from 2002 to 2017. The number of initiations of antitrust cases has decreased since the 1990s. After observing a peak in 1998 (the year when the first Directive came into effect), the number of antitrust cases decreased to one or no cases per year. This could be explained because of a change of jurisdiction (national competition authorities dealing with most of the antitrust cases of Member States).

With regard to location, cases during the analyzed period were concentrated in Germany, the United Kingdom, France, and Italy.

5.1 State Aid Cases

In the postal sector, state aid control has several objectives: to ensure a level playing field for postal operators, to promote competition between them, and to ensure that high-quality postal services can continue to be delivered at affordable prices. During the analyzed period, 47 cases were state aid procedures. Thirty-eight of those cases were initiated by the notification of Member States, and nine cases were initiated by the EC, following a complaint (most of the time, complainants were the competitors of the national USP arguing against unlawful state aids and potential cross-subsidization). The number of state aid cases has increased over the last 30 years: during the 1990s, there were only 2 decisions; but from 2000 to 2010, there were 25 decisions, 2.7 on average per year.

As can be observed in Fig. 2,[8] state aid proceedings during this time concerned mainly compensations granted to USPs for discharging the universal postal services obligations entrusted to them. Aids granted to guarantee territorial coverage (network aids) were the second most important type of aid analyzed by the Commission during the period. Eight out of 11 decisions on network aids were notified by the United Kingdom.[9] Only 3 among the 47 cases concerned aid measures for the distribution of the press; these took place in France and Belgium.

Out of 47 state aid decisions, the Commission found it necessary to open an in-depth investigation for only 17, which shows that the state aid control procedure is

[8] Two decisions concerned simultaneously three different types of aids. Each type of aid was considered when computing the shares.

[9] The United Kingdom undertook a series of measures during the 2000s in order to ensure that the post office counter network, Post Office Limited, will remain able to sustain a nationwide network of post offices, particularly in rural areas.

Fig. 2 State aid cases in the postal sector in Europe by type of aid, 1990–2017

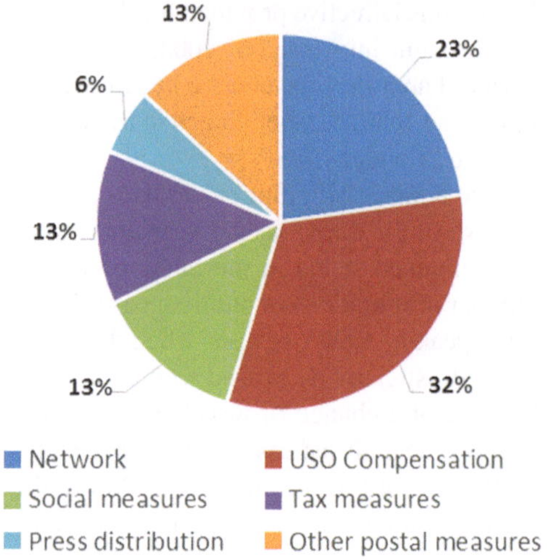

quite effective. With the decline in letter volumes, the role of national financing of the USO is increasingly being raised. Of in-depth investigations, six were opened on the financing of the USO, while none were opened regarding the postal operators' network.

Regarding final outcomes, 74% of the cases ended with a decision of the Commission that the measure was no aid, or the aid was compatible with the internal market rules. Only 9% of aid measures were rejected as unlawful by the Commission. Two out of forty-seven state aid measures were compatible, but implementation was subject to commitments. For example, the Commission authorized state aid on condition that the Member State ensures that it improves the definition of the parameters for calculating controlling and reviewing the compensation.

Nineteen percent of the state aid decisions were appealed to the General Court (9 of the 47 cases). Three of those appeals ended with an annulment of the EC's decision by the General Court. In the first case, the Commission's decision had authorized, after a preliminary examination, state aid from Belgium to La Poste.[10] The General Court found that the Commission had carried out an incomplete examination of the measure. The assessment of the compatibility with the common market of the notified measure raised serious difficulties, which should have led the Commission to initiate the procedure referred to in Article 88(2) EC (procedure allowing the Commission to examine the measure in depth).

The other two cases concerned state aid notified by Germany to Deutsche Post. The first case concerned a Commission's decision declaring state aid incompatible for reasons of overcompensation.[11] The European courts considered that the Commission had not verified that the notified aid was less than the total amount of

[10] General Court's decision (T-388/03) and Court of Justice's decision (C-148/09).

[11] General Court's decision (T-266/02) and Court of Justice's decision (C-399/08).

Deutsche Post's net additional costs relating to its SGEI missions. In essence, the Commission had not proved the existence of an unlawful advantage. The second case concerned a Commission decision declaring certain measures incompatible.[12] The General Court held that the assertion that pension costs are part of the costs that are normally included in a company's budget was not sufficient to establish the existence of an economic advantage for Deutsche Post. Also in this case, the Commission had not provided sufficient evidence for the existence of an unlawful advantage.

5.2 Merger Cases

The aim of merger control in the postal services market is to prevent effective competition from being hampered by merging companies, in particular in new market segments. During the analyzed period, 38 of the investigations carried out by the EC were merger control procedures. All cases were initiated by the notification of the companies involved. In the 1990s, the average number of merger cases was of 2.5 cases per year. Most of the cases during those years concerned international services and parcels. Concentrations were mainly led by Dutch and German operators and were aimed to organize the international delivery business.[13]

During the 2000s, the average number of cases per year decreased to two. The concentrations took place on parcels, mails, and various postal services. The average number of cases continued to decrease to 1.6 during the period 2010–2017. Those cases concerned mainly parcels and mails (see Fig. 3).

As Fig. 4 illustrates, 87% of the cases initiated between 1990 and 2017 were reviewed under a simplified procedure, and the EC decided not to oppose to the merger. On 5% of the cases, the Commission decided not to oppose after a simplified procedure, but remedies were required. Two mergers (5%) were cleared after undertaking and an in-depth, phase 2, investigation; one case required commitments.

Only one merger was prohibited, but the Commission's decision was canceled by the General Court and by the Court of Justice.[14] This case concerned the acquisition of TNT Express by UPS. The European court considered that the Commission failed to respect UPS's right of defense. The econometric analysis was based on a model different from the one that was the subject of an adversarial debate during the procedure, and for this reason the General Court annulled the Commission's decision.

[12] General Court's decision (T-143/12).

[13] For example, decision M.102 concerned the creation of a JV between TNT and five postal operators.

[14] Case M.6570: Acquisition of TNT Express by UPS, on the small package sector.

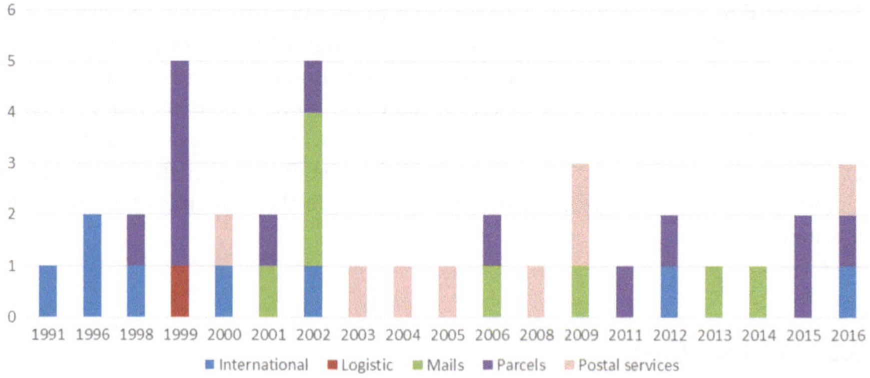

Fig. 3 Merger cases in the postal sector in Europe by market segment, 1991–2016

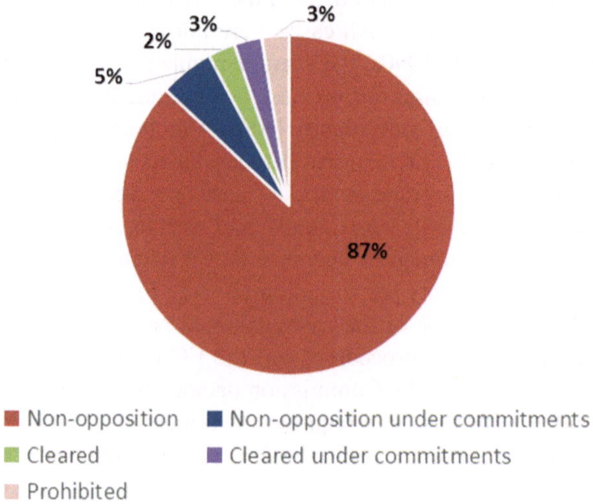

Fig. 4 Merger cases in the postal sector by final outcome: cases initiated between 1990 and 2017

5.3 *Antitrust Cases*

During the analyzed period, the EC only dealt with 11 antitrust cases. Seven investigations started after the filing of a complaint, and four cases were trigged by the EC's own initiative. This low number of cases is due to the fact that generally the EC deals with cases that have an impact on the entire EU. For example, the Commission examined on the basis of Article 101 TFEU agreements on terminal dues, which concerned all postal operators. National competition authorities deal with a majority of cases concerning postal operators, as the effects are mainly within a Member State.

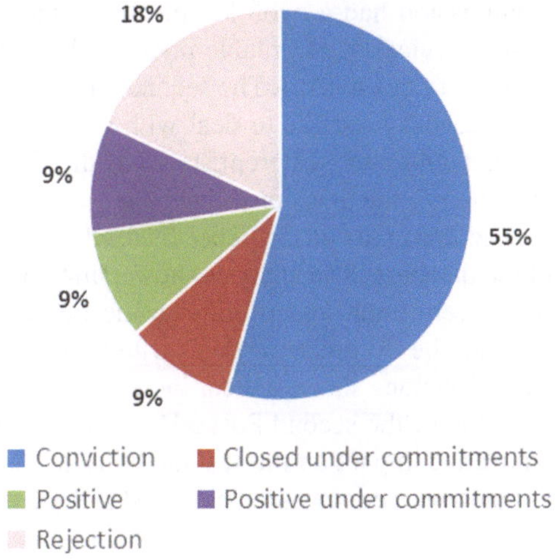

Fig. 5 Antitrust cases in the postal sector by final outcome: cases initiated between 1990 and 2017

The most important antitrust issues in the postal sector generally concern allegations that incumbent operators have engaged in abusive conduct to foreclose competitors. Out of 11 decisions, 9 concerned abuse of dominant position. Two main practices emerged: granting of selective and discriminatory rebates and refusal to give access to non-replicable parts of the postal network. In the case of abuse of a dominant position, it is not difficult to establish a strong market position, i.e., to satisfy the dominance requirement, since the incumbents tend to have a significant position in the local postal market.

As Fig. 5 shows, 55% of the cases ended with a conviction after finding an abuse of dominance. Those decisions concerned mainly mail services (hybrid mail, cross-border mail, B2B mail, and mail preparation). Two decisions ending with a positive outcome corresponded to the granting of an exemption to postal operators to sign an agreement to remunerate terminal dues (REIMS and REIMS II). The remaining cases were either closed by the Commission if the investigation did not proof any abuse of dominance or rejected.

6 Conclusion and Possible Extensions

This paper studied trends in competition case law in the postal sector during the last three decades, with the purpose to identify and understand (if existent) the link between the competition law trend and regulatory changes in the sector. To our knowledge, no other academic papers have attempted to analyze the EC's competition law decisions in the postal sector by studying their trend over time.

In the first part of the paper, we reviewed the main regulatory changes and market trends observed in the postal sector. This review confirms the particular context of the postal sector liberalization. When adopting the three Directives, the

Commission had a twofold objective: guarantee the maintenance of the universal postal services at affordable prices and gradually achieve the full liberalization of postal services market. The second part of the paper recapped the analytical framework used by the EC to deal with state aid, mergers, and antitrust cases. In fact, understanding the different stages of the EC proceedings was required to construct and analyze the decisions' database.

The third part of the paper focused on the results and lessons from the analysis of the database. The analysis shows, first, that competition cases reported by the EC have been much less prolific in the postal sector than in other network sectors. Second, the Commission deals with very few antitrust decisions. Third, the trend of EC's decisions shows a clear increase in state aid decisions that coincides with the adoption of the second Postal Directive. Reducing the reserved area may have had a negative impact on the sustainability of the USOs, so that Member States started to grant more compensations to USPs, triggering more inquiries by the Commission.

Bibliography

Batail, J. (2012). Quelle concurrence pour le secteur postal et quels effets? *Mission de contrôle auprès du Groupe La Poste.*

Boltron, F., Borsenberger, C., Joram, D., Lécou, S., & Roy, B. (2010). *Libéralisation & Services publics – Economie Postale.*

Copenhagen Economics. *Main developments in the postal sector (2013–2016).* Study for the European Commission, Directorate-General for Internal Market, Industry, Entrepreneurship and SMEs.

Eccles, R. (2013). Survey of competition law developments in postal services in Europe. In *21st conference on postal and delivery economics.*

European Commission. (1992). *Green paper on the postal sector.*

European Commission. (1998). *Notice from the Commission on the application of the competition rules to the postal sector and on the assessment of certain State measures relating to postal services.*

European Commission web site. http://ec.europa.eu/competition/index_en.html

Fédération du e-commerce et de la vente à distance, FEVAD. (2018). *Les chiffres clés.*

Gerardin, D., Malamataris, C. (2013). Application of EU competition law in the postal sector: Overview of recent cases. In *21st conference on postal and delivery economics.*

Hearn, J. (2017). *Regulation. Quo vadis?* The contribution of the postal and delivery sector: Between e-commerce & e-substitution (pp. 75–88).

Kjolbye, L., & Malamataris, C. (2016). Postal services and competition law: An overview of the EU and national case law. In *e-Competitions*, n°77572.

Valentiny, P. (2015). Anti-competitive practices, unlevel playing field after the full opening of the postal market. *Studies in International Economics, 1*(2), 50–70.

WIK Consult. (2006). *Main developments in the postal sector (2004–2006).* Study for the European Commission. Directorate General Internal Market.

WIK Consult. (2010). *Main developments in the postal sector (2008–2010).* Study for the European Commission. Directorate General for Internal Market and Services.

WIK Consult. (2013). *Main developments in the postal sector (2010–2013).* Study for the European Commission. Directorate General for Internal Market and Services.

Approaches to Assessing Vertical Mergers: A Review and Evaluation

Victor Glass and Stefano Gori

The Department of Justice (DOJ) is in the process of updating its non-horizontal merger guidelines, which have not changed since the mid-1980s. The work began in 2018, the year when the DOJ lost its case to prevent the AT&T/Time Warner merger from going into effect. The DOJ has reached out once again to the Federal Trade Commission (FTC) for its input. The FTC is a natural ally because it is responsible for consumer protection and preventing anticompetitive business practices (Royall et al. 2019). The DOJ believes that new guidelines would clarify its current positions on vertical mergers, which would benefit the business community. They will account for new economic insights into potentially anticompetitive effects of a merger at different points in the supply chain for a product of service. The agency had been waiting for the outcome of its appeal to block the AT&T/Time Warner merger (Perlman 2019). In February 2019, the wait ended when the DOJ decided to drop its case after it lost the case once again, this time before the US Court of Appeals (Snider 2019).

A need to update the vertical merger guidelines has been a widespread view within the academic community. Salop and Culley (2014) have suggested a compre-

The views presented in this paper are those of the authors and not of the affiliated institutions. We would like to thank Prof. David Sappington and Prof. Tim Brennan for having provided us fruitful insights and constructive comments ahead of our presentation in Dublin. We would like to thank Edward S. Pearsall and Michael Plunkett for having discussed our paper in Dublin and provided us advice on how to build on our results and improve our conclusion.

V. Glass (✉)
Rutgers Business School, Newark, NJ, USA
e-mail: vglass@business.rutgers.edu

S. Gori
Rutgers University, New Brunswick, NJ, USA

P. L. Parcu et al. (eds.), *The Changing Postal Environment*, Topics in Regulatory Economics and Policy, https://doi.org/10.1007/978-3-030-34532-7_20

hensive list of reforms. In Europe, similar concerns have been voiced about the spate of vertical mergers that involve major online platforms mainly Google, Apple, Facebook, and Amazon (GAFA) (The Economist, March 23, 2019 at 11).

A more fundamental question posed in this article is whether vertical mergers pose a particular risk when they involve information-intensive dominant platforms. "Big Data" is a key input in many industries for understanding customer needs and improving supply chain logistics. Processed data is sold as a service by itself, but it is also used to identify new market opportunities. Any merger could be seen as vertical when information is a major upstream input for improving company performance within a specified industry, or it can be viewed as a conglomerate merger when the information is used to expand into seemingly different industries.

This paper examines two companies outside the postal sector to understand the influence of Big Data on markets, looking at Amazon, which has acquired numerous vertically related companies, and the newly merged AT&T/Time Warner. The fear is that Amazon collects so much data that it has the capability of dominating markets and invading the privacy of the public. The AT&T/Time Warner merger, on its surface, is a standard vertical merger of a content provider (Time Warner) and a distributor of content (AT&T). One major sub-theme of the merger is the lack of customer data available to Time Warner to compete with online companies such as Netflix. Another is that AT&T will use information-enhanced content to expand into the 5G market.

The effect of Big Data on market structure and performance is not limited to major online platforms and media companies. European postal services, for example, have established digital platforms to offer a variety of online services, and some are expanding into telecommunications (Arlandis 2019). Stanford and Houk (2019) suggest postal services could expand into gathering sensor information for smart cities. Information sharing between a postal service and its customers such as Amazon could benefit both and, by doing so, cement long-term business relationships without the need to merge.

A key theme of this paper is that traditional vertical merger theories have not focused clearly on Big Data's effects on market behavior and performance. To fill the gap, a new "matrix" approach is introduced to examine the potential market imperfections caused by uneven availability of data. All this can be helpful for understanding the challenges that may confront postal companies attempting to expand into information-rich markets.

The paper is organized as follows. After this introduction, Section 1 summarizes the policy debates associated with Amazon and the recent AT&T/Time Warner merger. Section 2 introduces the matrix approach to regulation and antitrust that encapsulates economic theory in a network-engineering framework. The matrix approach traces information flows through broadband networks. Section 3 summarizes antitrust implementation issues. Section 4 focuses on European antitrust concerns and directions. Section 5 summarizes and concludes.

1 The Policy Debate About Vertical Integration

Amazon's growth is making more than a handful of academics and policymakers uneasy.[1] Amazon has become a huge and growing online platform. Amazon's annual revenue in 2017 was $232 billion, and it continues to grow annually by 30%. Its net profit margin was in negative territory during the 2012–2015 period, and yet, its stock price rose from $173 to $322 per share. As of March 29, 2019, its stock price is $1780 (Amazon financial data websites).

Lina Khan asked a rhetorical question, "Why would its stock price continue to grow while net profit margins remain modest?" Her answer is that Amazon's low-profit and profit margins portend future exploitation or abuses of market power when its platform is dominant (Khan 2016, p. 786).[2] Smart money is betting on it, according to Khan. Why else would its stock price be so lofty? Khan sees hints of abuse already. Amazon Prime has had the effect of reducing retail purchases from competitors (Khan 2016, p. 752). Amazon's aggressive pricing of e-books may be leading to consolidation of book publishers and fewer titles by unknowns (Khan 2016, p. 766–767). The size of its shipping business allows Amazon to negotiate heavily discounted delivery rates (Khan 2016, p. 775). Khan fears that with such a large presence, Amazon potentially has enormous informational power not only over customers and competitors but also over politicians, which could threaten America's way of life. Senator John Sherman said the objective of his bill, the Sherman Act, passed in 1890, was that the public should not submit to the king of production and trade (Lloyd 2006). Now, however, the issue is whether a king of information will dominate society by developing dossiers to influence policymakers.

Muris and Neuchterlein (2018, p. 5–8) dispute Khan's contention that selling products at low margins is a threat to long-term competition because the strategy will drive out competitors from the market. They contend that A&P resembles Amazon. A&P's innovative business plan allowed it to undercut local grocery store prices. Instead of focusing on prices, which would have favored A&P, the government charged A&P with substantially lessening competition. Lazonick (2018) suggests that Amazon's profits are rising and will rise because Amazon is the world leader in spending on research and development. Between 2014 and 2016, its high-paid professional staff rose from 18,266 to 30,433. This group is responsible for Amazon becoming the world leader in cloud computing, a new and high-margin market.

[1] For a more complete list, please refer to Wikipedia, *List of Largest Internet Companies*. Available at https://en.wikipedia.org/wiki/List_of_largest_Internet_companies.

[2] Petit (Petit 2016, p. 63) relates that platform leadership literature suggests that platforms like Amazon may use an "inducement mechanism" to steer external innovations toward a platform's complements to discourage other forms of innovation. He suggests that the type of innovation and spending on innovations should be an important element in an antitrust case.

This data wealth gives Amazon the ability to gather detailed information at different levels of the value chain. This type of leverage is a new phenomenon. For example, when Amazon buys a startup company, it may be functioning as a venture capitalist with deep pockets that can accelerate the development of new products, or it can be exploiting unwary startups that may have grown to compete with Amazon, itself. The list of Amazon's acquisitions is long and impressive (Wikipedia List of Mergers) and potentially troubling. More research is necessary to understand the effect of competing platforms using platform data for competitive advantage. A broader view would consider, for example, would Amazon lose business to eBay if it were perceived as an exploiter of its own platform data?

The AT&T/Time Warner merger was challenged in court for a more traditional reason. AT&T controls a large, physical part of the nation's broadband infrastructure that distributes, among other traffic, video content. Time Warner supplies programming content. The Department of Justice (DOJ) claimed providers of popular programming "have the incentive and ability to use (and indeed have used whenever and wherever they can) that control as a weapon to hinder competition." In this case, the merged company "can much more credibly threaten to withhold programming from rival [distributors]" and can "use such threats to demand higher prices and more favorable terms" (U.S. vs. AT&T, 2017, Complaint, p. 1–2). The DOJ admitted the timing of AT&T's push for higher prices was uncertain. AT&T could hold back from raising rates immediately because it could tap money from its cash cow, pay TV, until it pivots toward its long-term strategy (U.S. vs. AT&T, 2017, Complaint, p. 3).

The DOJ has since dropped its case after losing its appeal,[3] but the aftereffects of the merger are still being assessed. AT&T's stock price did poorly after the merger compared to competitors such as Comcast and Time Warner Cable (Glass 2019). AT&T raised prices for content at the same time a recent acquisition, DirecTV, was losing money (Lopez 2019); subsequently, Time Warner's top management left (Kafka 2019). The merger's aftermath could serve as a warning that culture clashes between merging companies can eliminate the value of any technical synergies from the combination.

A sub-theme for the merger was that Time Warner needed better information about customers to compete against fast-growing over-the-top competitors such as Netflix, Amazon, and Google. These companies are already vertically integrated. For example, Netflix owns thousands of servers that connect its customers to its content (Netflix Research).These "over the top" content providers are leaders in programming and distribution that allows them direct contact with customers (AT&T Pretrial Brief, p. 1 and p. 3). Another important implication of the merger is that it will influence conduct and performance in other markets. From this perspective, AT&T may be an important new large platform that can compete with Facebook, Google, and Amazon. Because information spans markets, the

---

[3]U.S. v. AT&T et al., No. 18-5214, (D.C.C., February 26, 2019). Available at https://www.cadc.uscourts.gov/internet/opinions.nsf/390E66D6D58F426B852583AD00546ED6/$file/18-5214.pdf.

same rules should apply to all large platforms. The key issue is whether additional rules are necessary when a platform also controls a substantial portion of the data transmission network.

2 The Matrix Approach to Vertical Mergers

Glass (2019) introduced a matrix approach to antitrust policy that places current antitrust literature into a new framework constructed from online network engineering principles. Specifically, the matrix approach employs the Open System Interconnection (OSI) framework used for developing online networks such as the Internet to analyze whether a merger is in the public's interest. The OSI model divides online networks into three basic layers: (1) the physical layer, (2) the transmission layer, and (3) the applications (final service) layer. The OSI approach is capable of simultaneously examining a merger's effect on particular markets and across markets at each layer of the network. In doing so, the matrix approach also calls into question traditional merger classifications because the effects of a merger's information gathering and processing and communications capabilities span many industries.

Besides the layering perspective, the OSI model naturally leads to categorizing products and services as either virtual or real. The virtual ones are built from bits of information. Voice, data, and video transmission fit into this virtual category. We would normally classify them as media products. Another given is that Internet Protocol communication networks process, transmit, and store information, which raises issues associated with network interoperability, privacy, security, and asymmetric information.

If applied to the recent AT&T/Time Warner merger, the matrix approach identifies key issues associated with information flows and interoperability of the networks being merged that are relevant for assessing mergers and that were not stressed in this case. The arguments in the case focused only on consumer welfare, which could be as hurt if the merged company had the ability to raise prices because of increased market power. A lingering question is why the merger was necessary for AT&T and Time Warner to develop more targeted information. Are there impediments to sharing data, including legal restrictions, which motivate mergers? Control over huge and growing proprietary databases is a controversial issue that raises social as well as competitive concerns.

From an OSI perspective, discussions of market power so far deal with the highest layer of the OSI model, the "applications layer," which deals with online input and product flows. Missing from the discussion are issues associated with the physical and transmission levels of the ISO model. For example, how will the AT&T/Time Warner merger potentially affect AT&T's ability to fund future upgrades to its physical network and proposed funding of the physical network required to roll out a 5G network? AT&T assumed that the merger will generate sufficient funds (Fung and Harwell 2016), but is this so? AT&T may also have the incentive and would have the ability to protect its investment in Time Warner content by reducing the quality of interconnections with its content rivals. This issue was also raised in the Federal Communications Commission's Business Data Service docket (Glass and Tardiff 2017). Not enough evidence was available to definitively say that AT&T tried to disadvantage competitors that use its network. In this case, the message is to monitor closely the behavior of the merged company because it controls an essential physical network.

The OSI model suggests that new measures of identifying markets and market power need to accommodate market changes often unforeseen. One set of measures that could work would focus on data gathering, processing, and utilization. Examples include personal information such as social security numbers and sensitive commercial data such as sales patterns of companies. Another set could focus on information transmission. An example would be blocking traffic from competitors. By contrast, the SSNIP test is largely a static concept. New and often surprising innovators such as Netflix create new markets that bleed older markets of their customers. How can one define a market using SSNIP when the future competitors are not even conceived of yet? Measures related to information control and flows are needed.

The matrix approach reinforces the idea of protecting access to essential physical facilities. It would also extend the concept to sensitive connections at the higher layers of the OSI model. The OSI matrix suggests general rules that cut across traditional industries for interconnecting networks and platforms, for privacy, security, and other information-related market issues. Special policies are necessary when a company such as AT&T controls an essential physical network. The reason is that by controlling the physical transmission network, AT&T knows the source and destination of all data packets that transit its network. It can even engage in deep packet inspection to examine the data payload being transmitted.

3 Antitrust Implementation Responses

It remains to be seen if the revised DOJ and Federal Trade Commission (FTC) published antitrust guidelines for upholding Section 7 of the Clayton Act (15 U.S. Code § 18), which prohibits mergers if they substantially lessen competition or tend to create a monopoly, will be consistent with the matrix approach recommendations. Historically, much of the analysis done by the FTC and DOJ follows similar methodologies for both horizontal and vertical mergers. Both examine market inputs and outputs, not information per se. The starting point is to predict how a merger will likely affect competition in a designated market. The two basic categories of inquiry are (1) market definition and measures of market power that provide the opportunity to lessen competition and (2) conduct that may raise prices, lower quality, reduce product variety, or inhibit innovation (U.S. Department of Justice and Federal Trade Commission 2010).

Vertical mergers and horizontal mergers differ in one crucial respect. Horizontal mergers eliminate a competitor that sells a substitute product. Vertical mergers combine firms that sell complementary inputs and final products. The main anticompetitive threats in this case are associated with foreclosure of competitors to critical inputs or to customers (Hoffman 2018). The matrix approach suggests that information gathering and transportation are two critical inputs in the online economy that produce informational power to improve company performance within an industry and the intelligence to expand into other industries. The traditional approach needs to be supplemented with measures of information power.

Argument on the limits of quantitative techniques that are primarily used for horizontal mergers are not new. Kaplow (2017, p. 1406) contends that the standard approach for antitrust investigations fails for many reasons. In his view, market power cannot be measured by a simple statistic because it has many dimensions and operates differently in different settings. For example, both cable and telecom companies are categorized as media companies that offer bundles of services—voice, data, and video—to increase network utilization. Customer profile data that includes choice of content selected, personal information, and customer online purchases from other vendors would improve marketing effectiveness.

Even a media-targeted information measure misses the value of information for entering new markets. AT&T was very eager to control movie content because it is viewed as the first "killer app" for 5G service (Glass 2018). The 5G market has enormous potential to open a new portfolio of markets:

> The fifth generation of wireless technology, 5G, promises to deliver billions of bits of information per second – Gigabit speed. With so much information transmitted and received, virtual reality will become commonplace, a 3D layer will be added to make your own imagined world even more real. Instantaneous biofeedback will keep you constantly in touch with your doctor or your virtual doctor. Smart homes will become smarter. Location and context aware sensors will become the chauffeur in your driverless cars. The list of enticing possibilities is long. (Glass 2018)

In the AT&T/Time Warner case, the issue is whether the merger will hasten the development of a competitive 5G market or allow AT&T/Time Warner to dominate markets associated with 5G. The crucial point is that information market power is hard to define and, even where it exists, its relationship with market conduct is not independent.

Liability for anticompetitive acts should depend on the nature of the act and the power of the company. A merged company may have a great deal of market power in the short run but may not act anticompetitively because of concerns regarding future entry. It should not be prevented from merging. If it does act anticompetitively after the merger, it should be fined heavily to recoup consumer losses and prevent further anticompetitive acts (Kaplow 2017, p. 1407). In Amazon's case, for example, the best strategy has been to moderate price increases to shield itself from antitrust allegations.

For market power to be a workable concept, Kaplow believes that the government should proceed by induction, first identifying the channels of market power and then applying them systematically to an assortment of anticompetitive practices in different settings. Even then, the government should develop a consumer (or societal) loss function and a threshold value or range of values for when the government should intervene (Kaplow 2017, p. 1407).

His prescription, if adopted, highlights the difficulties for developing antitrust guidelines for an online economy. Understanding the power of online information is in its infancy. Raw data may start out being processed for specific purposes but may lead to unexpected insights, some of them a threat to business and personal privacy. The neo-Brandeisian approach championed by Lina Khan becomes especially problematic if the channels of harm to society go beyond consumer welfare loss. A reliable index of societal harm would have to be developed that would account for changes in privacy, security, and secondary mergers that would reduce consumer choice (Lande and Averitt 2007).

4 European Concerns and Directions

Increasingly, global technology giants have been facing growing scrutiny over issues ranging from privacy and security to licensing practices and other types of allegedly abusive conduct. In the USA, the Federal Trade Commission is conducting a series of hearings aimed at addressing potential changes in competition and consumer protection policy considering the ongoing technological evolution. Furthermore, the agency has also launched a task force to focus broadly on the technology sector. In Europe, there are national initiatives but also initiatives at the European Commission level. For example, the UK government at the beginning of 2019 called for new rules for dominant digital platforms, and a panel, led by professor Jason Furman, called for a "code of conduct" to be applied to platforms (Perlman 2019).

The German authorities and politicians have pushed for a change in the law to require a dominant firm to share bulk anonymized data with competitors (The Economist, March 23, 2019, p. 11). The reason for these national initiatives is that online data has become a critical input for developing new services and targeting potential customers. European authorities perceive that concentrations of data can also be a weapon to foreclose markets and stifle innovation in a continent that does not have relevant domestic platforms. They are standing firmly on the principle that firms cannot lock out competition. This requires equal treatment for rivals who use their platforms.

In April 2019, the European Commission released a report authored by an expert panel comprising Prof. Jacques Crémer, an economics professor at the Toulouse School of Economics in France; Yves-Alexandre de Montjoye, an assistant data professor at Imperial College London; and Prof. Heike Schweitzer, a law professor at Humboldt University of Berlin, titled "Competition policy for the digital era" (Crémer et al. 2019). The report identified extreme returns to scale, network externalities, and the role of data due to technology as the three main characteristics of the digital economy that lead to the presence of strong "economies of scope."

These stimulate the development of ecosystems and give incumbents a strong competitive advantage (Crémer et al. 2019, p. 2).

They recommend that the assessment of market power has to be case-specific and must take into account insights drawn from behavioral economics about the strength of consumers' biases toward default options and short-term gratification. In line with the matrix approach, they believe the case-specific analysis should examine the access to data available to a firm versus its competitors and the sustainability of any such differential access to data (Crémer et al. 2019, p. 3–4). Their other basic recommendation is for company rules that prevent abusive self-preferencing. Companies would have a responsibility to ensure that their rules do not impede free, undistorted, and vigorous competition, on the platform, without objective justification (Crémer et al. 2019, p. 6). European Commissioner Margrethe Vestager, while presenting the report at a press conference in Bucharest, on April 4, 2019, addressed the issue of the importance of data: "…as data becomes increasingly important for competition, it may not be long before the commission has to tackle cases where giving access to data is the best way to restore competition" (Perlman 2019). And yet, open access could eliminate the incentive to gather data.

Two other issues are emerging in the analysis being carried out by economists in Europe: (1) the boundary between competition policy and regulation and (2) the distinction between vertical and horizontal integration. In the first case, the boundary is blurred for merger control. As a result, competition authorities often take actions more typical of regulators (Motta 2009, Preface xviii). In the latter issue, traditional antitrust policy distinguishes between horizontal and vertical mergers, but these categories are no longer adequate to characterize market power in an online economy because Big Data is an upstream input that spans the economy. Moreover, because voice, data, and video are data bytes, the definition of market in media cases could include content from many websites not traditionally associated with movies and television.

5 Conclusion

In our view, economists and policymakers are struggling to understand market power and anticompetitive activities in a digital world. The Internet is still in its infancy. In the future, more and more devices will be communicating information. One point is clear already: information concentration affects many markets and supply chains simultaneously. Key questions remain unanswered: Are online integrated platforms too big for others to grow? What types of rules will enhance online market performance? Will these rules improve a postal service company's prospects for participating in the online economy? The matrix approach to analyzing the performance and conduct of online platforms suggests that government policy should consider the technologically neutral rules for the online economy in its totality.

In the near term, it will be important to monitor what takes place in Europe. For example, it will be interesting to see what happens on the Spotify vs. Apple case, which raises issues of pricing the use of platforms and excluding competitors (Feldman 2019). Similar to the complaints of book publishers (Shaphard 2017), Spotify also claims Amazon is using its platform power to extract excessive fees and limit access to third-party apps that, in this case, makes Spotify less competitive with Amazon's streaming music service (Arcand 2019; Nicolau and Buck 2019).

Antitrust and regulatory policies should consider how the applications layer and the transportation and physical layers interact. Unlike historical companies that grew large because of efficiencies and innovative practices, the online platforms hold a great deal of more individualized data than was the case before data digitization became widespread. This informational advantage has allowed online platforms such as Amazon to exert monopsony-like power over suppliers. Will suppliers band together to lessen this power? If so, how will it affect the number of supply channels? In Amazon's case, if it actively competes against suppliers such as parcel delivery companies, will it cause suppliers to raise prices to other customers, and will parcel delivery rates rise in places where current suppliers have market power such as rural areas? Future policy should monitor online entities that are information reservoirs and transportation giants. In this context, a basic challenge of postal operators is to develop an information strategy that will avoid government concerns while at the same time allowing it to form new information links with companies such as Amazon to cement long-term relationships.

References

Amazon financial data websites: Stock Price: https://www.macrotrends.net/stocks/charts/AMZN/amazon/pe-ratio; Profit margins: https://www.macrotrends.net/stocks/charts/AMZN/amazon/profit-margins; TTM: Trailing Twelve Month Margin Industry Comparisons: https://www.zacks.com/stock/research/AMZN/industry-comparison; Revenue: https://www.macrotrends.net/stocks/charts/AMZN/amazon/revenue.

Arcand, R. (2019). *Spotify's antitrust case against apple, explained.* SPN. Available at https://www.spin.com/2019/03/spotify-apple-music-antitrust-complaint/.

Arlandis, A. (2019). *European postal operators' diversification strategies and implications for cost allocation.* Presented at the 2019 Conference on Postal and Delivery Economics.

Crémer, J., de Montjoye, Y. A., & Schweitzer, H. (2019). *Competition Policy for the digital era.* European Union. Available at http://ec.europa.eu/competition/information/digitisation_2018/report_en.html.

Feldman, B. (2019). Spotify takes on apple's anti-competitive behavior in Europe. *New York Magazine*. Available at http://nymag.com/intelligencer/2019/03/spotify-files-lawsuit-against-apple-in-europe-elizabeth-warren-google.html.

Fung, B., & Harwell, D. (2016). *Why AT&T's merger with Time Warner is such a huge deal*, Washington Post. Available at https://www.washingtonpost.com/news/the-switch/wp/2016/10/21/att-could-soon-own-almost-everything-from-hbo-to-cnn-to-dc-comics/?utm_term=.df221ab322b9.

Glass, V. (2018). *The FCC's push to speed-up 5G deployment by overhauling infrastructure regulation: What's at stake and what to expect?* Featured in three installments, Bloomberg Law: "A Primer on Wireless 5G Technology," "The FCC's Proposals and Industry Reaction," and "The FCC Acts to Spur Broadband Development." February–May.

Glass V. (2019). A Matrix Approach to Antitrust and Regulatory Policy: The AT&T/Time Warner Merger Revisited, Rutgers Business School Working Paper.

Glass, V., & Tardiff, T. (2017). What types of regulatory strategies work when a customers are likely to become competitors? *Rutgers Business Review, 2*(3), 295–314. Available at https://www.rbusinessreview.org/rbr020302.

Hoffman, B. (2018). *Remarks on vertical merger enforcement at the FTC* https://www.ftc.gov/system/files/documents/public_statements/1304213/hoffman_vertical_merger_speech_final.pdf.

Kafka P. (2019). Everyone who used to run Time Warner is out the door less than a year after AT&T paid $85 billion for the media giant, Recode, March 18, 2019. Available at https://www.recode.net/2019/3/18/18271285/warner-bros-sex-scandal-kevin-tsujihara-att-time-warner-top-executives-out

Kaplow, L. (2017). Article on the relevance of market power. *Harvard Law Review, 130*(5), 1303.

Khan, L. M. (2016). Amazon's antitrust paradox, *126 The Yale Law Journal*. http://digitalcommons.law.yale.edu/ylj/vol126/iss3/3.

Lande, R. H., & Averitt, N. W. (2007). Using the 'Consumer Choice' approach to antitrust law. *Antitrust Law Journal, 74*, 175. Available at SSRN: https://ssrn.com/abstract=1121459.

Lazonick, W. (2018). *The secret of amazon's success*, New York Times, November 19, 2018. Available at https://www.nytimes.com/2018/11/19/opinion/amazon-bezos-hq2.html.

Lloyd, M. (2006). *AT&T and whatever happened to antitrust.* Center for American Progress.

Lopez, M. (2019). *AT&T's DirecTV now to restructure pricing model, will raise price $10 per month*, March 11, 2019, Yahoo. Available at https://www.yahoo.com/entertainment/t-directv-now-restructure-pricing-192943782.html.

Motta, M. (2009). *Competition policy, theory and practice.* 12th printing.

Muris, T., & Neuchterlein, J. (2018). *Antitrust in the internet era: The legacy of United States v. A&P.* George Mason Law & Economics Research Paper No. 18-15. Available at SSRN: https://ssrn.com/abstract=3186569 or https://doi.org/10.2139/ssrn.3186569.

Netflix Research. *Streaming: Optimizing your viewing experience*. Available at https://research.netflix.com/business-area/streaming.

Nicolau, A., & Buck, T. (2019). *Spotify chief Ek warns of price rises if apple wins EU antitrust battle*, page 1 Financial Times, March 15th.

Perlman, M. (2019). *EU report calls for new antitrust rules for tech platforms, Law 360*. April 4th.

Petit, N. (2016). *Technology giants, the "moligopoly" hypothesis and holistic competition: A primer*, Draft. Retrieved from SSRN: https://ssrn.com/abstract=2856502 or https://doi.org/10.2139/ssrn.2856502.

Royall, M. S., Cunningham, R., Wilson, C., & Kapp, C. (2019). *Updated vertical merger guidelines may be on the horizon*. Washington Legal Foundation. Available at https://wlflegalpulse.com/2019/04/24/updated-vertical-merger-guidelines-may-be-on-the-horizon/.

Salop, S., & Culley, D. P. (2014). *Potential competitive effects of vertical mergers: A how-to guide for practitioners.* Georgetown University Law Center. Retrieved from //scholarship.law.georgetown.edu/cgi/viewcontent.cgi?referer= //scholar.google.com/&httpsredir=1&article=2404&context=facpub.

Shaphard, A. (2017). *Amazon steps up its battle with the book industry*. New Republic. Available at https://newrepublic.com/article/142616/amazon-steps-battle-book-industry.

Snider M. (2019). *Justice department loses appeal to block AT&T-Time Warner merger, won't appeal again, USA Today*. February 26. https://www.usatoday.com/story/money/media/2019/02/26/at-t-time-warner-merger-upheld-court-again-denying-doj-opposition/2990856002/.

Stanford, I., & Houk, A. C. (2019). *How the USO might help influence and enhance the growth of smarter cities*. In Presented at the 2019 Conference on Postal and Delivery Economics.

The Economist. (2019). *Europe takes on the tech giants, page 11*. March 23rd issue.

United States Court of Appeals for the District of Columbia Circuit United States of America, Plaintiff-Appellant, v. AT&T INC.; Directv Group Holdings, LLC; and Time Warner Inc., USCA Case #18-5214, Filed 08/06/2018. (2019). Retrieved from https://www.courthousenews.com/wp-content/uploads/2018/08/Government-ATT-Time-Warner-Appeal-Brief.pdf September 30, 2018.

United States Department of Justice and Federal Trade Commission. (2010). *Horizontal merger guidelines*. August 19, 2010. Available at https://www.ftc.gov/sites/default/files/attachments/merger-review/100819hmg.pdf.

United States of America (U.S.). Plaintiff, v. AT&T INC DIRECTV Group Holdings, LLC. Time Warner Inc., Defendants. (2017). Case 1:17-cv-02511, United States District Court for the District of Columbia, November 20. Retrieved October 1, 2018n from https://www.justice.gov/atr/case-document/file/1012916/.

Wikipedia. *List of mergers and acquisitions by amazon*. Available at https://en.wikipedia.org/wiki/List_of_mergers_and_acquisitions_by_Amazon.

(Un)Locking Parcel Lockers

Til Rozman

1 Introduction

Because of the development of the parcel business, innovative last-mile delivery solutions are growing in importance. Missed home delivery attempts are costly for parcel delivery service providers and inconvenient for the addressees. Parcel lockers for depositing and collecting parcels and small packages seem to be a possible solution. From the perspective of the postal operators, lockers reduce costs of delivery due to the higher hit rate and shared delivery costs for parcels that are dropped off simultaneously at the same location (Zurel et al. 2018). From the perspective of the addressees, assuming lockers are always accessible, the cost of collecting parcels from the parcel lockers are probably in the average lower compared to the situation where the addressees collect parcels at the post office or a pickup/parcel shop where parcels were delivered due to missed home delivery. In addition, delivering to and collecting from the parcel lockers can significantly reduce environmental pollution and traffic congestions (*ibidem*).

This chapter deals with implications of parcel locker developments for the scope of the sector-specific regulation in the EU countries. From the regulatory point of view, it aims at answering the following policy question: Should Universal Service Providers' (USP) parcel lockers be open to other operators and if so on what grounds? In the EU countries, there are, on the one hand, limited yet different and contradicting regulatory approaches to this question and, on the other hand, a silent majority of regulators that has not yet taken a formal position. This chapter

---

This chapter does not necessarily reflect the views of the institution the author belongs to.

T. Rozman (✉)
Agency for Communication Networks and Services of the Republic of Slovenia and University of Ljubljana, Ljubljana, Slovenia
e-mail: Til.Rozman@akos-rs.si

P. L. Parcu et al. (eds.), *The Changing Postal Environment*, Topics in Regulatory Economics and Policy, https://doi.org/10.1007/978-3-030-34532-7_21

aims to serve as one of the bases for answering this topical question and to spark a debate among EU countries on regulation of parcel lockers.

The chapter is organized as follows. In order to illustrate the most recent parcel locker developments, section 2 provides a picture of the increasing numbers of parcel lockers in many EU countries. Further, it identifies different and contradicting regulatory approaches in the EU countries. Section 3 discusses the regulatory question of whether USP's parcel lockers should be accessible to parcel competitors. After explaining the concept of essential facilities, this section builds on the leading jurisprudence and assesses whether the essential facilities concept applies to parcel locker facilities. Section 4 argues that sharing of parcel lockers generates a positive social outcome and that some regulation is unavoidable in order to promote non-economic public interests. However, general social regulation, for example, to reduce pollution and traffic congestion, should be prioritized over sector-specific regulation. The latter should play a supportive role. Section 5 concludes that developing a potential sector-specific regulation of parcel lockers should be cautious, yet innovative and future-proof.

2 Different Market Developments and Regulatory Approaches in EU Countries

2.1 Number of Parcel Lockers: EU Countries Overview

In the light of the abovementioned advantages, it is not surprising that the number of parcel lockers is increasing in many EU countries. Although the data are very limited, Table 1 clearly indicates significant differences between the EU countries regarding both the number of parcel lockers and the identity of the parcel lockers' operators. In five EU countries, the number of parcel lockers operated by the USP has increased by more than 50% from 2013 to 2017, while over the same period, the number of parcel lockers has decreased in only one country. Data on the parcel lockers operated by other postal service providers (OPSPs) indicate a similar trend; in four EU countries, the number of parcel lockers has increased by more than 50%, while only in two countries, the number has decreased.

Spain stands out in the total number of parcel lockers operated by its USP as well as in the percentage increase in the number of parcel lockers over the observed period.

Although Germany is missing in the table above, the number of parcel lockers and the maturity of the parcel locker market are significant in this country as well. In 2018, Deutsche Post DHL Group operated around 3,700 parcel lockers (Deutsche Post DHL Group, 2018). Comparing this with 3200 parcel lockers in 2017 (Deutsche Post DHL Group, 2017) and with 2650 parcel lockers in 2013 (Deutsche Post DHL Group, 2013) indicates the growing trend in Germany.

Table 1 Parcel lockers from USP and from OPSP in the period 2013–2017

	USP						OPSP					
Country	2013	2014	2015	2016	2017	Variation 2013–2017 (%)	2013	2014	2015	2016	2017	Variation 2013–2017 (%)
BE	–	–	150	150	151	1	–	–	1	2	2	100
BG	–	–	–	–	–	–	–	–	–	–	67	–
CY	–	–	2	3	3	50	–	–	–	–	–	–
CZ	–	10	15	5	5	–50	–	–	–	32	30	–6
DK	445	467	468	469	465	4	–	–	–	–	–	
EE	79	98	104	124	126	59	81	83	85	111	127	57
ES	–	–	403	2305	3110	672	–	–	–	–	–	–
FI	307	459	482	479	498	62	–	–	–	–	–	–
HR	–	–	–	–	–	–	–	–	–	–	2	–
HU	–	–	50	50	50	0	–	–	152	138	138	–9
IS	–	–	8	8	8	0	–	–	–	–	–	–
LT	–	–	–	–	–	–	–	121	131	184	238	97
NL	–	–	8	10	35	338	–	–	25	70	69	176
PL	34	117	120	120	118	247	283	100	–	–	–	–
RO	–	–	–	–	0	–	–	–	–	–	53	–
SI	–	–	–	–	24	–	–	–	–	–	56	–
SK	–	–	–	–	45	–	–	–	–	–	–	–

Source: ERGP (2018b, p. 84)
Notes:
1. Where no data are available for 2013 (or of zero value), the variation presented corresponds to the variation between 2017 and the first year for which there are data
2. Data regarding OPSP parcel lockers in Poland are not available from 2015 onward due to the fact that the network of parcel lockers was sold to, and then outsourced back, to an entity which is not a postal operator. The NRA of Poland is not able to collect data about this entity

Parcel lockers operated by noncarriers (e.g., white label companies)[1] are not included in the table above, although their number is significant in many EU countries. For instance, in the UK Amazon has installed over 500 parcel lockers, and InPost operates over 1000 parcel lockers (IPC 2018a).

Interestingly, there seems to be a relatively modest correlation between the number of parcel lockers and delivery preferences. According to the cross-border e-commerce shopper survey (IPC 2018b), parcel lockers were the most commonly used type of delivery location (for e-commerce parcels) in Finland (40%), Denmark (36%), and Latvia (35%). In countries among the highest total and per capita numbers of parcel lockers, Germany and Spain, preferences for parcel locker delivery are not among the highest.

[1] A white label company is one that does not collect, sort, and transport parcels itself, but only possesses parcel lockers or service locations where parcels from different, but not necessary all, operators can be picked up by consumers.

2.2 Different Regulatory Approaches in EU Countries

The shift from letters to parcels and the increasing number of parcel lockers operated by USPs, OPSPs, and noncarriers raise the question of the implications of these market developments to the scope of postal regulation and access practices. The issue of access practices regarding parcel lockers has been recognized as a topical one also at the ERGP level.[2]

At the moment, no comprehensive overview of the state of the legislation and practices regarding the regulation and access to the parcel lockers is available. However, a glance at national postal legislations in the EU countries suggests that postal lockers' specific legislations or regulatory decisions are still rare. Copenhagen Economics' 2018 study on the main developments in the European postal sector identified cases of sharing of parcel lockers among the USP and OPSPs in Belgium and Luxembourg and sharing of delivery network by OPSPs in Italy (Okholm et al. 2018). In Denmark, access to USP's parcel lockers is required by law (*ibidem*). Its study concluded:

> …that operators generally do not cooperate in building or sharing infrastructure. In a few cases, however, operators have engaged in cooperation initiatives to develop and/or share part of the postal infrastructure. (*ibidem*, p. 90)

In addition, the following three regulatory practices/decisions regarding the access to the parcel lockers have been identified. In Luxembourg, the USP refused to deliver to a noncarrier's parcel lockers. During an investigation, companies reached an agreement, resolving the dispute (Cullen International 2018). In Germany, access to the parcel lockers is not mandatory because "… parcel logistic systems involving the operational facilities are not seen as 'essential facilities'" (ERGP 2019, p. 33). In Spain, CNMC formulated an opinion that USP's parcel locker service is not part of the Universal Service Obligation (USO) and, consequently, access to the USP's parcel lockers has not been imposed (Cullen International 2016). However, CNMC held that if parcel lockers become essential in order to compete on the parcel market, CNMC would propose that access thereto is granted at the reasonable conditions and prices (ERGP 2019, p. 39). However, the very opposite situation is in Greece where parcel lockers are considered as part of the USP network to which providers of services which fall within the scope of the USO have access to (Regulation on access to Postal Network of the Universal Service Provider 2014).

The identified regulatory approaches clearly indicate that different views among NRAs are present at the moment. This, together with the silent majority of the NRAs that has not taken a formal position on the issue of access to the USP's parcel lockers, makes sharing of USP's parcel lockers a highly topical issue, especially for regulators and USPs.

---

[2]According to the ERGP Working Programme for 2019, working group is preparing a Report on the development of postal networks and access practices regarding infrastructure related to the parcel market (ERGP 2018a).

3 Should Parcel Lockers Be Open?

Market developments pose the question of whether USPs' parcel lockers should be accessible to rivals and under what conditions. To find an answer, I examine the essential facility concept and whether this concept is applicable to parcel lockers.

3.1 The Regulatory Question

In the EU countries, the number of parcel lockers is increasing, and the battle for first-mover advantage has started. However, the scarcity of the best micro-locations might become an issue. Assuming that the fixed costs of installing and operating are high, achieving the benefits of the economies of scale is crucial for the profitability of the parcel lockers. The full utilization of their capacities requires a sufficient quantity of parcels delivered thereto. Under these assumptions, control over the best-located parcel lockers constitutes a competitive advantage for the company but only if they are used frequently enough to surpass the break-even point. From the parcel locker operators' perspective, sharing weakens the competitive (first-mover) advantage of their holder but facilitates achieving economies of scale. From a broader policymaking and regulatory perspective, sharing of parcel lockers generates a positive social outcome, e.g., increased network coverage and positive environmental and urban logistic effects.

If these scale economies are significant and prime locations scarce, access to parcel lockers may raise antitrust and regulatory issues. One of them is the refusal to supply parcel lockers or give access to them. The fundamental question is whether parcel lockers are necessary for parcel delivery firms to compete effectively.[3] This invites consideration of the essential facilities concept in competition law.

3.2 The Essential Facilities Concept

Building on the freedom of contract and deriving from respect for property rights, the fundamental rule in market economies is that all companies, including dominant companies, are free to choose their trading partners (Dunne 2015). The essential facilities doctrine is an exception to this fundamental rule. It relates to a physical infrastructure which is required for market participation, but would not be economically feasible to duplicate. This doctrine specifies conditions under which the owner of an essential or bottleneck facility is mandated to provide access to that facility at

[3] In general, when examining whether a refusal to supply deserves its attention, the European Commission (2009) considers whether the supply of the refused input is objectively necessary for operators to be able to compete effectively on the market.

a reasonable price (OECD, 1996). In EU law, the essential facilities doctrine is interpreted narrowly, which is logical, given that this doctrine is an exception to the fundamental rule and exceptions must be according to the legal theory – interpreted narrowly.

In Oscar Bronner v Mediaprint[4] ("Bronner case"), the European Court of Justice (ECJ) held that a press company with a very large share of the daily newspaper market, and that operates the only nationwide newspaper home-delivery service, did not abuse a dominant position in refusing to allow the publisher of a rival newspaper to have access to that delivery service for appropriate remuneration.[5] ECJ developed a restrictive three-part test for assessing refusal to supply by a firm with a dominant position.[6] First, the refusal is likely to eliminate all competition in the market on the part of the person requesting access.[7] Second, the refusal cannot be objectively justified. Third, the requested access is indispensable to carrying on access seeker's business because there are no actual or potential substitutes. Unless all three conditions are met, refusal to supply does not constitute abuse of dominance under Article 102 TFEU.

When assessing whether refusal to supply constitutes an exclusionary conduct sanctioned under Article 102 TFEU, the European Commission had stated that one has to consider:

> "… whether the supply of the refused input is objectively necessary for operators to be able to compete effectively on the market. This does not mean that, without the refused input, no competitor could ever enter or survive on the downstream market. Rather, an input is indispensable where there is no actual or potential substitute on which competitors in the downstream market could rely so as to counter — at least in the long-term — the negative consequences of the refusal." (European Commission, 2009, p. 83)

The European Commission further justified this cautious and restrictive approach. A dominant's company's obligation to supply, even for appropriate remuneration, may harm investment and innovation incentives and, thereby, possibly harm consumers. Competitors may be tempted to free ride on investments made by the dominant company instead of investing themselves (*ibidem*).

Dunne (2015) argues that it is not the competitor but the competitive process that needs to be safeguarded. She identifies three major objections against the essential facilities doctrine (*ibidem*). First, an essential facilities doctrine would constitute

[4] Case C-7/97 Oscar Bronner v Mediaprint.

[5] *Ibidem*, p. 47.

[6] *Ibidem*, p. 41.

[7] Parcu et al. (2017) questioned the ECJ's position that a refusal to supply is an abuse if it risks eliminating downstream competition. ECJ's focus on whether the downstream competitor could be active in the downstream market only if it is supplied by the dominant company ignores the possibility that the downstream market is already competitive. For instance, the dominant company in the upstream market may have already supplied a number of companies in the downstream market with the indispensable upstream product or service. Therefore, we can assume that downstream market is already competitive. From an economic point of view, the new company seeking the indispensable upstream product or service is not necessary entitled to it.

excessive intrusion into the freedom of choosing trading partners, even if fair compensation for (mandatory) access is paid. Second, mandatory access can harm investment and innovation. Third, the process of determining the price and conditions of (mandatory) access is administratively complex, and there is a high risk of costly error.

Probably the most influential and famous critic comes from Areeda (1990) in which he offers six principles for limiting application of the essential facilities concept. Inter alia, Areeda argues that, first, mandatory access should be very exceptional and, second, that firm's facilities are essential only if they are critical to another firm's competitive vitality and that the other firm is essential for competition.[8]

3.3 *Are Parcel Lockers Essential Facilities?*

Building on the jurisprudence and theory mentioned above, it seems quite unconvincing to argue that parcel lockers are essential facilities. Assume that company A holds a dominant position in the parcel locker market and refuses to grant access to its network to parcel delivery in company B. Arguing that company A is not allowed to refuse access to B requires premise that parcel lockers are indispensable for providing parcel delivery services. Such argumentation would make little sense since it is clear that there are many not only potential but also actual substitutes for the delivery to parcel lockers (e.g., home delivery, delivery to alternative locations/parcel shops, etc.).[9]

Furthermore, there are no technical, legal, or economic obstacles preventing duplication of the parcel locker network. In many EU countries, parallel parcel locker networks already coexist (see Table 1). In the Bronner case, ECJ took the position that indispensability is not simply a matter of greater convenience for the access seeker and, furthermore, that the economic unviability of network duplication because of the (small) size of the access seeker is irrelevant. Building on this reasoning, parcel lockers cannot be defined as indispensable simply because it would be easier and more cost-efficient for parcel delivery services providers without owning parcel locker network to free ride.

Moreover, refusing access to parcel lockers can easily be justified. The number and size of parcel locker compartments are strictly limited, which make them incapable of accepting more or different-sized items than the number or size the compartments allow. In the case of a fully (or near fully) utilized parcel lockers network,

[8] The other four principles are as follows. First, duty to deal should exist only if it substantially improves competition. Second, refusal to deal is never unlawful itself. Third, refusal to deal with the intention to limit competition and to increase profits does not itself contaminate the conduct. Fourth, unless duty to deal can be explained and supervised, it should not be imposed.

[9] According to IPC (2018a, b), home delivery is still the most convenient (59%) and most frequently used (68%) delivery location.

its operator could reasonably refuse access due to the shortage of parcel lockers' compartments. The ECJ jurisprudence is clear that the shortage of a product is an objectively justified argument for a dominant company's refusal to supply.[10]

4 Should Parcel Lockers Be Regulated at All?

If parcel lockers are not indispensable for providing parcel delivery services, should they be regulated at all? To answer this question, policy goals and desired outcomes of a regulatory intervention need to be identified. General social regulation seems to be most fit for the purpose, with sector-specific regulation playing a supplementary role.

4.1 *Why Regulate?*

Building parallel parcel locker networks may create an inefficient use of resources. From the operators' perspective, sharing parcel lockers would better recover costs of investment. From the users' perspective, their needs would be better met, and users would benefit from wider choice since they could order a delivery to the parcel locker that is located most conveniently to them. To put it differently, sharing would increase network coverage.

Furthermore, environmental and logistic benefits would be achieved as well. Users would be able to collect parcels from the nearest parcel locker; in case that parcel locker is occupied, delivery would not be missed but rather would use the nearest available parcel locker of another operator. Building (too) many parallel networks is questionable also from the perspective of an efficient use of public space. The Swedish NRA has said that establishing "… parallel facilities…is unlikely to be sustainable …" (Zurel et al. 2018).

Positive environmental and logistic effects of delivery to parcel lockers, especially in case of their interoperability, are "side effects" of efficient delivery and collection of the parcels. CO_2 emissions and traffic congestion could be significantly reduced. There would be no missed deliveries and returns, and addressees could collect parcels from the most conveniently placed parcel locker at any time and not during traffic peak periods. Positive environmental and logistic effects of delivery to parcel lockers have been confirmed by the recent study comparing ecological aspects of deliveries to the individual addresses and deliveries to the parcel

[10] In the leading case, BP v Commission, Case 77/77, ECJ held, "A duty on the part of the supplier to apply a similar rate of reduction in deliveries to all its customers in a period of shortage without having regard to obligations contracted toward its traditional customers could only flow from measures adopted within the framework of the Treaty, in particular Article 103, or, in default of that, by the national authorities" (p. 34).

lockers (Moroz and Polkowski 2016). The study was conducted on the local level, for the Polish city Szczecin, and found that delivery in parcel locker produces approximately 20 times less CO_2 emissions and fuel consumption per parcel as compared with traditional delivery to the individual addresses. Moreover, a courier that delivers to parcel lockers travels half the distance and delivers ten times more parcels per day (*ibidem*, p. 383).

4.2 General Social Regulation as a Primary Instrument

The aforementioned benefits of parcel locker sharing are desirable, yet it seems that sector-specific ex ante economic regulation is not a conditio sine qua non for achieving them. If operators have economic interests for sharing parcel lockers (e.g., in order to recover investments), there is no need to impose an obligation on them to open parcel lockers for other providers since they already have (economic) incentives to do so. In this case, contractual freedom suffices to achieve the desirable outcome.

In case operators do not have an intrinsic interest to share parcel lockers, public policies and instruments for promoting more efficient and environmentally friendly transportation are the appropriate mean for indirectly stimulating parcel locker sharing. It is reasonable to assume that incorporation of negative environmental and traffic impacts into the price of mobility, including the transportation and distribution of parcels, would reduce pollution and traffic congestion and, at the same time, promote and stimulate parcel lockers sharing, thus contributing to better meet users' needs.[11]

In order to promote nonmarket values and to serve the identified noneconomic public interests, some regulation is unavoidable (Dunne 2015). However, instead of imposing mandatory access through sector-specific economic regulation, social regulation and taxation should come to the fore. Some of the possible measures are tax and other incentives for more efficient use of public space (by avoiding duplication of parcel locker networks) and for reducing pollution and traffic congestion (by minimizing path from the sender to the delivery location). Such measures and mechanisms to encourage sharing of parcel lockers are less restrictive and could be as or even more efficient for achieving the interoperability and cooperation between parcel locker networks than imposing mandatory access.

These types of general social regulation seem to be the most appropriate and proportional instrument to encourage parcel locker sharing on a voluntary (not mandatory!) basis. Such regulation could easily align with ongoing efforts of all the EU countries to achieve efficient use of public space and to reduce pollution and traffic congestions.

[11] For more details on positive effects of delivery to parcel lockers on reducing environmental, health and urban logistic externalities, see Zurel et al. (2018).

4.3 Sector-Specific Regulation as a Supplement

Prioritizing general social regulation over sector-specific regulation does not mean that the latter is irrelevant or per se inappropriate. Quite the contrary, sector-specific regulation should support and supplement social regulation in order to achieve desirable outcomes from promoting parcel lockers and sharing thereof, especially better meeting users' needs, providing more choice for users, and reducing pressure on USO financial sustainability). If sector-specific regulation allows USP to use parcel lockers for fulfilling its USO, this would most likely decrease USO cost. The PSD does not preclude defining parcel lockers – which enable sending, receiving, and generating proof of delivery for all postal items – as a point of contact (alternative to traditional post offices) or as an element of postal infrastructure or services provided within the scope of the USA (Article 11a PSD) to which a statutory or regulatory access regime applies.

The main question is whether defining parcel lockers as points of contact and/or elements of the postal infrastructure is desirable. Variation in national characteristics implies that a one-size-fits-all approach is not appropriate. Some USPs would likely oppose such a definition, whereas others would welcome an NRA initiative to interpret parcel lockers as points of contact or elements of the postal infrastructure within the scope of the USO. A USP's opposition would, most likely, be based on the view that parcel locker services are value-added (and not universal) services and constituting a competitive advantage that should not be regulated in the same way as a USO. On the other hand, a USP's support would, most likely, be based on the opportunity to reduce USO costs.

5 Conclusion

The principle of proportionality is an essential element of the NRA's assessment whether defining parcel lockers as (automated) points of contact and/or elements of the postal infrastructure is desirable. For such an assessment, the key question is whether the benefits resulting from defining parcel lockers as points of contact and/or elements of the postal infrastructure prevail over the downsides of such interpretation. This assessment should not be carried out in an "ivory tower." Active involvement of the USP into the assessment process will be vital. An NRA's decision is more likely to be well accepted and successfully implemented if the USP's views and positions are duly taken into account.

In the event of a USP's opposition, defining parcel lockers as (automated) points of contact and/or elements of the postal infrastructure would most likely lead to undesirable results, e.g., harmed investment and innovation incentives. In this case, regulatory intervention aiming to promote competition would not bring desirable benefits to the users. Where a USP supports including parcel lockers, a possible approach would be to, mutatis mutandis, apply the concept of regulatory sandboxes.

To develop regulation that keeps up with the fast pace of innovation, a special and temporary regulatory regime for testing parcel lockers as points of contact and/or elements of the postal infrastructure is a feasible compromise. Ideally, including parcel lockers into USO provisions for a trial period would promote a smooth transition.

Such an approach would be, at the same time, innovative yet cautious. A possible first step could be to identify already existing or evolving sharing practices and cooperation models and acknowledge them as desirable. Regulation aiming to promote usage and sharing of parcel lockers for better meeting the users' needs and for fulfilling USO could become an example of social innovation and, moreover, a good example of active collaboration between the EU countries NRAs, businesses, and citizens.

References

Areeda, P. (1990). Essential facilities: An epithet in need of limiting principles. *Antitrust, 58*, 841.

Cullen International. (2016). *Spanish NRA decides not to impose access to Correos' parcel lockers service*. Brussels: Cullen International.

Cullen International. (2018). *Luxembourg NCA closes refusal to supply case against post Luxembourg but keeps watching*. Brussels: Cullen International.

Deutsche Post DHL Group Annual Report 2013, 2017 and 2018.

Dunne, N. (2015). *Competition law and economic regulation*. Cambridge: Cambridge University Press.

ERGP. (2018a). *Working programme 2019*, https://ec.europa.eu/docsroom/documents/33027/attachments/1/translations/en/renditions/native.

ERGP. (2018b). *Report on core indicators for monitoring the European postal market*. https://ec.europa.eu/docsroom/documents/33143.

ERGP. (2019). *Report on the development of postal networks and access practices regarding infrastructure related to the parcel market*. https://ec.europa.eu/docsroom/documents/36162/attachments/1/translations/en/renditions/native.

European Commission. (2009). Communication from the Commission — *Guidance on the Commission's enforcement priorities in applying Article 82 of the EC Treaty to abusive exclusionary conduct by dominant undertakings*.

IPC. (2018a). *Delivery choice – Parcel lockers overview*.

IPC. (2018b). *Cross-border e-commerce shopper survey*.

Moroz, M., & Polkowski, Z. (2016). The last mile issue and urban logistics: Choosing parcel machines in the context of the ecological attitudes of the Y generation consumers purchasing online. *Transportation Research Procedia, 16*(2016), 378–393.

OECD. (1996). Policy Roundtables, The Essential Facilities Concept, https://www.google.si/url?sa=t&rct=j&q=&esrc=s&source=web&cd=2&ved=2ahUKEwiB98Gg6LnmAhWhPOwKHVvPA2EQFjABegQIBRAK&url=http%3A%2F%2Fwww.oecd.org%2Fcompetition%2Fabuse%2F1920021.pdf&usg=AOvVaw1XaGdtC3jDwbe5dIx5Ee6U

Okholm et al. (2018). *Main developments in the postal sector (2013–2016), study for the European Commission, Directorate-General for Internal Market, Industry, Entrepreneurship and SMEs, 2018*. https://publications.europa.eu/en/publication-detail/-/publication/d22799b5-bbb7-11e8-99ee-01aa75ed71a1/language-en.

Parcu, P. L., Monti, G., & Botta, M. (Eds.). (2017). *Abuse of dominance in EU competition law – emerging trends*. Cheltenham/Northamton: Edward Elgar Publishing.

Regulation on access to Postal Network of the Universal Service Provider. (2014). *Government affairs of the Hellenic republic*. Issue two, No. 728/6 (5), 29 September 2014.

Zurel, Ö., Van Hoyweghen, L., Braes, S., & Seghers, A. (2018). Parcel lockers, an answer to the pressure on the last mile delivery? In P. L. Parcu, T. Brennan, & V. Glass (Eds.), *New business and regulatory strategies in the postal sector. Topics in regulatory economics and policy*. Cham: Springer.

Can the Postal Market Afford Affordability? How to Assess It?

Henrik Ballebye Okholm, Bruno Basalisco, Julia Wahl, Gerdis Marquardt, and Martina Facino

1 Introduction

Mail volumes in European postal markets are declining. In the last 10 years, the number of letters sent in Europe decreased by 30%.[1] For postal operators, this reduction in mail volumes implies lower economies of scale in the delivery of mail and hence higher unit cost of delivery. Under current regulatory frameworks, operators will need to consider larger and more frequent increases in the price for letters to ensure a sustainable USO.

The trend in price increases raises the question for regulators and policymakers of whether letter mail prices will remain affordable for consumers. While the postal directive and national postal laws require tariffs to be affordable, they neither define affordability nor provide guidelines on assessing it. The concept of letter mail affordability is still relatively unexplored. Borsenberger et al. (2012) suggested that affordability matters for essential goods without substitutes which should be offered at a price that allows everybody to access it. However, they also note that defining what that means appears still remains difficult. Other papers discussed specific methods to evaluate affordability.[2] However, there is no review, to our knowledge, of the methods used in practice.

[1] Calculated as change in the number of letter-post items, domestic service, sent in 26 EEA countries and Switzerland between 2006 and 2016 from UPU database (Accessed 2 Nov 2018).

[2] Borsenberger et al. (2012) assess affordability by looking at household spending on postal services in France. Swinand et al. (2014) examine the response of lower-income groups to hypothetical postal price in Ireland, and Gough et al. (2017) also consider any cost or disutility incurred by the consumer in obtaining the service as part of the price of mail. See Section 3 for a more detailed discussion.

H. B. Okholm · B. Basalisco (✉) · G. Marquardt · M. Facino
Copenhagen Economics, København, Denmark
e-mail: bb@copenhageneconomics.com

J. Wahl
Copenhagen Economics, Brussels, Belgium

P. L. Parcu et al. (eds.), *The Changing Postal Environment*, Topics in Regulatory Economics and Policy, https://doi.org/10.1007/978-3-030-34532-7_22

We aim to fill this gap by investigating how regulators and operators assess and ensure affordability and trade-offs with other regulatory aims. We also discuss whether letter mail affordability is still a relevant concern. The paper is structured as follows. Section 2 reviews the purpose of the affordability principle and shows that ensuring affordability might conflict with other regulatory aims such as cost recovery orientation. Section 3 examines how EU regulators assess affordability and critically discusses three main approaches. Section 4 discusses whether the affordability principle will survive. We test the hypothesis that letter affordability is a shrinking problem due to the declining use of letters and consider alternative solutions to safeguard vulnerable consumers. We also investigate whether affordability is a growing concern for parcel mail. Section 5 summarizes our main findings.

2 The Affordability Principle and Other Regulatory Aims

Postal price-related regulation is common across many jurisdictions. In this paper we focus on the EU. Therein, price-related regulation is informed by principles set out in EU legislation. The EU Postal Service Directive (European Commission 2008, Directive 2008/6/EC) includes principles that tariffs should be cost-oriented, transparent, and non-discriminatory – as well as affordable (Art. 12). Thus, EU Member States must ensure that price increases comply with Article 12, which holds that "prices shall be affordable and must be such that all users, independent of geographical location, and, in the light of specific national conditions, have access to the services provided […]."

It must be stressed that neither the Directive nor national postal laws specify what these objectives entail. This creates ambiguities that are explored in this chapter. For this reason, we will leave open-ended the precise definition of affordability during this analysis and return to the matter of defining affordability at the conclusions stage. In the following, we discuss the definition of affordability in regulatory practice and compare it to affordability as defined in economic literature while considering regulatory challenges in its assessment.

2.1 Definition of Affordability

Only a few regulators have defined affordability. In the UK, *Ofcom* holds that "[a] universal postal service product, for example, a First Class stamp, would be 'unaffordable' if a potential residential customer was entirely excluded from purchasing it or faced significant hardship from purchasing it because of the price" (Ofcom 2013, p. 9). This is a relatively high bar, because significant hardship or being "entirely excluded" is an extreme circumstance. Yet vulnerability may be a key factor for some groups of individuals, even within societies where the average person has sufficient resources.

Since affordability is a rather subjective measure influenced by the interplay of many factors, defining affordability is difficult, as Borsenberger (2018) also found. Summarizing the discussion by regulators and economists, she noted that the affordability principle should ensure access to postal services for all consumers without imposing a high financial burden on consumers reliant on letter mail.

Affordability of sending letters depends on various factors. Naturally, it is linked to the price level, i.e., with higher prices, consumers may struggle to afford letters. Affordability depends also on the share of consumers' overall expenditure on postal services.[3] When consumers' total expenditure on letters is small compared to other goods, consumers' financial burden from sending letters is low. Furthermore, protecting consumers' accessibility to letter mail depends on whether they can use substitutes such as digital communication matters for the assessment of affordability.

Borsenberger et al. (2012) discussed affordability in the postal sector, drawing upon affordability discussions in other sectors including water and electricity. They stated that affordability means that an essential good, for which no substitutes exist, is offered at a price such that everybody can access it, i.e., pay for a socially desirable consumption level. Post can enhance the social integration of households, especially if they cannot communicate via other channels; this function may be one of the bases for policymakers' decision to deem affordability as one of the basic principles. Also, Borsenberger (2018) finds that affordability depends on the interplay of many factors such as consumers' level of consumption, preferences, income, and availability of substitutes.

While EU regulators have repeatedly emphasized letter affordability, in past regulatory practice, they focused mainly on applying cost-orientation rules as a tool inter alia to avoid monopoly rents. Also, ERGP (2014, 2018) reviewed how the tariff principles of Article 12 are adopted in practice but do not appraise affordability specifically. Only few regulators make explicit assessments of the affordability of letter mail, as described in Section 3 below.

2.2 *Regulatory Challenges in Assessing Affordability Following the Letter Volume Decline*

The decline in letter volumes and the resulting necessity for operators to increase prices create two challenges in price regulation for regulators and policymakers.

Firstly, adhering to the cost-orientation and affordability principle creates a trade-off. When unit costs for letter delivery increase due to volume decline, the two principles pull the letter price in different directions, as shown in Fig. 1.

[3] The European Commission stated: "a price for a universal service item could be deemed affordable in that it comprises a low proportion of household expenditure" (BIPT 2017, p. 23, Fn. 29–31).

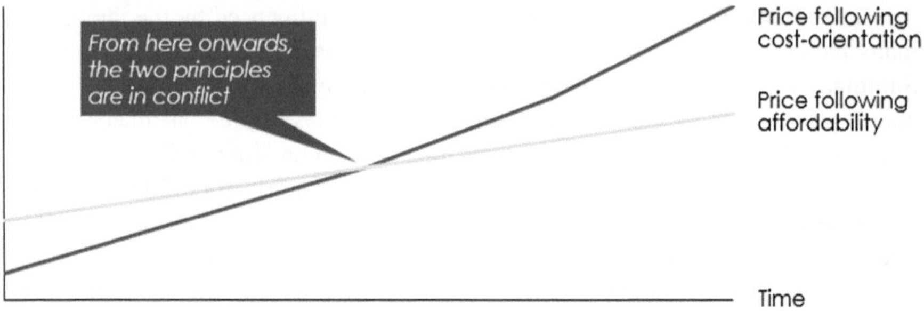

Fig. 1 Trade-off between the cost-orientation and affordability principle: Letter price. Note: This is an illustrative example. (Source: Copenhagen Economics)

Cost-orientation underpins various forms of price regulation, which often explicitly or implicitly accounts for the cost of providing the service to ensure that operators can cover costs. For instance, the efficiency factor (X) in the price-cap regulation (CPI-X) often reflects the potential for cost reduction.[4] When unit costs rise, letter prices that follow cost developments similarly increase. However, this creates a potential trade-off with the affordability principle. Price regulation requires a careful analysis to identify price levels that guarantee the sustainability of the USO (ensuring that cost is covered) while not imposing a significant burden on consumers (ensuring affordability).

Secondly, the right combination of price and service level in the USO also influences price developments and affordability. Consumers might be willing to give up a high level of service, e.g., accept slower letter delivery, to moderate or offset scheduled cost-related price increases. To identify possibilities to reduce the service level, regulators and policymakers need to assess changes in consumer needs and whether the cost of providing a high service level exceeds the consumers' valuation of it.

Regulators in Denmark, Norway, Sweden, Finland, and Italy have reduced the level of service in the USO to reduce operators' costs. They replaced the priority letter by a slower letter product (e.g., D + 2 to D + 4), achieving cost reductions in delivery. Some regulators changed the delivery requirements, for example, reducing delivery frequency of standard letters to once a week, three times a week, or five times a week in Denmark, Finland, and the Netherlands, respectively. Furthermore, regulators have decreased the service level in terms of accessibility, reducing the coverage density of branch network or lowering the cost of running a branch. For example, in the Netherlands, the government helped to reduce the number of post offices from 2000 to 1000 and the number of mailboxes from 19,000 to 8700 in 2015. In Denmark, all post offices have been converted into post-in-shop, e.g., a post office counter in the supermarket (Copenhagen Economics 2018).

[4] In some countries, e.g., Germany, the price-cap regulation is now defined as CPI + X (instead of CPI-X) since the declining mail volumes do not allow for further cost reductions.

3 Methods to Ensure Affordability

EU regulators do not follow a uniform approach in ensuring that letter prices satisfy the affordability principle. In the following, we discuss whether and how regulators assess affordability and critically review the three main approaches used in practice.

3.1 Affordability Assessment in Practice

Many regulators appear to monitor affordability without much intervention or undertaking extensive research on the topic. Some regulators decide whether to approve price increases without explicitly addressing affordability, while others take it explicitly into account. We can divide the approaches into three main groups.

The first group of regulators considers affordability fulfilled when prices are regulated by an ex ante approval or a price cap. Most European regulators follow this approach. Regulators in Belgium and Germany consider affordability satisfied when letter prices do not exceed the price cap.[5] The *Bundesnetzagentur* in Germany introduced a CPI-X price cap for individual letters under 1000 g (which since 2015 is in fact a CPI + X price cap due to declining mail volume). The price cap regulates the average price of letter products weighted according to their expected volume and has two goals. First, it should ensure an efficient service and (via the X factor) provide incentives that ensure that the operator will strive to improve the efficiency of service provision (dynamic efficiency). Second, it should ensure that prices do not grow faster than the general price level.

While, the price cap ensures that letter prices do not grow much faster than other consumption prices, it does not assess whether all consumers can afford letters. The price cap accounts neither for decreasing demand for letters compared to other consumption goods nor for differences in the development of costs to provide postal versus other services in the economy. Besides, a price cap may (directly or indirectly) yield benefits to bulk mail buyers, which is not within the scope of affordability concerns. Thus, a price cap, per se, has several limitations in its effectiveness and efficiency as a tool to ensure affordability.

A second group of regulators has assessed affordability when changing price regulation, i.e., in Denmark, Ireland, Italy, Sweden, and the UK. They found no concern with respect to affordability in their assessment for two reasons. The first reason is the decline in mail volumes, as regulators in Denmark, Ireland, and

[5] "Het Instituut gaat de betaalbaarheid en de kostenoriëntering na op basis van de price cap formule [The regulatory authority assesses affordability and cost orientation on the basis of the price cap]" (BIPT 2018, Loi du 26 janvier 2018 relative aux services postaux, Art. 18). "Universaldienstleistungen sind ein Mindestangebot an Postdienstleistungen [...], die flächendeckend in einer bestimmten Qualität und zu einem erschwinglichen Preis erbracht werden. [Universal services are a minimum set of postal services that are provided comprehensively, at a specified quality and at an affordable price]" (Bundesamt für Justiz 1997, Art.11 (1), Postgesetz vom 22. Dezember 1997).

Sweden concluded. Consumers' dependence on mail decreases as more people have access to and increasingly use alternative communication channels, such as e-mail. Thus, only a small portion of the population can potentially have affordability issues in the first place. Also in light of several years of decline in average postal volumes consumed per household, the latter spend only a small portion of their budget on letter mail products; even a significant increase in the letter price would not significantly impact overall household expenditure (CEM Institute – Voxmeter 2014; ComReg 2014, 2017).

The second reason is that consumers have access to alternatives, i.e., slower and thus more affordable letter delivery, as regulators in Denmark, Italy, and the UK concluded. The slower speed of non-priority products is often enough to meet consumers' needs because most communications traditionally fulfilled via express delivery are now fulfilled via e-mail. Even in the rare occasion that urgent delivery by mail is necessary, the average of surveyed consumers reports to be willing to pay a premium (Ministry of Transport 2011; Ofcom 2013; AGCOM 2015). That notwithstanding, what holds for the average consumer may not apply to a vulnerable minority and related affordability concerns.

A third group of regulators assess letter affordability explicitly either sporadically in conjunction with reviews of price regulations or regularly every year. Regulators in Spain, Portugal, and the UK apply three main approaches to evaluate affordability: (i) benchmarking of letter prices with other EU countries, (ii) analysis of household expenditure on letters as a proportion of total household expenditure or in comparison with other expenses, and (iii) direct consumer survey on letter usage and affordability.

3.2 *Discussion of the Main Approaches*

In the following, we discuss the three affordability assessment approaches used by (the third group of) regulators.

3.2.1 Price Benchmarking

To assess affordability, some regulators compare the price of the standard letter in their respective country with prices in other EU countries. Such price benchmarking gives regulators a good sense of how far prices of the country in question are from the EU average. Generally, prices below average are more likely to satisfy affordability.

For example, CNMC in Spain annually conducts a price benchmarking to assess letter affordability. In Spain, domestic mail volumes (USP and non-USP) declined by 16% from 2013 to 2016, and the standard letter price increased by 49% from 2013 to 2018 (Copenhagen Economics 2018). In its most recent assessment, CNMC compared, inter alia, the letter prices in Spain with the European average price for standard mail products (domestic and international). The regulator's conclusion was that the letter price of EUR 0.60 in Spain is affordable (CNMC 2017, 2018).

Price benchmarking is a simple method that can be conducted regularly and at low cost. By adjusting for purchasing power, prices can be compared across countries that differ in living standards and economic productivity. However, price benchmarking depends on the prices charged by other operators and monitored by regulators in market environments that may not be comparable to the market in question. Prices that meet the affordability criteria in one country may not be affordable in another country when consumer habits and needs differ. Regulators also may balance affordability differently with other regulatory aims such as cost-orientation. Since unit costs of delivery depend on many factors that differ across country, prices that are in line with all regulatory aims may vary by country.

3.2.2 Households' Postal Expenditure

Another method for assessing affordability is analyzing consumers' expenditure on letters and comparing it with overall household expenditure to identify how much burden letter price increases create for consumers. Borsenberger et al. (2012) examined household spending on post and the effect of price increases on household budgets with a focus on France. They tested for across-the-board price increases ranging from 2% to 10% and then considered the impact on the household consumption budget of the poorest (first decile) of the population. In doing so they summed both the direct impact of postal items purchased by consumers and indirect impact of cost increases in other consumer products for which postal services (i.e., bulk mail) are an input. The combined impact on the poorest citizens of a 2% postal price increase was of a yearly EUR 2.14 (0.01% of yearly expenditure); for a 10% postal price increase, this was a yearly EUR 7.38 increase (0.05% of yearly expenditure).[6] On this basis, that study concludes that the across-the-board postal price increases tested would not prompt affordability concerns in France, even on the poorest.

To interpret the above result, one can look beyond the postal industry. The same method to assess affordability of letters could also be used to evaluate affordability of electricity, gas, housing, and water. Borsenberger (2018) reviewed the threshold at which the share of household spending is deemed high enough to constitute an affordability issue and found that this differs across sectors and ranges from 3% to 30%.[7] Notably, even the lowest of these thresholds (3%) is a factor of six larger than the upper bound of the expenditure impacts found in Borsenberger et al. (2012) for the poorest citizens.

[6] While that study accounts for elasticity of single-piece and bulk mail, it flagged that its results may not account for potential longer-term demand decreases due to the price change.

[7] See Borsenberger (Borsenberger 2018, p. 105) for a review of affordability measurement in various sectors.

In Portugal, regulator ANACOM evaluated affordability in every price regulation period explicitly according to four measures: (i) family expenditure on postal services, (ii) postal service use and satisfaction monitored via surveys, (iii) whether price increases threaten the commercial profitability of users, and (iv) elasticity of demand and the risk that price increases could lead to strong demand/volume declines undermining the financial viability of the USO (ANACOM 2018, p. 11–12).

We focus on the first, key, assessment. ANACOM concluded that letter prices are affordable inter alia because, for the average household, expenditure on postal services amounts to 0.013% of yearly total expenditure and thus has only a "negligible weight in the shopping basket of Portuguese families." This finding relates to the average household and thus the impact on a vulnerable minority may be different. Furthermore, according to a survey conducted by ANACOM in 2016/2017, only 29% of the respondents had used postal services in the year before, spending on average EUR 1.79 monthly for the service and reporting to be satisfied with the price for postal communications (ANACOM 2018, p. 12).

Comparing expenditures for letters with total household expenditure is a direct way to assess affordability. An advantage of this method is that it captures changes in consumer habits and usage of letters instead of only focusing on the price. This matters, for example, when letter prices are high, but consumers send letters only sporadically, in which case affordability is unlikely to be an issue.

However, possible feedback effects are not part of the analysis. For example, lower usage of letters may stem from unaffordable letter prices. Also, high degrees of regulation, such as the price cap and four additional evaluation elements in Portugal, give little flexibility to operators while creating a large burden for regulators.

3.2.3 Consumer Surveys

Another method for assessing affordability is consumer surveys. This elaborate method can reveal consumers' perception of prices and provide deeper insights into consumers' habits in the use of letters. For example, surveys can provide information on consumers' ability to substitute mail with other means of communication, i.e., consumers' dependence on sending letters, and whether affordability should be a concern. Moreover, surveys can reveal how often consumers send letters and how much they spend annually on letter mail, thereby providing the basis for a measure of affordability.

Swinand et al. (2014) investigated affordability of postal prices in Ireland by examining the response of lower-income groups to several hypothetical price increases using survey data on income and living conditions as well as household budget. They defined affordability with respect to price changes and hold that a price increase creates affordability issues when substitution is not possible. They concluded that postal products make up a low share of consumers' budget and have low substitutability and low impacts on necessity products.

Ofcom in the UK has used survey-based methods to assess affordability of postal services in 2013, in addition to other methods.[8] In the UK, the letter mail volume declined on average by 3% per year from 2013 to 2016 (Copenhagen Economics 2018, p. 39). Ofcom's commissioned consumer study aimed, inter alia, at understanding consumers' usage of postal services, whether communication via letters is essential or can be substituted for it, and how consumers are affected if they cannot send mail due to high prices. The study was carried out via discussion groups, telephone interviews, individual interviews, and friendship pairs and specifically focused on vulnerable consumers (Ofcom 2013, p. 70–72).

In the study, Ofcom said that affordability is an issue when consumers send essential mail and get into financial difficulties as a result or when consumers cannot send essential mail and thus suffer a damage (e.g., reduced social contact, missing out on important dates). The regulator concluded that current letter prices are affordable in the UK because consumers send letters only rarely and the unit price is low, even though consumers consider some letters as essential (including official and commercial mail and letters to family and friends). Furthermore, the cost of postal items that are important to vulnerable consumers, such as Christmas cards, is too small to play a role. If consumers regard letters as too expensive, they avoid sending them and send, for instance, e-mails instead (Ofcom 2013, p. 73–75).

Using consumer surveys can provide wide-ranging insights into consumer's usage of postal services and the hardship they may incur from letter price increases. However, designing a survey to elicit households' views on affordability can be challenging. Asking consumers directly questions such as "Do you find letter prices affordable?" should be avoided because consumers may have different subjective interpretations of "affordability" (Borsenberger 2018). Furthermore, this method is very costly and can typically not be replicated regularly. This may create a problem when rapid changes in the market realities call for frequent adjustments of prices which the regulator must evaluate.

4 Will the Affordability Principle Survive?

In the following, we discuss whether the affordability principle will remain important for regulators and policymakers in the future. We argue that affordability of letters is generally a shrinking problem. While affordability may still be a concern for low-income and vulnerable consumers in specifically hard circumstance, they could benefit from alternative solutions. However, the affordability of parcel shipment may become a growing concern.

[8] To assess affordability, Ofcom has also analyzed data on consumers' postal send and spend patterns, expenditure on postal services versus total household expenditure, and considered also small- and medium-sized businesses (Ofcom 2013, p. 9–14).

4.1 *Affordability of Letters Is a Shrinking Problem*

The affordability of letters across Europe is a shrinking problem for two reasons. Firstly, affordability is a shrinking problem due to the declining use of letter mail. Communication in all EU countries is increasingly digitalized. In 2017, 99.9% of EU households (over 219 million) had access to at least one of the main fixed or mobile broadband technologies (IHS Markit and Point Topic 2018). More and more governments are providing their citizens with the opportunity to communicate digitally with public administrations. In 2017, consumers could communicate electronically with public institutions in one or more matters, historically sent via post, in most European countries; see Fig. 2. Consequently, letter volumes have been declining across Europe by on average 4% annually from 2013 to 2016 (Copenhagen Economics 2018) (Fig. 2).

Given the decrease in demand for letter mail, the expenditure on postal services has also been declining. European citizens spent on average more money on ice cream (EUR 24 per capita) than on post (EUR 15 per capita) in the last year.[9] This suggests that the expenditure on letters is small compared to overall household expenditure.

Due to the declining use of letter mail, regulators in Denmark, Sweden, and Ireland also recently concluded that letter price increases would not endanger affordability. In Ireland, the yearly mail volume decreased on average by 7% from 2011 to 2015. Regulator ComReg reviewed the price cap in 2014. They permitted an increase in rates (CPI plus 1.35%) and concluded that affordability is unlikely an issue due to the small number of sent letters. In 2017, the regulator abolished the ex

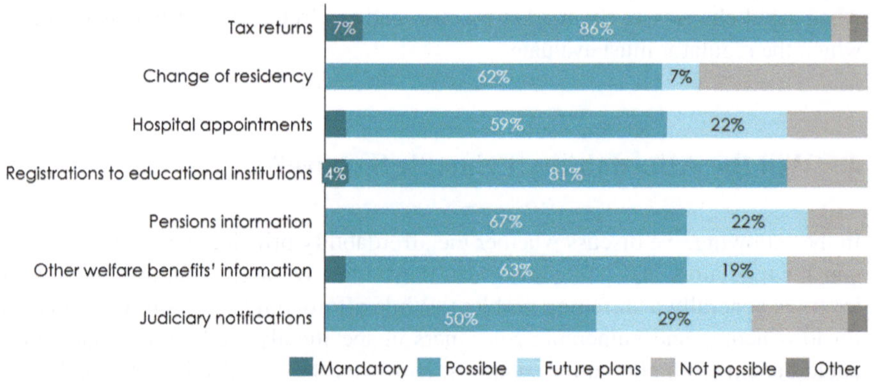

Fig. 2 Electronic communication with public institutions, 2017: Share of countries. Note: Data from the following 29 countries: AT, BE, HR, CY, CZ, DK, EE, FI, FR, DE, EL, HU, IS, IE, IT, LV, LT, LU, MT, NL, NO, PL, PT, RO, SK, SI, ES, SE, CH. (Source: Copenhagen Economics (2018, p. 35))

[9] Ice-cream expenditure is for 2019 (Statista) and postal expenditure is for 2017 (Eurostat).

ante price cap regulation and, to our knowledge, did not discuss the possible effect on affordability in the process (ComReg 2014, 2017).

In Sweden, regulator PTS moved from a mere CPI price cap to a CPI + X price cap in 2016. In the process, it studied individuals' preferences and access to digital alternatives. Based on the following findings, they concluded that affordability was not a concern. First, letter mail volumes declined on average by 4% from 2013 to 2016. Second, consumers' expenses on postal products are negligible compared to households' overall expenditure as 75% of consumers spent less than EUR 19.50 on letter mail. Third, a price increase of up to EUR 0.50 (i.e., up to 71%) would increase expenditure by up to EUR 14.40 (SOU 2016; Sveriges Riskdag 1998), deemed not concerning enough. We note that the above results reflect the impact on the average citizen, while impacts on a vulnerable minority may be different.

In Denmark, annual priority mail volume decreased on average by 32% from 2010 to 2017. Its regulator found a decline in mail volumes for all users in 2014 and that even frequent mail users had access to the internet and thus alternative communication channels. Therefore, the regulator made price increases possible by moving the price regulation from priority to non-priority letters (Transportministeriet 2010; CEM Institute–Voxmeter 2014). We note that reflections based on frequent postal users may miss the impact on any infrequent users among a vulnerable minority of citizens.

Secondly, affordability concerns are reduced due to the availability of slower mail products. While the price for priority mail is increasing, the availability of slower mail products limits affordability concerns. Priority mail used to be the main communication tool for private users and thus fell under the affordability principle. However, due to changes in user needs and increasing unit costs, many operators have introduced slower and cheaper mail products. Some regulators now consider it satisfactory for operators to provide at least one product that meets the affordability principle, even if it has lower quality than the previous standard.

For example, in Italy, the regulator made the D + 4 letter the new standard following a 10% annual letter mail volume decline from 2011 to 2015 (AGCOM 2015). In the UK, the regulator introduced a safeguard price cap for D + 3 ("second-class") letters to ensure the sustainability of the USO while keeping prices affordable (Ofcom 2013). In Denmark, the regulator made the slower D + 3 letter ("B-letter") the new standard to ensure affordability while allowing more flexibility for the priority A-letter (Transportministeriet 2010).

4.2 Affordability of Letters Might Still Be a Concern for Vulnerable Consumers

While affordability is a shrinking problem for most consumers, some consumers are more vulnerable and depend more on letter mail and may experience financial hardship. For those consumers affordability may still be an issue. Ofcom specifically considered low-income and vulnerable consumers in their assessment of affordability. They define vulnerable consumers as consumers who live in remote areas, are unemployed, over 65 years in age, have only limited Internet access, are disabled, or recently immigrated. Ofcom concluded that affordability can be a problem for "some consumers in very limited and specific circumstances [...] where a consumer suffers both significant financial difficulty or very low income, and has a frequent need to send post items they consider to be essential" (Ofcom 2013, p. 70–71).

While consumers that face especially hard circumstances should not become "citizens left behind," we recognize that poverty and vulnerability are much broader and more complex issues than what a single type of service (postal products) can address. Affordability of letters for the poorest and most vulnerable consumers is likely to be an issue insofar as the structural, wider socioeconomic factors that foster vulnerability are in place – even if the postal prices were to be eternally frozen or reduced. In this vein, Ofcom noted that "consumers in such circumstances would unfortunately have concerns about the prices of universal postal services, even at much lower prices" (Ofcom 2013, p. 28). The regulator, thus, concludes that letter prices in the UK are in line with the affordability principle, even when an affordability concern for a limited group of consumers persists. Also, in Sweden, the study for the regulator concludes that low-income groups would have affordability issues even without further price increases (SOU 2016).

General price regulation, which depends on other regulatory principles such as cost-orientation and USO sustainability, does not seems to be the most efficient – or effective – way to protect vulnerable consumers. Policymakers can find alternative solutions for those low-income and vulnerable consumers that cannot afford letter prices, as also the regulator in the UK and Sweden argue. Other measures such as subsidized envelopes or vouchers could ensure that vulnerable consumers have access to letter mail.

4.3 Affordability of Parcels May Become a New Debate

As opposed to shrinking affordability concerns related to letters, affordability of parcel delivery might become subject to debate in the future. The Postal Directive requires affordable prices not only for letters but also parcels that fall in the scope of the USO. Furthermore, the European Commission proposed affordability assessments for items outside the USO, especially related to cross-border delivery (European Commission 2016). With the importance of parcel delivery increasing and the role of letter mail decreasing, regulators and policymakers might call for different affordability assessments for the delivery of parcels compared to letters. This would require a careful assessment of the dynamics in parcel markets.

On the one hand, the increasing role of e-commerce in consumers' lives may be a policy argument for ensuring affordability of parcel delivery. Consumers are already increasingly buying goods online. The percentage of individuals that bought goods online increased by an average of 24 percentage points in the last 10 years in Europe.[10] Consequently, the question arises whether policymakers and regulators should be concerned with the affordability of parcels. Consumers' ability to have online access to "essential" goods, such as clothes and food, might hinge on the price they pay for delivery. E-commerce represents a viable alternative for consumers with limited access to physical stores, making the delivery of e-commerce parcels increasingly important. In rural areas, where retail stores are closing, consumers risk losing access to retail goods via physical stores.[11]

On the other hand, the increase in e-commerce, by growing demand (direct and indirect) for parcel services across many more routes, has allowed for greater scale of operations in parcel delivery (including in residential areas previously served with low density of traffic by parcel/express specialists). This enables gains in localized economies of scale and thus reductions in unit costs, promoting entry and resulting in increased competition in parcel delivery markets. When competition in the market keeps prices at an affordable level, additional regulation is unnecessary.[12] Price regulation for parcel delivery may create other challenges. Constraints on the delivery price may protect e-commerce companies relative to offline stores, especially since delivery costs are often hidden in the purchase price. Controversies may also arise regarding cross-border parcel and packets delivery, for example, regarding the terminal dues system.[13] An affordability assessment of cross-border parcel delivery must take into account how vital the access to goods in foreign markets is for consumers and whether domestic online and offline alternatives can serve consumers' needs.[14]

Whether affordability of parcel delivery will become a concern in the future and whether regulatory intervention is beneficial or detrimental will be an interesting topic for future research.

---

[10] Calculated as the difference between the percentage of all individuals having ordered/bought goods or services for private use over the Internet in the last 3 months in 2018 and 2008 (Eurostat data).

[11] For example, the number of retail stores in the UK has decreased by 18.4 per cent from 2012 to 2018 (Centre for Retail Research 2018). In the USA chains such as J.C. Penney, Macy's, Sears, Toys"R"Us, Mattress Firm, Bon-Ton, and Abercrombie & Fitch closed some of their stores in 2018 (Citylab 2018).

[12] ERGP (2014) concluded that the characteristics of the EU cross-border parcel delivery market do not call for ex ante regulation.

[13] See, inter alia, Okholm et al. (2017), Copenhagen Economics (2019).

[14] See Borsenberger (2018) for a discussion of the affordability of cross-border parcel delivery services.

5 Conclusion

Falling mail volumes and the resulting increase in unit costs force operators to consider larger and more frequent letter price increases to ensure a sustainable USO. However, under the current Postal Service Directive, operators and regulators must ensure that letter products are affordable. In this context, we have examined methods and relevance of affordability assessments and come to the following conclusions.

Regulators and operators assess and ensure letter affordability in different ways since no clear framework is in place. Most regulators indirectly ensure affordability through their price regulation. A few regulators conduct affordability assessments using (i) price benchmarking, (ii) considering the proportion of household expenditure on postal services, or (iii) conducting consumer surveys.

Based mainly on average effects, letter affordability is not a general concern for regulators and policymakers anymore due to the decline in mail usage. Some EU regulators address these developments via more flexible price regulations, allowing for letter price increases, and regard letter affordability not as an issue.

However, a common challenge is that either of the three above approaches mainly capture the impact of postal pricing on the average consumer. One way to sharpen the concept and application of affordability is to focus enquiries on these vulnerable groups, which some analyses have done. For example, this entails testing postal expenditure impacts on the poorest share of the population.

Finally, postal affordability is fundamentally linked with socioeconomic conditions of vulnerability which are a broader challenge than the postal regulatory task alone. This raises a set of key questions that in our view warrant further research. First, whether the postal affordability principle will remain relevant in fast-changing postal markets where parcels increasingly gain importance. Second, how the use, frequency, and dependence on postal services among the vulnerable consumers interact with the structural factors that drive the vulnerability itself: monetary poverty, lack of skills (including digital skills), and lack of inclusion in society. Third, whether the regulatory shift in attention toward parcel services and e-commerce may also be grounded in any related affordability challenges and whether specific vulnerability drivers (peripheral geographic location) may play a different role therein.

References

AGCOM. (2015). *Decree N. 396-15-CONS*. URL: https://www.agcom.it/documents/10179/2209608/Delibera+396-15-CONS/2dfc1d52-435c-44ac-a30a-5f989c762989?version=1.0. Accessed 5 Aug 2019.

ANACOM. (2018). *Decision on the price proposal submitted in the scope of the universal postal service by CTT – Correios de Portugal, S.A.* URL: https://www.anacom.pt/streaming/Decision23Mar2018PricesUPostal.pdf?contentId=1432743&field=ATTACHED_FILE. Accessed 4 Nov 2019.

BIPT. (2017). *Decision du conseil de l'ibpt du 21 mars 2017 concernant l'analyse de la proposition tarifaire de bpost pour les tarifs pleins a l'unite pour l'annee 2017*. URL: https://www.ibpt.be/public/files/fr/22251/Decision_pricing_2017_version_non_confidentielle.pdf. Accessed 7 Sept 2019.

BIPT. (2018). *Loi du 26 janvier 2018 relative aux services postaux, Art. 18*. URL: https://www.ibpt.be/fr/operateurs/postal/legislation/cadre-national/loi-du-26-janvier-2018-relative-aux-services-postaux. Accessed 5 Aug 2019.

Borsenberger, C. (2018). Are European cross-border parcel delivery services affordable? In *The contribution of the postal and delivery sector*. Cham: Springer.

Borsenberger, C., Joram, D., & Martin, L. (2012). Affordability of postal services addressed to households. In *Multi-modal competition and the future of mail*. Cheltenham: Edward Elgar Publishing.

Bundesamt für Justiz. (1997). *Art.11 (1), Postgesetz vom 22*. Dezember 1997.

CEM Institute – Voxmeter. (2014). *Analyse af danskernes brug af posttjenester. November 2014*. URL: https://www.trm.dk/da/publikationer/2015/analyse-af-danskernes-brug-af-posttjenester. Accessed 5 Aug 2019.

Centre for Retail Research. (2018). *Retail at Bay 2018. May 2018*. URL: http://www.retailresearch.org/retailatbay2018.php. Accessed 5 Aug 2019.

Citylab. (2018). *The 2018 Retail Apocalypse, in 6 Charts and a Map*. URL: https://www.citylab.com/life/2018/12/2018-retail-apocalypse-online-shopping-charts-maps/579112/. Accessed 5 Aug 2019.

CNMC. (2017). *Revision de precios de los servicios postales prestados bajo regimen de obligaciones de servicio universal para el año 2017*. URL: https://www.cnmc.es/ambitos-de-actuacion/postal/revision-de-precios. Accessed 5 Aug 2019.

CNMC. (2018). *Revision de precios de los servicios postales prestados bajo regimen de obligaciones de servicio universal para el año 2018*. URL: https://www.cnmc.es/ambitos-de-actuacion/postal/revision-de-precios. Accessed 5 Aug 2019.

ComReg. (2014). *Response to Consultation and Decision on price cap control for universal postal services. ComReg 14/59 and D05/14, 18 June 2014*. URL: https://www.comreg.ie/publication/response-to-consultation-and-decision-on-price-cap-control-for-universal-postal-services/. Accessed 5 Aug 2019.

ComReg. (2017). *Repeal of price cap control for universal postal services. Information Notice 17/18, 21 March 2017*. URL: https://www.comreg.ie/media/dlm_uploads/2017/03/ComReg-1718.pdf. Accessed 5 Aug 2019.

Copenhagen Economics. (2018). *Main Developments in the Postal Sector 2013–2016*. URL: https://www.copenhageneconomics.com/publications/publication/main-developments-in-the-postal-sector-2013-2016

Copenhagen Economics. (2019). *Throwing away the baby with the bathwater. Economic literature on global coordination vs unilateralism: Relevance to the UPU remuneration system and the future of the postal industry*. URL: https://www.copenhageneconomics.com/dyn/resources/Publication/publicationPDF/1/481/1552402124/copenhagen-economics-unilateralism-vs-global-coordination.pdf

ERGP. (2014). *ERGP report on tariff regulation in a context of declining volumes*. (14) 22 – draft report – tariff regulation. November 2014. URL: https://ec.europa.eu/docsroom/documents/14377/attachments/1/translations/en/renditions/pdf. Accessed 5 Aug 2019.

ERGP. (2018). *ERGP report on the application in access regulation of the principles of transparency, non-discrimination and proportionality as incorporated in the postal services directive*. PL (18) 27. June 2018. URL: https://ec.europa.eu/docsroom/documents/30521/attachments/1/translations/en/renditions/native. Accessed 5 Aug 2019.

European Commission. (2008). *Directive 2008/6/EC and amending Directive 97/67/EC*.

European Commission. (2016). *Proposal for a regulation of the European parliament and of the council on cross-border parcel delivery services, COM/2016/0285 final – 2016/0149*.

Gough, B., Kaneer, K., Cigno, M. M. (2017). The total price of mail: A consumer perspective. In: Crew M., Parcu P., Brennan T. (Eds.), *The Changing Postal and Delivery Sector*. Topics in Regulatory Economics and Policy, Vol 50, Springer.

IHS Markit and Point Topic. (2018). *Broadband Coverage in Europe 2017, study prepared for the European Commission*. URL: https://ec.europa.eu/digital-single-market/en/news/study-broadband-coverage-europe-2017. Accessed 5 Aug 2019.

Ministry of Transport. (2011). *Postal Services Act No. 1536 of 21 December 2010 as amended by Act No. 172 of 26 February 2014, unofficial translation*.

Ofcom. (2013). *The affordability of universal postal services. Report on findings 19 March 2013*. URL: https://www.ofcom.org.uk/__data/assets/pdf_file/0014/10445/affordability.pdf. Accessed 5 Aug 2019.

Okholm, H. B., Basalisco, B., Gårdebrink, J., & Boivie, A. M. (2017). An economic perspective on terminal dues. In *The changing postal and delivery sector* (pp. 79–96). Cham: Springer.

SOU. (2016). Som ett brev på posten, postbefordran och pristak I ett digitaliserat samhälle, *SOU, 27*. URL: https://www.regeringen.se/4a4611/contentassets/41de60c9a2d7428f899405d5f7d4f20a/som-ett-brev-pa-posten-sou_2016_27.pdf. Accessed 7 Sept 2019.

Sveriges Riskdag. (1998). Regeringens proposition 1997/98:127, Statens ansvar på postområdet. URL: https://www.riksdagen.se/sv/dokument-lagar/dokument/proposition/statens-ansvar-pa-postomradet_GL03127. Accessed 7 Sept 2019.

Swinand, G., Hennessy, H., & O'Meara, G. (2014). A demand system approach to affordability. In M. Crew & T. Brennan (Eds.), *Postal and delivery innovation in the digital economy. Topics in regulatory economics and policy*. Dordrecht: Springer.

Transportministeriet. (2010). *Aftale om sikring af befordringspligten på et liberaliseret postmarked*. URL: https://www.trm.dk/da/politiske-aftaler/2010/politisk-aftale-om-post. Accessed 5 Aug 2019.

A Note on "Postal Users' Needs" and Their Role in Postal Regulation

Felix C. H. Gottschalk

1 Introduction and Literature Review

In recent discussions on the reform of postal universal service obligations (USOs), frequent references are made to "postal users' needs" (sometimes also: "postal consumers' needs"). The notion has become an important ingredient in the postal policy debate, yet the notion itself and its implications have remained remarkably fuzzy. This article analyzes the notion, by classifying its use in the literature into two distinct concepts, and discusses them with respect to their strengths and weaknesses. We claim the two concepts serve different purposes and need to be distinguished thoroughly. However, in discussions, they are often mixed-up, resulting in a lack of clarity about the role of user needs in postal regulation.

The importance of the notion of "postal users' needs" is apparent in the large number of surveys claiming to empirically measure user needs in different countries. These studies are surveyed by the European Regulators Group for Postal Services (ERGP 2016). Results of the survey show great heterogeneity with respect to methods and focus. Currently, a new study on users' needs, commissioned by the European Commission, is in the making (WIK Consult 2019), again a sign of the relevance of the issue. Several authors have recently stressed more generally that postal USOs should reflect "users' needs" (see Confraria et al. 2017 and 2018). Other recent studies suggest that the current level of postal USOs exceeds the needs of consumers and suggested deregulation of the postal sector (see Cape and Groves 2017). Hearn (2018) makes the point for deregulation, arguing that postal services

I thank participants of the 27th Conference on Postal and Delivery Economics in Dublin and the editors Victor Glass and Pier Luigi Parcu for valuable inputs. Further, I thank Christian Jaag for introducing me to the world of postal economics with patience and rigor.

F. C. H. Gottschalk (✉)
Regulation Economist, Swiss Post, Bern, Switzerland
e-mail: felix.gottschalk@post.ch

P. L. Parcu et al. (eds.), *The Changing Postal Environment*, Topics in Regulatory Economics and Policy, https://doi.org/10.1007/978-3-030-34532-7_23

no longer can be regarded as "a good of basic economic interest," because users' needs could be fulfilled by new technological alternatives.

To the best of our knowledge, this article is the first to discuss the notion of users' needs and its role in postal regulation in its own right and to categorize different uses of the notion in the literature. In its newest report, ERGP states: "Considering the trends and developments described in the previous chapters of this report, a rethinking of the basic definitions and concepts is needed" (ERGP 2018). The contribution of this article may be interpreted in this vein.

The concept of "user needs" was already used in the Postal Services Directive of the European Union from 1997,[1] which states that the universal service shall remain "adaptable to the needs of users" (preamble) and "shall evolve in response to the technical, economic and social environment and to the needs of users" (article 5). Article 5 has often been interpreted in a way that universal service should evolve responding to *changing* consumer needs. However, in the strict sense of its formulation, the article also allows to see user needs as unchanging, but interacts with an evolving "technical, economic, and social environment" to necessitate changes in the universal service. These two poles also form the basis of the two concepts, which are identified and discussed in this article.

In the first meaning attached to the notion (concept 1), "user needs" is interpreted as a synonym for "consumer preferences" for satisfying these needs. This interpretation is used to inform the winding-down process of postal regulation about which reductions in USO scope are most consumer-friendly. In a variant of this concept, the notion is used to outline the services needed to guarantee societal participation of particular consumer groups ("vulnerable consumers") and thereby comprises normative considerations about social policy. Reflections on postal reform using either variant of this meaning are immanently status quo dependent and what is considered as user needs develops directly with changes in consumer behavior and in the regulatory status quo. In the second meaning attached to the notion (concept 2), consumer needs are understood as fundamental communication needs, which are technology-neutral and stable over time. Besides, they can clearly be distinguished from consumer preferences, which determine consumer choices. Based on this second concept, changes in demand for postal services in the last two decades do not necessarily have to be understood as being initiated by changing user needs, but rather by expanding possibilities for consumers, which result from new technologies. Concept 1 may be used to inform processes of gradual postal reform, whereas concept 2 is required when one wants to assess regulatory reform from a more comprehensive perspective without necessary reference to the status quo ("greenfield approach"). A good example of how both concepts appear in the debate without explicit distinction is provided through the discussions in ERGP (2016).

After this introduction, Sect. 2 will discuss some specific aspects of the notion of "user needs" and its use in the literature. This lays the base for the main part of the

[1] Directive 97/67/EC of the European Parliament and of the Council of 15 December 1997.

article, Sect. 3, where we present a categorization of the different usage of the term "user needs" in the literature into two distinct concepts and discuss both of them. Section 4 concludes.

2 Background

2.1 The Connection of Postal USOs and User Needs

In today's discussion on the development of postal USO regulation, user needs play a crucial role. Yet traditionally, postal USOs have been justified without direct reference to user needs. As analyzed notably by Cremer et al. (2001), the main justifications for USOs are the internalization of positive externalities and redistributive goals (e.g., regional balance). First, positive externalities occur when the societal value of providing specific (postal) services is greater than the sum of the attached private values. In the postal world, such externalities occur via network effects or the public value of the post office network. Generally, what is often referred to as the "social value" of the postal networks – on both the accessibility and the delivery side – can be represented as positive externalities. Second, USOs also serve redistributive goals by including measures like uniform tariffs, which redistribute wealth from urban to rural areas, from business to private consumers, from young to older users, etc.

Importantly, user needs do not seem to play an explicit direct role in these considerations. Needs are only relevant indirectly, when they have an impact on externalities or on redistributive goals. It will be argued in the remainder of this article that the two main concepts of user needs used in the literature have different connections to the justification of USO regulation. Concept 1 mainly connects through redistributive motives in the form of the protection of specific user groups, and concept 2 mainly connects through the positive externality of network effects, which occurs when mutual communication, which itself develops with the development of technology, is a vital ingredient to societal prosperity.

2.2 User Needs and Regulatory Needs

An implicit distinction is often made between primary user needs and regulatory user needs (regulation "needed" to fulfill user needs), while both are named "user needs." Regulatory needs are, when used in this sense, a consequence of primary user needs and are therefore not directly the kind of user needs discussed in this article. To make this clear, we suggest the following hypothetical example: "Postal users need access points (primary need), which are only provided when they are mandated by regulation. Users hence require (not: need) this kind of regulation." We also suggest an analogue usage of the term to future writers.

3 Two Concepts Behind the Notion of Users' Needs

This article categorizes the usage of the notion of "postal users' needs" into two groups, "concept 1" and "concept 2." The aim of this categorization is to bring clarity into the multifaceted use of the notion in the literature. Certainly, it simplifies and may correspond to some examples from the literature better than to others. The two concepts both have strengths, weaknesses, purposes, and areas of application; it is the purpose of this categorization to make readers aware of the importance of a coherent and appropriate application of the two concepts behind the notion of "postal user's needs."

Table 1 summarizes the two concepts briefly. Concept 1 puts the status quo of postal markets and postal regulation at the center of its considerations about user needs. Its purpose is to inform policy makers about how short-term postal reform can be designed as consumer-friendly as possible. Concept 2 has a broader viewpoint and analyzes user needs from the perspective of fundamental communication needs and may best be used to discuss bold or long-term reforms. This concept explicitly takes into account technological developments outside the postal sector.

In the following, we will discuss the two concepts in detail.

3.1 Concept 1: User Needs as Preferences and Dependencies

3.1.1 Description

The notion of users' needs founded on concept 1 typically appears in one of two ways: as a preference or as a social concern. Many of the studies surveyed by ERGP (2016) fall into the first category and usually rank USO attributes with respect to their importance to inform policy makers about how gradual USO-scope reductions in "the protracted winding-down process of postal regulation" (Hearn 2018) can be designed most efficiently, i.e., how a certain saving can be reached with the lowest loss in consumer utility. These studies claim to analyze user needs and the attributes ranking highest are typically named "core user needs" or similar. In fact, these rankings express preferences in the closest sense of the definition, which states that

Table 1 Two concepts of postal users' needs and their respective purpose

User needs concept	Character of users' needs	Main purpose of concept
Concept 1	User needs as preferences or dependencies; needs are revealed by consumer choices in the status quo of postal markets	Guarantee user-friendly design of gradual postal reform. Protect certain user groups from changes
Concept 2	Needs as fundamental communication needs	Guarantee that new technologies and alternatives to postal services are considered appropriately in long-term postal reform

a preference is "a greater liking for one alternative over another or others" (Oxford dictionary) or, in economics, "the ordering of alternatives based on their relative utility" (Wikipedia). Hence, what appears in the shape of "user needs" are essentially consumers' preferences – and should hence be treated as such. Most importantly, preferences are relative, whereas needs, when translated into minimum standards of communication, have absolute character. Although preference analyses serve the important purpose to inform policy makers about how reform can be designed in a consumer-friendly fashion, they do not necessarily have much to do with needs, which are defined as "require (something) because it is essential or very important rather than just desirable" – and are hence an absolute concept. A thorough distinction of minimum standards of communication (needs) and choices based on available standards or technologies is indispensable in discussions on the future regulation of postal USOs, because the insight that some consumers still prefer postal services to alternative means of communication may have very different implications than the insight that consumers require a minimum standard of communication.

In a related vein, but with different emphasis, other contributions express social concerns by focusing on particular user groups, which are considered to truly depend on postal services and hence would suffer most from USO-scope reductions (see, for instance, the respective passages in Copenhagen Economics (2017, 2018)). This emphasis has the aim to make policy makers aware of how gradual USO reforms can be carried out without neglecting the basicneeds, defined by a minimum standard, of "vulnerable" users. This point of view represents a paradigm shift in postal regulation, because it raises the question whether postal regulation should give up its principle of universality and instead focus on targeted measures for specific users.

In concept 1, the historical economic justification of USO regulation is reflected in the redistribution dimension. The protection of certain user groups from too fast changes can be interpreted as a redistributive, social policy in the form of establishing a minimum standard based on a social compact. The line to positive externalities is more vague here, but social policy could also increase societal welfare, for instance, when people who do not benefit directly from the protection may, nonetheless, positively value the protection of other consumers.

Variants of concept 1 could be considered expressed by studies from Portugal (ANACOM 2012) and Switzerland (BAKOM 2017), respectively, in which users are surveyed about their satisfaction with the current USO level. High levels of satisfaction are interpreted as a sign that the current USO fulfills users' needs, but – when user needs become more heterogeneous – potentially masks that some groups still require assistance. It can be doubted that the approach taken in these studies is useful to analyze postal reform in light of consumer needs, because they already make the implicit assumption that users need the services mandated by the current USO. More generally, user satisfaction based on immediate available choices is not a concept which is connected to user needs as minimum standards of communication in an unambiguous way. Hence, these approaches are not further considered in this article.

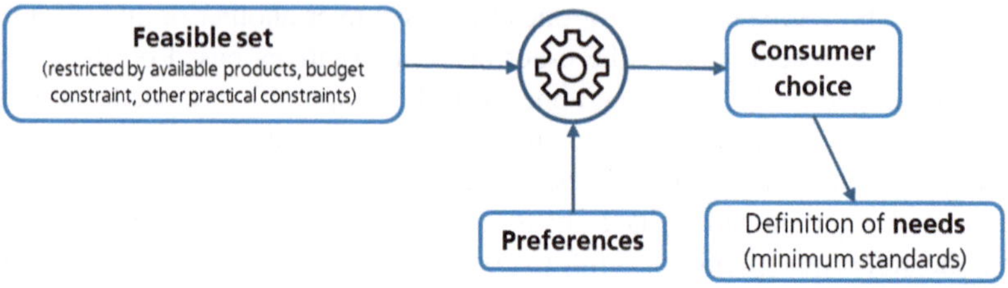

Fig. 1 The derivation of user needs in concept 1 in a consumer theory framework

3.1.2 Relation to Consumer Theory

In a simple representation inspired by microeconomic consumer theory (Fig. 1), users' needs are located at the end of the process that leads to consumer choice. Needs are identified on the basis of consumer choice. At the start of the decision process is the feasible set, a set of all possible realistic choices a consumer can make with respect to products and quantities to consume. The preferences of a consumer rank the options in the feasible set, leading among the possible choices to the most favored by the consumer. The task of policy in this understanding of needs is to guarantee that the consumer is able to repeat a former choice in a new period.

3.1.3 Discussion of Concept 1

We identify some considerable weaknesses of concept 1: status quo bias, the neglected endogeneity of new technologies, taking immediately available choices for needs, and expensive/inefficient regulation.

First, the concept is status quo biased, because user needs are determined based on actual consumer choice. Hence, when the current regulatory framework influences consumer choice, what is considered a need depends on the current regulatory framework instead of the other way round (needs should determine the regulatory framework). Current consumer choices may also be driven by habit or other factors.

Second, by focusing on the status quo of consumer choice, the concept neglects the endogeneity of new technologies. For instance, advocates of the concept often argue that postal services remain essential (and hence represent a "need" of users), because consumers still use them. In this vein, it is argued that an Internet penetration of below 100% was a sign for the fact that postal services were still "needed." But in this point of view, products outside the postal sector are taken as exogenous; precisely, it is assumed that postal users consume them independently of postal services. These arguments neglect that consumers live in a multi-product world, where the postal technology and other technologies compete with each other. But when postal services are part of a competitive multi-product world, the question arises whether high-quality and affordable postal services are by themselves an obstacle to the adaption of new technologies (i.e., higher Internet penetration). Users may make insufficient use of alternatives to postal products, such as email, as long as postal services are cheap and of high quality, i.e., but this may happen not because of "needs" but because they have a choice to use currently available postal services over technological alternatives. In other words, the current regulatory framework in the postal sector may influence the consumption choices of consumers with respect to other products. The disregard of this can be interpreted as a special form of status quo bias.

Third, when making use of concept 1, authors often fail to distinguish between preferences with respect to immediately available choices, which are mere rankings of alternatives, and needs. This has already been discussed above.

Fourth, concept 1 fails to consider the increasing costs of USOs in times of technological change, because of its implicit bias toward the status quo of postal markets. How expensive a status quo-fueled USO regulation can become with time, as technological alternatives to postal services progress and as net costs of USO provision are increasing, can be illustrated by the following example calculations. Although the postal USO may benefit many more users than those who are identified as vulnerable, it is clear that non-vulnerable consumers wouldn't require the USO. Hence, when it is agreed that only vulnerable consumers ultimately require the postal USO, the net costs of USO provision can be viewed as being caused only by vulnerable consumers (a point of view, which is compatible with concept 2, but rather not with concept 1). Copenhagen Economics (2017) undertook such a calculation and came to the conclusion that the costs of the USO per vulnerable consumer per year in Norway amounted to EUR 1,260 to 2,170, depending on the effective net costs of the USO. Using the authors' assumption on the share of vulnerable consumers, we calculated that the USO costs per vulnerable consumer in Switzerland amount to EUR 4,300 each.[2] The reason for these very high numbers is that the apparatus of the current USO concept serves all citizens and not only those who truly need it.[3]

3.2 *Concept 2: User Needs as Fundamental Communication Needs*

3.2.1 Description

Concept 2 considers users' needs as fundamental, technology-independent, communication needs – for instance, the need of a business to send an invoice to a client or the need of a person to receive a message by a public authority. The concept

[2] We assumed that Switzerland has the same share of vulnerable consumers as Norway as analyzed by Copenhagen Economics (2017). This implies 56,500 vulnerable consumers among the Swiss population of 8.484 m (2017, Federal Statistical Office), compared to 35,000 vulnerable consumers among the Norwegian population of 5.258 m (2017, Statistics Norway). The net costs of the Swiss USO amounted to CHF 271 m in 2018 (PostCom, annual report 2018).

[3] At the conference, somebody commented: This is like purchasing a car if you only want to have a device that displays the outside temperature.

thereby abstracts from the legacy of postal services. This concept is closer to the dictionary definition of needs – "require (something) because it is essential or very important rather than just desirable" – than concept 1, although it should be noted that needs as minimum communication standards develop with technology and are therefore not as stable as in this definition. Yet, it may be argued that they are comparatively stable and fix in the short-run. Further, concept 2 incorporates a cross-sectoral, multi-product world view on user needs. With respect to postal services, the concept asks what fundamental communication needs are satisfied by the postal services, but at the same time asks what other technologies/products could serve well those same needs or should be part of larger minimum standard communication USO. Concept 2 is well-suited for root-and-branch reviews of postal regulation ("greenfield" approaches) and for the assessment of cross-sectoral policy questions. For instance, concept 2 underlies the work by Jaag and Trinkner (2011, 2012), who discuss the idea of technology-independent, sector-overarching USOs.

With respect to the historical justifications of postal USOs, concept 2 strictly relates to the positive externalities produced by network effects, which occur when the fulfillment of individual communication needs also increases societal welfare.

3.2.2 Relation to Consumer Theory

In a simple representation inspired by microeconomic consumer theory (Fig. 2), users' needs are located at the start of the decision process. Needs are reflected in the feasible set as an additional constraint. A consumer excludes all options from the feasible set, which do not fulfill these needs. The task of policy is then to make sure that the feasible set includes all the possible options that fulfill the consumer's needs, given other constraints on the feasible set like the consumer's budget constraint. In contrast to concept 1, as needs in concept 2 enter the process "unfiltered," they can clearly be separated from the preferences, which determine consumer choice.

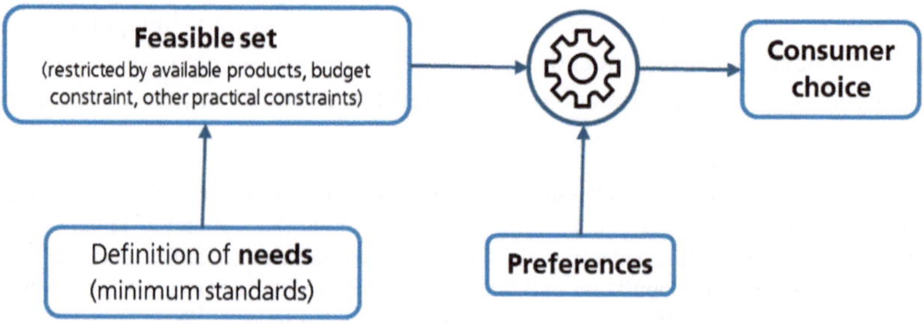

Fig. 2 The derivation of user needs in concept 2 in a consumer theory framework

3.2.3 Are User Needs Really Changing?

In countless contributions in the wide field of postal and delivery economics, it is referred to "changing user needs." But when user needs are seen as fundamental communication needs as in concept 2, doubts arise, whether changing consumer choices in a multi-product world, in times of rapid technological change, can necessarily be interpreted as changing consumer needs. Here lies a considerable difference between concept 1 and concept 2. Because concept 1 defines needs based on actual consumer choice, changes in consumer choice are necessarily interpreted as changes in consumer needs. This is not the case with concept 2, where user needs, in the form of fundamental communication needs, may remain unchanged, even when consumers change their choices with regard to the product quantity basked they consume.

We can use a simple microeconomic framework to show this. The situation is depicted in Fig. 3 which illustrates consumer choice in a two-product world with physical and digital mail in times of technological progress, which happens from the left to the right picture. The pictures display a two-product world with the quantity of physical mail on the vertical axis, and the quantity of digital communication (email, etc.) on the horizontal axis. Two indifference curves, $\overline{u}_1$ and $\overline{u}_2$, respectively, show combinations of quantities of both products (consumption bundles) that are equally valuable to the consumer. The quantities consumed are higher on curve $\overline{u}_2$, such that the utility on any consumption point on that curve is larger than on any consumption point on curve $\overline{u}_1$. The line *AB* in the left picture represents the budget line. The consumer can only afford consumption bundles within the area of the triangle *AB*0. The consumer chooses consumption bundle $\left(Q_1^p, Q_1^d\right)$, with quantity Q_1^p of digital mail consumed and quantity Q_1^d of physical mail, because it provides the highest possible utility given the budget constraint.

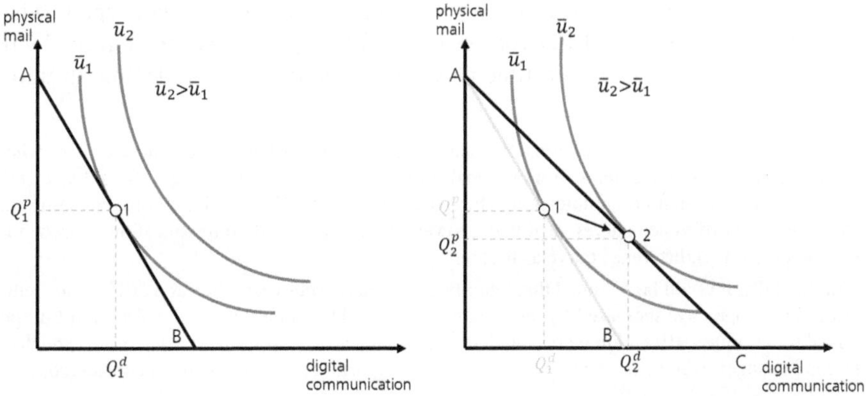

Fig. 3 Consumer choice in a two-product world with physical and digital mail in times of technological progress

We interpret technological progress as decreasing the costs of digital communication, where costs are not necessarily pecuniary but may also include improved usability that reduces the time and effort required for using digital communication.[4] Such technological progress is reflected in the difference between the left and the right picture. In the right picture, the former budget line *AB* has become *AC*, i.e., a consumer can afford more digital communication with the same budget as before.[5] The optimal consumption bundle is now bundle 2, $\left(Q_2^p, Q_2^d\right)$, which consists of less physical $\left(Q_2^p < Q_1^p\right)$ and more digital $\left(Q_2^d > Q_1^d\right)$ mail and lies on a indifference curve with higher utility than the curve on which bundle 1 was located. The important insight of this simple textbook exercise is that technological advances are not necessarily a result of changing consumer needs or preferences at all, but rather of a world of product innovation and development with changing relative prices.

Hence, in the progress of digitalization, consumer choices may change, even though consumer needs (and preferences) remain completely unchanged. For example, when consumers are not willing to pay for next day delivery anymore, the reason is not necessarily a change in users' needs to deliver or receive pieces of information, but only a change of "economic" choices given that e-mail is now available as a new alternative of rapid communication.

3.2.4 Discussion of Concept 2

Concept 2 of user needs seems to avoid the main weaknesses of concept 1, especially status quo bias. However, the concept may be more difficult to put into practice, because it implicitly requires to make assumptions about a hypothetical world without or with a different postal regulation and to include considerations about other technologies and sectors. Concept 2 also requires translating "needs" into minimum communication standards, which may be difficult to define and may change over time with changing available technology. Moreover, the concept is likely to justify bolder moves in postal regulation than concept 1, what will be likely challenged by advocates of the status quo. However, concept 2 will become more important with time as with continuing volume decline in tradi-

[4]One editor pointed out an additional rational for the argument that choices may change when needs are stable: improvements in digital mail (adding voice and video to text) would also shift demand toward digital communication. This could be depicted in the diagram by changing the shape of the indifference curves such that a lower amount of digital communication is needed to stay on the same indifference curve as before.

[5]Additionally, it could be assumed that letter prices increase (between 2013 and 2018 alone, letter prices in Europe have increased by more than 50% – see Deutsche Post, Letter Prices in Europe, 18th edition, June 2019). With increasing letter prices, the relative price between physical and digital mail changes even faster than when only decreasing prices of digital mail are considered.

tional mail markets, postal USOs become more expensive and new technologies become ever better substitutes for postal services. In the eyes of regulators and industry representatives these technological developments may require more and more greenfield approaches to postal reform. Such a greenfield approach was recently proposed by the European Regulators Groups for Postal Services (ERGP 2018). It will be important that those who will be carrying the analysis will acknowledge that such an exercise requires concept 2 as the underlying concept of user needs.

It is well established that – in order to completely understand the net costs of any universal service provision – it is necessary to consider a hypothetical scenario and compare it to the status quo (Panzar 2000). A related approach could be taken with respect to assessing changing regulatory needs and the most efficient regulatory regime from a greenfield perspective in the postal sector. The following list proposes a cascade that a greenfield approach to postal regulation would have to go through if it had the aim to fulfill user needs with the best suited policy. First, define the underlying, technology-independent, fundamental (communication) needs of users. Second, define hypothetical scenarios with different – potentially cross-sectoral – regulatory regimes (including the no-USO scenario). Third, analyze to what degree the needs collected in the first step would be served by postal and non-postal services in the scenarios defined in step two. Fourth, choose the preferred scenario among those analyzed in the third step.

4 Conclusion

This article provided an analysis of the frequently used notion of "postal users' needs" and stresses the importance of a conscious use of the term by researchers and regulators. We claim that the usage of the term in the discussion on postal regulation can be categorized in two concepts. In concept 1, which is the dominant concept in the literature, user needs are in fact an immediate representation of user choices or social concerns. In concept 2, user needs are considered to be fundamental communication needs. Concept 1 can be used for a consumer-friendly design of gradual postal reform. The article pointed out several conceptual weaknesses of this concept, especially its intrinsic status quo bias. Concept 2 provides a broader, non-status quo-dependent approach and is better suited for greenfield assessments to postal reform. With continuing technological progress, greenfield assessments to postal reform will become more demanded. As the analysis in this article has revealed, in carrying out such assessments, regulators and researchers should adopt the viewpoint of user needs as fundamental communication needs (concept 2) and avoid to identify user needs as past choices or dependencies formed by the status quo (concept 1).

Bibliography

ANACOM. (2012). *Survey on the use of postal services—residential population in December 2012.*

BAKOM. (2017). *Postversorgung in der Schweiz. Erhebung im Auftrag des Bundesamtes für Kommunikation BAKOM.* Schlussbericht vom 9. November 2017.

Cape, S., & Groves, P. (2017). Changes to the universal service: Influencing factors, impacts and regulatory implications. In *The changing postal and delivery sector* (pp. 257–269). Cham: Springer.

Confraria, J., Ribeiro, V. M., Franco, A., & Pereira, F. (2017). A case study of density of retail outlets in Portugal: Regulation and politics in postal markets. In *The changing postal and delivery sector* (pp. 97–114). Cham: Springer.

Confraria, J., Silva, F., Pereira, F., & Franco, A. (2018). Postal users' needs regarding accessibility to the postal network. In *The contribution of the postal and delivery sector* (pp. 187–205). Cham: Springer.

Copenhagen Economics. (2017). *Effects of changing the USO in Norway.* Final report for Samferdselsdepartementet.

Copenhagen Economics. (2018). *Main developments in the postal sector (2013–2016).* Study for the European Commission.

Cremer, H., Gasmi, F., Grimaud, A., & Laffont, J. J. (2001). Universal service: An economic perspective. *Annals of Public and Cooperative Economics, 72*(1), 5–43.

ERGP. (2016). *ERGP report Universal Services in light of changing postal end users' needs.*

ERGP. (2018). *ERGP (18) 49.* Report on developments in the postal sector and implications for regulation.

Hearn, J. (2018). Regulation. Quo Vadis? In *The contribution of the postal and delivery sector* (pp. 75–88). Cham: Springer.

Jaag, C., & Trinkner, U. (2011). *The future of the USO – Economic rationale for universal services and implications for a future-oriented USO.* Swiss Economics Working Paper.

Jaag, C., & Trinkner, U. (2012). *Defining and financing an intermodal USO.* Swiss Economics Working Paper.

Panzar, J. C. (2000). A methodology for measuring the costs of universal service obligations. *Information Economics and Policy, 12*(3), 211–220.

WIK Consult. (2019). *User needs in the postal sector. A study for the European Commission.* Presentation held at the Public Stakeholder Workshop Brussels. 29 January 2019.

The Economic and Social Utility of the Postal Infrastructure: Above and Beyond Postal Items Delivery

Claire Borsenberger

1 Introduction

Digitalization of the economy continues to shrink postal operators' (POs) historical core business – letter mail delivery. As a result, their economic performance is under pressure. Nonetheless, POs continue to be a key vector of socioeconomic development: with a global network of over 677,000 post offices and 5.3 million employees around the world according to UPU statistics, POs still facilitate economic activity and provide large benefits to the society in a variety of ways. Indeed, they have never been "just" mail or parcel carriers. Through their human and physical infrastructure, they have always promoted social and territorial cohesion and supported local economic development. When the economic sustainability of the postal universal service is threatened and the users' needs are questioned, it is useful to revisit the literature on the economic and social contribution of POs. This work is a first step toward documenting their current contributions to promoting the digital economy and supporting an aging population. The paper offers fruitful insights for revising the European Postal Directive.

Section 2 deals briefly with the evolution of POs' economic performance in recent years. Section 3 surveys studies about the historical role of POs and their social contribution larger than mail delivery. Section 4 shows that today, POs contribute to the promotion of e-commerce, the financial and digital inclusion of vulnerable people, the well-being of older people, the sustainability of the economy through the support of the social solidarity objectives, and the promotion of energetic

The opinion expressed in this paper are mine and do not necessarily reflect the position of La Poste. I thank Peter Denley and participants to the 27th Conference on Postal and Delivery Economics for their valuable comments.

C. Borsenberger (✉)
Direction of Regulation and Economic Studies– Le Groupe La Poste, Paris, France
e-mail: claire.borsenberger@laposte.fr

P. L. Parcu et al. (eds.), *The Changing Postal Environment*, Topics in Regulatory Economics and Policy, https://doi.org/10.1007/978-3-030-34532-7_24

transition, and the development of an environmentally friendly circular economy. Section 5 concludes.

2 The Direct Economic Value of POs Is Negatively Affected by the Digital Revolution

For approximately 15 years, the postal industry has been facing the digital revolution. The Internet and social media companies in particular such as Facebook and Twitter have profoundly changed the way people communicate around the world. POs' historical core business, the delivery of letter mail, is disappearing more or less quickly according to the country[1]: for instance, the number of addressed mail decreased by 90% in Denmark since 2000, by 50% in Finland since 2008, by 41% in Sweden since 2000, and by 45% in Ireland since 2007 and in France since 2004. On average, in advanced economies, mail volume declined by 31% between 2007 and 2017 (IPC 2018).

Meanwhile the way people purchase goods has also changed: e-commerce has grown rapidly with a few big economic actors dominating this new sector. Alibaba and Amazon together now accounting for more than one in every three euros spent online (IPC 2018). For POs, this evolution means many more packets and parcels to deliver than 10 years ago: between 2007 and 2017, on average, in advanced economies, parcels volume increased by 103% (IPC 2018).

Despite sometimes huge price increases of letter mail (on average, letter tariffs increased by 49% between 2012 and 2018 whereas consumption price index increased only by 8%[2]), POs' turnover in mail activity is decreasing and only partially compensated by increase in parcel delivery and logistics activities, which combined now accounted for over a third of the industry's revenue according to Holger Winklbauer, Chief Executive Officer of International Post Corporation.[3] Consequently, according to IPC latest figures,[4] over the last 3 years, the average EBIT margin of the postal industry has decreased, both on mail – due to increasing costs in maintaining national sorting and delivery networks – and parcel segments, due to strong competition on this vibrant market and the growing bargaining power of some customers, notably the biggest e-commerce retailers and marketplaces. Pressure on POs is also illustrated by the fact that listed POs[5] underperformed on the

---

[1] Posts in countries with the highest rates of digitalization saw among the sharpest declines in mail volumes.

[2] IPC (2018), *Global Postal Industry Report,* November, p. 40, Fig. 2.14.

[3] IPC (2018), *Global Postal Industry Report,* November, p. 7.

[4] IPC (2018), *Global Postal Industry Report,* November, p. 60, Fig. 70.

[5] Ten Posts are now listed on local stock exchanges: Deutsche Post DHL, bpost, PostNL, Österreichische Post, Poste Italiane, CTT Portugal Post, Royal Mail, Singapore Post, Post Malaysia and Japan Post.

stock exchange since 2014 compared to the MSCI World Index[6]: whereas listed posts have seen share prices fall by 15% on average since January 2014, the MSCI World Index has increased by 30%.[7]

3 The Real Value of Posts: Far Beyond Purely Economic Own Performance Indicators

The postal sector has always been an essential infrastructure that facilitates the functioning of the global economy.[8] Besides direct contribution to economic growth (through employment and the value added directly generated by postal activities as a final good), postal services, as an input entering in the production function of others services, contribute indirectly to economic growth and country's development. For instance, Hristova et al. (2016) analyzed the postal flows of 184 countries between 2010 and 2015[9] and found they are highly positively correlated with trade, GDP, life expectancy, and the Economic Complexity Index (an holistic measure of the production characteristics of large economic systems produced by the Observatory of Economic Complexity) and negatively correlated with the rate of poverty and the Human Development Index (a composite statistic of life expectancy, education, and income per capita indicators computed by the United National Development Program).[10] Deloitte Access Economics (2018) has recently estimated the economic contribution of Australia Post using an input-output model[11] to $6 billion in 2017 ($3.2 billion directly and $2.8 billon indirectly), representing 0.45% of the Australian GDP. Regarding employment, Australia Post directly employed around 26,500 full-time equivalent (FTE) workers in 2017 and indirectly supported

[6] The MSCI World Index is designed to represent the performance of large- and mid-cap stocks across 23 developed markets (Australia, Austria, Belgium, Canada, Denmark, Finland, France, Germany, Hong Kong, Ireland, Israel, Italy, Japan, the Netherlands, New Zealand, Norway, Portugal, Singapore, Spain, Sweden, Switzerland, the United Kingdom, and the United States). With more than 1,600 constituents, it covered approximately 85% of the free float-adjusted market capitalization in each country as of December 2018.

[7] IPC (2018), *Global Postal Industry Report,* November, p. 60. Fig. 71.

[8] See, for instance, Rogowski et al. (2017) who exploited two original datasets: one tracking the spread of postal services in countries around the world from 1875 to 2007 and the other describing the distribution of post offices across counties in the United States from 1845 to 1896 and found evidence of a positive relationship between the establishment of post offices and economic growth.

[9] In order to take into account of the fact that the number of daily items sent and received by countries can be highly dependent on the size of the population of a country, the authors normalized the volume per country's population.

[10] See Fig. 6, p. 12.

[11] Such a model captures both the direct contribution to the economy through Australia Post's operations and its indirect contribution through flow-on economic activity such as the intermediate inputs that are supplied by other firms and used in Australia Post's operations.

24,800 FTEs in other businesses and industries through flow-on economic activity (representing globally 0.6% of all FTE employments).

Moreover, several parts of the postal infrastructure generate huge positive externalities, increasing its contribution to the social welfare. For instance, a high-quality national address system brings a number of benefits: for citizens, it provides the guarantee of rapid access for the emergency services, a simpler connection to utilities networks, and a guarantee of more rapid deliveries; for local authorities and administrations, it facilitates a more efficient organization of public services and streamlined relationships with citizens; for businesses, it provides a reliable location, easy and rapid access for their customers, and the assurance that they will receive their goods hitch-free. In a study for the US Postal Service Office of Inspector General (2014), IBM has calculated that the additional revenues and reduced costs resulting from all the uses of the ZIP Code amount to close to $10 billion across the economy.

But the most important elements of the postal infrastructure are certainly the POs' physical (post offices) and human (carriers) networks. As well summarized by MacConnell (2015), "mail carriers (and women) always delivered much more than routine mail to their neighbors. (…) The country postman has been a social worker in real terms," and several studies have proved that the post offices network generates positive spillovers on the domestic economy by providing a stable anchor of centrally located economic and social activity that attracts and helps to keep jobs and shops. According to Zigelbauer et al. (2005), public buildings, including courthouses, libraries, and *post offices*, draw many people on a typical day, generating potential business for surrounding merchants and making downtowns more hospitable. On a more general way, as emphasized by Thisse and Wildasin (1992), "the most casual observation suggests that the location of public facilities can have a substantial impact on private sector locational choice." More recently, Anson and Gual (2008) examined if there is a causal link between the presence of Banco Postal and the local development, by considering the opening of a branch in a municipality in 2002 as a "treatment" for the municipality and using propensity score comparison methods[12] to estimate the impact of this openness on the economic situation of the municipality after this event. They also took into account regional effects by introducing dummies in their econometric model and found that in the municipalities in which a Banco Postal agency was introduced, the creation of new businesses increased by 23%, job creation by 14%, and the number of new banking agencies by 56% in comparison to the municipalities with no such agency.

By providing financial services in their post offices, POs fight against banking exclusion. According to Clotteau and Measho (2016), 91% of POs worldwide (183 out of 201) provide financial services, either directly or in partnership with other

[12] Propensity scores are an index that takes into account all the information on a given municipality in order to calculate the probability that she undergoes the "treatment." Using this index, the authors used the technique of the comparison of closest neighbors to compare the economic development level of a municipality that has been treated to those of another municipality that has a similar propensity score but that had not been treated.

financial institutions, to 1.5 billion people, making them the second biggest global player in financial inclusion, behind banks but well ahead of microfinance institutions, which account for "only" 200 million customers, and mobile money operators, which have roughly 150 million active customers. According to Anson et al. (2013), POs are better placed than banks to provide accounts to people excluded from the financial system, especially those in rural areas or precarious economic situations thanks to their very dense physical networks, their unique presence in rural areas and trusted status. Anson and Toledano (2010) pointed the fact that in emerging and developing countries, banks have been very reluctant to expand financial services toward poorer segments of the population. In this context, a significant number of POs have increased their market share in some segments of the retail banking business during the first decade of 2000s, addressing particularly populations typically unbanked or underserved by commercial banks. They presumed that this movement was accelerated after the 2008 global economic and financial crisis, since a number of Posts being more trusted than banks after the crisis. In industrialized countries too, full financial inclusion has not always been ensured by pure commercial banks. For instance, in the United States, where USPS does not provide financial services, the Federal Deposit Insurance Corporation (FDIC) estimates that 6.5% of households were unbanked in 2017, representing approximately 8.4 million households.[13] Last but not least, Anson and Toledano (2010) noted also that even with the emergence of new information and communication technologies and of mobile banking services, a physical and human network continues to be necessary to provide such inclusive banking and financial services.

Moreover, the postal presence (through the post offices network) has accompanied the presence of the State on the territory. Posts have been a tool to create a territorial unity and to uniform the timing of the circulation of information. They have contributed to the establishment of the ideas of equality and unity. According to the Office of Inspector General of USPS (2014), "for much of its first 200 years, [USPS] not only carried mail but also was deliberately used by the government to bind together and develop the nation." For most rural Americans in the nineteenth century, the post office was the only source of interactions they would have had with State institutions (Carpenter 2001; John 1995). According to Blevins (2015), postal systems provided a *sense of the state* in communities located far away from a nation's political and economic centers. In Canada, an even more diffusely settled land, the post office helped to bring "the various rural markets of Canada into an integrated national economy" (Amyot and Willis 2003). Today, at least in some countries, national POs remain closely linked to the State. In EU member states, POs are in charge of various services of general economic interest (such as the postal universal service, the transport and delivery of newspaper, the financial inclusion, the provision of State official documents – driving license, passport, and so on). Debates surrounding the closure of post offices in local community are an

[13] FDIC (2018), *2017 FDIC National Survey of Unbanked and Underbanked Households*, October.

example of the symbolic figure attached to POs, sometimes considered as the last public service, in the sense of the last State's representative.

4 The "New" Societal Contribution of Posts: Promoting a Digital and Aging Society in a Sustainable, Inclusive, and Human Way

One could think the social role played by POs through their human and physical networks is old-fashioned and is disappearing with mail volume decline. This is clearly not the case. According to a recent survey made by the Belgium postal regulator (BIPT 2017), the social role of the postman is still experienced as a fundamental element for staying in touch with the outside world. Especially vulnerable users are interested in having a permanent postman, so that they can establish a personal bond. In the same kind of spirit, according to Why5Research (2017), for some people (notably for elderly, vulnerable, or people living in rural areas), the postman keeps a social or watchdog role inherited from the past. Several quantitative studies[14] showed that people are willing to pay some amount of money to keep post offices opened. For instance, according to Deloitte (2018), on average Australians (aged 18+) are willing to pay $10.20 per year, in addition to the prices paid for purchasing Australia Post's products and services, in order to ensure the ongoing existence of Australia Post and the post office network. Even Australians who have not used postal services place a value on the broader community and social benefits: 82% value the existence of Australia Post's delivery services because other people can use them, and 71% value that other Australians can use the post office's broader services.

This could in part be explained by the aging of the population: according to MacConnell (2015), "as the rural population dwindles and ages, it is equally true that there are many isolated homes to whose doorstep the postman is the only daily caller. There are many recorded instances where their contacts with vulnerable persons led to the prevention of tragedies. They know their rounds, and they know the first names of the people behind the letter boxes. They are a crucial cog in the country wheel."

But aging is not the only factor explaining the attachment to the "postman's" presence. Paradoxically, the need of human interactions seems to grow with the digitalization of the society.[15] Indeed, Internet creates an illusion of a social

---

[14] Among the pioneer works on this topic, we found NERA's (2003 and 2009) cost-benefit analysis of UK rural post office services, a Postwatch Scotland (2006) survey on the importance of Scottish rural post offices. More recently, we can cite the Ellison et al. (2016) study dealing with the social value of UK Post Office network. NERA (2009) estimated the social value of Post Office Limited's network between £2.6bn and £11.7bn per year, and more recently the network's social value was estimated by Ellison et al. (2016) between £4.3 billion and £9.7 billion per year.

[15] Opinion polls reveal that a large amount of the population actually prefers human interaction. For instance, according to a SurveyMonkey survey conducted in November 2018 on 1,820 US adults aged

interaction rather than providing people with a real one. Whereas the digital technology has brought people together in many ways, by allowing them to easily connect with one another through just one click and to constantly stay in touch with their peers, relationships often lack of depth, generating loneliness feelings. Moreover, social media often induce people to conceal too much personal details, emotions, and facts, leading to a lack of intimacy, also detrimental to human interactions. Loneliness as well as lack of intimacy could lead to dangerous outcomes, such as addiction and self-harm.

Around the world, POs through their historic and strong settlement on territories, thanks to the trusted link formed with local population, are able to respond to this need of human interactions and to reach all people and in particular those facing the risk of social exclusion. They could (and some already do it[16]) promote an inclusive and human digital world in which all people, the oldest as well as the less skilled, have access to the best services.

4.1 Post's Involvement in an Inclusive and Human Digital Economy

As the number of services (including public ones) available (sometimes exclusively) online is increasing, solving the digital divide become more and more crucial. Indeed, the lack of access to the Internet and the literacy issue lead to a new form of exclusion affecting a significant proportion of the population, even in the most advanced countries. For instance, in France, 14 million people – 23% of the French population above 15 years old – are "far from the digital technology"; 11% of the population (40% of people aged 70 years or over and 46% of low-income people) have never connected to the Internet; 40% of the population (87% of people aged 70 years or over) do not use social networks (Facebook, Twitter, etc.); and a third of the population (70% of non-graduates) has never made an online administrative procedure.[17] Nevertheless, by 2022, all administrative procedures will be dematerialized in France.

Sheedy and Moloney (2015) and Eggrickx et al. (2018) have already emphasized the role that POs could play in digital inclusion. Sheedy and Moloney (2015) considered that "the local post office [is] an ideal candidate for not only introducing citizens and local business to the digital world but also for supporting them by providing training facilities at local post offices. NPOs have the reach to enable citi-

18–34, 35–46, and 65 and up exhibited that 42% of participants felt that they preferred in-person interaction over technological connections. Only 2% actually expressed a preference for interacting over social media (https://www.goboldfish.com/dangers-of-loneliness-we-want-human-interaction/).

[16] Since 2013 and the establishment of its current strategic business plan "La Poste 2020: Conquering the Future," Le Groupe La Poste has set itself the ambition of "becoming the first people-centered local services company for everyone, everywhere and every day."

[17] https://labo.societenumerique.gouv.fr/2017/11/16/vers-strategie-nationale-dinclusion-numerique/

zens, at local level, to get online by providing public access computing services in their postal branches. Furthermore, with 40% of the citizens over 55 using the local Post Office weekly and 55% of branches located in rural areas, NPOs are well placed to assist in bringing digital services to an increasingly disadvantaged section of society – the digitally excluded." Still today, POs remain for their users an indicator of national identity, and according to Asher et al. (2011), USPS in particular could continue "to bind the Nation together" in the digital age by embracing technological development and digitalization.

This is especially the case of POs that actively participate to their national e-government strategy and the digital transformation of the society by providing, for instance, digital identity (see on these topics Borsenberger et al. (2016, 2017), Eggrickx et al. (2018), and Gori and Parcu (2018)) or by accompanying every day the most vulnerable people toward digital autonomy. Concretely, some POs, like Le Groupe La Poste in France or Post Office Limited in the United Kingdom,[18] help to reduce the digital divide, both by giving access to the Internet inside some of their post offices and by training people to use online services. For instance, in French rural areas, at end-2018, digital tablets had been installed in more than 4,500 La Poste's Agence Communale service points. Available to customers on a free-of-charge self-service basis, these tablets provide access to banking and postal services, as well as to local public authorities and institutional partner websites, such as the CAF (family benefits fund) or Pôle emploi (the French national employment agency). With #stopillétrisme, La Poste provides skills to first-time digital users and raises their awareness about connected devices, security, and digital languages, by running workshops. For instance, in the post office Wilson in Saint-Etienne, 350 persons were accompanied, and 103 of them benefited from a digital training workshop between September 2018 and May 2019.

4.2 Posts' Involvement in an Elderly Society

Statistics and projections have long shown that the world population is aging due to improvements in life expectancy and a decrease in fertility. The global population aged 60 years or over numbered 962 million in 2017 (representing 13% of the global population) – more than twice as large as in 1980 when there were 382 million older persons worldwide – and is growing at a rate of about 3% per year, faster than all younger age groups. The number of older persons in the world is expected to more than double by 2050 and to more than triple by 2100, rising to 2.1 billion in 2050 and to 3.1 billion in 2100[19] (United Nations 2017).

[18] In the United Kingdom, Post Office Limited has also implemented a Digital Inclusion Programme aiming to reduce the number of British people who are not online (estimated to 8 million).

[19] Globally, the number of persons aged 80 or over is projected to triple by 2050, from 137 million in 2017 to 425 million in 2050. By 2100 it is expected to increase to 909 million, nearly seven times its value in 2017.

Currently, Europe has the greatest percentage of population aged 60 or over (a quarter) and a majority (93.4% in the Netherlands) of those persons live alone or with a spouse only, with no family support within reach, especially in rural and remote areas, and express a strong desire to remain in their home as they get older, to "age in place" (United Nations 2017; UNECE 2017). However, ensuring adequate and affordable care coverage, especially in rural and remote areas, is often problematic: lower population density and more geographically dispersed populations make it more difficult and expensive to create and maintain a comprehensive service infrastructure. Consequently, rural populations have less access to services and activities (including health and social care services[20]) or must travel longer to access to them whereas mobility decreases with age. Consequently, older people in rural areas may be confronted with higher risk of social isolation and feelings of loneliness and must struggle to access health services, whereas studies proved that people in rural areas often have a poorer health status (Unite for Sight, 2015). So, there is a need to develop modern policies for care as well as extending home-based services to enhance older persons' quality of life and overall well-being with care services tailored to their needs and to their desire to age at home.

This could be viewed as an opportunity for POs: with their extensive post offices network (especially in rural areas) and their network of carriers, POs have daily connections with customers, even the most isolated and less mobile people. Jersey Post is already engaged with aging populations: the service *Call&Check* enables postal employees on their usual postal rounds to check on the well-being of vulnerable members of society and to connect them with supportive community services. This assistance service for older people helps them to stay in their home for longer, which has been proven to have considerable mental and physical benefits for the individuals concerned. Moreover, it helps to relieve caregivers in their work and to reassure families. In light of *Call&Check*'s success the Government of Jersey has now made the service a fully approved and funded service for the island. In France, La Poste has launched a similar service called *Veiller sur mes parents* (*Watch over my parents*), which includes a regular visit from the local postman and a 24/7 helpline and offers a large panel of goods and services which help elderly people to remain autonomous, such as the digital tablet Ardoiz developed by Tikeasy, a subsidiary of Le Groupe La Poste, the delivery of meals at home, training workshops on road safety, and eco-driving for seniors organized by Bemobi, a subsidiary specialized in mobility advices. Having observed the success of La Poste and Jersey Post's initiatives, the Home Office has asked Royal Mail to support trialing a similar type of service in the United Kingdom, entitled *Safe and Connected*, and in several Belgian municipalities,[21] bpost proposes the *bclose* service in collaboration with the

[20] Healthcare corresponds to medical services provided by professional staff, whereas social care is mainly provided by local authorities, the private sector, and informal carers and consists of personal assistance aimed at increasing the recipients' well-being.

[21] Thirteen, seven, and eight Belgian municipalities used bclose services in 2016, 2017, and 2018 according to bpost annual report 2018.

local social services. Until now, these initiatives remain more or less at an experimental stage but one can expect they would grow in the next years.

4.3 Posts' Involvement in Sustainable, Circular, and Solidarity Economy

In recent years many people have begun to realize the need to change to mitigate the negative externalities of their practices on the environment. A 2012 World Wildlife Fund report estimated that by 2030 we shall need need the equivalent of two planets in order to sustain our lifestyles.[22] We need to come up with new economic models and new modes of consumption. One way forward in which consumption can continue in part, but through which the negative externalities are reduced or even eliminated, is through circular economic principles.

The circular economy is an economic system of exchange and production which, at all stages of the life cycle of products, is designed to use resources more efficiently and reduce the environmental impact, while promoting well-being for individuals. It is opposed to a linear economy, in which raw natural resources are taken, transformed into products and get disposed of. In general terms, circular economy refers to the reduction and optimization of the use of non-renewable natural resources through more efficient production and use of goods and services and by reducing waste, with the aim of increasing their resilience or sustainability of these resources. According to the World Economic Forum (2014), "a circular economy is an industrial system that is restorative or regenerative by intention and design. It replaces the end-of-life concept with restoration, shifts towards the use of renewable energy, eliminates the use of toxic chemicals, which impair reuse and return to the biosphere, and aims for the elimination of waste through the superior design of materials, products, systems and business models."

Despite its benefits for the environment, economy, and businesses, this model has been growing slowly. POs have a role to get things moving and many are already involved in the transition toward a circular economy. For instance, Le Groupe La Poste is committed to environmental transition both for itself and for its customers (companies, local authorities, individuals) and is developing a range of solutions to encourage the transition from a linear to a circular economy by supporting gradual changes in behavior and consumption patterns, developing new circular channels, especially shorter ones, supporting start-ups and social and solidarity economy structures that promote reuse of products and short delivery circuits, managing efficiently its energy resources, reducing and compensating its carbon emissions, promoting eco-mobility, and so on. The best example of this involvement for a more sustainable world is the establishment of the largest fleet of electric vehicles in the

[22] WWF (2012), Living Planet Report 2012.

world (by the end of 2017, more than 50% of postmen's rounds were traveled by non-motorized or electric transport).

Promoting the circular economy could be a business opportunity. For instance, among others, Le Groupe La Poste has developed office paper recycling service (Recygo): the paper is directly picked up from the offices by the postman; it is then delivered to Nouvelle Attitude, a subsidiary of Le Groupe La Poste that helps the long-term unemployed people to rejoin the workforce; Nouvelle Attitude then carries out the sorting of the paper, in order to enhance its value, before transmitting it to nearby paper recyclers located in France.[23] Other examples of this kind are given by Lithuania Post that has disposed boxes dedicated to the collection of used batteries in its post offices, to be recycled by a partner since 2012; Bosnia-Herzegovina Post that signed an agreement with a certified paper recycling company in April 2013 and put containers at the customers' disposal in every post office; Posti and Swiss Post that have adopted a recycling model for their work clothing; Correos that launched in 2013 a program to donate obsolete computers to NGOs, associations, and schools in Spain and in emerging countries; and POST Luxembourg that organized for the first time in November 2017 a solidarity action aiming at distributing abandoned parcels coming from Asia to charities (PostEurop 2015).

5 Conclusion

The postal service has historically provided a core social and economic infrastructure and has been the trusted provider of secure communication, payment, and delivery services between identified senders and receivers. This role of trusted provider has facilitated all aspects of commercial, social, and political developments of nations. Today, the postal sector is in a period of profound change. Technological developments, notably digitization, are challenging its traditional economic model. They are impacting the use of mail and the demand for parcel delivery services and modifying customers' expectations. As new technologies emerge, the postal network may no longer be needed in the same way than several decades ago.

Nevertheless, even if the historical core activity of POs is disappearing, POs remain key players of the economy: they provide numerous services that benefit the public both directly as part of their missions to deliver mail and parcels and indirectly as a by-product of their networks and daily presence. They remain a critical (physical, human, and electronical) infrastructure for generating economic growth, for an inclusive and effective economy.

Historically, POs have always successfully adapted their activity and network to changing needs and technology. But successful adaptation presumes identifying new needs through studies and then giving POs enough flexibility to adapt their physical and human networks to these new needs. As emphasized by the OIG (2014),

[23] Recygo made it possible to collect 635 tons in 2016 and 620 tons of paper for recycling in 2017.

"only an agile and adaptive infrastructure will be able to maintain self-sufficiency and serve the nation effectively."

Today, armed with a workforce that already visits citizens and businesses almost every day of the week and that enjoys a good reputation and confidence from elderly people, POs have the opportunity to develop their position in the silver economy. Mail carriers could be "look-outs" for isolated people, and social service workers who regularly visit isolated people, in partnership with public institutions. Moreover, thanks to their dense physical network in the heart of territories and thanks to their proximity with consumers, citizens, businesses, and public institutions, POs are natural partners and promoters of the circular economy. Again, POs can reinvent themselves provided that public authorities and regulators do not prevent these socially useful transformations with inappropriate regulation or constraints. It is time to accept changes in the postal service in order to guarantee the sustainability of POs.

References

Amyot, C., & John, W. (2003). *Country Post: Rural Postal Service in Canada, 1880 to 1945* Gatineau, Quebec: Canadian Museum of Civilization.

Anson, J., & Gual, L. B. (2008). Financial access and inclusion through postal networks: Evaluating the experience of Brazil's banco postal. In J. Toledano (Ed.), *Postal economics in developing countries*. Bern: Universal Postal Union.

Anson, J., & Toledano, J. (2010). Financial inclusion and postal banking: Is the survival of posts also there? In M. A. Crew & P. R. Kleindorfer (Eds.), *Reinventing the postal sector in an electronic age* (pp. 319–335). Cheltenham: Edward Elgar Publishing.

Anson, J., Berthaud, A., Klapper, L., & Singer, D. (2013). *Financial inclusion and the role of the post office*. Policy Research Working Paper 6630, World Bank.

Asher, D., Callan, J., & Marsh, B. (2011). The postal service role in the digital age-expanding the postal platform. In *Presented in the 19th Conference on Postal and Delivery Economics*.

BIPT. (2017). *Communication by the BIPT Council of 13 February 2017 regarding an overall analysis about postal needs in Belgium*.

Blevins, C. (2015). *The PostalWest: Spatial Integration And The AmericanWest, 1865–1902*. PhD Dissertation, Department of History, Stanford University.

Borsenberger, C., Klargaard, O., & Régnard, P. (2016). Personal data and privacy issues and POs stand. In M. A. Crew & T. J. Brennan (Eds.), *The future of the postal sector in a digital world* (pp. 261–270). Cham: Springer International Publishing.

Borsenberger, C., Klargaard, O., & Régnard, P. (2017). Digital identities: A good move for POs. In M. Crew, T. Brennan, & P. L. Parcu (Eds.), *The changing postal and delivery sector* (pp. 223–332). Cham: Springer International Publishing.

Carpenter, D. P. (2001). *The Forging of Bureaucratic Autonomy: Networks, Reputations and Policy Innovation in Executive Agencies, 1862–1928*. Princeton, NJ: Princeton University Press.

Clotteau, N., & Measho, B. (2016). *Global Panorama on Postal Financial Inclusion*. Bern: Universal Postal Union.

Deloitte. (2018). *Economic and social value of Australia Post*.

Eggrickx, B., Klargaard, O., Lefort, M., & Régnard, P. (2018). E-government: A curse or an opportunity for posts? In P. L. Parcu, T. J. Brennan, & V. Glass (Eds.), *New business and regulatory strategies in the postal sector*. Cham: Springer Nature.

Ellison, G., Piggott, L., Sutter, J., & Jones, S. (2016). *The social value of the post office network.* November.

Federal Deposit Insurance Corporation. (2018). *2017 FDIC national survey of unbanked and underbanked households.* October.

Gori, P., & Parcu, P. L. (2018). POs as "ground based" online platforms? In *New business and regulatory strategies in the postal sector.* Cham: Springer Nature.

Hristova, D., Rutherford, A., Anson, J., Luengo-Oroz, M., & Mascolo, C. (2016). The international postal network and other global flows as proxies for national wellbeing. *PLoS One, 11*(6), e0155976.

IPC. (2018). *Global postal industry report.* November.

John, R. R. (1995). *Spreading the News: The American Postal System from Franklin to Morse.* Cambridge, MA: Harvard University Press.

MacConnell, Cormac. (2015). The country postman is a social worker too. *The Irish Examiner.* 15th October.

NERA. (2009). *The social value of the post office network.* Report for Postcomm. August.

PostEurop. (2015). *The postal sector, leading the way in corporate social responsibility.*

Postwatch Scotland. (2006). *The importance of rural post offices: An assessment of the economic and social role of post offices in remote rural Scotland.* September.

Rogowski, J. C., Gerring, J., Maguire, M., & Cojocaru, L. (2017). *State infrastructure and economic development: Evidence from postal systems.* Working paper. December.

Sheedy, C., & Moloney, M. (2015). Digital inclusion: A role for POs in a smart world. In *Postal and delivery innovation in the digital economy. Berlin.* Cham: Springer.

Thisse, J. F., & Wildasin, D. E. (1992). Public facility location and urban spatial structure: Equilibrium and welfare analysis. *Journal of Public Economics, 48*(1), 83–118.

U.S. Postal Service Office of Inspector General. (2014). *The postal service's role as infrastructure.* RARC Report n° RARC-WP-15-003. December 15th.

UNECE. (2017). Older persons in rural and remote areas, *Policy brief on ageing*, n°18. March.

United Nations. (2017). *World population ageing 2017 – Highlights, report of the department of economic and social affairs.* Report ST/ESA/SER.A/397.

Why5research. (2017). *A qualitative study into consumer perspectives in the Belgian postal market.*

World Economic Forum. (2014). *Towards the circular economy: Accelerating the scale-up across global supply chains.*

Zigelbauer, R., Ryan, B., & Grabow, S. (2005). *The importance of government facilities in downtowns: An analysis of business establishments in Wisconsin's county seats.*

Beyond the USO: Reflections on Recent Decisions on Postal SGEIs

Alessandra Fratini and Manfredi Pucci di Benisichi

1 Introduction

The paper looks at some recent decisions of the European Commission, within the framework of EU competition law and State aid control, approving compensation granted to postal operators for the provision of services of general economic interest (SGEI) other than universal postal service. In 2018, the Commission authorized public compensation for the provision of a Data Boxes Information System, including the related operational support services and certain development services,[1] for the provision of high-density territorial coverage over and above the universal service obligation;[2] for the provision of various services (such as processing of social benefit and tax credit payments to the public, as well as national identity and licensing scheme applications, and providing universal payment facilities for public utilities and access to basic cash / banking facilities via the branch network).[3]

[1] Commission decision of 2/02/2018, C(2018) 561 final, State Aid SA.47293 (2017/N) Czech Republic – State compensations granted to Czech Post for the provision of the Data Boxes Information System over the period 2018–2022.

[2] Commission decision of 6/04/2018, C(2018) 1937 final, Aide d'Etat SA.49469 (2018/N) France – Compensation de la mission d'aménagement du territoire en faveur de La Poste pour la période 2018–2022.

[3] Commission decision of 20/02/2018 C(2018) 954 final, State aid SA.48224 (2018/N) United Kingdom – Compensation to Post Office Limited for costs incurred to provide SGEIs 2018–2021.

A. Fratini (✉)
FratiniVergano – European Lawyers, Brussels, Belgium
e-mail: a.fratini@fratinivergano.eu

M. P. di Benisichi
Poste Italiane, Rome, Italy

P. L. Parcu et al. (eds.), *The Changing Postal Environment*, Topics in Regulatory Economics and Policy, https://doi.org/10.1007/978-3-030-34532-7_25

The paper reviews the Commission's assessment of the above measures as regards two compatibility conditions: a genuine and correctly defined service of general economic interest and compliance with Union public procurement rules. Different from the Universal Service Obligation (USO), which is recognized by the EU as a genuine SGEI and whose direct entrustment is foreseen by the Postal Directive, additional public service missions granted to postal operators require a case-by-case evaluation as to whether those two conditions are met. Moving from the above precedents, the paper considers the potential for a recourse by Member States to "non-USO" SGEIs in the postal sector, in the context of the ongoing changes in markets and society and their consequences on the relevance and design of the postal network for public needs.

After an overview of the compatibility conditions under the 2012 SGEI Framework (section 2), the paper looks at the three recent Commission's decisions, with a focus on the genuine SGEI and compliance with EU procurement rules conditions (section 3), and the main takeaways about the role incumbent network/USO operators can play in the public interest (sections 4). Section 5 concludes.

2 The Compatibility Conditions Under the 2012 SGEI Framework

In accordance with Article 106(2) TFEU, the Commission may declare compensation for SGEIs compatible with the internal market, provided that certain conditions are met. The Commission has laid down the conditions according to which it applies Article 106(2) TFEU in a series of instruments, namely, the 2012 SGEI Communication,[4] the 2012 SGEI Decision,[5] and the 2012 SGEI Framework,[6] the latter being relevant for this paper as it sets out guidelines for assessing the compatibility of SGEI compensation that exceeds €15 million per year. Under the 2012 SGEI Framework, the compatibility conditions for public service compensation concern (1) the existence of a genuine SGEI; (2) the entrustment act; (3) the duration of the entrustment; (4) compliance with the Transparency Directive[7]; (5)

---

[4] Communication from the Commission on the application of the European Union State aid rules to compensation granted for the provision of services of general economic interest, OJ C 8, 11.01.2012, p. 4.

[5] Commission Decision of 20 December 2011 on the application of Article 106(2) TFEU on State aid in the form of public service compensation granted to certain undertakings entrusted with the operation of SGEI, OJ L 7, 11.01.2012, p. 3.

[6] Communication from the Commission: European Framework for State aid in the form of public service compensation, OJ C 8, 11.01.2012, p. 15.

[7] Directive 2006/111/EC on the transparency of financial relations between Member States and public undertakings as well as on financial transparency within certain undertakings, OJ L 318, 17.11.2006, p. 17.

compliance with Union public procurement rules; (6) absence of discrimination; (7) the amount of compensation and control of overcompensation; and (8) transparency.

The two conditions of interest for the postal SGEIs that are examined here are the first, a genuine and correctly defined service of general economic interest, and the fifth, compliance with Union public procurement rule. Compliance with these conditions is fairly straightforward in the case of compensation granted to postal operators for the USO, which on the one hand is unquestionably recognized as a genuine SGEI[8] and accurately defined in its scope by the Postal Services Directive,[9] with no need for the Member States to provide additional justifications, and on the other can be entrusted by Member States without a tender procedure via direct designation under the same Directive. By contrast, additional public service missions granted to postal (or network) operators require a case-by-case evaluation as to whether those two conditions are met.

As far as the first condition is concerned, as indicated in the 2012 SGEI Communication,[10] in the absence of specific EU rules defining the scope for the existence of an SGEI, Member States have a wide margin of discretion in defining a given service as such. However, EU Courts have ruled that there are certain minimum criteria common to every SGEI and that the inability of a Member State to demonstrate that a particular service fulfills those criteria constitutes a manifest error in defining this mission as an SGEI.[11] The Commission has further explained in the 2012 SGEI Framework that Member States cannot attach specific public service obligations to services that are already provided or can be provided satisfactorily and under conditions, such as price, objective quality characteristics, continuity and access to the service, consistent with the public interest as defined by the State, by undertakings operating under normal market conditions.[12] Recognizing the Member States' discretion, the Commission's authority is limited to checking whether the Member State has made a manifest error when defining the services as an SGEI, unless provisions of EU law provide a stricter standard. Pursuant to the 2012 SGEI Framework, Member States should also show that they have given proper consideration to the public service needs supported by way of a public consultation or other appropriate instruments to take the interests of users and providers into account.

As for the fifth condition, p. 19 of the 2012 SGEI Framework makes the compatibility of SGEI compensation conditional upon compliance with EU public procurement rules, where applicable. (The rules on public procurement apply when a public

[8] Article 3(1) of the Postal Services Directive (as amended) reads: "Member States shall ensure that users enjoy the right to a universal service involving the permanent provision of a postal service of specified quality at all points in their territory at affordable prices for all users."

[9] Judgment of 19 May 1993, Corbeau, Case C-320/91, EU:C:1993:198, p. 15; see also Article 7(2) of the Postal Services Directive.

[10] Communication on the application of the European Union State aid rules to compensation granted for the provision of services of general economic interest, cit., p. 46.

[11] Judgments of 12 February 2008, BUPA and Others v Commission, Case T-289/03, EU:T:2008:29, pp. 166–169 and 172; and of 15 June 2005, Fred Olsen, Case T-17/02, EU:T:2005:218, p. 216.

[12] Communication on the application of the European Union State aid rules to compensation granted for the provision of services of general economic interest, cit., p. 48.

authority decides to entrust the provision of a service to a third party against remuneration.) Aid will be considered compatible with the internal market on the basis of Article 106(2) TFEU only where the responsible authority, when entrusting the provision of the service to the undertaking in question, has complied – or commits to comply – with the applicable Union rules in the area of public procurement. This includes any requirements of transparency, equal treatment, and non-discrimination resulting directly from the Treaty and, where applicable, secondary Union law. Aid that does not comply with such rules and requirements is considered to affect the development of trade to an extent that would be contrary to the interests of the Union within the meaning of Article 106(2) TFEU.

Against this background, the next section reviews the Commission's assessment of the two conditions above in the context of the notified compensation for the provision of the Data Boxes Information System (Czech Post case), of high-density territorial coverage over and above the USO (La Poste case and Post Office Ltd case), and of various services via the branch network (Post Office Ltd case).

3 The Recent Commission Decisions

3.1 The Czech Post Case: DBIS

The case concerned the State compensations granted to Czech Post for the provision of the Data Boxes Information System (DBIS) and certain DBIS development services over the period 2018–2022. According to the Decision, DBIS is a public administration information service that can be used as an advanced electronic communication channel for internal communication within the public administration and for secured guaranteed communication between the public administration and citizens and companies.[13] The service is an electronic alternative and in some cases a replacement for conventional postal services, e.g., registered mail, giving equal legal effect to documents sent via physical means or electronically. Initially conceived as part of a wider eGovernment initiative in the Czech Republic, the DBIS is described as aimed at contributing to the increased efficiency and transparency of public administration processes.[14]

According to the decision, the Czech authorities submitted that the DBIS is "a service operated in the public interest, in order to provide a free, guaranteed, secure, efficient and accessible system for electronic communication between individuals and the public administration with a proof of delivery of the messages."[15] In addition, the system is operated by "a reliable State-controlled entity"; the service is free of charge at the point of use and its use mandatory for the public administration

[13] Commission decision of 2/02/2018, cit., p. 12.

[14] *Ibidem*, p. 16.

[15] *Ibidem*, p. 71.

bodies, all "benefits" that would not be ensured by a privately operated system. According to the Czech authorities, no operator would be interested in providing a free-of-charge service that would not be commercially viable. On the other hand, a private paid system "might compromise the secret and confidential nature of some communications (e.g., administrative decisions or court judgments, etc.) and would not guarantee a sufficient level of security of the communications which is very high."[16] The system would also risk not achieving sufficient economies of scale to ensure its maintenance in the long-term, thereby putting at risk the implementation of the Czech eGovernment policy.

Besides the strategic purpose, the Czech authorities also pointed to the specific benefits brought about by entrusting the DBIS service to Czech Post from the natural integration of physical and data communications, resulting from the dense network of physical post offices operated by the post in the Czech Republic.[17] The post offices are meant to play a key role in the success and optimal operation of the DBIS service since these offices provide support to the DBIS users (i.e., citizens) that may require assistance in the form of secure password recovery or conversion of electronic documents with confirmation of authenticity. The Commission was satisfied that the definition of the DBIS service as an SGEI was not vitiated by a manifest error.[18]

As to compliance with public procurement rules, the decision relies on the exemption provided for by Article 11 of the Public Procurement Directive (2014/24/EU),[19] which concedes that the Directive does not apply to the award of a public contract by a contracting authority to another contracting authority on the basis of an exclusive right, which they enjoy pursuant to a law, regulation, or administrative provisions which is compatible with the TFEU.

In that respect, the Czech authorities submitted that Czech Post is a contracting authority, *rectius* a "body governed by public law" within the meaning of Article 2(1)(4) of the Public Procurement Directive. Czech Post is wholly owned by the Czech State, has legal personality, is subject to managerial supervision by the Ministry of Interior of the Czech Republic, and was established for the specific purpose of meeting needs in the general interest, not having an industrial and commercial character. These interests include not just the USO *in primis*, but also other specific services for the Czech State, such as administration of cash pension payments, CzechPoint services, collection of payments for the Czech public television, and radio license fees.[20]

---

[16] *Ibidem*, p. 73.

[17] *Ibidem*, pp. 74–75.

[18] *Ibidem*, p. 77.

[19] Directive 2014/24/EU of the European Parliament and of the Council of 26 February 2014 on public procurement and repealing directive 2004/18/EC, OJ L 9, 28.3.2014, p. 65.

[20] *Ibidem*, pp. 116–118.

The exclusive right to operate the DBIS has been foreseen in two Acts and in a Government Resolution,[21] which meets the requirement under Article 11 above of the necessary legal basis. As to its compatibility with the TFEU, the decision moves from the acknowledgment that while Article 56 TFEU prohibits restrictions to the freedom to provide services, restrictions can be justified as an exception, among others, by the exercise of official authority under Article 51 TFEU, provided that the restriction (i) is appropriate for achieving the objective it pursues, (ii) is necessary to achieve the objective, and (iii) does not go beyond what is necessary.[22] In the case at issue, the Commission noted that the grant of an exclusive right to operate the DBIS to Czech Post:

(i) is appropriate "to achieve the objective of streamlining the communication between the public authorities with each other, and with the citizens, in the sense of increasing the efficiency of the communication, and enabling the conversion of paper-based documents into electronic form with the same legal effects of a certified copy so that all communications delivered by means of DBIS are granted the same legal value as acts delivered in writing";
(ii) seems necessary because the DBIS is a strategic service for the Czech State and some critical functions of the system, such as security and access to DBIS, must be controlled by the State; and
(iii) does not go beyond what is necessary, as Czech Post would be directly responsible for the implementation of the most critical functions, such as, for instance, system integration, security audit, website management, second and third level Service Desk, etc. but would contract the elements of the service over which there is no need to exercise strict State supervision, via a tender procedure, to an external provider.[23]

Based on the above, the Commission concluded that the DBIS service contract can be exempted from the public procurement rules under Article 11 of the Public Procurement Directive.

3.2 The La Poste Case: Territorial Presence

The case concerns the public compensations granted to La Poste for the period 2018–2022 for the fulfillment of its public service mission relating to territorial presence (*aménagement du territoire*). That is one of the "traditional" missions for La Poste, which is called to maintain a network of contact points across the national territory, to help reduce geographic and demographic inequalities by guaranteeing

[21] Article 14(2) of the Act No. 300/2008, together with Article 2(4) of the Act No. 221/2012, and Government Resolution No. 676 of 27 July 2016.

[22] Commission decision of 2/02/2018, cit., p. 114.

[23] *Ibidem*, pp. 119–121.

adequate access to (public) services (Fijalkow and Taulelle 2012). The territorial presence is built as an incremental mission compared to the universal service with the further, different objective of territorial development. It is a matter of maintaining a network of contact points, whose density goes above and beyond that required by the universal service obligation as defined by the French authorities, to ensure a given level of service accessibility to the entire population.

The Commission had consistently considered the French Post's obligation to participate in territorial planning by maintaining a postal presence and unprofitable public services, particularly in rural areas, a genuine SGEI since the *Banque Postale* decision.[24] For the purposes of the renewal of the measure in 2018, pursuant to the 2012 SGEI Framework, the continuous respondence of the service to the needs of users was proved by the French authorities on the basis of the consultations held on the draft *contrat d'entreprise entre l'Etat et La Poste* and the *contrat dit de présence postale territoriale.* The latter covers "the adaptation of the postal network to the diversified needs of the territories and to the economic constraints (notably by the integration of postal services in shared spaces, the experimentation of new forms of postal presence or pooling of services), the adjustment of schedules to customer expectations, the improvement of the postal offer and access to services (notably via the development of IT and digital solutions, social and digital mediation)" (unofficial translation from original in French).[25] In addition, a consultation with national and local representatives allowed to establish that the mission entrusted to La Poste is in line with users' expectations in relation to postal presence. Accordingly, the Commission reckoned that the *aménagement du territoire* mission conferred to La Poste is a genuine SGEI.[26]

When it comes to compliance with EU public procurement rules, the Commission considered that the territorial presence mission can be covered by the single provider exemption and be entrusted by means of a negotiated procedure without prior publication in accordance with Article 32(2)(b) of the Public Procurement Directive. Consistently with the previous 2014 decision,[27] the Commission accepted the French authorities' position that La Poste is currently the only operator capable of carrying out the territorial coverage mission, as it continues to be the only provider to have a unique logistics and retail network in terms of density and size.

---

[24] Commission decision of 21/12/2015, "Aide d'État N 531/2005 – France. Mesures liées à la création et au fonctionnement de la Banque Postale". In the decision, which concerned the transfer of the banking and financial business of La Poste to its subsidiary Banque Postale, the Commission found that La Poste was required by law to maintain a network beyond what was strictly necessary to meet the universal service obligation. That second SGEI is therefore a complementary mission to the universal postal service offering, which also addresses the density of contact points.

[25] Commission decision of 6/04/2018, cit., p. 43.

[26] *Ibidem,* p. 46.

[27] Commission decision of 26/05/2014, "Aide d'Etat n° SA.36512 (2014/N) – France – Des dispositifs compensatoires des missions d'aménagement du territoire, de transport et de distribution de la presse dévolues à La Poste", pp. 78–80.

In this respect, comparisons with other networks (in particular banks) continued to show that La Poste's network is the only one with a quality that meets the coverage requirements set by law. While local businesses (e.g., retail bakeries) exceed La Poste in terms of the number of establishments in rural communes, none of these types of businesses are present in as many municipalities as La Poste's points of contact, and, in any event, the locations of these alternative operators do not form a network. As such, these cannot be a viable and credible alternative to La Poste's network for the implementation of the territorial presence SGEI. The latter, as pointed out by the French authorities,[28] requires the entrusted operator to have a network of more than 17,000 contact points in the national territory and to meet criteria in terms of *maillage du territoire*, to ensure that at least 90% of the population in each department is at a reasonable distance from the closest contact point – no more than 5 km and 20 min by car under traffic conditions of the territory concerned. In the best of cases, "these operators could possibly perform some of the services incumbent on La Poste without, however, being able to carry out all of them" (unofficial translation from original in French). Accordingly, the decision concludes that the territorial presence mission can be covered by the exemption for the presence of a single provider, based on Article 32(b)(ii) of the Public Procurement Directive.

3.3 The Post Office Ltd Case: The Network SGEI and the Products SGEI

The case concerns the public compensation granted to Post Office Ltd for the period 2018–2021 to maintain a branch network above its optimum commercial size, meeting a number of specified access criteria (including, e.g., 99% of the UK population to be within three miles and 90% of the population to be within one mile of their nearest branch nationally; 99% of the total population in deprived urban areas across the UK to be within three miles; and 95% of the total urban population across the UK to be within one mile of their nearest branch in urban areas), and to provide a bundle of services through the branch network, namely, processing of social benefit and tax credit payments to the public; processing of national identity and licensing scheme applications; providing universal payment facilities for public utilities; providing access to postal services; and providing access to basic cash/banking facilities, especially for rural customers and those on social benefits.[29] Public compensation was to be provided only for the maintenance of the branch network, the Network SGEI, and not for the Products SGEI. The latter are financed according to

[28] Commission decision of 6/04/2018, cit., p. 59.

[29] Commission decision of 20/02/2018, cit., p. 10.

the terms of the commercial contracts between Post Office Ltd and its public or private counterpart.[30]

At the time of the notification, Post Office Ltd only owned and managed directly about 3% of the post offices, the remainder (97%) of the network offices being owned and managed by independent third party businesses, who have entered into agreements with Post Office Ltd to manage a post office, often co-located alongside another retail business (e.g., selling stationery, food, newspapers, and magazines). The irrelevance, for the purpose of the State aid assessment, of the ownership of the offices is an application of the principle of "neutrality" of the Treaties as regards public or private ownership of undertakings, enshrined in Article 345 TFEU.

The public service obligation of Post Office Ltd to maintain a post office network above its optimum commercial size and to provide a bundle of services through that network had already been recognized by the Commission as a genuine SGEI in previous decisions.[31] In addition, the UK authorities justified that obligation with regard to a number of public needs, such as the public need for a local, accessible, and secure serviced office environment, in particular for those people (*including the vulnerable, elderly, rural dwellers and deprived urban dwellers*)[32] that cannot travel independently for long distances due to the cost or health impact of travel and/or the availability of transport and/or cannot easily access such services via alternative channels such as Internet or telephone services.

There is also a public need for the possibility of completing multiple over-the-counter transactions in the same space (the post office), given that retail areas are frequently widely dispersed and public transport links are irregular in many parts of the UK. In addition, the UK authorities stated that they attach a social policy requirement to the SGEIs at stake.[33] In their view, post offices remain a key part of the social fabric of communities, especially where an ever-increasing share of public communication is made through digital means that cannot be accessed easily by certain segments of the population. Finally, post offices act as a source of general information and advice on public services, which is particularly important in rural and deprived urban areas, as well as for vulnerable groups.

Consistent with the approach in the La Poste's decision, the public needs for the Network SGEI entrusted to Post Office Ltd were confirmed by a public consultation and independent research commissioned by the UK.[34] The Commission noted that those public needs would not be met under normal market circumstances, this market insufficiency being the standard justification for State intervention. Based on the

---

[30] *Ibidem*, p. 75.

[31] Commission decisions of 28/03/2012, "State aid SA.33054 (2012/N) – United Kingdom, Post Office Limited (POL): Compensation for net costs incurred to keep a non-commercially viable network for the period 2012–15 and the continuation of a working capital facility", pp. 55–56; and of 19/03/2015, "State aid SA.38788 (2015/N) – United Kingdom, Compensation to Post Office Limited for costs incurred to provide SGEIs 2015–2018", pp. 84–93.

[32] Commission decision of 20/02/2018, cit., p. 77.

[33] *Ibidem*, p. 78.

[34] *Ibidem*, pp. 83–87.

above, the Commission concluded that the Network SGEI does constitute a genuine SGEI and that the UK did not commit a manifest error in its definition.

In relation to public procurement rules, the Commission considered that the Network SGEI is covered by the sole provider exemption, as it was the case for La Poste's territorial presence mission. In that respect, and consistently with its previous decisions on earlier compensations for the same mission,[35] the negotiated procedure without prior publication in accordance with Article 32(2)(b) of the Public Procurement Directive, which was followed to entrust Post Office Ltd with the Network SGEI, was justified under EU public procurement rules. The beneficiary continued to remain the only operator with the necessary characteristics to provide the Network SGEI, with no reasonable alternative or substitute to provide for the same public services. As put forward by the UK, Post Office Ltd is the only operator with the ability to meet the geographic access criteria of the Network SGEI, as well as the quality and capacity needs of the UK and the expectations of the SGEI users; to offer the bundle of different services like the Products SGEI by means of a single, cohesive network; and to perform a social and economic role for local communities across the country.

For the Products SGEI, on the other hand, the decision recalls the commitment, undertaken by the UK in the previous decisions and renewed for the future, to ensure compliance with EU procurement rules of all public contracts of Post Office Ltd for the provision of services that are part of the Products SGEI. In that context, the Commission acknowledged the review run by the UK authorities of all Post Office Ltd's contracts falling within the scope of application of the Public Procurement Directive because they were concluded with a contracting authority subject to public procurement rules and had an aggregate value in excess of the relevant EU threshold. That review showed that while the Master Distribution Agreement with Royal Mail was covered by the sole provider exemption (consistent with Article 40(3)(c) of Directive 2004/17/EC and Article 50(c) of Directive 2014/25/EU, the applicable Utilities Directives),[36] the other contracts had been tendered by the relevant contracting authority in a manner compliant with EU public procurement rules. That was the case for the contracts relating to (i) the sale and processing of fishing rod licenses for the Environment Agency; (ii) biometric data capture for the UK Border Agency; (iii) travel ticket services for transport to London; (iv) Online Identity Assurance Framework Agreement and Call-off contract with the Cabinet Office; (v) Front Office Counter Services (FOCS) framework; (vi) the Driver License and Motor Tax Applications Services for DVLA; and (vii) passport check and send services for Her Majesty's Passport Office. That shows that the "unicity" of the provider for the purposes of compliance with public procurement rules has to be proved, on a case-by-case basis, against the features of the specific service being outsourced by the public authority concerned. The Commission was

[35] See 2012 decision, p. 67, and 2015 decision, p. 102.

[36] Directive 2014/25/EU of the European Parliament and of the Council of 26 February 2014 on procurement by entities operating in the water, energy, transport, and postal services sectors and repealing Directive 2004/17/EC, OJ L 94, 28.03.2014, p. 243.

thus satisfied that the EU public procurement compliance criterion under p. 19 of the 2012 SGEI Framework was met in this case.

4 Main Takeaways

The three cases summarized above concern public compensations granted for different services by Member States (the Czech Republic, France, the UK) that have legal, social, and historic traditions unquestionably very far apart. That in itself proves "the diversity between various SGEIs and the differences in the needs and preferences of users that may result from different geographical, social or cultural situations," which Protocol (No 26) on services of general interest ranks within the shared values of the Union in respect of SGEIs.[37]

Yet, their analysis allows to draw three common takeaways on the role of the incumbent postal network/USO operator as provider of services designed to address the public needs. The first takeaway is the fact that incumbent network/USO operators can play a relevant role in the public interest when dealing with service offerings outside the traditional scope of postal services. The incumbent network/USO operator, be it publicly or privately owned, is a trustworthy partner for the State when it comes to providing SGEIs. This legitimacy is the result of a combination of features such as its ability to ensure the delivery of the service itself, its intrinsic reliability, and, more in general, its naturally trustworthy capacity in the area of official, but also commercial and private communications.

The second takeaway is the confirmation of the incumbent network/USO operator's capacity to operate in the communication domain, whether the communications are conventionally physical, converted from physical to digital or from digital to physical, or also digitally native. That seems to imply not only its trusted role for running an SGEI, as noted above, but also the confirmation of its reliability for handling digitally native communications, including those involving intrinsically sensitive data, to the benefit of the public at large.

The third takeaway is the pivotal role of the network offered by the incumbent/USO operator. Beyond the universal service and the USO, courts have confirmed the postal network as a unique asset for the purposes of the State's public interest objectives. This uniqueness enables the offering of services as heterogeneous as public administration services, ticket sale services and financial services, with the guarantee of their ubiquitous accessibility throughout the territory. An extraordinary nationwide presence made up of brick-and-mortar offices but also of the ability to organize the ubiquitous provision of services so as to ensure the appropriate level of services at all places and for all customers, irrespective of their administrative structure.

[37] Consolidated version of the Treaty on European Union – Protocols – Protocol (No 26) on services of general interest, OJ L 115, 09.05.2008, p. 308.

The ensuing considerations are associated with the societal evolution that most European countries are experiencing. The increased age of a growing part of the society limits a hard and definitive transition to digital. At the same time, the territorial convergence to cities leaves large zones of the country that cannot be served under commercially viable conditions. With this in mind, it will be important to manage transition phases to ensure equal services at equal conditions, in compliance with the solidarity principle.[38] While digital transition is unstoppable, it has to be borne in mind that a range of un-digitalized population will likely remain so without having the possibility to convert to digital. A mid-to-long period management will be required to ensure common service availability.

Regarding the distribution of services in scarcely populated areas, in the absence of (unlikely) disruptive transformations, it will be difficult and non-economical for market-oriented services to establish and flourish. In these circumstances, the entrustment of SGEIs and related public compensation would address market failures (and/or government failure) by providing support for social objectives that would not otherwise be economically viable (Bacon 2017). Where market failure may lead to suboptimal provision of public goods, there is a case for public intervention in terms of imposing SGEI obligations on network/USO operators as providers of last resort (Sauter 2008). The connection between public administration and providing equal quality services, particularly to vulnerable users, could shape itself well to a postal operators' silhouette.

5 Conclusions

The decisions reviewed in this paper acknowledged the genuine SGEI nature of the services being compensated. This sheds some light both on the fundamental changes that are taking place in postal users' preferences (Czech Post case) and on the role that a local, accessible, and secure environment can play for a wide range of public needs other than postal services (La Poste and Post Office Ltd cases). The decisions also recognized, by conceding the EU public procurement compliance either under the exercise of official authority under Article 51 TFEU or the "sole provider" exception under the Public Procurement Directive, the unique position of the postal network/USO operator when it comes to the ability to meet the required geographic access criteria and to perform a social and economic role through a single, cohesive, and good-quality network.

[38] The EU Treaties explicitly refer to solidarity in a number of provisions, including the values (Article 2 TEU) and objectives of the Union (Article 3 TEU), and particular policies where the "principle" or "spirit" of solidarity is to be applied. The Charter of Fundamental Rights in the EU adopts solidarity as the title of Chapter IV for provisions that include rights at work, family life, welfare and health.

References

Bacon, K. (2017). *European Union law of state aid.* Oxford: Oxford University Press.
Fijalkow, Y., & Taulelle, T. (2012). La Poste en milieu rural: une gestion entre rentabilité et aménagement du territoire. *Sciences de la Société, 86*, 34–49.
Sauter, W. (2008). Services of general economic interest and universal service in EU law. In *European law review, no. 2, 2008*. London: Sweet & Maxwell.

How the USO Might Help Influence and Enhance the Growth of Smarter Cities

V. Ian Stanford and Adam C. Houck

1 Introduction

The rise of the "smart city" concept has reshaped citizen engagement with government. It seeks to transform how publicly owned assets can be utilized and repurposed to improve the quality of infrastructure management, social services, and emergency response within cities. Around the world, cities are looking for ways to use Internet-connected technologies to develop solutions to common strategic issues such as poor air quality and aging-in-place populations. While there are key examples of smart cities globally such as Dubai and Singapore, adoption has been slow and has not lived up to expectations in most other locations.

Meanwhile, postal operators (POs) face continued financial pressures resulting from volume and revenue declines in traditional letter mail products. The growth seen in packages from global e-commerce cannot offset these losses, putting significant pressure on POs to identify new revenue streams to survive. Some POs have diversified and expanded into non-core postal functions such as financial and other government services to create new revenue streams, often using legacy postal infrastructure to deliver these new services.

Universal Service Obligations (USOs) make POs ideal partners for providing government services, including partnering with smart cities. The asset-rich physical

The views expressed are those of the authors and do not necessarily represent those of the USPS Office of Inspector General (USPSOIG), or IBM Global Business Services. We would like to thank Michael Plunkett from PostCom and Paula Gori from the European University Institute for their helpful comments and suggestions.

V. I. Stanford (✉)
USPS OIG, Alpharetta, GA, USA

A. C. Houck
IBM Global Business Services, Washington, DC, USA

P. L. Parcu et al. (eds.), *The Changing Postal Environment*, Topics in Regulatory Economics and Policy, https://doi.org/10.1007/978-3-030-34532-7_26

networks and geographic coverage provide access and scale which are difficult to replicate. However, smart city initiatives have not proliferated at the rate expected. The traditional barriers to this expansion have included financial return on investment (ROI), expertise in data and related technologies, and public perception. In addition, as explored in this paper, the selection of the underlying business model is critical.

This paper examines causes for the lack of growth in smart cities in the USA. It also explores possible alternative business models, inspired from platform economics, for successful PO smart city partnerships. Finally, it investigates how the relative strictness of the USO definition could improve or hinder the prospects of POs providing services to smart cities. The lessons learned from the US example can be applied to POs around the world facing similar choices. To gather information on current developments in smart cities initiatives and technologies, in-depth interviews were conducted with subject matter experts from related fields to supplement other research performed.[1]

The next section provides some background and examines the causes behind the slow growth seen in smart cities. Section 3 explores how applying principles from platform economics could create superior incentives for cities, POs, and other stakeholders when compared to traditional business models, helping drive greater growth in smart cities. Section 4 examines the current debate on redefining the USO and how regulators could affect a PO's ability to offer smart city services depending upon how strictly they define the USO. Conclusions are presented in Section 5.

2 Review and Background of Smart Cities

The Internet of things (IoT) agenda abstractly defines a smart city as "a municipality that uses information and communication technologies to increase operational efficiency, share information with the public and improve both the quality of government services and citizen welfare" (Rouse 2019, online, no page number). Overall, most of these solutions fall into one of four areas: transportation and infrastructure management, social services, emergency response, and public safety. Examples of smart city solutions include equipping lampposts with auditory sensors to aid in gunshot triangulation and outfitting city government vehicles with technologies to analyze the ride quality on city streets and detect potholes. For each solution, the underlying goal is to outfit existing city assets with applicable technologies to collect data that city governments can use to better address their pain points, such as properly deploying police to crime scenes and dispatching work crews to fix potholes. As the needs and capabilities of cities are heterogeneous, the IoT agenda

[1] Seven subject matter expert interviews were performed from March to May 2019 representing a variety of cross-background experience. The roles of those interviewed include Chief of Civic Innovation and Technology, Industry Research Director, Managing Director, and Former Postal Industry Executives.

definition of a smart city does not necessarily apply everywhere and must be considered within the greater context of available smart city solutions.

Identifying and implementing smart city solutions are important today and will likely become more important in the future. The reasons for this are rooted in demographic shifts and changing citizen expectations. Re-urbanization will exacerbate the current pressures of constrained city budgets and force the creation of innovative new offerings to solve known city challenges. A 2016 McKinsey report posited that the share of the global population living in urban centers will reach 60% by 2030, up from 50% in 2015 (Bouton et al. 2015, online, no page number). Some of these city challenges, such as vehicle congestion and the cost of maintaining aging infrastructures, have existed for some time and have gone mostly unresolved. For example, the cost of congestion is felt by more than just city administrators. "A five-minute delay for each UPS vehicle, every day, costs UPS $105 million annually in additional operating costs" (Straight 2017, online, no page number). Public safety concerns, like congestion, affect a significant number of, if not all, city residents and must be addressed.

Most cities are still analog in a digital world, which creates challenges, opportunities, and incentives. For example, ride quality on city streets is often measured and tracked via handwritten notebook and journal entries instead of utilizing accelerometer technology to more precisely measure and record road conditions. Political incentives exist to utilize tax revenues more efficiently and improve the quality of living in cities. Beyond improving day-to-day city operations, additional incentives exist that create long-term benefits for a city that must be explored. City governments, such as those in Charlotte, North Carolina, and Louisville, Kentucky, are working to become thought leaders in smarter cities to attract residents, especially younger generations such as millennials, and to attract companies. Attracting new companies fuels the infrastructure development cycle and can help put the city on a sustainable growth trajectory. Overall, the direct and indirect benefits from smarter cities initiatives accrue across several areas: citizens, governments, private industries, and, within the context of this paper, POs.

As reported by Ted Smith (2018), venture capitalist Kevin Fong separated viable investments into two categories: painkillers and vitamins. Painkillers "are must-haves and if your community is in pain, it will prioritize relief above all else" (Smith 2018, online, no page number). Gas leak emergencies and gunshot detection are examples of painkillers. Alternatively, a vitamin "is a solution for a problem the customer does not know they have" (Ibid.). Vitamins deliver a less concrete vision of the future compared to solving an immediate problem that a painkiller addresses such as public safety. An example of a vitamin might be installing Wi-Fi in city parks or solar powered trash compacting cans in densely populated urban areas. As Smith states, "the longest list on every city mayor's desk is nothing but vitamins. This is not to say that vitamins are not good – quite the contrary, they are very good for you, but they are nearly impossible to sell or invest in if there is a pain problem or even the possibility of a magic pill solution" (Ibid.). This difference is important if one considers the political implications of delivering better outcomes for citizens and citizens agreeing on the correct mix of painkillers and vitamins. Indeed, governments must be careful to not push vitamins to the populations that least need them especially when they are denying painkillers to the most in-pain populations. An undesirable imbalance of painkillers and vitamins might help explain why smart city solution adoption has been slow and piecemeal, not living up to expectations.

A few strong examples of smart cities exist globally including Dubai and Singapore. However, the proliferation of smart cities overall has not lived up to expectations due to governance, prioritization, and financial challenges. Evidence suggests more centralized governance models for cities such as Dubai and Singapore pave the way for clear, autonomous action to drive smart city agendas forward, unlike more democratically run cities. Notwithstanding the political implications, quicker action can be taken to pursue smart city solutions when authority is centralized. Another political element not to be overlooked is the risk appetite for experimentation. Experts confirmed that in the US, the most successful locations experimenting with smart city solutions, such as Louisville, Kentucky, have been given "permission to fail" by city leadership, understanding that not every initiative will succeed.

From a prioritization point of view, experts believe that many smart city ideas have been shelved because services to address basic city functions regarding homelessness and overcrowding have taken priority. When these core city functions compete for the same resources as smart city initiatives aimed at quality of life issues like expanding broadband access or easing traffic congestion, the quality of life issues often take a back seat. While the Great Recession officially ended in 2009, many city governments in the US were dealing with the aftermath for several years after. Smart city programs can be even harder to get off the ground when their benefits do not accrue evenly across the economic spectrum and favor economically stable areas over communities in need. Programs that are successful often fit into cities' larger strategic development plans.

Perhaps most importantly, the financial uncertainty of how to fund smart city solutions has created a significant barrier to progress. Typically, smart city initiatives start as small scale pilot projects, sometimes located in specifically defined smart city development zones that might be as small as two city blocks. Programs this small rarely have the kind of economic impact to be financially self-sustaining. Instead, many smart city programs rely on grants and other types of external funding provided by state and federal governments, universities, and private donors. However, when these funding sources run dry, even the best ideas have a hard time getting started. Some technology companies that look to partner with cities have been willing to accept the savings realized by cities as payment or to use the free press generated by high-profile initiatives as a marketing expense, but it is rare that these initiatives will pay for themselves.

POs, like cities, have faced significant budget challenges over the last decade. As traditional letter mail volumes have declined globally, packages have become a growth area, accounting for 30% of the revenue share and 4.2% of the volume share in the US (USPS 2018, online, no page number). However, these packages generate much lower margins in highly competitive markets. To continue funding their delivery networks in the face of declining volumes, POs are exploring several supplemental markets for products and services that leverage existing assets, address a currently unmet market demand, and provide additional revenue streams. These markets include financial services at Deutsche Post and Japan Post, logistics services at Royal Mail and SingPost, communication services at An Post and La Poste, and government services at Poste Italiane and An Post.

While the US Postal Service (USPS) has experimented with some smart city solutions in the past, the challenge of generating a viable ROI on smart city projects has endured. In an industry where federal/state/local grant and other funding models have caused confusion, the seminal question of how to generate ROI has likely hindered significant progress. This is a critical question for cities and POs operating in a regulated industry and needs further exploration. There are multiple potential business models that cities, POs, and technology companies could pursue in this space. Choosing the correct business model could serve to reduce investment risk, create more positive network externalities for POs, employees, citizens, and governments, and have a significant impact on the proliferation of smart cities.

As detailed by USPS OIG (2016), "the U.S. Postal Service, with its ubiquitous physical network, could provide cities with an unparalleled means to collect the data that can be used for smart cities initiatives." The physical network of USPS is immense; 232,372 vehicles, 34,772 total retail offices, 497,157 employees, and over 143,000 collection boxes provide a significant competitive advantage that would be cost prohibitive to try and replicate (USPS 2019, online, no page number). Instead of investing to reproduce the scale, cities could partner with POs to use their physical networks to help solve smarter city challenges. The USPS OIG paper also suggests several such pilot opportunities including using Internet-connected sensors mounted on mobile postal assets including postal delivery vehicles that could collect data on road, bridge, and even underground water pipes as well as stationary sensors on post offices and collection boxes that could monitor air quality. Beyond the physical network, the scale of technology and data gathering efforts involved with smarter city initiatives should provide good opportunity for cities to partner with USPS, given the scale of its existing data infrastructure.

The trusted brand status POs enjoy is another asset that can benefit both cities and POs in the development of smart city solutions. It is clear this trust is an asset that has served POs well over the decades. The integrity of the mail supply chain, guaranteed by law, has placed POs in a position where citizens and businesses trust the actions of POs.[2] Trust is just as important today in the letter and parcel delivery business and, given the growth in startups such as Uber, Lyft, and Postmates, evidence would suggest this trust can be immediately earned in the delivery industry. Therefore, it is not antithetical to assert the public's trust in a PO's delivery business could be transferred to some segment of smart cities solutions. Additional research is needed to explore this transferability to better understand which services require

[2] For example, the privacy and security nonprofit research center the Ponemon Institute has consistently ranked USPS as the most trusted government agency in the USA and as a top 10 most trusted business for information security. https://about.usps.com/publications/annual-report-comprehensive-statement-2013/annualreport2013_018.htm.

the highest levels of trust and the PO's ability to meet those requirements. Trust as it relates to a PO's brand is critical. One former USPS executive interviewed for this paper noted "one cannot underestimate the importance of brand at USPS anytime partnering is considered; USPS exerts very strong control over its brand." The lack of third-party advertisements on USPS delivery vehicles is an illustration of this tight brand control. It is likely USPS has been unwilling to accept the risk of diluting its trusted brand image by offering advertising for other firms. Indeed, trust and brand perception can exert both positive and negative influences on the opportunity to partner on smart city solutions. On the positive, USPS and other POs could lend strong brand image and trust to smart city solutions which could help fuel the growth in these new areas. Negatively, POs could be too selective in partnering on smart city solutions, seeking to overly protect the brand. This could create stronger headwinds against the growth of these solutions, as discussed in Section 3.

Indeed, even with this trusted brand position, the concerns of cities must be addressed. If the governance, perception, and prioritization challenges can be solved, financial barriers to action are still significant. The next section explores challenges surrounding the potential business models chosen for smart city solutions, from both a traditional and a platform economics standpoint, and will explore whether platform models could be superior compared to traditional.

3 Applying Principles of Platform Economics to Smart City Business Models

In 2016, USPS OIG identified five potential smart city pilot projects around the USA and highlighted several barriers that USPS could face in getting smart city projects off the ground. It expanded on three significant barriers that must be overcome: selecting the correct business model, providing adequate data security, and overcoming regulatory barriers. The final two concerns are relatively straightforward. The National Institute for Standards and Technology (NIST) has a framework for government agencies to ensure cybersecurity, which should be the minimum standard that government agencies should follow in the USA. Similarly, the European Union (EU) has its own privacy rules that would apply to European POs interested in providing similar smart city services. Additionally, regulatory allowability is also largely out of the PO's hands and a factor of policymakers and regulators. In the USA, the 2006 Postal Accountability and Enhancement Act (PAEA) prohibits USPS from offering "non-postal" products, though some allowances are made for non-postal or postal-adjacent services that meet the needs of other federal government agencies. Examples include the ability to take passport photos and accept passport applications for the USA State Department. It is unclear, however, whether this same allowance would immediately apply to state or local government entities as well. Recent postal reform legislation has considered providing USPS greater authority to pursue non-postal revenue generating opportunities, but ultimately this is an exogenous factor out of the PO's control.

One aspect that the PO can more readily control is the business model it would select for a potential smart city service. The 2016 USPS OIG white paper proposed three potential business models: "space leaser," "data collector," and "full-service provider." As a "space leaser," USPS would rent out space on its assets and infrastructure for third parties to attach sensors and other equipment; USPS would collect fees for leasing this space. A "data collector" approach would include greater involvement from USPS and its employees, requiring them to perform additional actions in standard operating procedures, potentially generating higher revenues from business partners. In this case, USPS would collect, manage, and own the data but might seek external help in processing and analyzing. As a "full-service provider," USPS could offer its own suite of smart cities solutions, similar to La Poste's Digital Hub, and seek to capture greater market share and revenue. However, the paper stopped short of providing objective criteria that USPS, or any PO, should use to choose among these options.

Classical economic models of production lean toward the full-service approach, where the amount of sellable data collected by USPS is a function of its labor and capital. Considering that much of the data collection will be done passively (i.e., sensors on trucks) or through minimal marginal effort by employees during their regular duties, the cost of labor should be relatively low. Meanwhile, the expenditure of capital, including purchasing the sensors and data storage infrastructure, would likely be expensive. However, as explored in Section 2, using existing postal infrastructure to house the sensors can drive down the cost when compared to starting such a business from the ground up.

The classical production model does not account for some important aspects of this smart city business. For instance, it cannot explain which sensors the PO should purchase and install across their network to meet the demand for these services. As a result, the PO would likely have to constantly monitor city RFPs and invest in technology on a small scale through individual pilot programs with specific cities that might not generate substantial revenues, at least at the start. Additionally, the model does not explain how a PO would acquire the technical expertise to maximize the value of the data it is collecting. Confirmed through expert interviews, these concerns have caused USPS to shy away from offering these types of services in the past. A former USPS executive has stated that the issue of generating enough revenue from a smarter city business to finance the investment is perhaps the most significant hurdle. This revenue challenge is not unique to POs; evidence also suggests technology companies have had a difficult time generating sufficient revenues from partnerships with smart cities, given the increasing financial constraints on city budgets.

Alternatively, the field of platform economics provides an example of how a PO can provide smart city services that meet all these challenges, both for themselves and for other partners in the market. Instead of purchasing sensors and selling data collection services directly to individual cities, a PO could simply create a platform that connects technology providers and cities looking for smart data services. For example, a company that specializes in making sensors that monitor road conditions could join the platform and install its sensors on postal delivery vehicles in 20 of the largest metropolitan areas in the US. Likewise, another technology company that specializes in a different type of sensor, air quality monitors for instance, could join the same platform and install their sensors on post offices in the same 20 cities. Then, each of the cities would be able to access the platform and look for the combination of data services that meet their individual city needs and objectives. Some may select a single data collection service, while others might decide they want multiple services. Instead of cities incurring the cost of researching individual technology solutions and both parties dealing with the transaction costs associated with developing small-scale pilot projects that are eventually scaled up, this platform would provide a link between data collectors and data users, already scaled to meet the needs of city governments and any other users that might be interested in purchasing the data services. This two-sided network business model is similar to the PO's core business model, where the post serves to connect both collectors and users of data, just as it does senders and receivers of mail. Similarly, the technology companies would pay to be on the network, primarily through rental fees for access to the PO's physical assets for data collection. Meanwhile, cities could gain access to the platform for free, which would attract a critical mass of platform users, which Parker and Van Alstyne (2005) point out is essential to any platform business model's success.

This type of business model presents four clear advantages. First, by creating a national platform for smart city data collection, a PO could attract multiple technology providers and multiple cities simultaneously, creating a critical mass of participants. Instead of attempting to squeeze profit out of a single city through a single, limited pilot program, technology providers can immediately start offering smart data services on a national scale with multiple cities as customers.

Second, greater flexibility is created by the actual demand for services. In this model, the PO does not decide what data is collected. It simply offers its infrastructure to become a trusted mobile data collection lab for technology companies. If this data collection platform remains provider agnostic, where any tech company willing to pay can join, then the innovation on the platform will be driven by the private tech companies competing for business through the platform. This is akin to the generation of new apps on Apple's and Google's platforms. This should result in greater flexibility and variety in the services offered on the platform.

Third, the data expertise resides with technology providers. While POs are often highly trusted institutions, cybersecurity and privacy are major concerns in many parts of the world when data collection is considered. In this model, technology companies can utilize their expertise to provide confidence among potential smart city clients that their citizens' data will be secure from hacking and other data threats. Additionally, they would be allowed to sell analytical services to any other client that could access the platform. Both POs and city governments often lack the in-house expertise to effectively manage and analyze large quantities of data outside their core competencies. In this way, technology companies can bring in additional revenue and leverage their own core competency.

Lastly, this model maximizes positive social externalities. By enabling a larger-scale proliferation of data gathering technology, a platform business model creates positive social externalities, enabling services that make people's lives better through improved city operations. Moreover, POs serve all parts of the country, rich and poor. Often, smart city programs are subject to criticisms because that they tend to benefit the wealthiest citizens in small, affluent parts of cities. However, partnerships between posts and smart cities have the potential to maximize smart city benefits for segments of society that are most in need of improved government services.

As explored in Section 2, posts are potentially desirable partners for smart city initiatives given their rich physical infrastructures. The amassing of these assets is rooted in meeting the USO. While meeting the current demand for mail and packages remains important, POs often seize on opportunities to improve the technologies that operate their physical infrastructures, such as upgrading to electronic or Internet-connected vehicles, to continue fulfilling their delivery obligations in a rapidly changing digital world. This could have the added benefit of increasing their attractiveness to potential smart city solutions partners. In the case of USPS, the organization is in the middle of such an opportunity now, as it looks to update its entire vehicle delivery fleet over the next few years (Zwahlen 2019, online, no page number). The next section explores how current debate on the state of the USO and potential changes to its definition could have significant effects on a PO's ability to aid in smart city initiatives.

4 How the Strictness of the USO Influences Postal Operators' Ability to Deliver Smart City Services

The requirement to provide citizens with universal access to postal services enables the extensive physical networks that make POs potentially attractive partners for smart cities. While almost all countries have a designated Universal Service Provider (USP), the specifics of the USO vary substantially by country (Ambrosini et al. 2006). The USO is traditionally evaluated as a balance among three elements: scope, quality, and affordability (Accenture 2008), which cover how often a PO must deliver, how quickly mail and packages must move through the network, where retail facilities are located, and how much POs can charge, among other things. While most large countries impose and enforce their own USOs through national regulatory agencies, the EU with its Postal Directive in 1997 addressed to member states, placed minimum conditions and service standards that all EU members must impose on their USPs. Nations are also free to impose higher standards if so desired.

In the wake of postal market liberalization in Europe during the late 1990s and early 2000s, regulators considered how USOs could be maintained in a liberalized postal market with a mix of public and private competitors. The worry was that, without clarity, private operators would favor service in areas that were more profitable while leaving behind areas that were less profitable. This would force the USP to have the sole responsibility for delivering mail to these less profitable areas. In some cases, this required better specifying the elements of the USO, so POs charged with providing universal service would have a clear idea of their requirements.

In the US, the USO is not explicitly defined in any single statute (Task Force Report 2018). While the basic statute instructs the USPS to provide mail service that is "prompt, reliable, and efficient," and covers "all areas" where people live, neither a minimum number of days, minimum delivery standards, nor a maximum price is specified (39 USC 101(b)). Consider this in contrast to the European General Directive on Postal Services which specifies 5 days of delivery service and explicitly identifies the size and weight requirements of packages that qualify for universal service. The recent Presidential Task Force issued a report on the USPS suggesting that some elements of the USO should be more specifically defined to provide more clarity and better enable USPS to understand and control costs. This notion was echoed in recent public congressional hearings by some other officials and regulators in the postal industry, though the specific details remain under debate.

How the USO is specified carries strong implications for the success of a smart city platform. Interviews with smart city administrators as well as previous research on the topic (USPS OIG 2016) reveal that overall quality of network coverage and frequency of data collection are critically important issues for cities looking to collect the most accurate data for the provision of services. These two elements relate specifically to the scope element of the USO. As mentioned previously, the advantage of POs in this space is that they conduct regular routes that cover significant geographic areas on regular, almost daily schedules. This stands in contrast to private delivery providers that typically follow routes that are optimized daily to reduce their costs. As a result, these companies possess a much lower quality of network coverage which can strengthen the PO's competitive advantage. Imposing a required minimum number of delivery days for a postal USP in statute would give cities a sense of how often data would be collected and potentially be an indicator of the quality of that data. Also, as the number of days covered increases, the types of smart city services could be diversified, potentially attracting more technology companies and cities to the platform. However, the decision about what specific smart city services are offered, whether they be painkillers or vitamins, is left up to the cities and technology providers, not the PO acting as a platform, whose only role would be those of facilitating the data collection and connecting tech companies with interested cities.

Formally mandating equal levels of service for urban and rural customers is also an important USO feature of which smart government advocates should be aware. While this paper focuses on smart city solutions, some state governments like Illinois are exploring becoming "smart states," with data-driven tools improving the delivery of government services to all residents, not just city dwellers (Maddox 2016). However, attracting these users to the platform would require USPS to continue offering equal levels of service to urban and rural customers, including to remote areas where last-mile delivery is most expensive. As private delivery carriers often charge higher rates for deliveries in rural areas, these residents are often already reliant on USPS for affordable service. Thus, USPS is better positioned compared to competitors to collect frequent and accurate data in these more remote locations.

Additionally, properly defining the other elements related to service quality and affordability appears just as important, as cities would only engage in a platform that they thought would be around for years to come. To continue offering high quality and affordable service to all areas of the country, the Presidential Task Force concedes that offering non-postal products and services may be necessary and should be considered as a part of postal reform along with USO specification. The ability for USPS to leverage its network assets in the creation of a smart city platform could create a virtuous cycle that would, itself, help fund universal mail service.

The USA is not the only country reconsidering USO requirements in the near future. By withdrawing from the EU as a part of the Brexit process, the UK would no longer be subject to the European Postal Directive on Universal Mail Service. As the UK government considers whether to keep or alter its USO requirements, advocates for smart cities in the UK should consider how those regulatory changes could impact the ability of Royal Mail to act as a partner or platform in the provision of smart city services.

5 Conclusion

When it comes to capturing the potential of smart cities, both POs and city governments have important roles to play, and they could support each other. Strong USPs in the postal sector have an opportunity to utilize their network assets to create platforms for smart city data collection services that could benefit themselves, private tech companies, city governments, and all residents. However, in many jurisdictions regulatory changes must be considered to make this a reality, including in the USA. In several countries, the window of opportunity for policy change has been opened but advocates for smart cities in the USA may not even realize that this moment exists or that they should take a keen interest in postal reform legislation likely coming before Congress during the next few years.

It is clear that the development of these information platforms will not be easy. Indeed, there are critical questions about the level of openness in the network and how a PO should incentivize participation that are not addressed in this paper. This paper, however, addresses two critically important points for stakeholders. First, in opting for a platform-based business model over a standard production model, posts can help overcome a significant barrier to the expansion of smart city programs that seems to have stalled in recent years. Second, while any level of universal service provision makes a PO an optimal partner for cities in data collection initiatives, the current postal policy debate in the US and other countries means that smart city advocates must push for action and engagement now in order to influence the role POs should play in the growth of smart city initiatives.

References

Accenture. (2008). *Postal Universal Service Obligation (USO) international comparison: International postal liberalization – comparative study of US and key countries*. Report prepared for the U.S. Postal Service. https://about.usps.com/universal-postal-service/accenture-report.pdf.

Ambrosini, X., Boldron, F., & Roy, B. (2006). Universal service obligations in the postal sector. In M. A. Crew & P. R. Kleindorfer (Eds.), *Progress toward liberalization of the postal and delivery sector. Topics in regulatory economics and policy* (Vol. 49). Boston: Springer.

Bouton, S., Knupfer, S., Mihov, I., & Swartz, S. (2015). *Urban mobility at a tipping point*. September 1, 2015. Web. March 10, 2017.

Maddox, T. (2016). Illinois seeks to become the Nation's first smart state. *TechRepublic*. https://www.techrepublic.com/article/illinois-seeks-to-become-the-nations-first-smart-state/.

Parker, G. G., & Van Alstyne, M. W. (2005). Two-sided network effects: A theory of information product design. *Management Science, 51*(10), 1494–1504.

Presidential Task Force on the United States Postal System. (2018). *United States postal service: A sustainable path forward*, December 2018. https://home.treasury.gov/system/files/136/USPS_A_Sustainable_Path_Forward_report_12-04-2018.pdf.

Rouse, M. (2019). *Smart city*. July 1, 2017. Web. April 2, 2019.

Smith, T. (2018). *The problem with most 'smart city' projects is they're vitamins instead of painkillers*. October 31, 2018. Web. April 9, 2019.

Straight, B. (2017). *Inside the true costs of congestion*. May 19, 2017. Web. May 2, 2019.

United States Postal Service. (2018). 2018 10-K form. https://about.usps.com/who-we-are/financials/10k-reports/fy2018.pdf.

United States Postal Service. (2019). *Fun facts*. https://facts.usps.com/size-and-scope/.

USPS Office of Inspector General. (2016). The postal service and cities: A 'smart' partnership. https://www.uspsoig.gov/sites/default/files/document-library-files/2016/RARC-WP-16-017.pdf.

Zwahlen, C. (2019). *USPS completes next-generation delivery vehicle tests*. Trucks.com, May 3, 2019. https://www.trucks.com/2019/05/03/usps-completes-next-generation-delivery-vehicle-tests/.